Collaborations with the Past

Collaborations with the Past

RESHAPING SHAKESPEARE ACROSS TIME AND MEDIA

Diana E. Henderson

Cornell University Press   Ithaca and London

First published 2006 by Cornell University Press

Printed in the United States of America

Library of Congress Cataloging-in-Publication Data

Henderson, Diana E.
    Collaborations with the past : reshaping Shakespeare across time and media / Diana E.
Henderson.
        p. cm.
    Includes bibliographical references and index.
    ISBN-13: 978-0-8014-4419-7 (cloth : alk. paper)
    ISBN-10: 0-8014-4419-5 (cloth : alk. paper)
    1. Shakespeare, William, 1564–1616—Adaptations. 2. Shakespeare, William,
1564–1616—Film and video adaptations. 3. Scott, Walter, Sir, 1771–1832. Kenilworth. 4.
Woolf, Virginia, 1882–1941. Mrs. Dalloway. 5. Shakespeare, William, 1564–1616. Taming of
the shrew. 6. Shakespeare, William, 1564–1616. Henry V. I. Title.
    PR2880.A1H46 2006
    822.3'3—DC22   2006006243

Cornell University Press strives to use environmentally responsible
suppliers and materials to the fullest extent possible in the publishing
of its books. Such materials include vegetable-based, low-VOC inks
and acid-free papers that are recycled, totally chlorine-free, or partly
composed of nonwood fibers. For further information, visit our website
at www.cornellpress.cornell.edu.

Cloth printing   10 9 8 7 6 5 4 3 2 1

For Alaine, Joyce, and Geoffrey Henderson
"not of an age, but for all time!"

Contents

Acknowledgments

This book is nothing if not a testament to collaboration. I must begin by thanking Barbara Hodgdon, William Carroll, Kate McLuskie, Peter Donaldson, Stephen Tapscott, Shankar Raman, and Douglas Lanier, all of whom have given me specific, useful advice for improving its shape and direction. Many other colleagues and friends have read sections and the whole of its earlier incarnations, and I thank them all. I am grateful to the Wade Fund, the Cambridge-MIT Institute, the Old Dominion Fellowship fund, Dean Philip Khoury, and the Open University (UK) for their assistance and sponsorship while developing this project. My students have taught me much about the works I discuss here; most notably, Joyce Wongkung Lee and Sarah Wall-Randell contributed insights about *Jane Eyre* and *Cymbeline*, respectively. Scores of colleagues have made this process and product better. I cannot name them all, but for sustaining support, mentorship, and good conversation over the years, I warmly thank Emily Bartels, Mary Crane, Tony Dawson, Lowell Gallagher, Jean Howard, Marina Leslie, David Scott Kastan, Pat Parker, Jim Siemon, Val Wayne, and Paul Yachnin.

Happy collaborations in the workplace are not easy to sustain. I am blessed to ply my trade in the company of literary scholars who combine deep intelligence with true kindness on a daily basis. Pete Donaldson has been the Platonic ideal of a valued colleague and mentor: patient, tireless, insightful, and wise. I owe him much, not least my job. Shankar Raman, my twin in Renaissance drama, dazzles with his brainpower, energetic commitment, and willingness to help me find an argument. Ruth Perry and Mary Fuller make each season a cause for celebration, and Jim Buzard indulges my delusion that we're still graduate students. Stephen Tapscott and William Uricchio make me happier—and I suspect, by osmosis, smarter—

x   each time we talk. Wyn Kelley, Henry Jenkins, Noel Jackson, Jim Cain, David Thorburn and John Hildebidle have provided daily models of professional, teacherly devotion, and Alvin Kibel makes me laugh (and sing) and then think harder. Along with many esteemed colleagues in Women's Studies, Theater Arts, and across the Institute—and our off-the-charts students—they make coming to work a pleasure.

Although each has changed substantially, earlier versions of portions of this book have appeared in print: "Othello Redux? Scott's *Kenilworth* and the Trickiness of 'Race' on the Nineteenth-century Stage," in *Victorian Shakespeare*, volume 2: *Literature and Culture*, ed. Gail Marshall and Adrian Poole (Palgrave Macmillan, 2003); "A *Shrew* for the Times, Revisited," in *Shakespeare, The Movie, II: Popularizing the Plays on Film, TV, Video, and DVD*, ed. Richard Burt and Lynda E. Boose (Routledge, 2003); "Rewriting Family Ties: Woolf's Renaissance Romance," in *Virginia Woolf: Reading the Renaissance*, ed. Sally Greene (Ohio State University Press, 1999); and "The Disappearing Queen: Looking for Isabel in *Henry V*" in *Shakespeare and His Contemporaries in Performance*, ed. Edward Esche (Ashgate, 2000). I thank all these editors, who have also helped me to continue developing my essays beyond the format in which they first appeared. Similarly, I am appreciative of the colleagues and students at MIT, the Harvard Humanities Center, Boston University, the University of New Hampshire, Northeastern University, the University of Pittsburgh, and many, many conferences who have enriched my thinking. The staffs (and collections) of the Folger Shakespeare Library, the British Library, Widener Library, the Theatre Museum in Covent Garden, the Museum of Television and Radio, the Shakespeare Centre Library in Stratford-upon-Avon, and the MIT libraries have helped me enormously and often. At the Royal Shakespeare Company, Thea Jones, Roger Mortlock, Tom Piper, and Michael Boyd have been especially generous and helpful. Julie Saunders, Briony Keith, Douglas Purdy, Laurel Landers, and Jan Ellertsen have all provided essential office support and good cheer.

At Cornell University Press, Bernie Kendler worked hard on my behalf, and Peter Wissoker has patiently kept me on track; many thanks to Susan Tarcov and Teresa Jesionowski for their meticulous, thoughtful assistance. On my many trips to work at the British Library, Tessa Forbes has been a gracious host and good friend. Michael Krass and Blair Brown provide both hospitality and the performing arts "reality check" that a scholar of drama sorely needs. In Boston, Maria Koundoura, Jumbi Edulbehram, Tara Raman, and Mihir and Uma have provided nourishment to both body and spirit. Many more should but cannot be listed, but I will at least name Fred and Jenny Greenwell, Binky and Guy Sellars, Diana Lewis and Robin Barnsley, Sara Withers, Helen Dodds, Frances Keck, Rita Foisie, Kathy Eden, Virginia Jackson, Mary Loeffelholz, Ishrat Chaudhuri and Mark Sheldon, Jay Parini and Devon Jersild, Don Wyatt, Paula Schwartz, Ruma Dutta and Maarten, Paul, and Loes Nijhoff Asser, Michael Krass (deservedly, again), and—my anchor in the practical world—Bill Pierce.

Collaboration begins at home. I have had the joy and privilege of growing up in a household presided over by a Virginian of indomitable spirit and good sense, who nevertheless (or therefore?) always took the chicken neck. Without her, her mother, her sisters, and their tradition, I doubt I would ever have arrived where I am. On that journey, I have been sustained by the love and unflagging support of my sister and brother—who quite rightly give me grief when I act like an academic. I can only say thank you.

D.E.H.

Collaborations with the Past

Shake-shifting

An Introduction

> He to whom the present is the only thing that is present knows nothing
> about the age in which he lives.
>
> Oscar Wilde, "The Critic as Artist"

Shakespeare, Mon Amour

This is a book about the bearers of Shakespeare: those artists who have
transported plays by an Elizabethan Englishman into modern Anglo-
American culture, and in the process helped transform both him and it. Focusing on four exemplary instances in which his plays were reconceived
within distinctively modern narrative forms (novels, films, video) and in the
radically altered modern theater, the book examines the simultaneously delightful and uneasy results of collaborating with the past. It further argues
that we cannot help but do so, and thus must continue to seek the most helpful, self-aware routes through this tricky process of diachronic collaboration;[1] performance cannot simply forget about history any more than the humanities can fail to address the present moment. Or, more correctly, we do
so at our peril, and to our collective loss. For as Oscar Wilde's Gilbert argues
(in paradoxical fashion), a critical eye on the past is essential for those who
would be truly modern. Better to struggle, as did novelists as different as Sir
Walter Scott and Virginia Woolf, with the legacies of a troublesome history;
better to imagine, as have filmmakers and Shakespeare himself, selective
glimpses of a past that art can and cannot represent, even as we indubitably

---

1. Jeffrey Masten directed me to Bill Worthen's verbal use of this phrase. In his own theoretical usage, Masten would efface "the author" more completely than I do; see his *Textual Intercourse: Collaboration, Authorship, and Sexualities in Renaissance Drama* (Cambridge, UK, 1997),
10. I retain the somewhat ungainly modifier to distinguish my usage from normative (syn-
chronic) assumptions about collaboration, discussed below.

1

2   reshape its meaning. We still learn from the struggles and glimpses. Using his plays as a kaleidoscope, modern artists shake up Shakespeare, cutting his glassy essence to bits in order to create newly evocative patterns. They turn back to Shakespeare in order to remake him in our own image—often with spectacular results. But they also teach us to see that image and the past anew.

William Shakespeare wrote poetic stories for the stage. Many of his plays were palpable hits; some were not. He died. Or rather, a man died and "Shakespeare" lived on and kept growing, becoming, as centuries passed, the bearer of English history, an encyclopedia of phrases, a source of profound inspiration, and fodder for many professions. Often and variously told, the story of how this came to pass is a fascinating one, and *Collaborations with the Past* is indebted to those accounts as well as to surveys of Shakespeare's modern history and appropriation.[2] But this book tells a different story: it refocuses attention on some key writers, directors, and actors who have kept "Shakespeare" at center stage. This story highlights the rewards, choices, and responsibilities of re-creating culture across time and media, and the ingenuity and difficulties of a collaborative model of artistic process. It is thus as much about art in the modern world as it is about the figure, legacy, and plays of William Shakespeare.[3]

The idea of collaboration lies at the heart of this book because it lies at the heart of the artistic process, both modern and early modern, more accurately capturing the practice of Shakespeare and his inheritors than does the notion of isolated genius. We know that in his day, Shakespeare collaborated with John Fletcher; Thomas Middleton added witch scenes to *Macbeth*; and respect for playwrights was not much greater than is reflected by the producer-manager exchange in the comic film *Shakespeare in Love*: "Who is that?" "Nobody. The author." Despite the rise and always prematurely pre-

---

2. Rather than overwhelm the reader with compendious (and redundant) references in these notes, with a few key exceptions I include relevant general studies that are not being quoted directly in the bibliography only. Marjorie Garber, *Shakespeare After All* (New York, 2004), 5, recently anticipated my chapter title in her passing reference to Shakespeare's plays themselves as cultural "shifters." I'm interested in the people as well as works doing the shifting.

3. This book's case-study approach bears affinities to works by Peter Donaldson, Peter Erickson, and Marianne Novy, although their focus is more specific to one medium, type of writer, and/or era. My emphasis on the mixed messages of collaboration—the political and aesthetic tensions of that polysemous process—differs from primarily celebratory accounts of modern reclamation, on the one hand (Novy, Patsy Rodenberg), and a presumption in much contemporary performance studies that turning back to Shakespeare is fundamentally nostalgic, tragic, evasive, or deluded, on the other (Susan Bennett, Sue Ellen Case, Elin Diamond, Dwight Conquergood, and in places Joseph Roach). I cite many works on modern re-visions in the bibliography and chapters to come.

dicted decline of Bardolatry in intervening centuries, theatrical directors still collaborate on the script (John Barton's *The Wars of the Roses*); screenwriters still insert scenes (the fantastic digital sequences in Peter Greenaway's *Prospero's Books*); and sometimes they still actively dissociate themselves from the "author" (the publicity surrounding Richard Loncraine's *Richard III*). But even when trying to represent him "faithfully," of course the context has changed utterly, and thus the need for Shake-shifting. More often than not, modern artists invoke Shakespeare as precisely what he could not be in his own time: a source of unquestioned artistry and authority. Then they either celebrate and market that power or struggle against his institutional associations and codified performance traditions as well as the time-bound aspects of the plays themselves.

Between early and post-modernity, Romanticism wrought profound changes in the conception of the artist, including more active assertion of special poetic access to extrasocietal sublimity, and veneration for the meditative figure of solitary genius. For historically minded scholars, such an image is obviously at odds with Shakespeare's writing practice and profession as a player (though not, perhaps, with his character Hamlet); the figure of "the Bard" carries more than a trace of cultural back-formation. Yet as Marjorie Garber remarks, "Every age creates its own Shakespeare," and these attributes become entwined with the modern figure of Shakespeare from the early nineteenth century onward.[4] Within this context, to regard Shakespeare as a collaborative writer becomes a more destabilizing, even threatening claim than to acknowledge, say, his being John Fletcher's (superior) writing partner. Many who grant Shakespeare's co-author status at the site of creation nevertheless actively police the distinction in quality between his writing and that of his many playwriting contemporaries, cherishing the mystical dimension of his achievement. I will return to certain ironies

---

4. Garber, *Shakespeare After All*, 3. Gary Taylor, *Reinventing Shakespeare* (New York, 1989), remains an invaluable account of this process, focusing on critical and institutional uses of the Bard, as does Hugh Grady, *The Modernist Shakespeare: Critical Texts in a Material World* (Oxford, 1991). On the later eighteenth and nineteenth centuries, see Jonathan Bate, *Shakespeare and the English Romantic Imagination* (Oxford, 1986) and *Shakespearean Constitutions: Politics, Theatre, Criticism, 1730–1830* (Oxford, 1989); Michael Bristol, *Shakespeare's America, America's Shakespeare* (London, 1990); Michael Dobson, *The Making of the National Poet: Shakespeare, Adaptation, and Authorship, 1660–1769* (Oxford, 1992); Gail Marshall and Adrian Poole, eds., *Victorian Shakespeare*, 2 vols. (Houndmills, UK, 2003); Richard Foulkes, ed., *Shakespeare and the Victorian Stage* (Cambridge, UK, 1986); Adrian Poole, *Shakespeare and the Victorians* (London, 2004); and Richard W. Schoch, *Shakespeare's Victorian Stage: Performing History in the Theatre of Charles Kean* (Cambridge, UK, 1998). On the modernist era, see Michael Bristol, *Big-Time Shakespeare* (London, 1996); Thomas Cartelli, *Repositioning Shakespeare: National Formations, Postcolonial Appropriations* (New York, 1999); and Richard Halpern, *Shakespeare among the Moderns* (Ithaca, 1997).

4   in the historical timing of Shakespeare's emergence as the preeminent figure of solo authorial genius, but here want to suggest what was (and often still is) perceived to be at stake in preserving this figuration.

As an illustration, one can hardly do better than to look at a literally Shake-shifting painting entitled *The Edge of Doom* (1836–38; see figure 1). Samuel Colman (or Coleman; 1780–1845) of the Bristol school specialized in landscapes both biblical and fantastic, in each case showing a penchant for scenes of destruction (of Pharaoh's host and the Temple, to name two). In this particular apocalyptic fantasy, he imagines devastation closer to his English home. As buildings topple and artworks fall in a conflagration of orange, the statue of Shakespeare installed in Poet's Corner at Westminster Abbey remains standing, dwarfed yet unperturbed by its solitary, central stability: in time, Westminster may crumble, Guido Reni may tumble, but our Bard is here to stay. Long before T. S. Eliot published *The Wasteland*, one discerns the fears of cultural disintegration that form one of several continuities in the long modern era, linking British Romanticism, late Victorianism, and modernism. Amidst this perception of chaos come again, Shakespeare is called upon to embody something that will, we desperately hope, last. Future Shock meets Will Power: the still point in a turning world, Shakespeare is the only remaining universal constant to help anxious (especially British) moderns shore up their fragments against impending ruin.

This melancholy fantasy remains potent. What charms me about Colman's vision, however, is the more layered self-consciousness of its artistic representation: here, "Shakespeare" is always already an aesthetic (re)construction, that famed eighteenth-century statue itself being a romanticized image rather than a representation from life. Carved by Peter Scheemakers after a design by William Kent, it was dedicated in 1741 and, according to Jonathan Bate, "effectively marks the canonization of Shakespeare."[5] Furthermore, David Garrick would use it—as well as himself—as the model for the Shakespeare statue at Stratford unveiled at his 1769 jubilee. As such, the statue is more a testament to the collaborative labor of "modern" theatrical marketing that transformed Shakespeare into a secular idol than a tribute to any stable, originary author. Likewise, though in a more somber register, Colman's painting truly is a modern fantasy. His upright icon of Genius Preserved stands, like Brave Little Britain, against cataclysmic forces that would render individual human actions pointless. But by representing that genius as a later generation's statuary, Colman acknowledges Shakespeare's collective construction in time. Such an illusion of stony presence, like the

5. Bate, *Shakespearean Constitutions*, 27.

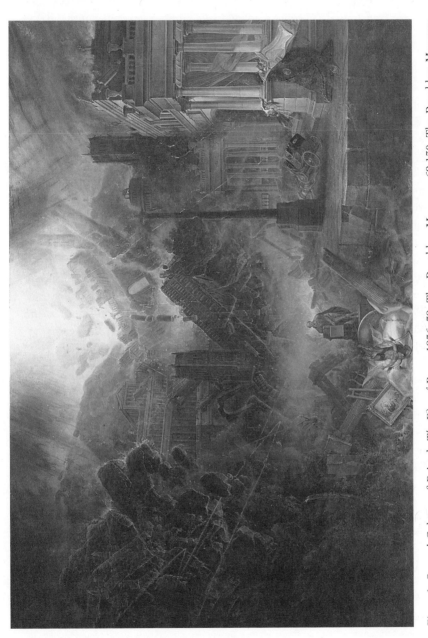

Figure 1. Samuel Colman of Bristol, *The Edge of Doom*. 1836–38. The Brooklyn Museum, 69.130. The Brooklyn Museum Fund. Reprinted by permission.

6   imaginary artwork *The Tempest*'s Ariel conjures from a dead man's bones in "Full fathom five," manifests the rich and strange way in which mortal bodies are transmuted (in time) into symbolic compensation (against time) — even when the body was never quite "there" in the first place. This progressive process of enshrinement complicates the statue's symbolic stasis and the reactionary fears that otherwise dominate the landscape. As ignorant armies clash, this icon of Shakespeare actually shadows the way in which the exceptional One can serve vicariously to epitomize and empower the increasingly numerous and invisible many. Shakespeare, like the Love he describes in sonnet 116, must bear it out, for us, "even to the edge of doom."

At a more superficial level, however, it was the simpler idea of Shakespeare as the singular genius on a pedestal that caught the popular imagination, continues to spark hero worship, and funds Globe reconstructions around the globe. Despite scholarly challenges and cinematic spoofs, the collaborative "player" still hovers aloft in most people's mind as the sole unchallenged self-justifying name in English literature. Nowhere is this inheritance more evident than in Harold Bloom's success with *Shakespeare: The Invention of the Human.*[6] That Bloom's reenergized Bardolatry (appropriate from a scholar who earned his credentials finding personal *agons* and "strong" misreadings in Romantic poetry) received such an enthusiastic mass-market reception testifies to the continued potency of the genius figure, as well as to the cultural role of the *New York Times* and our enduring fascination with fictional characters. Some of this Shakespeare worship is attributable to sheer enjoyment and desire, of course, which is in no way at odds with a larger historical explanation emphasizing the simultaneous marginalization and elevation of the aesthetic.[7] After all, in the case of Shakespeare's *writing* there is (to misquote Gertrude Stein) a there there — or as the early nineteenth-century critic William Hazlitt put it, "People would not trouble their heads about Shakespear, if he had given them no pleasure, or

---

6. Harold Bloom, *Shakespeare: The Invention of the Human* (New York, 1998). For a very different version of Shakespeare as inventor of the modern self, see Joel Fineman, *Shakespeare's Perjured Eye: The Invention of Poetic Subjectivity in the Sonnets* (Berkeley, 1986). Michael Wood's BBC television series *In Search of Shakespeare* (2003) pursued its genius-spirit with breathless enthusiasm, and Fiona Shaw made the Bard's case as greatest of all *Great Britons* (2002): see Roberta Pearson and William Uricchio, "Brushing Up Shakespeare: Relevance and Televisual Form," in *A Concise Companion to Shakespeare on Screen*, ed. Diana E. Henderson (Oxford, 2006), 197–215.

7. For a more expansive treatment of this topic, see Terry Eagleton's *The Ideology of the Aesthetic* (Cambridge, MA, 1990); see Grady, *Modernist Shakespeare*, 79ff. on Adorno's location of the aesthetic applied to Shakespeare studies. Joseph Roach reclaims the word aesthetic in "its eighteenth-century meaning: the vitality and sensuous presence of material forms"; *Cities of the Dead: Circum-Atlantic Performance* (New York, 1996), xiii.

cry him up to the skies, if he had not first raised them there. The world are not grateful *for nothing*."[8] Yet this recognition is just the starting point for analysis, not its conclusion. There is another, more generally compelling reason for the persistent attraction of the Romantic model of authorship, for imagining free-spirited (if sometimes garret-bound) souls who invent new worlds and ourselves out of whole cloth: our continued consciousness of human agency and responsibility in the creation of art, persisting even after cultural theorists such as Roland Barthes and Michel Foucault posited the collective "death of the author." Despite the power of much of their critique and the criticism that followed from it, one must concede that reports of the author's death have been greatly exaggerated.[9] Authorial biographies (such as Stephen Greenblatt's *Will in the World*) sell better than ever, capturing the truth that art is indeed made by particular human beings whose individuality still fascinates us. It is this directly human dimension that the terminology of diachronic collaboration also acknowledges, yet in so doing it redirects attention toward a different space and model from that of isolated genius.

Crucially, as both artistic professionals and postmodernism remind us, along with great labor there are unpredictable, uncalculated dimensions involved in any creative production, and those serendipitous aspects often result from many voices and hands converging. The magic of creativity, in other words, is a social event, even when a genius is in the room. Especially but not only in collective art forms such as theater and filmmaking, artists are conscious that collaboration is messy, exhilarating, and inevitable. Awareness of this reality makes attribution and judgment of the artistic product more difficult and scholarship that ignores these complexities less useful to those who would analyze and understand art's cultural work. Collaboration better understood—that is, with greater attention to exceptional,

---

8. Bate, *Shakespearean Constitutions*, 9.

9. Greenblatt's and Louis Montrose's New Historicism of the 1980s and 1990s emphasized the involvement of early modern artistic texts in hierarchical power networks, debating their capacity for subversion; see also Steven Mullaney, *The Place of the Stage: License, Play, and Power in Renaissance England* (Chicago, 1988); Jean E. Howard, *The Stage and Social Struggle in Early Modern England* (New York, 1994); Leonard Tennenhouse, *Power on Display: The Politics of Shakespeare's Genres* (New York, 1986); and Christopher Pye, *The Regal Phantasm: Shakespeare and the Politics of Spectacle* (New York, 1990). On Shakespeare's power and place in the contemporary marketplace, see Bristol, *Big-Time Shakespeare*; Richard Burt, *Unspeakable ShaXXXspeares: Queer Theory and American Kiddie Culture* (New York, 1998); Marjorie Garber, *Symptoms of Culture* (New York, 1998); Terence Hawkes, *That Shakespeherian Rag* (London, 1986); Barbara Hodgdon, *The Shakespeare Trade: Performances and Appropriations.*(Philadelphia, 1998); Bryan Reynolds, *Performing Transversally: Reimagining Shakespeare and the Critical Future* (New York, 2003); and W. B. Worthen, *Shakespeare and the Authority of Performance* (Cambridge, UK, 1997).

8   individuated artistic agency working within a particular social nexus—can
help bridge the gap between popular discourse and what historical accounts
and theatrical experience tell us about modern artists' conceptions regarding
Shakespeare. For unlike the disembodied vocabulary of much theoretical
writing on intertextuality or the zero-sum economics implied by "appropriation," collaboration focuses attention on the connections among individuals,
allowing artists credit and responsibility, but at the same time refusing to
separate them from their social location and the work of others.[10] It also
makes a space for emotion as part of art's appeal and reality, both for its creators and for its audiences. By focusing on diachronic collaborations with
Shakespeare—instances that require modern artists to work with an exceptional absent presence, if ever there was one—the chapters that follow try to
address artistic complexity without becoming incoherent, and to educe the
sociopolitical resonance of specific, personal choices without oversimplification. *Collaborations with the Past* thereby illuminates both the multiplicity and
the richness of "Shakespeare" for moderns, and the problems his collaborators seek to alter or carry, from his world into our own.

To some, this notion of collaborating with a dead man may still seem odd,
but we speak of the literary present tense for a reason: the textual traces,
oral traditions, and now screen images that adhere to "Shakespeare" keep
him alive and accessible, and it is in this sense that theatrical artists often
speak of collaboration. To actors bringing words to life, usually without
their author present, the distinction between a playwright's being dead or
alive can be moot; indeed, sometimes the benefits of greater temporal distance become obvious, allowing more space for interpretive creativity without interference from revising writers or proprietary estates. For novelists
too, the distance both formal and temporal from a long-dead playwright can
be liberating. With head-to-head competition out of the question, a posi-

---

10. "Associated with abduction, adoption, and theft, appropriation's central tenet is the desire for possession. It comprehends both the commandeering of the desired object and the process of making this object one's own, controlling it by possessing it"; Jean I. Marsden, ed., *The
Appropriation of Shakespeare: Post-Renaissance Reconstructions of the Works and the Myth* (London,
1991), 1. Bate (*Shakespearean Constitutions*) invokes a less power-based etymology of appropriation; see also Hodgdon, *Shakespeare Trade*; Christy Desmet and Robert Sawyer, eds., *Shakespeare
and Appropriation* (New York, 1999); and Deborah Cartmell, *Interpreting Shakespeare on Screen*
(London, 2000). While appreciative of the Marxist critique inherent in much scholarship using
the term, I wish to attend to noneconomic dimensions of this process without the implication
that they are epiphenomenal, and within a less deterministic overarching framework. Martha
Tuck Rozett, *Talking Back to Shakespeare* (Newark, DE, 1994), prefers "transformations" as "a
recognizable class of inventions located within the larger category of appropriations and intertextual traces" (8–9), but admits such distinctions are not always clear. Reynolds (*Performing
Transversally*) likewise stresses a potential for multiplicity in interpretation, though his transver-
sal theory focuses more on the critic's role in reception.

tively collaborative attitude is easier to achieve. It can also be easier to discern, for being free from the fear of plagiarism charges, writers are more apt to invoke the narratives and lines of Shakespeare directly. Indeed, given the way many artists speak and write, Shakespeare may be the most popular collaborator around. In my experience working with and talking to directors, actors, and designers alike, this is how theater practitioners tend to regard him. In the online press kit released with Michael Radford's *The Merchant of Venice*, the director is quoted as joking that he "wrote the script with my collaborator William Shakespeare. He just contributed the dialogue, the plot, the story, and the characters and I did all the rest";[11] the only thing that might be regarded as atypical here is the director's humorous self-deprecation. Certainly for some artists—though for many more academicians—Shakespeare will on occasion seem the Law of the Father, the inevitable test, or the stony monument. But far more often he resembles an imaginary friend.

Nor is this sense of social relationship and talk about dead authors as collaborators confined to Shakespeare alone. Here is a British director explaining his production of Christopher Marlowe's infrequently staged *Dido, Queen of Carthage* at the American Repertory Theater: "'I want people to meet this wonderful man,' director Neil Bartlett says of Marlowe. 'My work is very personal, so the stories that I tell and the writers I collaborate with matter to me hugely.'" Soon his interviewer adopts his vocabulary:

> And, indeed, as he speaks, it feels as if Marlowe comes alive in the room, the unseen collaborator in what Bartlett calls "this strange and wonderful beast," the tragic story of a proud Carthaginian queen and the warrior who abandons her to found Rome. . . . What the collaborators share, Bartlett says, is "the idea that theater should be gorgeous, extraordinary, passionate. I'm not making this up. That's Marlowe."[12]

That's Marlowe, that's Bartlett: in the wink of an eye, centuries disappear and sensibilities correspond, even as the artwork itself remains "strange and wonderful" in its otherness. Bartlett's emphasis on a dominantly two-person exchange reveals the affective bond informing one's choice of a diachronic collaborator. Yet Marlowe's presence still hovers in the world of "as if," just as Bartlett knows he must make drastic alterations in order for Marlowe's

11. "The History of the Project" 7, http://www.sonypictures.com/classics/merchantofvenice/index_site.html.

12. Louise Kennedy, "Dido Puts in a Rare Appearance," *Boston Globe*, 4 March 2005, http://www.boston.com/ae/theater_arts/articles/2005/03/04/dido_puts_in_a_rare_appearance/

rhetorically based play for Elizabethan boy actors to work in a modern the-atrical space and meet a modern audience's expectations.

And thus the skeptic may still challenge whether the term "collaborator" accurately describes the dead man in this partnership. The choice seems to run one way only, and Marlowe may be rolling in his unmarked grave at the gushing tribute aimed in his direction. Clearly, being alive has its advantages: when Blair Brown describes working on a film of *Hamlet* as a "hierarchical collaboration," the person at the top of that hierarchy is assuredly the director/star Campbell Scott, not the much-beloved Bard.[13] Nevertheless, I stand by the choice to name Shakespeare (especially) as collaborator for three reasons beyond the later artists' stated perceptions. One derives from his time of creation, another from our moment of reception, and a third from the word itself.

In producing art for a buying public, Shakespeare like any other professional artist chose to become part of a collaborative economy, making his work accessible for a wide audience to enjoy on stage and (if Lukas Erne and others are right) on the page.[14] Given that Shakespeare himself "borrowed" insouciantly and often from earlier playwrights, printed books, and circulated manuscripts, he could not help but expect his words to recirculate in new forms and fora—nor did he leave evidence of concern about that possibility (as rare Ben Jonson did).[15] Thus in his writing as in his participation

13. See Brown's comments in Diana E. Henderson, "Learning from Campbell Scott's *Hamlet*," in Henderson, *Concise Companion*, 80, and 77–95, on the consequentiality of knowing about actual artistic practice.

14. In the latest twist to the long-running debate over the artificially constructed dichotomy "text versus performance," Lukas Erne's *Shakespeare as Literary Dramatist* (Cambridge, UK, 2003) builds on Peter Blaney's careful study of the book trade to argue that Shakespeare (and his company) did in fact have use and interest in play publication, usually about two years after initial performance. One hopes this historicist argument will help advance the experiential awareness that the two categories are neither opposed nor identical, but rather resemble a Venn diagram with a whole range of possibilities in practice. On the complexities of print, text, and performance of Shakespeare, see especially W. B. Worthen, *Shakespeare and the Force of Modern Performance* (Cambridge, UK, 2003).

15. Arguably the linked sonnets 110 and 111, which complain that his "public means" of life have led to "strong infection," could be read as moments of Jonsonesque disdain for the commercial theater, although both tenor and vehicle focus more on acting than on writing, and the rhetorical context (allowing his beloved—and himself—to hold Fortune accountable for his bad behavior) displays more wit than worry. On early modern collaboration and textuality, see (among many) Gerald Eades Bentley, "Collaboration," in *The Profession of Dramatist and Player in Shakespeare's Time, 1590–1642* (Princeton, 1986); Masten, *Textual Intercourse*; Leah Marcus, *Puzzling Shakespeare: Local Reading and Its Discontents* (Berkeley, 1988) and *Unediting the Renaissance: Shakespeare, Marlowe, Milton* (New York, 1996); Margreta de Grazia and Peter Stallybrass, "The Materiality of the Shakespearean Text," *Shakespeare Quarterly* 44 (1993): 255–283; Stephen Orgel, *The Authentic Shakespeare, and Other Problems of the Early Modern Stage* (New York, 2002), *Imagining Shakespeare: A History of Texts and Visions* (Houndmills, UK, 2003), "What Is a

as sharer and actor with the Lord Chamberlain's (later King's) Men, Shakespeare's behavior was in practice collaborative, social, open-ended, and inviting.

A second and more fundamental reason to use the term collaboration derives from the insight of critically-minded artists since (at least) Wilde and T. S. Eliot, namely, that later artists reshape our perceptions of what came before, with each "individual talent" (in the words of Eliot's famous essay) affecting our reception of the entire "tradition." Even more overtly than in the case of the nondramatic poet, a playwright's art comes to us filtered and reshaped by the productions, performance traditions, and editions that try to recapture evanescent events.[16] The later works provide the lens through which Shakespeare comes into view, and thus to life—and in that second life, Shakespeare (Will he, nil he) becomes a collaborator in conveying the opinions, visions, and emotions of the Shake-shifters. It is now a literary critical commonplace to acknowledge the regularizing, codifying hands of eighteenth-century textual editors from Alexander Pope to Edmund Malone in creating our "modern" Shakespeare; likewise, performance historians have documented the myriad ways in which the gestural and verbal contributions of actors from Thomas Betterton and Colley Cibber to Laurence Olivier and Kenneth Branagh have shaped audience assumptions and expectations when they approach a Shakespeare play. The pleasures of Shakespeare discerned by Hazlitt change over time and place, and the cultural work of each new artistic production contributes to the specificity of those pleasures.

The point is not that later artists have altered a static object, as the "thinginess" of the critical term "appropriation" (and often the artists' own vocabularies) would suggest. They haven't, because "it" was never so stable and determinate in the first place: even the production of the First Folio— the text now venerated by actors and collectors "this side idolatry"—was a

---

Text?" *Research Opportunities in Renaissance Drama* 26 (1981): 3–6; Laurie Osborne, *The Trick of Singularity:* Twelfth Night *and the Performance Editions* (Iowa City, 1996); and Gary Taylor and Michael Warren, eds., *The Division of the Kingdoms: Shakespeare's Two Versions of* King Lear (Oxford, 1986).

16. John Russell Brown puts it well: "In the theatre everything is subject to revaluation, every time a play is performed; this is the nature of the medium. An assurance that this or that interpretation or mode of performance is the only one that is appropriate to a dramatic text will not come easily. . . . If any critic of Shakespeare attempts to 'fix' a play, he will do so most readily by ignoring its theatrical element—that is, by wholly unwarranted simplification"; *Shakespeare's Plays in Performance* (New York, 1993), 200–201. On theoretical problems inherent in analyzing performance, see the essays in Janelle G. Reinelt and Joseph R. Roach, eds., *Critical Theory and Performance* (Ann Arbor, 1992), especially Forte, States, and Roach; and J. C. Bulman, ed., *Shakespeare, Theory, and Performance* (London, 1996).

12   group effort involving Shakespeare's acting partners John Heminges and Henry Condell (performing on the writer's behalf seven years after his death) as well as typesetters and printers, known and anonymous.[17] Further to twist Stein's memorable phrase, the there that *was* there was never so definitive as a single book or set of lines, but rather (like her hometown, Oakland) relied—and continues to rely—upon the collective work of naming, associating, and investing material realities with human significance. The symbiosis, if not convergence, of critical and creative processes that Wilde celebrates in "The Critic as Artist" could thus find no better illustration than in Shakespeare's posthumous career.

Finally, if one wishes to examine the sociopolitical as well as aesthetic consequences of that career, as this book will indeed do, no word seems more appropriate than collaboration, with its checkered twentieth-century history. Though of Latin origin, the word in English is itself a creation of the long modern period. According to the *OED*, the first compound using *labour* to signify a fellow worker ("Wilberforce and his co-labourers") appeared in the mid-nineteenth century, only a year before the first recorded usage of the word *collaboration*. That 1860 instance exemplifies what remains the *OED*'s primary definition: "united labour, co-operation; especially in literary, artistic or scientific work." But twentieth-century political speech set the word against the word, giving collaboration a bad name. Though "collaborationist" was first used negatively in the struggles among socialist factions following the 1917 Russian Revolution, until Marshal Pétain's adoption of the term to inaugurate his French wartime government in the summer of 1940, "collaboration" still had predominantly positive associations. In the aftermath of World War II, however, to "collaborate" gained a second, "specialized" meaning: "to co-operate traitorously with the enemy." No longer unambiguous, the tainted word's antithetical definitions also epitomized the strenuously maintained though increasingly tenuous modern distinction between artistic and political thought.

Webster's Dictionary (1965) helpfully provides yet another definition, one that serves as the third term for moving beyond this compartmentalized stalemate: "to cooperate with an agency or instrumentality with which one is not immediately connected." This definition opens up the possibility of a temporal as well as spatial interpretation, and thus of diachronic collaboration. As already noted, it usefully challenges more static and unidirectional

---

17. Numerous studies on textual reconsiderations and their theoretical implications appear in this book's bibliography. Hugh Grady compares Taylor and Wells's Oxford editions with the late nineteenth-century "disintegrators"; "Disintegration and Its Reverberations," in Marsden, *Appropriation of Shakespeare*, 114.

ways of talking about artistic relationships (from the narrow "source study" to what Harold Bloom himself rightly deemed the amorphous ubiquity of "influence").[18] It does not necessitate the complete displacement of the earlier work or artist by the latter, nor does it presume a positive or negative stance toward either the artwork in question or the relational process: instead, it holds open the possibility of moving either way, both temporally and judgmentally. Thus in addition to being more open to what Gilles Deleuze and Félix Guattari would call the polyvalent "flows" of history and desire, it also encourages both artist and critic to pursue more nuanced analyses of specific texts, within a context where both process and products are multidimensional.[19] Even in the political world, we need to examine the particulars of the case before we can confidently judge its dominant register: UN Secretary General Kofi Annan's strategic emphasis on "collaboration" in his first meeting with the U.S. Congress signaled a willingness to confront that difficulty (little could he know in 1997 just how fraught that particular working relationship would become).[20] Finally, by carrying in itself a contradictory history, the word makes space for what I will emphasize in the coming chapters as the "uneasy" (dominantly sociopolitical) dimensions of working with Shakespeare across time and media, enmeshed though they are with the celebratory, empowering incentives that prompted diachronic collaboration in the first place.

Because of the complexity of this collaborative process, an analysis of artists' sociopolitical location is neither distant from nor anathema to a literary or formal understanding of art itself. Denial of this reality results in the polemical stances of both a Harold Bloom on the right and anti-authorial theorists on the left, both of which are ultimately unsatisfactory, failing to describe adequately their putative object of inquiry. The multidimensionality that Bloom sees in literary art is absolutely fundamental, but his own preference for the solitary mind (which in *The Anxiety of Influence* he posits as essential to poetic sensibility as well) precludes his acknowledging several dimensions of art—most notably, the social and political—that are every bit

18. Harold Bloom, *The Anxiety of Influence*, 2nd ed. (New York, 1997), passim.

19. Deleuze and Guattari regard their collaborative practice as one way to remain open to the flow; "Deleuze and Guattari Fight Back," in Gilles Deleuze, *Desert Islands and Other Texts, 1953–1974* (Cambridge, MA, 2004), 216–29. Although they are right to say that their brand of revolutionary utopianism in *Anti-Oedipus* resists becoming yet another "university industry," I find their mind-stretching machinery describes ontological conditions we in that industry need to confront. Speaking with Michel Foucault, Deleuze asks, "Who speaks and who asks? It's always a multiplicity, even in the person that speaks or acts. We are all groupuscles. There is no more representation. There is only action, the action of theory, the action of praxis, in the relations of relays and networks" (*Desert Islands*, 207).

20. Broadcast on *The News Hour* (PBS), 24 January 1997.

14   as important to its creation as are the formal, spiritual, or psychological aspects he cherishes.[21] Conversely, theorists of power who privilege a hegemonic state or other social apparatus in the conceptualization and judgment of art, or fans of popular culture who celebrate the marketplace as if it were synonymous with democracy, often deplore or dismiss the quirky "swerves" and "high" cultural dimensions of creativity that Bloom is so adept at venerating (if not mystifying).[22] An analytic method that neither turns art into religious faith nor denies the particularity and inner life of its makers can better explain the experience and appeal of artistic (re)production.

In the following chapters, I draw on several models of artistic analysis that carry different emphases from—or indeed are at odds with—my own: call it a critical example of uneasy collaboration. Despite the unsociable spirit and deeply idiosyncratic taxonomy of his six "ratios" of influence in *The Anxiety of Influence*, for example, Bloom nevertheless remains perhaps the "strongest" theorist of creative misprision and willful, productive dialogue between artists and their forebears. His accounts of repetition and discontinuity (*kenosis*) and completion and antithesis (*tessera*) overlap with some of the dynamics I identify in the Shake-shifting of Sir Walter Scott and Virginia Woolf respectively, yet Bloom's full-blown narrative associated with each ratio fails to describe the mutually reinforcing aspects of these collaborations,[23] nor do these examples confirm the particular logic of his competitive vision as regards the triumph of the will (and Will). Whereas he builds on Freudian as well as Nietzschean foundations, my chapter on *The Taming of the Shrew* finds in Freud the narrative pattern that troubles modern collaborations with Shakespeare's play. I will, however, follow Bloom's lead

21. See, for example, Bloom's lamentation that "Shakespeare's solitude has vanished" and his desire to be "alone with Shakespeare"; *Anxiety*, xxxv–vii. As Jonathan Bate concludes regarding the Romantic "privatization" of Shakespeare, "if 'political' is understood in its broad sense . . . then the valuation and appropriation of Shakespeare is always political"; *Shakespearean Constitutions*, 204. Although Bate is here emphasizing critical reception, among the Romantics as after, critical and artistic practice are deeply enmeshed. Within a phenomenological frame, Deleuze's meditation on the (never truly deserted) desert island, as a metaphor that captures the dynamic play between isolation and re-creation within the mind of a creator, is ultimately more compelling than Bloom's isolationism; Deleuze, *Desert Islands*, 9–14.

22. Bloom stands alone, like Abdiel, against a shadowy "School of Resentment"—equated with all who would in any way consider "Shakespeare culture-bound by history and society"; his amusing reduction of most other academic approaches to "state power is everything and individual subjectivity is nothing" sees a desert in a grain of truth; *Anxiety*, xv–xviii. See Kenneth Bleeth and Julie Rivkin, "'The Imitation David': Plagiarism, Collaboration, and the Making of a Gay Literary Tradition in David Leavitt's 'The Term Paper Artist,'" *PMLA* (2001): 1349–1363, on Bloom's "sexual" as well as "aesthetic policing of his theory" (1350).

23. Rather than attempt paraphrase of Bloom's arcane descriptions, I refer interested readers to *Anxiety*, 14–15, 49–92.

in suggesting different strains or emphases exemplified by the four chapters that follow, albeit with a much less exclusive or rhetorical focus and without aspiring to his pleasingly vatic opacity.

Two more recent studies analyzing performance and new media bear a closer kinship to *Collaborations with the Past*. Both Joseph Roach's *Cities of the Dead*, with its influential discussion of "surrogation," and Jay Bolter and Richard Grusin's *Remediation* take on the challenge of understanding the artistic process as an instantiation of larger cultural phenomena, across time and art forms. Focusing on the figure of the actor (though drawing parallels with generational changes in academia), Roach attends to the emotions involved in "surrogating" or standing for one's elders— as well as those involved when watching such surrogation. The artists working with Shakespeare in the dominant Anglo-American tradition have less to worry about (in terms of either "his" feelings or the likelihood of his or their complete displacement) than do many of the circum-Atlantic performers in Roach's study, and as a result the collaborations in this book do not in all instances share their elegiac, even tragic tonalities. *Remediation*, by contrast, tends to accentuate the positive more definitively than do the chapters here, a difference that again correlates with the attention accorded (or in Boulter and Grusin's case, not accorded) to the sociopolitical dimensions of representation. Boulter and Grusin find formal continuities across media over time, but of necessity (given their panoramic sweep) pay less attention to the contradictory dimensions of their examples or to the consequentiality of particular changes. Indeed, working from an overgeneralized premise that we seek an "immediacy" that now depends, paradoxically, upon hypermediacy, they mention but tend to avoid serious engagement with the complicating insights of literary (or Brechtian dramatic) theory.

Nevertheless, in exploring medial hybridity and refunctioning, *Remediation* rightly contests apocalyptic fantasies regarding the fate of older art forms in the wake of the new (at this moment, the digital revolution in particular); such fantasies have lasted longer and loom larger than Samuel Colman of Bristol's reputation. Precisely in order to illustrate comparable connections and commonalities across media within the long modern era, *Collaborations with the Past* unconventionally brings together instances of theatrical, novelistic, and screen collaboration with Shakespeare, giving special attention to the remediated representation of gender and nationhood. The rationale for choosing to focus on these narrative forms is multiple. In addition to their being the dominant media of fictional storytelling during the nineteenth and twentieth centuries, novels, plays, films, and television have played to diverse audiences that regularly challenge notions of high/low or

16   popular/elite cultural divisions. Moreover, they have become increasingly intertwined through cross-media recycling and adaptation, through formal remediation, and through the movement among them of creative artists as practitioners. This context cries out for a comparative media approach.

Valuable work has been done on the formal qualities of and distinctions among particular media in recent years. The specific apparatus of the camera, the kinetic immediacy of the stage, and the illusory stability of print have all warranted the extensive critical attention they have received. As in scientific analysis, the process of isolating a limited set of variables and rigorously delimiting a phenomenon produces greater clarity and insight. Yet it is also more obvious than ever that media, like authors, do not work in isolation, except within the parameters of scholarly analysis. As Bolter and Grusin remark generally,

> No medium today, and certainly no single media event, seems to do its cultural work in isolation from other media, any more than it works in isolation from other social and economic forces. What is new about new media comes from the particular ways in which they refashion older media and the ways in which older media refashion themselves to answer the challenges of new media.[24]

Here, at the level of the medium, is a partial analogy to diachronic collaboration between art makers. Instead of focusing on the differences among media, then, this book strives to relocate modern narrative forms within wider cultural conversations, in order to reveal the range of work that artistic collaborations with Shakespeare perform. Rather than viewing the larger field of inquiry as a simply patterned aggregation of similar discrete artifacts, it suggests a complex set of relationships requiring modes of inquiry more analogous to systems design than to simple problem solving—that is, the kind of multicontextual analysis and synthesis traditionally associated with the humanities.

Not surprisingly, crucial political categories and social divisions are played out and challenged in modern Shake-shifting. And not only where one might expect—in self-proclaimed radical productions or oppositional revisions such as Aimé Césaire's *Une Tempête*, for example—but also in "mainstream" novels and films that superficially appear more interested in continuity than in disruptive challenge. By focusing on these less obvious instances, *Collaborations with the Past* attempts to reduce the predictability

24. Jay Bolter and Richard Grusin, *Remediation: Understanding New Media* (Cambridge, MA, 1999), 15.

(but not the importance) of political representation as an artistic concern and encourages analysis of the dominant culture as itself deeply fractured. Such a perspective encourages more possibilities for local change, while suggesting how Shakespeare may seem both of and more modern than his time in a way distinct from generalizing appeals to the now-troubled language of "universality."

Each of the following chapters draws from one of the four subgenres into which Shakespeare's works are now conventionally divided (tragedy, romance, comedy, history), gesturing at the range of the field.[25] Just as importantly, they highlight different modes of diachronic collaboration. In their totality, the chapters provide a selective but representative "history" of Shake-shifting in the mainstream of Anglo-American modernity; because the chapters themselves will be sites for more focused, deep analysis, it will be helpful here to introduce their arguments within that larger historical context.

Brave New World

The first two case studies explore the recurrence of Shakespearean narrative and citation in novels by Sir Walter Scott and Virginia Woolf (with an unacknowledged assist from Charlotte Brontë), writers emblematic of prose Romanticism and modernism, respectively. Not coincidentally, "Bards of the Borders" begins in the early nineteenth century, when, in the wake of the French Revolution and Napoleonic wars as well as the ongoing Industrial Revolution, a sense of radical change generated the energies and systems conventionally deemed to constitute the modern era. Something new emerged: "modern" now signified not merely "of the present" but also a particular historical configuration of institutions and attitudes. These changes likewise affected the conceptualization and representation of Shakespeare, most notable in his overt political deployment in the service of the imperial nation-state (as in John Philip Kemble's anti-French additions to *Henry V*) and in a more thoroughgoing acknowledgment of historical distance from

25. The First Folio divides the plays into comedies (including *The Winter's Tale*), tragedies (including *Cymbeline*), and histories. In the late nineteenth century Edward Dowden posited a fourth category of "Romances," which has become standard and remains useful even now that the shelf life of his biographically based interpretation has expired; it helps distinguish the tone and technique of *Cymbeline* from those of both the earlier comedies and the tragedies. For Walter Scott, by contrast, such a distinction between romance and tragedy was not transparent (at least within the formal criticism of Shakespeare).

18 his world (as in the gradual shift from contemporary to period costuming).[26] Kemble's elaborately "historicized" costumes and sets established a precedent for a century of lavishly pictorial stage productions, culminating in the spectacles of Charles Kean, Charles Calvert, and Herbert Beerbohm Tree.

Paradoxically, it was at the very moment when Shakespeare was recognized as being historically distant that critics felt he also had to be "recovered" for modernity—or else lifted out of history altogether. Thus the Renaissance London theater writer became the prophetic Bard, either prescient or all-knowing, be the topic human nature, politics, gender relations, or the great globe itself. Within this context several writers wrestled with the relationships between Shakespeare's modernity and historicity. Whereas the essays of Charles Lamb and (the postrevolutionary) Samuel Taylor Coleridge transport Shakespeare into a sublime netherworld of the imagination, the writings of William Hazlitt and Sir Walter Scott constitute two attempts (from very different political positions) to have it both ways: to credit Shakespeare with bardic foresight while retaining his historicity as a model for worldly involvement.[27]

Scott took up the challenge, moreover, in the form that would become the quintessential modern literary genre, the novel. As its name implies, this was the new fictional form for the increasingly literate public, the citizenry as audience. Despite (or because of) its eighteenth-century associations with the feminine and fanciful, Scott turned to the novel—and specifically, the novel as historical romance—when he rewrote Shakespeare's tragedy of a marriage undone. "Bards of the Borders" relates Scott's *Kenilworth* to its Shakespearean pre-text, *Othello*, as well as to its immediate historical context, revealing a particularly rich case of political and artistic adaptation. Reconsidered in concert with the contemporary "whitening" of *Othello* on

26. I paint with broad brushstrokes. The ancient/modern debate informed the interpretation of Shakespeare from the beginning: Francis Meres's *Palladis Tamia* (1598) hailed him through the standard authorizing move of the day, comparison with ancient writers in which he and his contemporaries become their modern match or equivalent. Such competitive comparisons, however, did not directly address a qualitative difference in the nature of the world in which the writers composed, nor did they see historical change as a critical factor shaping the terms of evaluation. Likewise, Restoration productions certainly found (or added) topical political allusions, but without the consciousness of historical distance as a problem to be overcome or as so clear a testament to the myth of a continuous national identity (the *mentalité* of Kemble and his heirs).

27. On the simultaneous rise of historicism and the transcendent bard, see Howard Felperin, *The Uses of the Canon: Elizabethan Literature and Contemporary Theory* (Oxford, 1990), 9–15. Bate provides a thorough, sympathetic exposition of Hazlitt, and also discusses Lamb's "private, individualistic notion of 'authorship': Lamb refuses to admit the possibility that much of Shakespeare's power may derive from the fact that he is not in the Romantic sense an 'author' at all"; *Shakespearean Constitutions*, 133.

the stage, the Romantic aestheticization of Shakespeare as disembodied poetry, and the political and economic deterioration of Scotland, *Kenilworth* becomes a more complicated cultural document than either its stage adaptations or modern critics have allowed.

Self-consciously altering both Elizabethan history and Shakespeare, *Kenilworth* removes blackness from the *Othello* plot and substitutes a submerged
Celtic tragedy at the borders of its historical romance. At the same time,
Scott elides his authorial position with Shakespeare's; he thereby creates an
authoritative voice through which to express (muted) discontent with the
treatment of the Celtic fringe within Britain and to vindicate his participation within a market economy that undermined his Romantic codes of
honor. Rather than invoking Shakespeare as a mystical and transcendent
Bard, Scott in fact resurrects the playwright as figure and source for his own
border position: trying to link poetic vision with financial success, ethical
critique with endorsement by the elite, and (selective) political sensitivity to
"racial" otherness with mainstream popularity. By veiling his criticisms of
contemporary society in Shakespearean cloth, Scott collaborated with and
succeeded within the dominant English culture of his day, becoming its most
popular and esteemed author. The nineteenth century reproduced Scott's
construction of himself as a latter-day Shakespeare in critical commentaries
and on the stage — but in most cases it did so by ignoring the Scotsman's politics entirely. As with the Romantics' apotheosis of a transcendent Shakespeare, this interpretation removed Scott from the turmoil of the present
day, but came at a price.

As this chapter's examination of both chosen and market-impelled aspects
of collaboration reveals, modern forms of artistic circulation may undermine, even as they encourage, the figure of the singular author. Furthermore, Scott's noncompetitive model of diachronic collaboration, in which
his substitutions supplement rather than challenge the aptness of Shakespeare's representational choices (implicitly apt in his own day), does not
question the earlier writer's continued primacy. While this strategy allowed
Scott to be perceived as the necessary supplement for his own times, eventually his comparative humility contributed to making him and not Shakespeare seem the expendable figure — even as his own Shake-shifting contributed to the nineteenth century's vision of the Bard.

Across the Atlantic, Shakespeare's perceived modernity was even more
important, allowing him to become, Michael Bristol suggests, the classic author for American culture. Ralph Waldo Emerson (Harold Bloom's acknowledged master in Shakespeare criticism) put "the argument in its
strong form, namely that Shakespeare is actually an institution-maker, the

man who 'wrote the text of modern life.' "[28] But at the same time as Shakespeare was being hailed as protomodern, he was becoming the icon of continuity with the past that we saw graphically (and precariously) displayed in Colman's painting.

This cultural need for stability also made itself felt, backhandedly, in the name given to those late nineteenth-century scholars who recognized the collaborative dimension of Shakespeare's art: the "disintegrators." In that these scholarly amateurs acknowledged evidence of other hands in the composition of some plays within the canon, they disturbed the unity of the authorial figure in which the wholeness of their culture was reposited. Refining their methods, the newly professionalized "scholarly technologies" of the early twentieth century further threatened, as Hugh Grady has documented, to "disintegrate the Bard of the Romantic Age." A counteremphasis on the formal integrity and thematic unity of Shakespeare's plays took shape in response to this perceived threat, in the work of such critics as G. Wilson Knight, the American New Critics, and Northrop Frye.[29] Thus these moderns continued to look to Shakespeare as a marker of integrity and order, seeking comfort in an insecure new world.

Certainly Mr. Ramsay in Virginia Woolf's *To the Lighthouse*—like the eminent Victorian upon whom his daughter modeled the character—looked to Shakespeare (and Scott) for such reassurance. But as a more forward-looking—and female—adherent of modernism, Woolf took a position that was more complicated, and the discontinuities within her diachronic collaborations show it. For her, release from the long shadows of past masters (Milton's bogey in *A Room of One's Own*) promised new freedoms and her own moment in the sun. Yet she also felt a poetic kinship and opportunity in supplementing one master's vision—a "conflicted, dialectical" route indeed, but one leading to the "big time" in its more profound sense.[30] Thus Woolf's seri-

---

28. Bristol, *Shakespeare's America*, 3. Bloom cites Emerson's essay "Shakespeare; or, The Poet" approvingly in the preface to his revised edition of *Anxiety*, xiii–xiv, as he explains Shakespeare's absence from that volume.

29. Grady, *Modernist Shakespeare*, 30. Of T. S. Eliot's criticism, Halpern writes, "Historical allegory emerges in the shadow of historicism—or rather, *as* its shadow." Invoking Walter Benjamin's interpretation of baroque allegory, Halpern claims that modernist allegory is ultimately "not a salvific project but a juxtaposition of losses"; *Shakespeare among the Moderns*, 9. While he discerns the fruitfulness of the "conflicted, dialectical interplay between past and present" in modernist allegories (*Shakespeare and Modernity*, 4, 14), Grady underscores their conservative motivation: viewing "capitalist civilization as empty, bureaucratic, and soulless," these poet-scholars "celebrated a defunct past somehow recreated through art and literature in the present"; *Modernist Shakespeare*, 180.

30. See Bristol, *Big-Time Shakespeare*, 6–10, citing Bakhtin as the culmination of his observations on Woolf.

ous playfulness as a Shake-shifter best exemplifies novel modernist possibilities: the impulses that distinguish the newer aesthetic from Victorian
melancholia, but also a stronger desire to "correct" the Shakespeare Myth
than is found in Scott's *Kenilworth*. Focusing on her uses of *Cymbeline* within
Mrs. Dalloway, "A Fine Romance" explores both the difficulties and the possibilities this collaborative strategy entails for Woolf's attempt to re-gender
the author figure and the novelist's sentence. So contextualized, her explicit
turn back to Shakespeare's romance (rather than that of her "foremother" in
fiction, Charlotte Brontë) becomes more comprehensible—despite Woolf's
advocacy of a social order at odds with that celebrated in his plays.

Whereas Scott drew upon the plot of one of the most popular tragedies
for his popular fiction, Woolf cited *Othello* yet chose a lyric from a late play to
serve as a leitmotif within her high modernist novel. The dirge from *Cymbeline* echoes in the minds of Clarissa Dalloway and Septimus Smith, linking
two characters who never meet yet serve as literary doubles. The echo extends beyond local allusion into narrative structure. Shakespeare's world of
romance animates *Mrs. Dalloway*, leading Clarissa, like *Cymbeline*'s Imogen,
to rediscover lost "siblings": in this instance, the beloveds of her adolescence, Sally Seton and Peter Walsh. These youthful intimates supplanted
her dead sister Sylvia but were in turn superseded when Clarissa became
Mrs. Dalloway. Woolf's use of *Cymbeline* similarly reveals a pattern of romanticizing her own inheritance as a writer: she "recovers" a lost Renaissance and a kindred spirit in Shakespeare. But while *Cymbeline* combines
two notions of romance compatible in the Renaissance, *Mrs. Dalloway* more
clearly ironizes the relationship between the conventional love-and-
marriage plot and the ancient motif of lost and recovered siblings.

In claiming this fraternal bond for herself, Woolf collaborates with the
past in order to reconstruct it radically. She makes the Bard a double substitute: Shakespeare replaces her own lost sibling, her brother Thoby, who encouraged her first encounters with *Cymbeline* before dying young; and
Shakespeare supplants female forerunners in the genre of the romantic
novel—most notably, Charlotte Brontë—whose Victorian voices jarred with
Woolf's attempts to realize a modernist aesthetic. Shakespeare becomes the
dead brother whose elegy she sings without the interference of patriarchs
and flawed foremothers, without generational and historical strife, and without the marital closure of *Cymbeline*'s own romance plot. The elegy known as
Mrs. Dalloway thus concludes with a reanimated female presence as cultural
collaborator.

This alliance, like the other diachronic collaborations explored here, has
ambivalent consequences. Some of these Woolf acknowledges within the

22   novel. In the most sardonic instance, Septimus Smith's changing response to *Antony and Cleopatra* implies that interpretation of Shakespeare is primarily a projection of one's own psychic needs and obsessions, or even delusions. Such projections, moreover, can become tools for nationalist and military manipulation—and may lead ultimately to self-victimization and death. Woolf's own motivations for collaborating with Shakespeare, of course, take her in a more creative direction. Yet in affiliating herself with a male author and deploying the distancing techniques of romance, Woolf strives for "impersonality" as an artist at the expense of political consistency and immediacy: at several points within *Mrs. Dalloway*, the author's socialist and feminist sympathies are blunted, if not undermined, by inherited attitudes and artistic patterns. Like Clarissa Dalloway's inability to empathize with the inelegant woman who tutors her daughter, Woolf's harsh appraisal of Brontë's artistry reveals a limit to "sisterhood." More importantly, her silence about the common ground between the family romances of *Mrs. Dalloway* and *Jane Eyre* could be deemed the triumph of sound over substance, or even (if one were inclined to judge) the betrayal of political alliance.

    Woolf's quarrel with the constraints of the Victorian novel, however, went deeper than style alone: in her attempts to bring a poetic awareness of internal thought and everyday life into the novel form, perhaps she could not afford to see Brontë's allegorical intelligence. Given her more obvious differences from Shakespeare in sex and genre, it may have been easier to meditate upon and borrow from his alien medium in the services of a fresh vision. Having escaped the dutiful daughter's role, Woolf managed to create a dialectical relationship with Shakespeare that derives not from defensive misprision but from careful, attentive reading: at least in this instance, her "swerves" and alterations become necessary accompaniments, not displacements, and create a space capacious enough for cohabitation. Indeed, the success of Michael Cunningham's *The Hours* suggests that the age of Woolf-shifting has likewise arrived.

    The novel form has been said to epitomize modernity in its "low mimetic" resemblance to everyday life;[31] if so, the desire to collaborate with Shakespeare's poetic drama conspires against this movement toward the immediate and the mundane. These "Novel Transformations" instead look back across time to Shakespearean tragedy and romance in order to defamiliarize

---

31. Northrop Frye's differentiation of the novel could be said to discount the comparably "low mimetic" qualities of city comedy, and obviously simplifies a range of modern practice; see *Anatomy of Criticism: Four Essays* (Princeton, 1957), 34. Nevertheless, as shorthand for the representational shift to more temporally and socially immediate events enacted by recognizable, less than heroic characters, the distinction remains useful.

and enliven the present. The generic melding of romance and mundane modernity or historicism, in fact, links *Kenilworth*, *Jane Eyre*, and *Mrs. Dalloway*, works that would otherwise seem worlds apart. Ian Duncan describes romance (as it developed during the later eighteenth century) "as modernity's vision of worlds it has superseded, charged with a magic of estrangement, peril and loss: a cultural uncanny."[32] A romanticized past certainly haunts major characters within these novels, most notably the Cornishman Tressilian in *Kenilworth* and the title character in *Mrs. Dalloway*; each remembers an estranged beloved from earlier years, an alliance with whom would have symbolized—within the logic of the novels—a more idealistic political vision. *Jane Eyre*'s Rochester serves, until his happy ending, as their cynical foil. Yet on further examination, the sense of the past conveyed by these novels in their entirety is neither more nor less perilous than their sense of the present, and the time periods are not so easily kept separable. The books struggle with both history and their own modernity; Shake-shifting helps blur the distinctions.

It helps blur their societal location too. Because of their regional identifications or sex, these novelists wrote from what were both privileged and marginalized positions within the British Empire. While all three novelists have at various times been central to the English literary canon, none fully inhabited the idealized "universal" subject position of British modernity. None was an "Englishman"—that figure humorously lauded in Gilbert and Sullivan's *H.M.S. Pinafore* but taken for granted by the nineteenth century as the normative voice of authorship. Scott, Brontë, and Woolf had to cross national and gendered borders, as well as the distance of time and medium, to claim Shakespeare as their own. Their ambiguous locations were both a motivation for and product of that turn: the figure of the Bard helped shape fictions that are authoritative and yet temporally fluid, collusive yet rebellious, historically and politically specific without being thwarted or silenced by their liminality. Thus these authors' conceptions of nationhood, as well as gender and "race," become part of their Shake-shifting, defying attempts neatly to divide aesthetic decisions from political ones.

Further, the afterlife of these novels, like Shakespeare's work, challenges static categorization of high versus low, or elite versus popular culture. *Kenilworth* was wildly popular and respected in its day but both its prestige and its readership have faded, whereas *Mrs. Dalloway* began "highbrow" but is

---

32. Ian Duncan, *Modern Romance and Transformations of the Novel: The Gothic, Scott, Dickens* (Cambridge, UK, 1992), 9. On the use of Shakespeare in modern romance novels, see the online version (especially) of Laurie Osborne, "Romancing the Bard," http://www.colby.edu/personal/l/ leosborn/POPSHAK/.

24 now more widely read — and seen — than ever (with spinoffs such as a 1997 film and *The Hours* in turn adapted for the screen).[33] The reception history of *Kenilworth* and *Mrs. Dalloway* might even seem to epitomize the fate of two contrasting aesthetics during the course of the twentieth century, culminating in the triumph of literary modernism. It might symbolize the shifting fortunes of reading in an increasingly visual culture, as time pressures and the narrative potential of film conspire against the pleasures of the rambling three-volume historical novel. And indeed, in turning from novels to screen (as well as stage) collaborations with Shakespeare, this book follows the trajectory of twentieth-century popular culture, as it shifts from a "modern" to a "postmodern" era in which cutting and fragmentation are the given tools of the trade rather than the doom of art.

But this would be an overly simple story. For *Jane Eyre* likewise was a "triple decker" yet remains among the most popular novels of all time — nor are bulky best-sellers by James Michener so far from Scott's prose narratives. Moreover, as will quickly become apparent, the shift of medium from page to screen does not guarantee a more radical, or even progressive, praxis, in either aesthetic or political terms. Nevertheless, one striking pattern does emerge from this reflection: the novels remaining popular are those that are *perceived* as sites for debate and intense response rather than as simple rollicks. Even those readers who find the last volume of *Jane Eyre* anticlimactic and St. John Rivers insufferable tend to admit that their existence helps make the novel much more substantial than the legions of Harlequin romances spawned from volume 2. And it was only after Sir Walter's *Kenilworth* had been reduced and patronized by the real-life equivalents of *To the Lighthouse*'s Charles Tansley that it fell out of fashion. In this regard, the difference between the dominant method of Shake-shifting in Scott's and Woolf's novels may also have played a part. At least on the surface, Woolf's "corrective" mode of diachronic collaboration seems the more creative, radical, different. In emphasizing the numerous layers of substitution within *Kenilworth* I have tried to suggest that this judgment might still be a fruitful topic for debate. Nevertheless, even if one concedes that the pleasure of

---

33. On the cultural afterlives of Woolf, see Brenda Silver's book. In what might be viewed as a poignant or reactionary response to Woolf's popularity, a 2004 MLA call for papers by the International Woolf Society tried to sustain some highbrow space for academic analysis: they sought papers on "How Woolf motivates and informs contemporary intellectual artistic work (e.g., Sontag, Schaberg, Atwood). No pop culture or Cunningham!" *MLA Newsletter* 36, no. 1 (2004): 25. See, however, Scott Cutler Shershow on the impossibility of "an autonomous or self-contained elite or popular culture"; "New Life: Cultural Studies and the Problem of the 'Popular,'" *Textual Practice* 12, no. 1 (1998): 43. On cultural quotation, see the books by Douglas Bruster and Martin Harries.

Scott's novels is less challenging and of more narrowly historical interest now, the contrast between these two exemplary Shake-shifters reinforces our awareness of the varying artistic possibilities and the representational complexity involved in novelistic collaboration with Shakespeare. And each played an important role in bearing the Bard forward, his vitality renewed, into the future that is our present.

Thoroughly Modern Shakespeare?

From Shake-shifting as a means of "self-authorization" within the modern form of literary storytelling par excellence, "Media Crossings" turns to the more overtly collective processes of modern performance on stage and screen. After all, the truly novel art forms of the twentieth century appeared in cinema halls and homes, on film and television. Working in these media requires collaborating not only with a dead playwright but also with many living co-workers and the more immediate demands of an audience.

"Shakespeare" came in on the ground floor of the new screen technologies, providing stories and prestige. The earliest films transposed, onto celluloid, silent vignettes of famous performances by the most acclaimed Shakespearean stage actors of their day. Beerbohm Tree as King John, Sarah Bernhardt and Johnston Forbes-Robertson as Hamlet: akin to Woolf's literary citation of lines from *Cymbeline*, these were visual citations of stage productions. Soon the popularity of narrative shorts encouraged the frequent use of simplified plots derived from Shakespeare's plays as well, silent films with a few of his lines distributed among the title cards. But whereas Scott's plot and line borrowings, like Woolf's citation of the dirge, had been only the beginning of a self-conscious thematic reconceptualization of Shakespearean narrative, these films aspired to nothing more (or less) than a seeming translation to the new medium—even when in fact they drastically altered both story and theme. Like the traveling stage productions that crisscrossed continents throughout the nineteenth century, the silent cinema made Shakespeare a modern entertainment, experienced by audiences in their (mediated) present across Europe and North America. And among the most popular of plays in this mass media crossing—attracting such early film luminaries as D. W. Griffith, Douglas Fairbanks Sr., and Mary Pickford—was *The Taming of the Shrew*.

What's so funny about taming a shrew? The newness of the medium does not entirely obscure the oddity of selecting this most old-fashioned of comic stories, as advertised by its title. And just as Woolf differentiated her form of

26   romance from the gendered conservatism of Shakespeare's endings, film-makers (working with actual women rather than boy actors) did omit some of the more humiliating aspects of his sixteenth-century farce. But especially with the coming of talkies (and with them a presumption that His Master's Voice should be preserved), updating *Shrew* as a modern romantic comedy took concerted effort. "The Return of the Shrew" explores the nature of that challenge, both on film and later on television, by emphasizing the use of the camera to direct audience attention to Kate's unscripted possibilities. Else-where I have surveyed the ideological problems that persist in screen *Shrew*s, and I recontextualize some of that material here with a more partic-ular focus on their sources of pleasure.[34] More fundamentally, though, this chapter adds an entirely new dimension to that analysis by considering how certain films and videos wrestle with the possibilities of narrative rupture and psychological depth—two quintessential markers of twentieth-century storytelling.

And thus the analyst turns to Sigmund Freud. His clinical essay "A Child Is Being Beaten" provides a fruitful and unexpectedly exact parallel text to Shakespeare's tale of wife taming. As Freud describes (or rather, con-structs) a three-stage beating fantasy based on his interviews with a handful of patients, he reveals the creative work involved in stitching together a his-tory—even as he argues for its empirical truth and "necessity." Freud trans-forms what appears to be a disconnected, aggressive vision into a narrative premised upon female masochism. His clinical method, along with its gen-dered ideological assumptions, returns quite vividly in Jonathan Miller's commentary about the BBC/Time-Life television *Shrew* he directed. But just as importantly, Freud's manner of papering over the evident gaps in his ac-count reveals—when read against the therapeutic grain—the possibility of an alternative interpretation, and thus highlights what is at stake in choos-ing either disruption or determinism when telling a story. Through close ex-amination of the mixed media messages of the televised docudrama *Kiss Me, Petruchio* (in which the video cuts undermine the actors' attempts at consis-tent psychologizing) as well as Franco Zeffirelli's feature-film *Shrew*, chap-ter 3 illustrates how modern collaborators with the camera dramatize and finesse the difficulties of (yet again) taming a shrew. Bricolage, fragmenta-tion, jump cuts and more: in multimedia art forms, there are many ways to tame a narrative besides changing the script. But there are also ways in

---

34. Diana E. Henderson, "A Shrew for the Times, Revisited," in *Shakespeare, The Movie, II: Popularizing the Plays on Film, TV, Video, and DVD*, ed. Richard Burt and Lynda E. Boose (Lon-don, 2003), 120–39.

which the dynamics of an inherited tripartite narrative creep in even when the script does change—as *Ten Things I Hate About You* (not to mention some of the best Golden Age Hollywood film) demonstrates. Collaborating with another era's comedy remains a tricky, often divisive business, and remediation has the potential to reinforce residual ideologies as well as reframe them.

Scott and Woolf used Shakespeare to complicate their novels' modernity, but adapting his comedies does not encourage similar layering: instead, the genre of comedy—with its emphasis on bodily presence and accessibility—tends to efface temporal distance. Even when performed in period costumes, comedy's attention to crass realities and characters of "the middling sort" conspires to create the world as familiar. This tendency is aggravated by screen technologies that, especially in their early years, caused rapture and enjoyment precisely because they produced the illusion of transporting the viewer to another location, as if "you were there." As in director Bartlett's conjuration of Marlowe, the audience collaborates with the illusion, knowing that the performers are two-dimensional reproductions of actors elsewhere yet willing themselves to (semi)-inhabit their space-time continuum. Like theatrical performances, film and television are witnessed in the present moment, with their spectators experiencing the story (*pace* flashbacks) as if it were now occurring, its pace and sequence outside their control. At least, this was the "first run" or broadcast experience that until recently pertained: now, video and DVD recordings are diminishing the theatrical parallel by giving watchers more control—leading them back, perhaps ironically, to an experience that is closer to reading a (picture) book. Nevertheless, even now, if one gives oneself over to the artistic medium as most filmmakers practice it, two worlds come together phenomenologically, encouraging the audience to forget their distance. Only when the film has become "dated" (a document frozen in the time of production and visibly alien from the time of its witnessing) do we tend to focus upon its temporal remove—and at that point, if it is not judged an outright failure, the film's story and emotions have usually taken a backseat. Hence Jonathan Miller's difficulty in invoking historicism, his self-consciousness about reproducing the past on screen, in order to inoculate a televised comedy from accusations about the antiquated gender politics being represented. Hence too the more typical way in which actresses playing Kate validate their own act of collusion with an extreme form of ideological "self-discipline" by finding contemporary analogies and rationales (Pickford, Elizabeth Taylor, and Meryl Streep all attempt this). Psychological realism, then, tends to supplant other possible frames (and frame stories) for understanding Shakespeare's comedy, and film's conventional strength in conveying this type of acting serves thereby to perpetuate an old wives' tale.

In discussing directors, screenwriters, actors, and cameras, "The Return of the Shrew" addresses the challenge of attributing credit and responsibility in art forms that are far more obviously group collaborations than are novels. People are still making choices when they re-construct stories as their own, and to ignore their artistic agency would be patronizing and evasive. This chapter therefore makes critical judgments about the coherence of some participants' decisions, even as it recognizes the limits and problems (both contingent and systemic) that they confront. Such judgments are introduced less as a reflection upon individual reputations than as a means of illustration: by suggesting the ways in which particular choices deny or acknowledge their participation in Shake-shifting, we make the ethical stakes involved in artistic collaboration more apparent. Indeed, the "throughline" ultimately shared by this great variety of screen *Shrew*s is their resort to some mode of justification for collaborating with this overtly tricky text in the first place: the layers they add and the solutions they find vary, from medial to psychological to narrative re-vision, but all implicitly acknowledge more of a problem than Woolf's discontinuous practice ever evinces. The greater the perceived difficulty in making the audience laugh, the greater the urgency of Shake-shifting.

If *The Taming of the Shrew* has been important since the early days of screen Shakespeare, *Henry V* has played an even more dramatic, and unexpected, role in the success of Shakespeare at the movies. First Laurence Olivier's 1944 film established the actor as director and star of a respected, popular film based on Shakespeare, which buoyed both the British film industry and the Shakespeare trade. Then in 1989, Kenneth Branagh's low-budget *Henry V*, a conscious remake with a difference, heralded a new age of popularity for film Shakespeare (followed soon after by his *Much Ado About Nothing*, Franco Zeffirelli's *Hamlet*, and Baz Luhrmann's *William Shakespeare's Romeo + Juliet*, to name but a few popular successes). "What's Past Is Prologue" considers both the reasons for and the consequences of this unlikely pattern of success for an unlikely genre, the English history play. As in the film versions of *Shrew*, the desire to focus on psychologically realistic, or at least plausibly modern, characters leads to significant cutting, in both the textual and the film editorial sense. And again, collaborating with an inherited ideology—involving the nation as well as gender—has ethical consequences. Furthermore, just as the screen *Shrew*s carry forward the gender issues raised in "A Fine Romance," the selective reproduction of Shakespeare's his-

tory revives issues earlier explored with reference to "race" in "Bards of the
Borders." When *Henry V* is fitted into the twentieth century's cultural frame,
the particulars of the past are transmuted into allegories of a (misrecog-
nized) present, often diminishing those on the losing side of history even
more absolutely than did Shakespeare's version(s). Focusing on the present
can thus perpetuate inherited hierarchies more blindly than do attempts to
reproduce the past "faithfully."

Listed among the dead in *Henry V* is Davy Gam, Esquire; not listed among
the missing in Kenneth Branagh's film is the First Folio's French Queen.
The historical original behind each name could be considered a political collaborator in the twentieth-century sense of the word. Focusing on their figuration in Shakespeare's text, "What's Past Is Prologue" looks back into political history and forward to performance history in order to reveal their
intertwined dramatic and political significance for the conception of "England." Not only do these marginal characters blur the boundaries of the
English nation through their actions and alliances, but they also recall a
larger Franco-Welsh alliance that for a time effectively challenged the narrative destiny of "Harry England." Although Davy Gam, a Welshman, appears
in *Henry V* only as a name, it is a name to conjure with—since the historical
Daffyd ap Llywelyn fought against another Shakespearean conjuror, Owen
Glendower, before fighting and dying at Agincourt. And that same Glyn
Dŵr (to de-Anglicize the story nominally) had been supported by the
French King Charles as the true Prince of Wales, direct rival to Henry of
Monmouth. Shakespeare's Lancastrian tetralogy dramatizes the transforma-
tion of formidable opponents into traitors and (subordinated, fitful) allies,
and *Henry V* completes that task in great measure through the representation
of Davy Gam's living surrogate Fluellen and the French Queen Isabel.

Isabel provides an alternative route toward understanding the play's gendered state relationships. That route demands another foray into the contentious forest of late feudalism, in order to understand how she acquired
the duplicitous name of Isabeau de Bavière. The Queen's "foreign" origins
and alliances led to her vilification by French historians, a structural hazard
for women of high birth. Her representation in *Henry V* thus bears directly
upon that major worry for the English king: the legitimacy of inheritance
from the female. But only by recovering the specifics of the historical record
does Shakespeare's distinctively double action become fully apparent; as in
the case of Dafydd made Davy, the playwright simultaneously resurrects
and simplifies the representation of political collaborators. Attending to the
English-Welsh-French triangulation of the political landscape, "What's Past

Is Prologue" highlights the cost of choosing to focus on single oppositions or one action alone: the coin of this imaginative realm has more than two sides.

While much of *Collaborations with the Past* focuses exclusively on reworkings of Shakespeare, this analysis of *Henry V* circles back to Shakespeare as himself the diachronic collaborator, reworking chronicles of an earlier age to fit his "modern" concerns. Changes intervening between his time and Henry's led Shakespeare to represent feudal factions as emergent nations and to enlist border figures in their service. But his play also registers the uneasiness, or at least the effort, of this attempt to divide the world between enemies and friends—a process in which Welshmen and Frenchwomen are both vital and threatening. Even in Elizabethan times, the borders were unstable, and the wistful epilogue of *Henry V* would have recalled for its audience not only past failures but also present precariousness when kingdoms were at stake. Nevertheless, only traces of the (French) Queen's threatening history are allowed to ripple across the superficially calm waters of act 5. Especially when compared with Shakespeare's historical pre-texts, then, *Henry V* looks like a masterpiece of selective memory. If modern performances make their own partial selections from his work, they are only following the master.

Yet in each case, one sees less by looking complacently through "modern" eyes. The text carries complex traces of memory's unruliness, of the knowledge that there was once a life-and-death struggle over the ending of this story and that competing perspectives persist. To reduce that perception to mere celebration of either nation or king, as the nineteenth century did and many productions still do, erases more than the play's "dramatic" side: it also erases the losing sides. Until recently, Shakespeare's success in shaping Henry's history (appealing to modern investments in national defense and psychological characterization) displaced attention from the roles of the Welsh and French in establishing the king's legitimacy. In performance the Queen—if not omitted entirely—was often (as in Olivier's film) trivialized, and Fluellen played for laughs. Branagh's "usurpation" of the female part, taking some of Isabel's lines for himself and cutting her character, is thus ultimately more conventional—more consonant with Shake-shifting stage and film traditions—than is the unusual texture his film accords to the representation of Fluellen by Ian Holm. Likewise, Paul Scofield invests the French king with the painful knowledge of historical memory: the gendered complexity may disappear, but not the cost of war. Nevertheless, both this film and contemporary stage productions continue to struggle with what has become a nationalist ur-text; even when attempting to shift sympathies, they often end up replicating the narrative's quasi-magical determinism. Clearly both the *Henry* feature films have been marketplace, and in most quarters critical, successes. But chapter 4 concludes by looking to the future and the open question of how artists might avoid the pitfalls of collaboration as political endorsement without sacrificing the pleasures of this text. If the rehistoricizing mode of Olivier's *Henry* was propagandistically patriotic and that of Branagh's individualistically psychological, surely other ways of representing war and identity now beckon.[35] As one means of challenging the thinking that creates easy heroes and enemies, we might do worse than look again at some of Shakespeare's more shadowy collaborators from the past.

The two chapters of "Media Crossings" focus on stories that have played unusually important roles in the historical process of making Shakespeare a screenwriter—a radical Shake-shift indeed. And while the turn from allusive novels to "direct" screen adaptations may surprise, there is much common ground in these narrative arts; indeed, the surprise of the mainstream screen versions might be that aesthetically they feel more of a piece with the "modern" concerns of prose fiction than with the postmodern realizations of such Shake-shifting films as Peter Greenaway's *Prospero's Books* or Michael Almereyda's *Hamlet*. This resemblance may support the intuition that words matter more in a screenplay when Shakespeare is on the writing team. If so, it provides some basis for the practices within the subdiscipline of screen Shakespeare studies that align it as much with literary criticism as with mainstream modes of cinema studies. In any event, the movement from novels to films reinforces the inadequacy of formalist presumptions about what media "can" do—and even about which media are best employed for modern collaborations with Shakespeare.[36] It also refuses the literalism of much discussion of textual "fidelity" in favor of identifying potential sites of fidelity—or infidelity—to the spirit of the Shakespearean ur-texts: for those

35. See my essays "Performing History: *Henry IV*, Money, and the Fashion of the Times," in *A Companion to Shakespeare and Performance*, ed. Barbara Hodgdon and W. B. Worthen (Oxford, 2005), 376–96, and (especially) "Meditations in a Time of (Displaced) War: *Henry V* and the Ethics of Performing History," in *Shakespeare and War*, ed. Paul Frannsen and Rosalind King (forthcoming).

36. In introducing her powerful readings, Courtney Lehmann's *Shakespeare Remains* (Ithaca, 2002) implies that film is the superior, indeed only form adequate to capture Shakespearean "remains"—a variation on a theme dating back to Alfred Hitchcock's 1930s essay rebutting Granville Barker. While reasonable as a defense for Hitchcock's profession and important in the development of film scholarship, such absolute formalism does not stand up to close scrutiny. I am not emphasizing the distinctions among various screen technologies as a theoretical issue, although I address them within the particular studies. In addition to many singleauthored contributions, see the essay collections on screen Shakespeare edited by Boose and Burt, Mark Thornton Burnett and Ramona Wray, Richard Burt, Diana Henderson, Russell Jackson, Courtney Lehmann and Lisa S. Starks, and Robert Shaughnessy.

32   interested in creative collaboration, this is the more rich and revealing territory to explore.

Back to the Future

> *Nevill Coghill* But . . . can the play [*Sweeney Agonistes*] mean something you didn't intend it to mean, you didn't know it meant?
>
> *T. S. Eliot* Obviously it does.
>
> *NC* But can it then also mean what you did intend?
>
> *TSE* I hope so . . . yes, I think so.
>
> *NC* But if the two meanings are contradictory, is not one right and the other wrong? Must not the author be right?
>
> *TSE* Not necessarily, do you think? Why is either wrong?[37]
>
>   *T. S. Eliot: A Symposium*

Many years ago, when I began conceptualizing this cross-medial, cross-period reconsideration of modern Shake-shifting, there was little critical bibliography, much less an adequately interdisciplinary framework in which to pose the questions. Much has changed since then, with Shakespeare on screen and adaptation studies too numerous even to mention, and emergent programs in comparative media studies. Yet the synthetic work involved in exploring literary, performance, and screen media within common sociopolitical and artistic contexts, which I consider a crucial step forward, still raises some eyebrows, or perhaps seems to tread on too many specialists' toes. At the same time, a burgeoning cross-disciplinary interest in the word and idea of "collaboration" may have blunted some of its critical edge by now, with everyone from therapists to scientists to feminist performance artists selecting out its laudatory associations.[38] For me, however, the continuing value of the term lies precisely in its mixed messages.

---

37. I have reformatted this conversation, recorded by Coghill and reproduced in the 1948 volume, from its citation in John Russell Brown, *Shakespeare's*, 208.

38. A keyword search of "collaboration" in the MLA bibliography reveals 1306 entries, the vast majority of which date from the past fifteen years. The fields range from creative writing to robotics, but especially well represented are studies of women's writing, language acquisition and teaching, oral history, linguistics, autobiography, and drama. In women's studies and drama particularly (and in allied practices such as women's theatrical collectives), there has been ample debate and reevaluation of the term: for example, alongside Bette London's *Writing Double: Women's Literary Partnership* (Ithaca, 1999), and Elizabeth Peck and JoAnna Mark, eds., *Common Ground: Feminist Collaborations in the Academy* (Albany, 1998), one now finds Lorraine York's *Rethinking Women's Collaborative Writing* (Toronto, 2002). Among recent meditations on literary collaboration, see Bleeth and Rivkin; Michael Moon; and the discussions in *PMLA* 116, no. 2 (2001), *PMLA* 117, no. 5 (2002), *Australasian Drama Studies* 42 (2003): 14–25, and *Theatre Topics* 13, no. 1 (2003). Collaborative process has also become a popular term in psychological

Mixed and multiple: for although representative taxonomies and histories are valuable, they are never exclusively "right." Like performance and Shake-shifting itself, their use value must ultimately be determined by an ever-changing audience. For those who find categorization a helpful means of signposting, I have emphasized the more benignly substitutional logic of Scott's Shake-shifting as distinct from the revisionism of Woolf's; the justificatory logic in screen *Shrew*s perforce takes Woolf's mode a step further, whereas arguably the rehistoricization of the screen *Henry*s at times takes Scott (and Shakespeare's play) a step backward in privileging one version of the past—though at other moments the camera's work provides glimpses of multiplicity. Indeed, substitution, revision, justification, and rehistoricization to some extent appear in every act of Shake-shifting, and thus these emphases are in practice never fully separable. It is equally "right" to stress the shared thematic links among these chapters based on representational concerns. Conventionally, the work of gender becomes associated primarily with the psychological and domestic realms, whereas the work of nation (and with it categories of ethnic or racial distinction) becomes increasingly external and political. This tends, over time, to perpetuate naturalized gender distinctions while making historical/political thought seem artificial and distanced from the psyche; indeed, though academicians often speak as if we have done away with the stability of all such categories, in Anglo-American society the normative opposition between the sexes remains (to make a gross generalization) an even more stably entrenched psychic constant than are distinctions among ethnic identities—which is not to diminish the consequentiality of any social category but rather to delineate a different relationship within each one's history and performance.

Although the following chapters present a range of Shake-shifting models and historical exempla, some will discern in them a zest for particulars and induction at odds with the tendency in much scholarship to declare the wholesale applicability of a formally deductive (though usually not a priori) hypothesis. This emphasis on particulars is less a goal than a means to achieve balance: the particulars do ground and lead to generalizable opinions in the Aristotelian sense. I write at a time when many feel compelled to choose either the archive or theory, either the veneration of historical detail or the claim for present significance: this seems to me a loss, and an unnecessary one. Thus *Collaborations with the Past* attempts to bridge some of the artificial divides within current scholarly debate by avoiding overly grand claims and getting on with the particular work at hand. This also allows

---

counseling; on co-authoring the therapeutic narrative, see Steven Friedman, ed., *The New Language of Change: Constructive Collaboration in Psychotherapy* (New York, 1993).

34   space for the "swerves" that Bloom celebrates, the movements of what Deleuze and Guattari call the flow, to which they add the hypermodern praise of the human as machine. Less invested in the radically utopian versions of revolution they envisioned, *Collaborations with the Past* favors a peaceable way forward and may therefore be open to accusations of another (neo-Fabian?) form of utopianism in believing that local shifts can create great art and collaborative reform can bring about significant political improvement—including, though certainly not limited to, a serious place for that art in society.

"The paradox of the restoration of behavior," writes Joseph Roach, "resides in the phenomenon of repetition itself: no action or sequence of actions may be performed exactly the same way twice; they must be reinvented or recreated at each appearance. In this improvisatorial behavioral space, memory reveals itself as imagination." Roach begins his innovative study with a narrative that emphasizes the loss and pain involved in remembering the past. Nevertheless, "surrogation" encompasses not just historical loss but the positive possibility of re-membering or reimagining that disjointed past: "Like performance, memory operates as both quotation and invention, an improvisation on borrowed themes, with claims on the future as well as the past."[39] Roach suggests (as does the playwright August Wilson) that the way for the oppressed, excluded peoples of circum-Atlantic history to transform both past and future lies in political gestures that undermine and replace the dominant culture's white Eurocentrism.

Such work challenges those who argue that the only escape from historical suffering and injustice is to break with the past, to create avant-garde art free of all "nostalgia";[40] equally, it serves as an important corrective to the canonical study of dramatic literature alone, removed from its social contexts and consequences. Roach's scholarship and Wilson's drama should certainly give pause to those who would turn back to history simply to celebrate. Yet in studying fractures within the "mainstream," one realizes that it is not only by going "outside" that one can displace a simplified idea of literary tradition (or the historical past) as a sacred, unchallengeable given.[41]

---

39. Roach, *Cities*, 29, 33.
40. Nostalgia is Susan Bennett's key word in *Performing Nostalgia: Shifting Shakespeare and the Contemporary Past* (New York, 1996). See also Diamond, and Rozett's rhetorical emphasis. I also depart from Worthen's critique of Kate McLuskie at the conclusion of *Shakespeare and the Force of Modern Performance*, which seems too quick to dismiss the possibility of a more thoroughgoing, critical yet generative interaction between contemporary performance and (material) historicity.
41. Michael Bristol puts this well: "[N]o tradition is actually a stable form; the dynamic character and the potentially radical instability of tradition is an inherent feature of this sociocultural phenomenon rather than some sort of contingent aberration or symptom of breakdown. Finally, tradition is concrete, and even sensuous in its vital manifestations. Tradition is

Without diminishing the vast material distance between a Walter Scott and an Ira Aldridge, a production at the Globe and one by the Company of Women, there remains truth in the deconstructive insight that the monolithic core was never that, the tradition always being a jumble of pieces and prisms available for radical, sometimes magical shifting. Authorship is *always* a collaboration and a struggle—and some of the richest "traditional" works revel in that struggle. Ignorance of this past is no solution—as the case of *Henry V* most directly demonstrates. Utopian escape, revolutionary assault, passive veneration: all are inadequate to this slippery subject, the hybrid collaborations at the very core of English literature and Shakespearean performance.[42]

History and performance need to maintain their difficult dance. Precisely because the dominant culture of global capital effaces the past, encouraging us to look no further than this year's model and to throw out the old, the more challenging action now may be to look back with care. The reenactment of centuries-old scripts serves a communal function. Some speak of the past as burden, the weight of tradition to be lifted, while others romanticize it, hoping for continuity and a place in the story. For most people the feeling is doubled, signaling the desire both for coherence and for freedom. In this self-consciously comparative modern world, virtually everyone who can read this page feels some measure of psychic or social exclusion as well as entitlement, and the difference between trivial and consequential exclusion often gets lost. Looking at temporal—and, crucially, plural—otherness thus can be as eye-opening as attending to the "others" constructed by our contemporaries. It can change the scale and specificity with which we explore differences, replacing a debilitatingly static model of present-tense disaffection with an appreciation of dynamic struggle over time. It is more difficult to resist, or indeed to see, the cultural frame in which one is born than the

above all *praxis*, it occupies the ethical dimension and the social life-world"; *Shakespeare's America*, 49.

42. Of the venerators, Bristol suggests: "The celebration of a world of priceless meanings that exist in a horizon 'beyond ideology' is a mode of resistance to the imperialism of market relations. . . . Unfortunately it is also a denial of the institutional and social reality in which both Shakespeare and the people who read his work are embedded"; *Shakespeare's America*, 25. Nor are those who perform less embedded. The struggle to break free of the past does not address the larger problem, suggested by Pierre Bourdieu's work in *The Field of Cultural Production*, as to whether there can be effective ruptures (in this case, through performance) without a transformation in the surrounding cultural fields of power. Indeed, the focus on theatrical intensity as bodily presence may be in great part a reaction formation to the larger cultural shift of attention toward more overtly mediated—especially screen—modes of performance and communication. As Mary Louise Pratt remarks of the autoethnographic mode (in words that may be re-applied to performance theorists and literary critics), it "involves partial collaboration with and appropriation of the idioms of the conqueror"; *Imperial Eyes: Travel Writing and Transculturation* (London, 1992), 7.

36   ones that went before; studying the past results in some of the same salutary effects of imaginative dislocation and re-vision as are discovered through spatially constructed geographical encounters or creative improvisations. Valuable though it can be, looking only at the latest crop of Shakespeare teenflicks (or their art-house cousins) isn't a wide enough screen.

    Like the artists studied here, we pick and choose our Shakespeares, and through that labor another story emerges. Frozen in time on the page or screen, some of those collaborations continue to speak, but denuded of their immediate moment and surroundings; we are left to supplement the traces. In recovering that past, the present takes on greater clarity and contrast. But the proof must be in the telling. A writer lifts a pen. Enter the multiple forces—political and economic, psychological, formal, and technical—that serendipitously transform imagination into memory. Let the collaborative play begin.

Part One

NOVEL TRANSFORMATIONS

Bards of the Borders

Scott's Kenilworth, *the Nineteenth Century's*
Shakespeare, and the Tragedy of Othello

I am glad you like Kenilworth [it] is certainly a splendid production more
resembling a Romance than a Novel and in my opinion one of the most interesting works that ever emanated from the great Sir Walter's pen.

Charlotte Brontë to Ellen Nussey, 1 January 1833

I'm glad you are writing about Scott, if only to keep me in countenance,
who have just bought the Waverley novels in 25 large volumes, and am
thought a sentimental mug—or is it muff?—by my friends in consequence.
They say its because he was read aloud by my father when we were children—not altogether, I think.

Virginia Woolf to Hugh Walpole, 20 August 1928

Re-viewing *Kenilworth*

No author can match Sir Walter Scott for shifting fortunes, both monetary and literary. In a letter to a friend written the year of *Kenilworth's* publication (1821), Scott accurately observed, "I have had . . . more of fame and
fortune than mere literature ever procured a man before."[1] Jane Austen had
playfully agreed with that appraisal when *Waverley* first appeared in 1814—
and on the basis of his poetry alone: "Walter Scott has no business to write
novels, especially good ones.—It is not fair.—He has fame and profit enough
as a Poet, and should not be taking bread out of other people's mouths.—I
do not like him, & do not mean to like *Waverley* if I can help it—but fear I
must."[2] Beyond the witty concession of his likeability and the comic twist

1. Cited in Marshall Walker, *Scottish Literature since 1707* (London, 1996), 111.
2. Jane Austen to Anna Austen, cited in *Walter Scott: The Critical Heritage*, ed. John O. Hayden (London, 1970), 74.

39

40   that Sir Walter was to be among Austen's first crucial defenders in print, there would be a sad irony in Austen's words; a decade later, Scott's publishers went bankrupt. As a secret partner in the business, Sir Walter became a massive debtor overnight.[3] Out of a sense of gentlemanly honor and duty, he refused to take advantage of bankruptcy to cancel his debts, instead writing relentlessly for profit from 1826 until his death six years later—a demise undoubtedly hastened by overwork.[4] Perhaps this much-praised choice now seems utterly misguided, transferring a personal code of conduct to modern market transactions. But to the nineteenth century it served as an heroic model, a dignified acting out of values that Scott's fictions praised in past ages and saw wanting in a morally diminished if not bankrupt present.[5]

As for those novels, Charlotte Brontë's verdict in a letter written two years after Scott's death spoke for the age: "For Fiction—read Scott alone [:] all novels after his are worthless."[6] Ina Ferris, tracing the novel's historical elevation as a genre, argues that "the decisive move from literary outsider to literary insider was initiated by Scott's series of historical fictions."[7] Even his political antagonist Francis Jeffrey reflected during the 1840s: "The *Novels* of Sir Walter Scott are, beyond all question, the most remarkable productions of the present age; and have made a sensation, and produced an effect, all over Europe, to which nothing parallel can be mentioned since the days of Rousseau and Voltaire; while, in our own country, they

---

3. Ina Ferris notes that Austen's "first important notice did not appear until the 1815 review of *Emma* in the *Quarterly* by Walter Scott" (the review actually appeared in March 1816). *The Achievement of Literary Authority: Gender, History, and the Waverley Novels* (Ithaca, 1991), 55.

4. John Sutherland, *The Life of Walter Scott: A Critical Biography* (Oxford, 1995), 296–301, stresses Scott's engagement in questionable business dealings, and the dubious consequences of Scott's sense of honor. Yet one must admit the moving quality of his belief and its involvement with his Scottishness, recorded in his journal on 7 March 1829 (a day after remarking he would need ten years to get clear and would "have little chance of it"):

> No—I will not be sport of circumstances. Come of it what will *I'll bend my brows / Like highland truis* and make a bold fight of it—
>
>   The best o't the warst o't
>   Is only just to die.

The quotation derives from Robert Burns's "Epistle to Davie, a Brother Poet." Cited in Iain Gordon Brown, ed., *Scott's Interleaved Waverley Novels: An Introduction and Commentary,* (Aberdeen, 1987), 45.

5. Byron wrote to Stendhal three years before the financial crash: "I have known Walter Scott long and well, and in occasional situations which call forth the *real* character—and I can assure you that his character *is* worthy of admiration—that of all men he is the most *open,* the most *honourable,* the most *amiable.* With his politics I have nothing to do; they differ from mine. . . . I say that Walter Scott is as nearly a thorough good man as man can be, because I *know* it by experience to be the case"; in Paul Henderson Scott, *Walter Scott and Scotland* (Edinburgh, 1994), 7.

6. *The Letters of Charlotte Brontë,* vol. 1: *1829–1847,* ed. Margaret Smith (Oxford, 1995), 131.

7. Ferris, *Achievement,* 1–2.

have attained a place, inferior only to that which must be filled for ever by
the unapproachable glory of Shakespeare."[8]

During the nineteenth century, *Kenilworth* was among the most popular of
these novels. "Momentously, *Kenilworth* was retailed by [Archibald] Constable in three 'luxurious' volumes, octavo, at a guinea-and-a-half. It thus set
the pattern for fiction for the next three-quarters of a century. . . . It was
also a supremely influential text for what was to become a Victorian industry—the lusty Elizabethan romance."[9] It received more than fifteen reviews
during its first two months in circulation and ranked among the most read
and respected of the Waverley novels for generations. Scott's son-in-law and
biographer J. G. Lockhart declared that *"Kenilworth* was one of the most
successful of them all at the time of publication; and it continues, and, I
doubt not, will ever continue to be placed in the very highest rank of prose
fiction."[10]

Kenilworth's translation across media was equally remarkable. Thirty stage
versions were produced during the five years after its publication—the first
two in London within weeks of its appearance in print. According to H.
Philip Bolton, *Kenilworth* generated about 120 dramatic productions and
twice that many "derivative dramas": operas, Kenilworth pageants, and
even an equestrian spectacular featuring M. Pablo Fanque.[11] Jerome
Mitchell, noting that "[n]ext to Shakespeare [Scott] inspired more libret-
tists and composers than did any other single writer," lists eleven operas
based on *Kenilworth* (among Scott's novels, a number equaled only by *Ivanhoe*).[12] And even in 1901, a historian indignant at its "inexcusable" factual errors conceded: "It may be said with safety that the popularity of 'Kenilworth,' if even equalled, has not been surpassed by that of any other volume
included in the 'Waverley' series."[13] The power and portability of this text
were great indeed.

8. Ibid., 15. In Owen Dudley Edwards, Gwynfor Evans, Ioan Rhys, and Hugh MacDiarmid, *Celtic Nationalism* (London, 1968), MacDiarmid goes further: "It is simply a fact that, in
seminal influence on other literatures, three Scots have exceeded all English writers put together, not excluding Shakespeare, namely 'Ossian,' Sir Walter Scott, and Lord Byron" (308).
The irony of including a forger (Ossian) does not deter him.

9. Sutherland, *Life*, 247. Duncan observes that this price "fixed a ceiling that publishers
and circulating libraries together would prop up for the next seventy years" (*Modern Romance*,
179).

10. J. G. Lockhart, *Life of Sir Walter Scott* [abridged] (Edinburgh, 1853), 485.

11. See H. Philip Bolton, *Scott Dramatized* (London, 1992), 394–421. Beatlemaniacs will recognize Pablo Fanque from *Sgt. Pepper's* "For the Benefit of Mr. Kite . . ."

12. Jerome Mitchell, "A List of Walter Scott Operas," in *Scott and His Influence*, ed. J. H.
Alexander and David Hewitt (Aberdeen, 1983), 511.

13. Philip Sidney, *Who Killed Amy Robsart? Being Some Account of the Life and Death, with remarks
on Sir Walter Scott's* Kenilworth (London, 1901), 1, 9.

But time has done what the threat of bankruptcy could not, vastly diminishing Sir Walter's reputation. Complete sets of the Waverley novels now sell for pennies a volume in used bookstores. The most venerated and most popular writer of his day is hardly read by the general public and occupies a position of comparatively low standing in the critical canon.[14] Some of the novels set in Scotland have regained scholarly attention, and Hollywood acknowledged *Rob Roy* worth another go in 1995; but to find a reader, much less a serious discussion, of *Kenilworth* is no longer an easy task.[15] In 1995, John Sutherland observed, "Canonically, of course, the novel is an outcast. There cannot be a graduate course in the Western World where it is taught, and the MLA bibliography confirms that few modern scholars have wasted their valuable time on the novel." Yet after this harsh artistic judgment, even Sutherland conceded *Kenilworth*'s sociological importance and mass popularity as "an achievement . . . worthy of studious examination" (*Life*, 248).

I take seriously Sutherland's proposed task of relocating *Kenilworth* within its culture, but for a more complicated set of reasons. First, Scott is himself a more interesting collaborator than is often granted, both diachronically and politically, in that his location (and attitudes) shift between the literary center and national border territories. But equally to the point, illuminating the work of Scott also illuminates the modern work of Shakespeare. In order to understand how the nineteenth century saw the Bard, we need to look not only at the texts and productions of his plays but also at the forms in which readers and theatergoers came to know "Shakespeare" and at the associations they brought. In this regard, no influence was stronger than the beloved works of Scott. Oversimplifying or forgetting *Kenilworth* ignores one highly influential re-vision of the Renaissance that intervenes between early and late modernity, and lessens our understanding of key changes in the cultural interpretation of Shakespeare. For Scott was not merely an occasional quoter and borrower here, as in his other Waverley novels; Shake-shifting is fundamental to the very structure and vision of *Kenilworth*, just as Scott soon became fundamental to the nineteenth century's vision of Shake-

---

14. David Hewitt argues, "The fundamental reason for the decline in his reputation is common to most Scottish writers: too many people do not see why they should be interested in Scottish literature and history"; "Walter Scott," in *The History of Scottish Literature*, ed. Douglas Gifford (Aberdeen, 1988), 3:65. Ferris links the decline with Scott's border position vis-à-vis a gendered readership (*Achievement*, 12–13). One might also blame his verbosity and the footnotes, prefaces, and condensed type of later printings, which make the novel appear far more daunting than did the first edition. As this chapter shows, some condescension also derives from intellectual simplification of Scott's work and his manner of Shake-shifting.

15. Stephen Arata's essay is a happy exception, though he too focuses almost exclusively on the Elizabethan entertainments; "Scott's Pageants: The Example of *Kenilworth*," *Studies in Romanticism* 40, no. 1 (2001): 99–107.

speare. *Kenilworth* plays a major role in creating a venerable yet flexibly "modern" Shakespeare, a figure of use both to the Scottish novelist and to the British literary culture that would love and honor Sir Walter's novels alongside sweet William's plays.

A specter haunts Scott's historical novel: the uncanny presence of Shakespeare's *Othello*.[16] *Kenilworth; A Romance* centers on the domestic tragedy of a couple who elope for love and are thwarted by the supersubtle ways of a rigid court culture. The lovers here are Sir Robert Dudley (anachronistically referred to by his later title, the Earl of Leicester) and his first wife, Amy Robsart. Scott's reconstruction of their lives derives in part from scurrilous Elizabethan sources such as *Leicester's Commonwealth*; but the manner and mood reveal the equally powerful influence of Shakespeare's drama in general and *Othello* in particular. Like Desdemona, Amy is framed by the false accusations of infidelity constructed by her husband's trusted follower, Varney (with the aid of his Roderigo-like assistant, Michael Lambourne), and the scenes of temptation, inquisition, jealous rage, and manipulated pseudo-"evidence" repeatedly echo and mimic Shakespeare's play. Having borrowed *Othello*'s central trio of a jealous husband, his villainous henchman, and a slandered wife, the novel likewise culminates in the wife's murder.

Indeed, *Kenilworth*'s melodramatic focus on this unfortunate wife overwhelms Scott's famed antiquarianism, threatening his position as the manly, "healthy" alternative to what was perceived to be a feminized gothic tradition.[17] Although contemporaries praised Scott for freeing the novel from its "morbid" character by turning to history, it is actually the combination of this Shakespearean ghost narrative with a ghost-haunted eighteenth-century ballad by the Scottish poet William Julius Mickle, "Cumnor Hall," that provides Scott's story line. This twofold literary ancestry, from a Scot and an Englishman, aptly captures Scott's border position as a British writer; it also signals his conscious attempt to displace the simpler political tribute to Queen Elizabeth that his publisher desired. Rather than focus primarily on the Queen (who does not even make her appearance until volume

16. Given frequent acknowledgment of parallels, the absence of sustained analysis surprises. Wilmon Brewer, *Shakespeare's Influence on Sir Walter Scott* (Boston, 1925), 321–328, describes general character and narrative resemblances, finding them "remarkable" but not really exploring why or how so.

17. On the gothic and Scott's role in "masculinizing" the novel, see Ferris, *Achievement*, 10ff., Duncan, *Modern Romance*, 11–13, and Fiona Robertson, *Legitimate Histories: Scott, Gothic, and the Authorities of Fiction* (Oxford, 1994). Ferris argues that "Scott displaced the whole plot of courtship which had remained central to the proper novel, shifting it to the periphery of narrative interest. . . . That shift . . . was decisive for the kind of authority granted to Scott" (98). If so, *Kenilworth* stands as a problematic case, returning to an historical moment when a woman ruled the public sphere and interweaving a domestic drama as its tragic focus.

44 2), Scott delves into the corrupt court and affairs of the heart. His desire to retell the *Othello* story is so great that he resurrects the historical Robsart, who died under suspicious circumstances fifteen years before the 1575 entertainments at Kenilworth castle, so that she can attend them—only to then kill her off again.[18]

Moreover, Scott's desire to include Shakespeare directly in his novel results in the equally blatant—and more generally recognizable—anachronism of pretending that the Bankside theaters were thriving before they had in fact been built. Although the playwright was just eleven years old at the time of the Kenilworth pageants, he appears in Scott's novel at mid-career, petitioning Leicester on behalf of the theaters against the bear baiters.[19] Like Sir Walter himself, this Shakespeare is both a man of business and an influential, beloved writer. Other characters, including Sir Walter Raleigh and Queen Elizabeth as well as a picaresque ex-performer called Wayland Smith, consciously cite his plays at key moments. Raleigh recites the "virgin of the west" speech from *A Midsummer Night's Dream* in praise of Elizabeth, as the courtiers reflect on her fame in future ages. The Queen not only quotes from *Troilus and Cressida* to describe Amy's abandonment of her earlier suitor, Tressilian, but decides the petition in favor of the actors because the words of Shakespeare—aptly enough, mediated by the earlier Sir Walter—echo in her thoughts.[20] Lower down the social scale, Wayland had "swaggered with the bravest of them all, both at the Black Bull, the Globe,

18. These anachronisms are the basis for a modern Philip Sidney's accusation that *Kenilworth* "has poisoned with its cleverly-woven plot the dry facts of history" (*Who Killed*, xiv); he notes the slanderous unreliability of both Ashmole's *Antiquaries of Berkshire* and *Leicester's Commonwealth*, although himself citing Elizabethan accounts written by Spanish ambassadors as if they were "dry facts." Compare Elias Ashmole, *The Antiquities of Berkshire* (London, 1719), 1:149–54.

19. This anachronism sparked objections at the time of publication and staging. See G. Creed, *The Drama; or, Theatrical Pocket Magazine*: "The error, although trifling to the mere novelist reader, is of the utmost consequence to the correct historian; and I am surprised that the learned author of these admirable works should have made so glaring a mistake" (1 January 1822, 231).

20. I condense greatly: "At the command of the Queen, that cavalier [Raleigh] repeated, with accent and manner which even added to their exquisite delicacy of tact and beauty of description, the celebrated vision of Oberon. 'That very time I saw . . .' . . . The verses were not probably new to the Queen, for when was ever such elegant flattery so long in reaching the royal ear to which it was addressed? But it was not the less welcome when recited by such a speaker as Raleigh." Elizabeth soon after "murmured over the last lines as if scarce conscious that she was overheard, and as she uttered the words, 'In maiden meditation, fancy free,' she dropt into the Thames the supplication of Orson Pinnit [the bearbaiter]" (176–77). When the Queen tries to comfort Tressilian by quoting *Troilus*, she observes: "You smile, my Lord of Southampton—perchance I make your player's verse halt through my bad memory" (163). The historical Southampton would have been two years old at the time. Citations from Walter Scott's novel refer throughout to *Kenilworth: A Romance*, ed. J. H. Alexander (Edinburgh, 1993).

the Fortune, and elsewhere," before the audience's apple throwing led him to renounce his "half share in the company" (102–3). At one point he sings Caliban's song, thus moving *The Tempest* back in time thirty-five years (126).[21] In calling attention to Shakespeare's poetry at the expense of historical accuracy, the antiquarian Scott obviously knew what he was doing — but do we?

Modern critics dismiss *Kenilworth* as a jingoistic attempt to laud "merrie England" for Britain's post-Union edification, despite its author's complex feelings about the history of Scotland's subsumption; for them, the novel's anachronisms are just part of that "lusty English romance" genre. But a careful reading of the entirety of *Kenilworth* does not substantiate such a simple position. Nor, conversely, will it support the Scots diplomat Paul Henderson Scott when he tries to declare Sir Walter's independence from England, asserting that "none of Scott's ideas or attitudes are derived from Shakespeare" and that his Shakespearean "allusions, hints, similarities and overtones" are deployed merely as "surface ornament."[22] As the *Kenilworth* anachronisms testify, Sir Walter goes out of his way to announce Shakespeare as source — indeed, everyone's source. Inverting chronology, Scott's Leicester remarks that Shakespeare's poetry is beloved by Sir Philip Sidney.[23] Only by transforming history into romance can Scott achieve his goal of making Shakespeare the indisputable artistic fountainhead of the Elizabethan Renaissance — and more.

Scott's stress on the role of fiction within his historical novel is consistent with his focus on Shakespeare and other literary antecedents as mythic sources for an ethical tradition to support his ideal of a British nation, quite distinct from what he clearly presents as the corruption of its political center, the English court. Scott also calls attention to the model of Shakespeare's English history plays as works that rewrite antecedent narratives to con-

---

21. Similarly, when Smith adopts a peddler's disguise, he decides to "give them a taste of Autolycus" and sings "Lawn as white as driven snow" (202). The character's own name hearkens back to Wéland the Smith of Old Norse and Anglo-Saxon legend, as Scott obliquely signals when Wayland tells Tressilian, "I was bred a blacksmith" (103).

22. Henderson Scott, *Walter Scott*, 36.

23. Leicester greets him: "Ha, Will Shakespeare — wild Will! — thou hast given my nephew, Philip Sidney, love-power — he cannot sleep without thy Venus and Adonis under his pillow!" (168). The Earl initiates the quotation from Oberon: "There are some lines, for example — I would my nephew, Philip Sidney, were here, they are scarce ever out of his mouth — they are in a mad tale of fairies, love-charms, and I wot not what . . ." (175–76). Thus Shakespeare's verse implicitly "influences" Sidney's *Astrophil and Stella*, the poems in actuality echoed by Shakespeare's lyrical plays. Fittingly, the book-length attack on Scott's historical inaccuracies was penned by another Philip Sidney, who finds the "Venus and Adonis" allusion a "gross error, inexcusable even in fiction" (*Who Killed*, 9).

46   temporary ends. He invokes them to finesse the issues both of antiquarian
       purism and direct political intervention. Scott's collaboration with Shake-
       speare is thus multiply helpful, modeling the transformative power of art as
       well as its potential to comment indirectly on societal disorders.

           But the relationship between these bards, across time, medium, and na-
       tional borders, is politically uneasy as well as mutually reinforcing. For
       Scott's personal investments complicate the nationalist agenda that an Eng-
       lish Shakespeare supports. Sir Walter draws on the popular potential of
       Shakespeare—popular in the sense of carnivalesque and of the common
       people, as well as market-pleasing. This image resonates with Scott's wish to
       be the "minstrel of the Scottish borders," preserving the oral ballad tradition
       in the wake of Britain's attempts to obliterate Scottish popular culture by
       law after the Jacobite risings. Yet Shakespeare was by Scott's day increas-
       ingly the Bard of high culture and identified with Englishness per se. In at-
       tempting to elevate the status of the novel and be heard within British halls
       of power, Scott borrows authority along with story lines and quips, compli-
       cating if not compromising his claims of alliance with the people of Scotland.
       This, along with his dismay at the consequences of the French Revolution
       and his opposition to workers' movements, has led Nicola Watson to dismiss
       his politics as simple "Tory nationalism."[24] Though less obviously than do his
       novels set in Scotland, *Kenilworth* nevertheless attests to Scott's mixed posi-
       tion regarding Englishness and its history and uses Shakespeare to fortify
       that border position.

           What follows is an exploration of the relationship between *Kenilworth* and
       the nineteenth century's *Othello*—and its continuing consequences for how
       we read Shakespeare and (don't) read Scott. By reformulating and diverg-
       ing from *Othello*'s social specificity, Scott expresses his own concerns about
       "race" and the relationship between core and periphery within the British
       state. Scott's rewriting, aptly enough, is a doubled one: on the one hand, his
       erasure of blackness from the story responds to and promotes the nine-

       ───────────────────────────

       24. Watson's account relies heavily on evidence from Kemble and Malone yet evaluates
       Scott's "entire *oeuvre*," claiming Scott's aim in *Kenilworth* was a "comparable injection of 'authen-
       tic' historical detail, underwritten by the authority of Shakespeare, into the suspect discourse of
       fiction" in order to "instate a vision of an Edenic, post-revolutionary Britain." This cannot ac-
       count adequately for the text's conscious anachronisms or patterns; Nicola J. Watson, "Kemble,
       Scott, and the Mantle of the Bard," in Marsden, *Appropriation of Shakespeare*, 73–92. Similarly, in
       Dobson and Watson's excellent general study of the cult of Elizabeth, the brief account of *Ke-
       nilworth*—acknowledged as "a yardstick for fictive representations of both Elizabeth and the
       newly christened 'Elizabethan' age in Britain, America, and on the Continent until about
       1860"—oversimplifies the representation of the court and ignores Scott's characteristic irony;
       Michael Dobson and Nicola J. Watson, *England's Elizabeth: An Afterlife in Fame and Fantasy* (Ox-
       ford, 2003), 112–17.

teenth century's "whitening" of Othello in performance and critical commentary, part of the process whereby Shakespeare's texts become a repository of transhistorical aesthetic value removed from the political issues (such as new colonial encounters or black slavery) of either time period. On the other hand, Scott substitutes another ethnic conflict he would have viewed as "racial," albeit at the edges of his main plot: the marginalization of Celtic culture. This substitution, which locates the Celt in an already lost world less sullied by modern market relations, gendered disruption, and political corruption, allows Scott to position himself both as a latter-day Bard of the borders and as Shakespeare's ally in ambivalently chronicling nation building. But whether this subtler second move of Scott's was perceived, much less influential, remains a topic for debate. In examining *Kenilworth*'s own afterlives onstage, and later critical comparisons between Scott and Shakespeare, one confronts the dimensions of diachronic collaboration beyond authorial control: an artwork's particularity and initial life becoming involved with, if not overwhelmed by, the received meanings that accrue through modern mass circulation and media transformation.

The Text's the Thing

Kenilworth's anachronisms and self-conscious fictionality make more sense if one recognizes the problems Scott has in celebrating Elizabethan history. This difficulty is seldom acknowledged in criticism, which continues to portray the novel as upholding the grandeur of merry old England. While signaling the novel's links to Shakespeare, Sutherland, for instance, claims:

> Thematically, *Kenilworth* was a celebration of English nationhood—a pageant in prose. . . . Scott was inspired by the build-up to the Coronation of [George IV in] July 1821. . . . As such *Kenilworth* has no more artistic durability than a 1953 Coronation mug. The novel also shows [Scott] for the first time measuring himself as the modern Shakespeare—his nation's laureate in fiction. . . . *Kenilworth* was a main source of the cult of Elizabethanism that was to flourish in nineteenth-century Britain and which is still periodically revived by opportunistic politicians and nostalgists. (*Life*, 247)

Certainly such a cult of Elizabeth was to gain strength with the 1837 ascension to the throne of another long-lived queen, and reading *Kenilworth* as a tribute to Good Queen Bess would be understandable if one were familiar only with the pageants Scott's work spawned. Or indeed familiar with a fascinating poem that preceded Scott's rendering, although he did not ac-

48   knowledge it: Anna Liddiard's 1815 *Kenilworth: A Mask*, written in Ireland and overt in celebrating not only Elizabeth but Wellington's victory over Napoleon.[25]

Yet such a characterization fails to register the fact that within Scott's novel nearly every episode at or involving Elizabeth's court is ambiguously tainted by venality, vanity, mercenary corruption, or conscious evil. Neither does it capture the novel's tonal variety. Even the title page of *Kenilworth*'s three volumes signals Scott's playfulness, with a tease to forestall criticism. Quoting Richard Brinsley Sheridan, the epigraph reads, "No scandal about Queen Elizabeth, I hope? *The Critic*." Like the Irish playwright, Scott pokes fun at those who would sanctify the Tudor Queen, even as he strives to please a predominantly English audience.

Flat veneration of Elizabeth's court would in any case be unlikely from a Scots-identified author so cognizant of history and fresh from writing two novels, *The Monastery* and *The Abbot*, about England's northern neighbor during the sixteenth century. As *Kenilworth* appeared on the heels of a British production of Friedrich Schiller's *Maria Stuart* at Covent Garden (December 1819) and was influenced by Sophia Lee's *The Recess* (1785), Scott's first readers might in fact have expected their era's most famous Scot to echo those works' romanticization of Mary Stuart and consequently to blame or pathologize the English queen.[26] In his 1831 Magnum Opus introduction, Scott himself recalled that, having just written a novel involving

25. Scott wrote to Constable, 6 September 1820: "Please, not say a word about K. the very name explains so much that some knowing fellow might anticipate the subject"; *The Letters of Sir Walter Scott*, ed. H. J. C. Grierson (London, 1932–37), 397. But this "fellow" Liddiard had done so, and it seems odd that Scott would be unaware of her four-canto poem citing his "Don Roderique." Liddiard shared Scott's romanticized antiquarianism and passion for Britain (and Wellington); she was similarly writing from the Celtic fringe in the wake of Waterloo (to see which battlefield Scott took his first trip abroad). Furthermore, her poem was published by Scott's London publisher, Longman. Given contemporary assertions of Scott's inadequately acknowledged debt to Coleridge's unpublished *Cristabel* in *The Lay of the Last Minstrel*, perhaps he "forgot" Liddiard. Her *Kenilworth* is a remarkable historical document, revealing just how much *more* romanticized, simplified, and patriotic a contemporary rendering of Kenilworth could be, in the aftermath of war with France. Her masquing Merlin looks into the future to see Victory "Exulting claim each gallant Chief, her Son— / Immortal both!—a NELSON!—WELLINGTON!" By contrast, Scott's Merlin simply halts battles between the historical "aborigines" and invaders within Britain, and Scott mentions Wellington only parenthetically: "they alighted at an inn in the town of Marlborough, since celebrated for having given title to the greatest general (excepting one) whom Britain ever produced." As for Europe, Liddiard vaunts, "ENGLAND shall save them—SLAVERY expire." (It is worth remembering that Bonaparte abolished the slave trade in French territories.) See J. S. Anna Liddiard, *Kenilworth: A Mask* (London, 1815), 63, 107. I have found no other discussions of this text or its possible connection to *Kenilworth*.

26. See Robertson, *Legitimate Histories*, 7, on Lee; H. Philip Bolton, *Scott Dramatized*, 376, on Schiller. A direct connection was achieved on the stage: Mrs. Bunn played Queen Elizabeth with great success in both *Maria Stuart* and one stage adaptation of *Kenilworth*.

Mary, he began writing about Elizabeth with "the prejudices with which a Scottishman is tempted," "a prejudice almost as natural to him as his native air."[27] Traces of earlier pro-Stuart portrayals do appear in *Kenilworth*'s representation of Elizabeth as lovelorn and tormented by her pathetic desire for Dudley, who uses her to advance his political ambitions. Yet the novel also praises the queen for "sound policy, in which neither man nor woman ever excelled her" (166). While Scott criticizes what he sees as the intrusion of gendered personal weaknesses into public affairs, he seldom presents such "foibles" alone:

> Queen Elizabeth had a character strangely compounded of the strongest masculine sense, with those foibles which are chiefly supposed proper to the female sex. Her subjects had the full benefit of her virtues, which far predominated over her weaknesses; but her courtiers, and those about her person, had often to sustain sudden and embarrassing turns of caprice, and the sallies of a temper which was both jealous and despotic. (210)

Considering his sources Scott is remarkably evenhanded, neither enraptured by the cult of Elizabeth nor vilifying her. This is consistent with Scott's historicism but also with his Tory veneration of monarchy (a belief leading him to encourage his own Hanoverian monarch to represent himself in Edinburgh as, absurdly, a tartan-wearing "Jacobite").[28] Consequently, the portrayal of Elizabeth is not the primary site of allegory regarding the comparative merits of Scotland and England, despite an obvious opportunity.[29] This is a far cry, however, from saying *Kenilworth* is a celebration of the political state of Tudor England.

While monarchism may mute criticism of the Queen, the English courtiers are not spared. Most are represented as venal if not outright dishonest—especially those associated with Leicester. The Earl himself is not exempt, despite recognition of his virtues and his structural position as the

27. Scott as cited by Andrew Lang, ed., *Kenilworth*, by Sir Walter Scott (New York, 1893), xxvii.

28. See Sutherland, *Life*, 258, and James Buzard, "Translation and Tourism: Scott's *Waverley* and the Rendering of Culture," *Yale Journal of Criticism* 8, no. 2 (1995): 53–54. Scott's Highlands pageantry succeeded, despite the scorn of educated Whigs (even Scott's admiring son-in-law Lockhart called it an "orgy of Celtification"); they failed to comprehend its popularity. George IV was, for a' that, the first British monarch to visit Scotland since Charles I.

29. The only monarchic comparison concerns Elizabeth's giving of offices and refers not to Mary but to her offspring: "That wise Princess was fully aware of the propriety of using great circumspection and economy in bestowing those titles of honour, which the Stewarts, who succeeded to her throne, distributed with such imprudent liberality as greatly diminished their value" (302). The context suggests irony, as we are witnessing knighthoods assigned despite the Queen's doubts—including one to the villain Varney. Sir Walter's title of baronetcy (awarded six months after *Kenilworth*'s publication) was ironically just such a Stuart creation.

50   Othello-like figure. Leicester's desire to advance his courtly ambitions leads him to keep his marriage to Amy secret, a choice from which the narrative's tragedy in part derives.[30] Nor, despite the arch-villainy of the Earl's trusted attendant Varney, is the corruption confined to just one courtly faction. Ostensibly upstanding English "nobles" praise the alchemical poisoner Dr. Alasco, and almost everyone seems to fear and hire "intelligencers" to spy at court and in countryside alike.[31] (That the rule-proving exception is another self-made literary Sir Walter—Raleigh—hardly seems coincidental.)[32]

The repeated emphasis on hypocrisy emanating from the center of English power even bears upon the public displays of pageantry and courtesy described, so impressive in themselves. Thus while the Queen's behavior is distinguished from that of her self-serving and immoral courtiers, she too is wrapped within a larger web of competing interests and policy, which poisons the world beyond court as well. The state of England, in short, strips decent men of their ethical accountability and allows the wicked to thrive.[33]

30. Scott adds a dash of *Macbeth* here and in two chapter epigraphs. Given Shakespeare's quasi-nationalist "rehistoricizing" representation of an independent Scottish king as villainous usurper, Scott's citation could be deemed another sign of border-crossing political collaboration.

31. Scott anticipates recent popular interest in Elizabethan spy systems across media (Charles Nicholls's book *The Reckoning*, Shekhar Kapur's film *Elizabeth*, Wood's televised *In Search of Shakespeare*). Innkeeper Gosling worries, "there be intelligencers every where" (197; see also 150, 269), and betrays Wayland and Amy (237); Wayland narrowly escapes witch hunters (109ff.). The Sussex faction lives as if in an armed camp, and Amy finds her husband's home an "ill-ruled place" full of threats (314). Scott wrote to his son Charles, "our eye is enabled to look back upon the past to improve on our ancestors' improvements and to avoid their errors [?] This can only be done by studying history and comparing it with passing events" (*Letters* 7:734). One senses that Scott is using the past in this way in *Kenilworth*, just as in his less "romantic" novels (*Redgauntlet* refers to George III's "secret police"; Sutherland, *Life*, 268). Douglas Gifford calls attention to Scott's "bitter comment on the hypocrisies of aristocracy and power" in other Waverley novels; "Myth, Parody, and Dissociation: Scottish Fiction, 1814–1914," in *The History of Scottish Literature*, ed. Douglas Gifford, 3:222.

32. Sussex and his follower Walter Blount are presented as relatively benign, if comically unfamiliar with courtly manners, and thus also "outsiders." Blount's name echoes that of the honorable—but dead—soldier whose grinning displeases Falstaff in *Henry IV, Part 1*.

33. Blount fears Raleigh too will become entangled: "These court-tricks, and gambols, and flashes of fine women's favour, are the tricks and trinkets that bring fair fortunes to farthings, and fair faces and witty coxcombs to the acquaintance of dull blocks and sharp axes" (180). The historical Raleigh's disgrace over the Throckmorton affair and his life's end in the Tower give proleptic weight to Blount's worries. Scott's more sinister reading of the Elizabethan court is reinforced through allusion to Spenser's *Faerie Queene*. Like Gloriana dispatching Red Crosse Knight, Elizabeth sends Raleigh with Tressilian to rescue Amy; "He is a young knight besides, and to deliver a lady from prison is an appropriate first adventure" (377). But the death of Amy reveals just how unlike Spenser's Faerieland this England is. Repeatedly, petty facts undermine the mythic rhetoric that accompanies them (150, 155). When Dudley is lauded hyperbolically, the next paragraph describes Varney, reminding one of both his and his master's corruption (287). The novel, David Punter argues, contains a "'masterly' . . . patterned deconstruction of the male hero: at each step down the line more and more of the outward grandeur of the self is peeled away"; but he also notes that "aspects of the triumphalist self in command of history co-

Only by ignoring this narrative and tonal context can one transform the book—or even volume 3, in which the Kenilworth festivities finally take place—into a mere memento of royalism. It is certainly not the representation of court politics that earns this novel the generic subtitle "A Romance." Rather, as Sir Walter Raleigh's singular superiority attests, it is specifically, and perhaps only, the literary and dramatic legacy of "merry England" that entitles it to continued veneration. And in that kingdom, Shakespeare rules. After Leicester addresses Shakespeare within the novel, Scott makes this explicit: "The Player bowed, and the Earl nodded and passed on—so that age would have told the tale—in ours, perhaps, we might say the immortal had done homage to the mortal" (168).

From the very start, fiction takes priority over history, both structurally and as ethical source.[34] Announcing, 'It is the privilege of tale-tellers to open their story in an inn," Scott traces a literary genealogy for his Cumnor tavern back to Chaucer, with Elizabethan England producing the first rival to the Host of the *Canterbury Tales*: "since the days of old Harry Baillie of the Tabard in Southwark, no one had excelled Giles Gosling in the power of pleasing his guests" (4). Even Her Majesty is introduced through—or rather, surrounded and overwhelmed by—comparison with "mine host."[35] Like many other chapters, the first bears an epigraph from an early modern play, and the good fun to follow comes straight from that era's drama. The book's initial dialogue presents "the myrmidons of the bonny Black Bear," John Tapster and Will Hostler, echoing the comic exchanges of *Henry IV* most obviously. So too does the jesting Gosling when, like Falstaff after the Gadshill robbery, he retrospectively claims to have recognized his younger relative Lambourne, whom he regards (with accuracy) as a rogue.[36] Indeed, Chaucer and Elizabethan drama provide the opening "frame" for this Scott

---

exist in this fantasy of a male world which is insecure"; "'To Cheat the Time, a Powerful Spell': Scott, History, and the Double," in *Scott in Carnival*, ed. J. H. Alexander and David Hewitt (Aberdeen, 1993), 10. The deconstructive pattern obliquely embraces the Queen—and other cultural subtexts.

34. I would not overstate the antithesis, since Scott regarded literature as representing historical truths. Nevertheless, the sources and domains associated with history as conventionally defined—the workings of political power through the state apparatus, the understanding of social structures derived from archival data—are not the stuff of merriment.

35. The narrator effuses: "[S]o great was his fame, that to have been in Cumnor, without wetting a cup at the Bonny Black Bear, would have been to avouch one's-self utterly indifferent to reputation as a traveller. A country fellow might as well return from London without looking in the face of majesty" (1–2).

36. For extensive echoes of Falstaff and Hal, see 5, 12. The first chapter's epigraph comes from Ben Jonson's *The New Inn*. Among Shakespeare's plays cited in other chapter epigraphs are: *The Merchant of Venice*, *The Merry Wives of Windsor*, *The Taming of the Shrew*, *Richard II*, *A Midsummer Night's Dream*, and repeatedly *The Winter's Tale*, *Macbeth*, and *Richard III*. Several other quotations from unspecified "Old Plays" are most likely Scott's creations.

novel unusual in having no explicit framing device. Carrying the logic of a literary frame further, *Kenilworth*'s first edition closes with two stanzas of Mickle's "Cumnor Hall," a ballad about Robsart's death aligned with the gothic aesthetic that Scott likewise (*pace* Carlyle) incorporates into his historical romance.[37]

What negotiates between the two visions superimposed upon Elizabethan England, between the vital world of dramatic allusions and the ruined melancholia rooted in more recent literature imagining that era, is *Othello*: a verbally rich tragic play authentically of the period that is nevertheless centered on a domestic conflict congenial to melodramatic reinterpretation.[38] Moreover, the troublingly absent presence of *Othello*'s story of "race" makes the novel more than escapism. *Kenilworth* becomes an important historical document in its own right, an exemplary case of early nineteenth-century diachronic collaboration in all its complexity. The literary past being used humorously, sentimentally, and even sensationalistically in the frame becomes a route back to history in a more significant sense: it is a means of comparing past and present, representing struggles still pertinent in Scott's day. Granted, the disconnected citations from Shakespeare and other Elizabethan drama may function like the picturesque in landscape: serving to make the past a charming, quaint "other" to messy, corrupt modernity.[39] But the sustained structuring use of *Othello* works more directly to address the relationships between then and now. It is not a consistent point-to-point correlation: this is after all a three-volume novel, not a play. Nevertheless, the echoes are powerful and incessant, creating a pattern that encourages the reader to scrutinize the comparison with Shakespeare's story. Once we recognize that Scott is Shake-shifting *Othello*, his distinctively nineteenth-century vision and its consequences become clearer.

It is the Cornishman Tressilian, Amy's former suitor and loyal friend, who introduces the pattern of verbal and structural echoes. When he and we first encounter Amy hidden at Cumnor-Place, Tressilian informs her of her fa-

37. This framing was obscured in the 1831 Magnum Opus edition by the removal of the two stanzas (another stanza remained as the last chapter's epigraph); however, Scott reprinted the entire ballad at the end of his introduction. Gothicism appears as soon as Tressilian and Lambourne approach the ruined monastery where Amy Robsart is immured. The skeptic Varney chides Forster: "canst thou not make the out-of-doors frightful to her, with tales of goblins? — thou livest here by the church-yard, and hast not even wit enough to raise a ghost, to scare thy females into good discipline" (38–39).

38. Virginia Mason Vaughan's analysis of *Othello* offers a corrective to those who would encode the domestic as uninvolved with the state and its politics; the tendency to split the two is itself in great part a nineteenth-century legacy. *Othello: A Contextual History* (Cambridge, UK, 1994).

39. See Buzard, "Translation," 37–41.

ther's illness. As with Brabantio before him, old Robsart's decline has been prompted by his daughter's stealing away with her paramour (inaccurately believed to be Leicester's attendant Varney rather than the Earl himself). Identified with a feudal model of household relations despite his nineteenth-century vocabulary of free will, Tressilian speaks on Hugh Robsart's behalf: "'With thy will—thine uninfluenced, free, and natural will, Amy thou canst not chuse this state of slavery and dishonour—thou hast been bound by some spell—entrapped by some art—art now detained by some compelled vow.—But thus I break the charm—Amy, in the name of thine excellent, thy broken-hearted father, I command thee to follow me'" (33). But neither the command nor the accusation of witchcraft has any more accuracy or effect than do those made by Brabantio in 1.3 of *Othello*. Like Desdemona, Amy has eloped, is in love with her husband, and will remain devoted to him until her death. Her romance defies traditional notions of community and familial obligation.

But whereas Desdemona's elopement leads her away to the contested margins of empire, Amy's leads her to its center. Brought up in Devon, then hidden by Leicester at Cumnor-Place (outside Oxford), she finally escapes from Varney and morose Anthony Forster's confinement in order to pursue her husband to Kenilworth, where the Queen's court has come to visit. That trajectory, the opposite of *Othello*'s, reinforces the novel's more obvious location of threat at the very core of "civilization." There is no "Turk" without. More clearly than in Iago's case, the villain is thoroughly identified with the court. And because both Amy and Tressilian, the "good" figures recalling Desdemona and (in some aspects) Cassio, hail from the southwest of England,[40] the center's corruption is less qualified. Queen Elizabeth, like Shakespeare's Duke of Venice, attempts to render fair judgments, but she is more easily misled (even duped) by her courtiers, who work for their own ends rather than those of the nation. Foremost among them are Leicester and Varney.

The link between Varney and Iago has long been noted yet hardly interrogated. In Varney, Andrew Lang observed in 1893, "Scott presents us with the character nearest to Iago of any in romance, and the villain's power and resource are so great as almost to extort admiration"; to those who deplored "the absence of any touch of human feeling" in him, Lang retorts, "he has not less than Iago."[41] Indeed, he has a bit more. Like his fictional ancestor, Varney gets the first "soliloquy" (explicitly labeled as such), but in it he re-

40. The historical Raleigh came from the southwest—another connection with Scott's favored characters.
41. Lang, ed., *Kenilworth*, xxiv, xxv.

54 veals his own—slight—vulnerability. He has made one "fatal error" in confessing his own desire to Amy, since which "I cannot look at her without
fear, and hate, and fondness, so strangely mingled, that I know not whether,
were it my choice, I would rather possess or ruin her." Having announced a
heterosexual motive for this villainy, the soliloquy then shifts to improvisatory plotting: "My lord's interest—and so far it is mine own—for if he
sinks, I fall in his train—demands concealment of this obscure marriage . . .
I must work an interest in her, either through love or through fear—and
who knows but I may yet reap the sweetest and best revenge for her former
scorn?—that were indeed a masterpiece of courtlike art! . . . let her confide
to me a secret, . . . and, fair Countess, thou art mine own" (45). Bearing
traces of both Iago and Thomas Middleton's De Flores (while expressing
Scott's own interest in "interest"), Varney is nonetheless more comprehensible and fallible and thus a less haunting figure of evil.[42] At the same time, he
is recognized as a "highly qualified" courtly attendant, "being discreet and
cautious on the one hand, and on the other, quick, keen-witted and imaginative"; also like Iago, he has been of much past service to his master.[43]
Throughout the novel, Varney demonstrates his ability to outwit his betters
and evade exposure, twisting the unanticipated to advance his sinister purposes. He is artful before the queen when accused of abducting Amy (158),
and he enjoys improvising in tight spots.

Varney transforms Tressilian's honorable visit, like Cassio's to Desdemona, into an occasion to disrupt the Earl's marriage. First he suggests to
Amy that Leicester might be jealous, a concern she dismisses. Her words
echo Desdemona's in stressing love's absolute quality and her intention "to
speak the truth to my lord at all times, to hold up my mind and my thoughts
before him as pure as that polished mirror; so that when he looks into my
heart, he shall only see his own features reflected there" (55; compare *Othello*
1.3.253ff., 3.4.25ff., and 141ff.). Varney retreats, but suggests "mentioning
Tressilian's name to my lord, and observing how he bears it" (55)—a seem-

42. Charlotte Brontë's correspondence with Ellen Nussey reveals the latter had been upset
by Varney's wickedness: "I was exceedingly amused at the characteristic and naïve manner in
which you expressed your detestation of Varney's character, so much so indeed that I could not
forbear laughing out when I perused that part of your letter: he is certainly the personification
of consummate villainy and in the delineation of his dark and profoundly artful mind Scott ex-
hibits a wonderful knowledge of human nature as well as surprising skill in embodying his perceptions so as to enable others to become participators in that knowledge"; *Letters*, 1:131.
43. Varney, "sprung from an ancient but somewhat decayed family, had been the Earl's page
during his earlier and more obscure fortunes, and . . . had afterwards contrived to render himself no less useful to him in his rapid and splendid advance to fortune; thus establishing in him
an interest resting both on present and past services, which rendered him an almost indispensable sharer of his confidence" (62). Compare William Shakespeare, *Othello*, ed. E. Honigmann,
Arden ed. (Walton-on-Thames, 1997), 1.1.27ff.; all subsequent citations refer to this edition.

ingly "honest" bit of misguiding advice. In private conversation with Leicester, Varney works similarly by indirection to separate the Earl from Amy. Immediately after the Earl leaves, the villain cynically apostrophizes:

> "I am glad thou art gone," thought Varney, "or, practised as I am in the follies of mankind, I had laughed in the very face of thee! Thou mayst tire if thou wilt of thy new bauble [Amy]. . . . But of thine old bauble, Ambition, thou shalt not tire, for as you climb the hill, my lord, you must drag Richard Varney up with you; and if he can urge you to the ascent he means to profit by, believe me he will spare neither whip nor spur. . . . And thus he, who in the estimation of so many wise-judging men can match Burleigh and Walsingham in policy, and Sussex in war, becomes pupil to his own menial; and all for a hazel eye and a little cunning red and white. . . . Well, my lord, I order your retinue now; the time may soon come that *my* master of the horse shall order mine own." (64–65)

Both in Varney's dismissiveness of Leicester's love and in the inversion of servitude, one recognizes Iago's accents: "I follow him to serve my turn upon him. / We cannot all be masters, nor all masters / Cannot be truly followed"; "In following him, I follow but myself" (1.1.41 ff.). And here too during his scornful taunting, the attendant imagines his master a horse — though, crucially, not one from Barbary.

Consequently Leicester and Amy's next meeting is shaped by Varney's words. Asking permission to tell her unhappy father of her marriage, she omits the news of Tressilian's visit she intended to share. Her innocent suppression, like Desdemona's denial that she misplaced her handkerchief, will ultimately undo her. When Leicester himself mentions "that yonder Cornish man, yonder Trevanion, or Tressilian," Amy's defense of her rejected suitor reinforces the worries Varney created. The Earl's reasons for Shakespeare-echoing hyperbole ("I would rather the foul fiend intermingled in our secret than this Tressilian!") are in fact initially political. He fears that Elizabeth — entering the narrative significantly for the first time, as a blocking agent — would cast him out if she heard of his marriage. But Amy has been encouraged to perceive jealousy, and Leicester's angry response leads her to "forget" the visit: "something there was that I would have told you, but your anger has driven it from my recollection" (66–67). It will be Varney's later revelation of this visit that helps convince the Earl of his wife's infidelity and thus seals Amy's fate.[44]

---

44. As in *Othello*, the vertical axis from heaven to hell is invoked relentlessly. Varney is repeatedly linked with the devil, several characters realizing that he is an "inhuman dog" even before his murders of Lambourne (his Roderigo) and Amy; see 159, 170–71, 193, 281. That such recognitions have no effect on Varney's social standing reinforces the sense of political irony, which culminates in Elizabeth's knighting "Sir Richard" while he schemes to "remove" Amy.

And what of the Othello figure himself, the Earl of Leicester? As one
would expect in a novel, the central couple in *Kenilworth* are more "low
mimetic" than in Shakespeare's tragedy, in that they display obvious shortcomings or pettiness along with their virtues. The Earl's ambitiousness un-
dercuts the absoluteness of his devotion, while Amy's choice of lover
(though not the quality of her love) is criticized: the narrator laments her
"caprice which preferred the handsome and insinuating Leicester before
Tressilian . . . —that fatal error, which ruined the happiness of her life"
(249). Throughout, Scott entertains a baser conception of his jealous husband figure.[45] What remains clear is that the Earl shares Othello's propen-
sity to trust his male servant over his wife, an error leading him to murderous jealousy. These traits and situational parallelisms seem sufficient in the
novelist's mind to ground extensive allusion to—indeed, virtual quotation
from—Shakespeare's play.

Thus *Othello* comes to the fore in volume 3, where Varney orchestrates
Leicester's "temptation" and maddening.[46] Like his literary forebear, Varney
acts as if his thoughts were being dragged out of him reluctantly, rhetorically
involving Leicester in his own undoing (183ff., 306). The novelistic process
of persuasion is less compact than in *Othello*'s bravura 3.3, but Scott similarly
interweaves incidents with private dialogues between the men, thereby emphasizing how the villain turns all to advantage. Several of these incidents
became so popular, onstage and among the nineteenth-century readership,
that they attained a pseudohistorical credibility.

The most famous such episode is Amy's public discovery in the gardens at
Kenilworth, after her escape from Varney's propositioning and poisoning at
Cumnor-Place. Amy fortuitously encounters Queen Elizabeth alone in a
grotto, pleads for protection, and asserts that Leicester knows the truth of
her state. The Queen, detecting her favorite's deception (in professing both
ignorance in this matter and love for his sovereign), drags Amy to confront
the Earl. Fearing for her husband, Amy then recants:

> Amy, . . . who saw her husband, as she conceived, in the utmost danger from
> the rage of an offended Sovereign, instantly, (and, alas! how many women
> have done the same,) forgot her own wrongs, and her danger, in her appre-

45. Moreover, and crucially, he removes the factors of societal "otherness" partially mitigat-
ing Othello's errors in judgment. I shall return to Scott's complex motives in changing the cul-
turally liminal figure of a military Moor into a court favorite.
46. The section of the novel most remote from these concerns is the first part of volume 3:
when Scott presents the Kenilworth pageants his historical research takes over, including such
specifics as "It was the twilight of a summer night, (9th July, 1575)." He quotes directly from
the contemporary account in Robert Laneham's letter. Arata, Sutherland, and Dobson and
Watson focus their attention here. In terms of the novel's overarching shape, *Othello* is most em-
phatically invoked at the start and conclusion of the main plot.

hensions for him, and throwing herself before the Queen, embraced her knees, while she exclaimed, "He is guiltless, Madam—he is guiltless—no one can lay aught to the charge of the noble Leicester." (322–23)

Like the dying Desdemona, who at the price of imperiling her soul lies to protect her husband from the accusation of murder, Amy forgets the cost of marital devotion (as the narrator openly laments). Even here, the gesture might reunite the couple were it not for Varney's (un)timely appearance. Amy's vague accusation that he "has sown dissention where most there should be peace" leads the court to believe her mad, and she is removed (323–24). The immediate threat to his plots avoided, Varney commences to reshape Amy's appearance in the Earl's mind. "As Varney . . . took especial care to be silent concerning those practices on the Countess's health which had driven her to so desperate a resolution, Leicester, who could only suppose that she had adopted it out of jealous impatience . . . was not a little offended." There is an echo of Othello's "I will deny thee nothing, / Whereon I do beseech thee grant me this, / To leave me but a little to myself" (3.3.83–85) when the Earl impatiently muses: "I have made her sharer of my bed and of my fortunes. I ask but of her a little patience . . . and the infatuated woman will rather hazard her own shipwreck and mine" (327).

In context, the increasingly pronounced echoes of *Othello* constitute an artful recasting of characters, moods, and devices. Varney relentlessly goads Leicester into doubting Amy, whether she speaks out or retreats; like Desdemona's unfortunately timed defense of Cassio, Amy's vigorous idealism on Tressilian's behalf is turned against her. Varney, "with well acted passion," again employs Iago's method ("Ha! I like not that!"), his comparable "Alas! my lord," forcing Leicester to query, "wherefore alas, Sir Richard?" When Leicester asserts his willingness to face ruin for love, Varney reluctantly insinuates before moving to open, audacious accusation with "zeal" (compare *Othello* 3.3). Finally, Varney turns innocent information into "evidence" of illicit behavior, and Leicester (trying to "examine coldly and warily—coldly and warily" as he contemplates punishing "deeply") is caught:

> again compressing his lips, as if he feared some violent expression might escape from them, he asked again, "What farther proof?"
> "Enough, my lord," said Varney, "and to spare."

The Earl adopts the rational stance of a dispassionate seeker of evidence, even as his repetitions signal the emotional struggle already disorienting him: "but it is false, false as the smoke of hell! Ambitious she may be—fickle and impatient—'tis a woman's fault; but false to me!—never, never—the proof—the proof of this!" A crucial slippage sets the stage for tragedy: the

58   falseness of accusation shifts to become the falseness of infidelity. On cue, Varney produces a female accessory equivalent to Desdemona's handkerchief, explaining:

> "he obtained possession of one of her gloves, which, I think your lordship may know."
>
> He gave the glove, which had the Bear and Ragged Staff, the Earl's impress, embroidered upon it in seed-pearls.
>
> "I do, I do recognize it," said Leicester. "They were my own gift. The fellow of it was on the arm which she threw this very day around my neck!"—He spoke this with violent agitation.

Like the handkerchief, the glove becomes a fetish: the husband's gift circulating among men provides "ocular proof" of the wife's own overly free circulation.[47] But whereas Othello's familial gift carries "magic in the web" through associations with witchcraft and the foreign, this love token is marked with Leicester's heraldic identity. It thus reinforces his cultural centrality rather than liminality and reminds us that Amy's vulnerability as well as goodness derives in great measure from her unfamiliarity with corrupt courtly ways.

    The fetish in each work, fortuitously "found," drives the gift giver to distraction. The parallels with *Othello*'s acts 3 and 4 compound: in the phrasing and imagery, the tragic irony of the speaker's misattribution of infamy, his lightning shifts from doubt to certainty to "just" vengeance to mourning. Mirroring Othello's "the pity of it, Iago," Leicester laments, "Be it so—she dies!—But one tear might be permitted" (339). Enflamed by what he "sees," the Earl "will have her blood" (346): "She shall die the death of a traitress and adultress, well merited both by the laws of God and man!" (340). He descends into bestial obsession akin to Othello's seizure, complete with "foam": "the Earl's rage seemed at once incontroulable and deeply concentrated; and while he spoke, his eyes shot fire, his voice trembled with excess of passion, and the light foam stood on his lip" (344). Reversing assignments from *Othello*, Leicester plots to kill his supposed rival, while Varney prepares to take Amy back to Cumnor and her death.[48]

---

47. *Kenilworth*, 330–38. See *Othello* 3.3 and 3.4 passim and 4.1.1–43, 90–92, 167–210.

48. As do Othello and Iago after sealing their pact, these two differ in their success at masquerade, signaling the henchman's more thoroughgoing evil. Varney pretends to be in light spirits (342), whereas Leicester's "actions and gestures, instead of appearing the consequence of simply volition, seemed, like those of an automaton . . . his words fell from him piece-meal, interruptedly . . ." (343). As Othello can no longer contain his passions, so too the distracted Earl; see 345ff. as well as 328, 357, 366, 380.

In a final twist Leicester laments his haste, sending a letter via the Roderigo-like Lambourne to delay Varney: Varney simply murders Lambourne as well. Soon enough the Earl, who thought that by trying to kill only Tressilian he "restricted the instant revenge which was in my power, and . . . limited it to that which is manly and noble," learns the greater scope of his error. He discovers too late that "I have been made to believe a man of honour a villain, and the best and purest of creatures a false profligate" (357, 368). Like Othello, Leicester tries to distinguish between murder and sacrifice, justice and revenge, but discovers he has failed to do so because he trusted the male "insider" who served him treacherously.

The Shake-shifting continues to the novel's end. At Cumnor, Varney craftily imitates the sounds of Leicester's arrival, prompting Amy to rush out to greet him: in so doing, she plunges through a false floor to her "accidental" death. This device is the stuff of contemporary gothic romance and melodrama; nevertheless, by making the death suspicious rather than overt wife murder, Scott gestures back to the historical Leicester (whose wife fell down a staircase).[49] More important, Scott's tragic logic remains similar to that of *Othello*: it is precisely Amy's devotion to her husband, her "virtue," that undoes her. Even the hypocrite Forster is appalled by Varney's callous perversion of that goodness, crying out against the "incarnate fiend" that "if there be judgment in heaven, thou hast deserved it. . . . Thou hast destroyed her by means of her best affections" (390). For Desdemona and Amy, wifely loyalty kills. In such episodes, Scott reinforces what he regards as the "essence" of the Shakespearean ur-text, while adapting it to his own times and purposes.

Varney reiterates Iago's remorseless delight in his own villainy: "instead of expressing compunction . . . [Varney] seemed to take a fiendish pleasure in pointing out to them the remains of the murdered Countess, while at the same time he defied them." Scott then retreats slightly from this absolute triumph of evil, rejecting Shakespeare's remarkable choice to end without the villain's death. But even here some of *Othello*'s haunting quality lingers, for Varney remains proud and unrepentant. Realizing that suspicions will thwart his courtly ambitions, he takes his life by drinking a poisoned potion before bed: "nor did he appear to have suffered much agony, his countenance

49. Scott chose to forgo one detail in Ashmole that would have increased the surface resemblance to *Othello*: Varney and Forster's "first stifling her, or else strangling her" in her bed before throwing her downstairs (*Antiquities*, 149–54). Cited in Scott's 1831 introduction, it must have reinforced the connection between Amy and Desdemona. The means of execution match Scott's emphasis on Varney's Iago-like calculating wit and coldness. Scott also deletes Ashmole's Faustian account of Varney's dying misery, in which he cries, "all the devils in hell did tear him in pieces" (see also Lang, ed., *Kenilworth*, xxix–xxx). *Kenilworth*'s Varney, like Iago, remains smug.

60   presenting, even in death, the habitual expression of sneering sarcasm" (390–91). Varney succeeds in his plots and escapes public humiliation.[50]

Where Scott departs most radically from the conclusion of *Othello* is in the fate of the jealous husband. When Leicester learns of Amy's loyalty and admits his marriage to the Queen, he regains some equanimity by imagining he will be able to restore his married life—but this is before he learns that Varney has executed his command of murder. At this point the narrator announces, "It is time, however, to leave these intrigues" (378), pursuing the tragedy to Cumnor. Having so fully elaborated the events leading to Amy's demise, the novel ends almost abruptly, like her life. In the most perfunctory of gestures, one paragraph tells of the Earl's subsequent career, and only a single sentence mentions that "Leicester retired from court, and for considerable time abandoned himself to his remorse." There is no description or direct speech that aspires to match Othello's farewell. While that internally divided warrior kills himself, Leicester lives on to thrive at court "once more distinguished as a statesman and favourite." The narrator suggests "something retributive in his death" if it resulted, as rumored, from "a draught of poison, which was designed for another person" (391).[51] Contrasted with Varney's proud suicide, Leicester's survival and compromising nature appear all the more ignominious.

This impression is reinforced by the fate of the two other men who loved Amy: her father follows Brabantio to the grave "very soon after," and, despite inheriting Robsart's land and being induced by Elizabeth to come to court, nothing removes Tressilian's "profound melancholy. Wherever he went, he seemed to see before him the disfigured corpse of the early and only object of his affection." Abandoning Lidcote-Hall and England, Tressilian departs with Raleigh for Virginia, and "young in years but old in griefs, died before his day in that foreign land" (391–92). Although he is unimpeachably virtuous and steadfast in attempting to save Amy, the mere fact of her death (and his inability to prevent it) destroys Tressilian, whereas the man responsible for that death suffers only a temporary setback in his brilliant career. The fates of Cassio and Othello are thereby reversed.

What are we to make of this radical departure from the story of one who "loved not wisely but too well"? On one level, it is clear: Scott presents the

---

50. Varney's pride hearkens back to Marlowe's portrayal of another Kenilworth inhabitant, *Edward II*'s deposer Roger Mortimer (whom Scott mentions repeatedly in recounting the castle's history).

51. Scott shifts to more cynical commentary in the novel's last oblique reference to one of its historical sources. That "other person," according to Ben Jonson's slanderous account (also cited in the 1831 introduction), was Leicester's later wife, whom he was likewise trying to murder.

leading courtier of Elizabethan England as ethically weak and politically 61
self-serving. He is worthy of neither Amy's domestic devotion nor Elizabeth's public promotion, yet receives both. At the very zenith of the English
court, Leicester symbolizes the superficiality of England's "greatness," a
contrast between glorious image and hollow center that has been suggested
locally in scene after scene. The contrast with *Othello* thus makes all the more
vivid the inadequacy of reading *Kenilworth* as the literary equivalent of a
coronation mug.

Re-staging *Othello*: Race, Theatricality, and the Marketplace

> In studying the play of Othello, I have always *imagined* its hero *a white* man. It
> is true the dramatist paints him black, but this shade does not suit the man. It
> is a stage decoration, which *my taste* discards, —a fault of color, from an artis-
> tic point of view. I have, therefore, as I before stated in my *readings* of this play,
> dispensed with it. . . . Othello *was a white man!*
> Mary Preston, *Studies in Shakespeare: A Book of Essays*

To see how Scott's novel goes beyond the truism that power corrupts,
however, we need to confront the social categories that my analysis has thus
far addressed only in passing. From the outset, there has been a shift of geographical perspective relevant to the novel's rethinking of "race" and nationhood. Unlike *Othello*, in which the action begins at the hub of the Venetian
empire before moving outward, *Kenilworth* approaches the courtly center of
power gradually. It does so for the most part in the company of a character
who serves as Scott's surrogate and guide through the plot, the Devonshire-
bred Cornishman Tressilian. Tressilian is "peripheral" both ethnically and
geographically: he comes from the borders of England rather than from its
Saxon "core"; it is his traditional code of honor, associated with the border
culture, that incapacitates him at the modern court.[52] It is thus he who bears
Scott's memories of cultural "otherness."

Of course, to readers today, the most glaring difference in Scott's
retelling is the obliteration of Othello's most obvious form of difference, his
"race." How was this possible? Some might argue that without a difference
of ethnicity or cultural origin, Leicester cannot really figure Othello at all
but is simply a jealous husband. Others might find confirmation for the

---

52. On insider/outsider relations in *Othello*, see Michael Neill's book and the articles by Edward Berry and Carol Thomas Neely. For more on the basic social science model of core and
periphery in developing states, and on the "Celtic fringe" in Britain specifically, see the books
by Michael Hechter and Linda Colley.

view that one can talk about *Othello* without "playing the race card," as if the hero's perceived blackness were but one of many traits available to be performed (like Othello's mature age, ignored in recent performance treatment).[53] But the former position must ignore too much of *Kenilworth's* text to be sustained, whereas the latter view derives in great part from the work of the novel itself, when considered along with related contemporary developments in the theater and criticism. In other words, to efface the matter of race is to reiterate unconsciously a version of those nineteenth-century positions. Scott's "whitening" of *Othello* is thus far more than an antiquarian issue.

The text sends clear signals of Scott's consciousness of this alteration. Most telling is the scene directly following Varney's first "soliloquy," as the novel begins its overt echoing of *Othello*. Here Amy receives from Leicester a necklace of "orient pearl" with the posy "For a neck that is fairer" (38), recalling Othello's final self-comparison to the "base Indian" who "threw a pearl away, / Richer than all his tribe" (5.2.345–46).[54] Her rooms include "some cushions disposed in the Moorish fashion," as well as four candlesticks each of which "represent[s] an armed Moor, who held on his left arm a round buckler of silver"; the point is reiterated when she goes into "the withdrawing apartment" with her Emilia surrogate, Janet, "where the Countess playfully stretched her upon the pile of Moorish cushions, half sitting, half reclining, half wrapt in her own thoughts, half listening to the prattle of her attendant" (47, 49). As the immediate prelude to Leicester's first appearance, the gift and cushions serve to remind us of what has been repressed from the text of *Othello*—a difference that, whether viewed predominantly as religious, geographical, or ethnic, is repeatedly indexed by blackness.

53. Note the youthful Othellos of Laurence Fishburne in Oliver Parker's 1995 film and David Harewood at the British National Theatre (1997–98). On Othello and other jealous husbands on the Restoration stage, see Vaughan. While addressing the subtleties of "blackness" below, my aim is not to reify Othello's race but to emphasize its social weight as a marker of his "otherness." As Barbara Everett points out—aptly recalling Spanish/Berber contexts in contradistinction to sub-Saharan Africanness—"Othello's colour, which is to say his external being, is to some degree . . . a matter of social assertion and reaction"; *Young Hamlet: Essays on Shakespeare's Tragedies* (Oxford, 1989), 197. Others have criticized her oversimplification in bracketing the "external being"; my point would be that even she, as an historicist critic, acknowledges the social importance of being what other characters—and eventually he too—will call "black."

54. The Quarto reads "Judean"; an editorial debate has raged since Pope's day, with Boswell (the Scot whose edition Scott prized) favoring "Indian," as did Coleridge. Scott also knew the editions of Samuel Johnson, Nicholas Rowe, and George Steevens (who includes a lengthy disquisition on the topic), and probably Malone; having written the life of John Dryden, he would also know that Dryden referred to the story of the Indian (see Furness's New Variorum edition (Philadelphia, 1886), 327–31, M. R. Ridley's Arden edition (London, 1958), 196n, and Honigmann's edition, 342–43). The gift carries extra weight because this is the scene in which Amy and Leicester's relationship is first established.

Othello was perceived as akin to other jealous husbands on the Restora-   63
tion stage—even as he continued to be played in extreme blackface. At the
same time, he was costumed as an English officer, stressing the military context for his marital distrust. Although Scott alters this martial representation
(making Leicester the courtier in explicit contrast to his bluff warrior rival,
Sussex), not only domestic jealousy but an "Englished" appearance carries
over into *Kenilworth* from *Othello*'s earlier theatrical contexts. With this national shift comes space for other political conflicts closer to Scott's heart.
Before turning to that Celtic subtext, however, we first need to examine the
novel's most overt alteration. To do so requires stepping back from the level
of textual detail that made Scott a delightful read and that has here provided
the ocular proof, as it were, of *Othello*'s influence. It demands delving into
the historical context of *Kenilworth*, to comprehend its Shake-shifting in contemporary terms, as well as its legacy and its own causation. For whether he
would or no, Scott's choices squarely locate him as a key participant in a
phenomenon with wide-ranging consequences for how audiences came to
think about the genius of Shakespeare, and more generally for literary interpretation itself as a cultural practice. To understand this historical moment
and Scott's place in it, then, we must turn to a theatrical and critical process
taking place during the years of *Kenilworth*'s composition and first circulation: the process of gradually "whitening" Othello.

In an important sense, if Scott had not written *Kenilworth*, someone else
would have had to invent a white Othello for the nineteenth century. While
Mary Preston's words have been cited to show how racism could lead to ab-
surdity in readings of *Othello* after the U.S. Civil War, what remains less recognized is just how pervasive and influential were kindred attitudes earlier
in the century in Britain—and how they continue, less directly, to shape interpretive practices. They testify to many nineteenth-century readers' desire
to extricate Othello from the contemporary associations obvious in retelling
the story of a black man once "taken by the insolent foe / And sold to slavery" (1.3.137–38). Some would see here a particularly ugly instance of ethical avoidance (or in Preston's case, conscious racism) within modernity's
larger tendency to separate art from the political and mundane. It is easy to
gasp or cringe at the "reasoning" that supports this woman from Maryland's
version of "washing the Ethiop white," but it is simply less skillful in expression than, not different in its assumptions from, the commentaries of Coleridge, Charles Lamb, Hazlitt, and others whose critical legacy remains
powerful.[55] Their ideas, in turn, were generated in great part by their re-

55. Dympna Callaghan calls Preston a Southerner; while sympathetic to the Confederacy,
Preston actually lived (ironically) in a "border state." Ridley cites Preston ("a lady writing from

64   sponses to what they saw at the theater. For although many tie the dominance of racialized discourse to the competing renditions of Tommaso Salvini and Henry Irving late in the century, racialism played an important role in the staging of *Othello* much earlier, during the period of British debates over abolition throughout the Empire of both slave labor and the slave trade.[56] This was, moreover, the time when other race-based anthropological theories were gaining ascendancy among European intellectuals, including

---

Maryland") as "the reductio ad absurdum" of the "tawny Moor" line of criticism also invoked by Coleridge—to Ridley's surprise, although he does not explore that connection or avoid racial stereotyping (see Ridley, ed., *Othello*, li–liii). Traces of Ridley's manner of explaining away an implicit presumption that blackness equals baseness persist; Honigmann, while acknowledging the play's involvement with racism, turns to the 1600–1601 portrait of the lighter-skinned, "aristocratic face" of the Moorish ambassador to stress his nobility and concedes that one (presumed white actor) might manage the role "if he wears European clothes and has darkened skin of indeterminate hue" (a makeup artist's quandary; see Honigmann, ed., *Othello*, 2–3, 14–17). Part of the problem here results from dehistoricizing race, obvious in a leap from early modernity to a Paul Robeson remark to support the race-based association of Othello's blackness with a more passionate nature (20–21). Yet even the historicist Everett presumes that a too-dark appearance would somehow "hide the play of expression" in performance (*Young Hamlet*, 198) and fails to acknowledge that the racial politics of intervening centuries prevent our replicating only the Renaissance meanings of Moorishness—especially in "live" performance. While a twenty-first-century production might stress the text's Arabic possibilities to effect within our era of misunderstandings between dominantly Christian and Islamic nations, my point is that the early nineteenth-century turn to the tawny Moor involved both an historically specific act of avoidance through orientalism, and implicit or explicit racism in relation to blackness.

    56. My aim here accords with Virginia Mason Vaughan's: "to show *Othello* not simply as a product of a cultural milieu but also as a *maker* of cultural meanings, part of a complex negotiation between each episteme's cultural attitudes, its actors, and their audiences" (*Othello: A Contextual History*, 7). However, our location of an historical shift in the function of "race" differs significantly. For Vaughan, racialized discourse becomes dominant in *Othello* interpretation only after the American Civil War; she notes that William Charles Macready (touring the antebellum South) does not connect his representation of the noble Moor with the slavery that disturbed him (135–80). Whether this be Macready's failing or a cautionary reminder of cultural inconsistencies remains arguable, but the shaping consciousness of racialism appears earlier (and more extensively than in individual instances such as Thonas Rymer's *Short View of Tragedy* (1693), which did not alter the blackface playing tradition). Nevertheless, Vaughan and Adrian Poole ("Northern Hamlet and Southern Othello? Irving, Salvini, and the Whirlwind of Passion," *Shakespeare and the Mediterranean: The Selected Proceedings of the International Shakespeare Association World Congress [Valencia, 2001]*, ed. Tom Clayton, Susan Brock, and Vincente Fores [Newark, DE, 2004]) rightly locate a shift in the 1870s, when English audiences identified Othello's "otherness" with the Italianate passion of Tomasso Salvini's performance: this awareness came through contrast with Henry Irving's by then more familiar "English" style as heir to Kemble and the Keans. (In an ironic twist, Irving's Cornish accent, which emerged when he was excited, was interpreted by Gordon Craig as "the same good rich English . . . spoken in the days of Robin Hood, and long before and after"; see Wes Folkerth, *The Sound of Shakespeare* [New York, 2002], 3–4.)

    As of 1772, anyone previously enslaved was free on the soil of territorial Great Britain, but it was not until 1807 that British participation in the slave trade ended. William Wilberforce was pushing for abolition within all British territories by 1821, the year of *Kenilworth*'s publication, and was leading an antislavery society (along with Thomas Buxton) by 1823. The abolition bill cleared Parliament and received royal assent in August 1833, and all slaves within the British Empire were officially freed in 1838.

pseudosciences elevating Aryans and Normans above "darker" peoples (including Celts and Jews, to name two "races" relevant to Scott's novels). At the bottom of these racist hierarchies were Negroes.

Such associations of blackness with baseness appear in the English responses to Ira Aldridge, the one famed black actor to play Othello across Europe during the 1820s and 1830s and again at mid-century. Some London reviews of his Coburg performance are as physically race-based as can be conceived, the *Times* of 11 October 1825 asserting that "owing to the shape of his lips it is utterly impossible for him to pronounce English."[57] When Aldridge returned to debut at Covent Garden in 1833—the year Britain finally abolished slavery within its empire—the *Times* was slightly less overt: "His accent was unpleasantly, and we would say vulgarly, foreign"; "when by chance (for chance it is, and not judgement), he rises to a higher strain, we perceive in the transition the elevation of rant."[58] The charge of vulgarity elides questions of nationality, class, and taste with race, a blurring even more pronounced in the 13 April *Atheneum* review: having claimed to hold "no ridiculous prejudice . . . because he chances to be of a different colour from ourselves," the reviewer nevertheless concludes, "In the name of propriety and decency, we protest against an interesting actress and lady-like girl, like Miss Ellen Tree, being subjected . . . to the indignity of being pawed about by Mr. Henry Wallack's black servant."[59] The "lady-like" English "girl" is being pawed by a triple threat: American, black, servant. The actor-producer relationship of Aldridge and Wallack has been reduced to servitude alone, obviously influenced by the fact that slavery was a major political issue.[60] Although the performances were well received by audiences and the famed British Othello Edmund Kean, Aldridge's appearance in London was cut short by the pro-slavery lobby, and he was effectively exiled from performing in the capital for twenty years.[61] His reception in the provinces and on the continent, especially in Russia, was generally

57. See Julie Hankey, ed., *Othello,* Plays in Performance series (Bristol, 1987), 80.

58. Ruth Cowhig, "Blacks in English Renaissance Drama and the Role of Shakespeare's *Othello,*" in *The Black Presence in English Literature,* ed. David Dabydeen (Manchester, UK, 1985), 18.

59. Ibid., 20.

60. Aldridge did work as a backstage attendant to Wallack, a sad reminder of the many challenges he faced and overcame in becoming a major actor. On Aldridge's remarkable career, see Errol Hill, *Shakespeare in Sable: A History of Black Shakespearean Actors* (Amherst, 1984), 17—20; Lois Potter, *Othello. Shakespeare in Performance series* (Manchester, 2002), 108–18; Joyce Green MacDonald, "Acting Black: Othello, Othello Burlesques, and the Performance of Blackness," *Theatre Journal* 46, no. 2 (1994): 231–49; and Herbert Marshall and Mildred Stock, *Ira Aldridge: The Negro Tragedian* (1958; Carbondale, 1968).

61. If Ruth Cowhig is correct in identifying the *Atheneum* reviewer as John Hamilton Reynolds, Keats's friend and correspondent, there is a direct connection with Romantic authorial circles; "Blacks," 20.

66   warmer; the same association that caused trouble in London endeared him to those fighting to abolish Russian serfdom. What is clear is that everywhere Aldridge went, he went as a nineteenth-century black man as well as Othello, evoking among audiences their responses to the contemporary dilemmas of slavery.

Two decades later, the *Atheneum*'s comments on Aldridge's return as Othello (to the Lyceum in 1858 and the Haymarket seven years after) remained mired in the presumption of racial inferiority that the slave system had required. Three years before the U.S. Civil War began, the London paper averred that "it is impossible Mr. Aldridge should fully comprehend the meaning and force or even the words he utters"; and on 26 August 1865, after the Emancipation Proclamation and the South's surrender at Appomattox, an attempt to adapt to new political realities still grotesquely echoes the slurs of Shakespeare's Roderigo: "We may claim this black, thick lipped player as one proof among many that the negro intellect is human, and demands respect as such."[62] These responses partially explain why, despite (or precisely because of) the obsessive sexual fantasies associated with Turkish harems in Victorian pornography, a "tawny Moor" came to be viewed as more noble and appropriate for *Othello* than a black man (even if the performer "beneath" was white). Whereas the former might be sexually threatening, he remained powerful, even princely, while the latter was indelibly associated with servitude and race-based slavery.

Performance history reveals that the "whitening" of Othello had begun during the decades prior to *Kenilworth*'s publication: John Philip Kemble to some extent and Edmund Kean famously chose to present what was considered a more attractive Turkish-influenced figure. Kemble's cuts retain hints of dangerous sexuality consistent with English fantasies of exotic others, while diminishing emphasis on Africa or blackness.[63] Kemble was also lauded for emphasizing Othello's Moorish garb, a performance choice erroneously thought to be new.[64] Indeed, Kemble went so far in this direction that his devoted biographer James Boaden thought the performance "grand and awful and pathetic, but he was European: there seemed to be philosophy in his bearing; there was reason in his rage . . . the professional farewell

62. Hankey, ed., *Othello*, 80; Cowhig, "Blacks," 21.

63. Following Marvin Rosenberg (*The Masks of Othello* [Newark, DE, 1992], 47–48), Hankey (*Othello*, 50) finds it surprising that Kemble kept the coarse reference to the "beast with two backs" when he cut the "black ram" and "Barbary horse" slurs; but this surprises only if one presumes, as she does, that his criterion was sexual (versus racial) decency.

64. See Vaughan, *Othello*, 93–134; Rosenberg, *Masks*, 16–53; Bonnie Nelson's article; and Potter on *Othello*'s earlier performance history. On the performance of 5.2 in particular, see the article by James Siemon.

of Othello, came rather coldly from him." In terms of the ethnogeographic   67
stereotypes then current, Boaden implies that Kemble went too far north in
his desire to escape association with putative Negro savagery.[65] Tellingly, it
was Kemble's decision to retain at least Othello's black complexion that
prompted some criticism in the press, not the cuts or the costume. Thus the
Public Advertiser review (29 October 1787) concludes: "We must approve his
dressing Othello in Moorish habit . . . but is it necessary the Moor should be
as *black* as a native of Guiney?"[66]

Twenty-seven years later, Edmund Kean answered that question in the
negative. In 1814 he began performing as a "tawny Moor" or Arab, becoming the most celebrated Othello of the period; adding to the myth, he would
eventually die after collapsing in the role (while playing opposite his son
Charles as Iago, a month after seeing Aldridge). Keats praised Kean, and
Hazlitt responded to his performances as both Othello and Iago in several
essays. Indeed, Kean's was the production that shaped many Romantic authors' ideas about the part—and through it, the limits and possibilities of
Shakespeare onstage. At first, Hazlitt found Kean's "lofty-minded Moor"
wrong because he "was not fierce," but by October 1817 the critic admired
his representation of suppressed passion.[67] Loftiness and soulfulness were
nevertheless perceived to be at odds with blackness.

The Romantic critics' writings repeatedly testify to the impact of Kean's
performance choices. Hazlitt stresses Othello's "eastern magnificence," and
Coleridge in his 1822 *Table Talk* similarly avers that "Othello must not be
conceived as a negro, but a high and chivalrous Moorish chief."[68] Both Coleridge and Lamb discount Othello's blackness, Lamb finding it "an intolerable obstacle to a true appreciation." In his 1811 essay "On the Tragedies of

65. Boaden cited in Hankey, *Othello*, 49. Boaden's biography of Kemble was well known to
Scott, who wrote a lengthy review essay of it for the *Quarterly Review* (1826).

66. Cowhig, "Blacks," 15. This particular critic's concern might have derived from attention
to Berber coloration—although contextual evidence and contemporary allusion suggest otherwise.

67. Hankey notes, "[A]bout 1817 . . . his performance reached the ideal of the period as ex-
pounded by the romantic critics" in his "new inwardness, a new preoccupation with Othello's
soul." *Othello*, 56–57.

68. Samuel Taylor Coleridge, *Table Talk* (London, rpt. 1884), 29. More radical politically
and more appreciative of the theater, William Hazlitt takes a slightly different tack in "On Mr.
Kean's Iago" for *The Examiner*, 24 July 1814, although he shares the race-based assumptions of
Lamb and Coleridge. Hazlitt comments on Desdemona's love as "nature erring from itself,"
confessing that "we are a little of Iago's council in this matter." In a footnote, he adds: "If Desdemona really 'saw her husband's visage in his mind,' or fell in love with the abstract idea of 'his
virtues and his valiant parts,' she was the only woman on record, either before or since, who
ever did so"; *Shakespeariana*, 62:505–6). Whether this is a misogynist throwaway or simply conveys worldly skepticism about the superficial nature of attraction remains moot.

68   Shákspeare," Lamb deems Desdemona's love admirable when he is reading
      but "revolting" onstage because of Othello's color:

> I appeal to everyone that has seen *Othello* played, whether he did not, on the
> contrary, sink Othello's mind in his colour; whether he did not find something
> extremely revolting in the courtship and wedded caresses of Othello and Des-
> demona; and whether the actual sight of the thing did not overweigh all that
> beautiful compromise which we make in reading. . . . What we see upon the
> stage is body and bodily action; what we are conscious of in reading is almost
> exclusively the mind, and its movements.[69]

Coleridge confidently invokes history as the guarantor for his interpretation: "as we are constituted, and most surely as an English audience was disposed at the beginning of the 17th century, it would be something monstrous
to conceive this beautiful Venetian girl falling in love with a veritable negro."
Of course, what Shakespeare and his audience conceived is not so sure as
the racism of Coleridge's own statement.[70] Julie Hankey asserts: "The distinction between a Negro and a Moor which Coleridge seized upon to support his belief that Shakespeare could never have made a 'barbarous *negro*
plead royal birth' was not current in Shakespeare's day."[71] Early modern
perceptions of race and ethnicity have been the subject of much recent debate. But it is nonetheless certain that Shakespeare chose to accentuate
color in constructing Desdemona and Othello's love as one that crosses multiple cultural boundaries.[72] In denying Othello's blackness, the nineteenth

69. Charles Lamb, *The Portable Charles Lamb*, ed. John Mason Brown (New York, 1949),
577.
70. Hill, *Shakespeare in Sable*, 9; Cowhig, "Blacks," 17. See Coleridge's interpretation of Jo-
hann Friedrich Blumenbach's hierarchy of races, with Caucasian at the top, Negro at the bottom, and Malays between (*Table Talk*, 50–51; Blumenbach altered his theory in some particulars between his 1775 and 1795 editions). According to George W. Stocking Jr., *Victorian
Anthropology* (New York, 1987), 26–27, Blumenbach posited blackness as a "degeneration"
from Caucasian man (although others counter that his Negro is the more primitive, originary
form); his racial theory "was the most widely accepted in the pre-Darwinian nineteenth century," although Georges Cuvier's 1817 tripartite division moved toward a polygeneticist challenge. Blumenbach was published in England in 1817 as well: see *The Anthropological Treatises of
Blumenbach and Hunter*, ed. Thomas Bendyshe (London, 1817), 19ff. Sudipto Chatterjee and Jyotsna G. Singh discuss the racial complexities of performing *Othello* in nineteenth-century Calcutta and Petrius Camper's theories (translated in 1784, with a new English edition in 1821);
Nancy Stepan surveys the idea of race in British science well into the twentieth century.
71. Hankey, *Othello*, 13.
72. As Max Bluestone observes: "The source for *Othello* [Cinthio's novella] hardly mentions
the racial differences between Othello and Desdemona, but the play emphasizes his blackness
and her whiteness"; *From Story to Stage: The Dramatic Adaptation of Prose Fiction in the Period of
Shakespeare and His Contemporaries* (The Hague, 1974), 122. Many argue that religion and geography were more relevant to perception and categorization than was skin pigmentation. On
shifting conceptions of "race" and blackness during the early modern period, see the essays in
Margo Hendricks and Patricia Parker; Callaghan's article; Kim Hall; Eldred Jones; Neill; and
Mary Floyd-Wilson. Shankar Raman communicates the difficulty of talking about "race" with-

century in one sense also erases Shakespeare's authorial mark. The Romantics' unreflective, anachronistic presumption of black inferiority thus impeded their attention to Shakespeare's emphasis, their vision of the more acceptable "tawny Moor" being informed by a distinctively nineteenth-century orientalism.

The point is worth stressing because this was the moment when Coleridge and Lamb helped develop a mode of interpreting Shakespeare that privileged putatively "transcendent" reading over the vicissitudes of live performance. It is less often recognized how directly this preference for text over performance was involved with—and in some measure derived from—their race-based repugnance at seeing a "black" Othello onstage.[73] That preference in turn was one fundamental premise in the development of an aesthetic that continues to shape much criticism.[74]

Lamb's remarks serve as one salient example of his general principle privileging reading: "how many dramatic personages are there in Shakspeare . . . improper to be shown to our bodily eye! Othello, for instance." Lamb elaborates that it is far preferable to read about than to see "a young Venetian lady of the highest extraction . . . wedding with a *coal-black Moor*—(for such is he represented . . . though the Moors are now well enough known to be by many shades less unworthy of a white woman's fancy)."[75] "Less unworthy"—even when Othello was embodied by a white man with lighter brown makeup, the ocular proof that he had not been conceived as white like him proved a sticking point for Lamb, impeding identification and hence, he went on to argue, proper understanding of the transcendent subjectivity he sought in Shakespeare. If it was necessary to ignore or alter Shakespeare's textual signals in order to transport his plays into an aesthetic domain separated from sordid political realities, so be it.

---

out reifying the European constructs one is trying to critique; see his final chapter. On Renaissance conceptions of Moors, see books and articles by Emily Bartels; Anthony Barthelemy; and Jack D'Amico. On *Othello*, see Honigmann, ed., *Othello*; Arthur L. Little Jr.; Neely; Karen Newman; Martin Orkin; Potter; Camille Wells Slights; Vaughan; and Daniel J. Vitkus.

73. See Terry Eagleton on the rise of the aesthetic category during this period, and the complex links between its abstraction and "the middle class's struggle for political hegemony"; *The Ideology of the Aesthetic* (Cambridge, MA, 1990), 3.

74. Gary Taylor directly connects Hazlitt's and Coleridge's resistance to seeing *Lear* onstage with both the political situation (the play was not performed during the last decade of George III's madness) and their idealization of Shakespeare (making them reluctant to see "the character's physical frailty" complicate their vision of the poet's strength and power; *Reinventing Shakespeare*, 153, 160). In the case of *Othello* even more than *Lear*, performance undermines these critics' wishful self-construction through identification with a powerful yet sensitive character. By forcing the viewer to see the embodied character as different, performance interferes with the process of self-transformation from a particularly located white male Englishman into a universalized sympathizing subject.

75. Italics his; Lamb, *Portable*, 575–76.

70   These, then, were the theatrical and critical trends in play when Scott created *Kenilworth*. He himself preferred the acting of Kemble to Kean, his reasons befitting his characteristic mixture of old-fashioned antiquarian and romanticist attitudes. Like the English poets, he looked for nobility and inwardness and found that the large renovated Theatres Royal demanded too broad an acting style, a scale of gesture that in Kean's case he also associated with ill breeding.[76] But even if not swept away by the Kean craze, Scott was well aware of both the performances and the criticisms of *Othello* being generated as he wrote *Kenilworth*. Indeed, anyone even minimally interested in theater would have been aware of the huge to-do surrounding Junius Brutus Booth's brief stint as Iago opposite Kean's Othello in 1817. While in retrospect we can discern 1817 as a turning point in shaping Romantic critical attitudes (including those about *Othello* and Shakespearean performance more generally) and also as a key moment in the development of nineteenth-century racial theory, what made the 1817 season most remarkable at the time was the contract dispute and battle of the London Theatres Royal for the body of Booth. The incident serves as a reminder of the interpenetration of commercial with artistic and political concerns in the production of Shakespeare, another intrusion from the crass "modern" world that would both motivate and undermine the Romantics' attempts to retreat with the Bard into an alternative world of aesthetic majesty. The role of the marketplace was an equally powerful phenomenon affecting Scott's work and his Shake-shifting, and hence this tale of egos and money merits recollection.

On February 18, Drury Lane revealed that it had become the beneficiary of Booth's disagreement with the management at its competitor, Covent Garden. The Drury Lane playbill announced, "Mr. Booth is engaged at this Theatre, and will make his first appearance on Thursday, in the character of Iago, in the Tragedy of Othello. Othello, Mr. KEAN." According to the following Saturday's playbill—always hyperbolic but in this case aptly so—Booth's debut was a grand success. The play "performed on Thursday to an overflowing Audience, was honour'd throughout with unbounded Approbation, and announced for Repetition THIS EVENING amidst the loudest and

---

76. In reviewing Boaden's *Life of Kemble*, Walter Scott lamented that the enlargement of Drury Lane and Covent Garden made Garrick's naturalness impossible: "[A]ll the nicer touches of fine acting—the smile however suppressed—the glance of passion which escaped from the actor's eye . . . the whisper which was heard distinctly . . . are all lost or wasted in the huge halls. . . . Extravagant gesture must be used; excess of rant must be committed by the best actors in their finest parts"; *Critical and Miscellaneous Essays* (Philadelphia, 1841), 3:55. It is revealing of the author's romanticization of the lost past that Garrick died when Scott was eight years old and that Kean would be praised precisely for his naturalness.

most enthusiastic Acclamations of unanimous Applause; the Demand for Places being beyond all Precedent, —in order therefore to accommodate the numerous Parties who have hitherto been disappointed, it will be repeated on MONDAY and TUESDAY." But it was not to be: Booth pled ill, and was soon back performing in competition at Covent Garden. His contract dispute had been resolved. Booth's reversion, however, caused enough public outcry to initiate a playbill war, its most notable document being "Mr Booth's Appeal to the Public."[77] Alas, poor Booth, he hadn't imagined that he "should be made the first dreadful example of public Indignation" at an actor for non-appearance in the history of the theater. The scandal of course insured his celebrity, as well as the production's. The artistic triumph of Kean-versus-Booth onstage, however, was sacrificed: it was only a one-night stand, whereas the commercial rivalry lived on. Henry Wallack (later Aldridge's patron as well as Leicester in the Drury Lane production of *Kenilworth*) stepped in as Iago, and five more *Othello*s were performed during the spring season.

As Kean continued to perform Othello, he rotated it in his repertory with Thomas Southerne's dramatization of Aphra Behn's *Oroonoko*: this was the other play in which Kean had been starring at the time of the Booth hubbub. It was hardly coincidental that Kean chose simultaneously to impersonate another racially "other" tragic hero who kills his beloved.[78] *Oroonoko*, with its expressed opposition to the slave trade, was also reportedly playing "to a brilliant and overflowing Audience, and honoured with the most enthusiastick Applause" (20 February 1817 playbill). In concert with his support for Ira Aldridge, Kean's repertory choices imply his progressive racial politics. That is, while celebrity marketing made certain plays popular and some viewers found his Moor more acceptable for racist reasons, Kean's own mo-

77. [Junius Brutus Booth], "Mr. Booth's Appeal to the Public," 26 February 1817, Theatre Museum Archive, Covent Garden, London. Booth announces that he was badly received at Covent Garden the night before owing to his reversion and "not performing at Drury-Lane on Saturday last." He tries to redeem his damaged reputation by asserting that management knew of his illness by 3:00 p.m. that Saturday, "which was time sufficient to have had Hand-bills printed . . . and prevent my being the cause of any disappointment to the audience"; "Had I thought that such an unfair advantage would have been taken of my Illness, and that it would have been insinuated from the Stage, that my Indisposition was feigned . . . I would, at all hazards have performed, even tho' Death had been the consequence." Playbills cited from the archives of the Theatre Museum, Covent Garden, London.

78. See the article by Margaret W. Ferguson and Neely, "Circumscriptions," on the complexity of reading "race," gender, and colonial positions in (Southerne's adaptation of Behn's) *Oroonoko* and *Othello*, respectively; see also Roach, *Cities*, 152–61, on *Oroonoko*. Edward Young's 1721 *The Revenge*, with the Moor Zanga as its defiant villain, was also in Kean's and Aldridge's repertory with these roles; Hazlitt found this deceiving slave "more in conformity to our prejudices, as well as to historical truth" (Potter, *Othello*, 13–14).

72   tivations seem at odds with this interpretation. The gap between the actor's beliefs and the reception of his "tawny Moor" foreshadows a similar irony in the differences between *Kenilworth* and its stage adaptations. It likewise reinforces the difficulty involved in evaluating the political impact of "modern" Shakespeare, and the consequent inadequacy of flat praise or blame. This celebrated production of *Othello* thus epitomizes the interplay of theater's political, artistic, and commercial dimensions, even as it serves as a cautionary reminder that success in one dimension may undermine success in another.[79] The subversive or challenging aspects of Kean's choices were dwarfed in the moment by a commercial row, and in retrospect by the lasting textual impact of more conservative, racially biased interpreters.

Meanwhile, the ex-Iago Booth went into a slow decline and eventually emigrated to America. He fathered both Edwin, the greatest American tragedian of his day, and John Wilkes, named for the eighteenth-century advocate of English liberties who demonized the Scots as ethnic "others." That younger Booth would become notorious for assassinating Abraham Lincoln at Ford's Theatre, five days after the Confederacy's surrender spelled the end of the black slave system in the United States. From England to America, from John Bull to John Wilkes Booth, from the death of Othello to the death of Lincoln: politics and performance intertwined, even as the Romantics retired into their studies, hoping to read Shakespeare transcendently and finding instead a mirror of their own images, politics, and ideals. In the library as on the stage and within the marketplace, race mattered.

Celtic Twilight, Shake-shifting Substitution

Whaur's yer Willie Shakespeare noo?
                    Anonymous audience member responding to
                    John Home's Scottish play, *Douglas* (1756)

the cause is lost for ever

                                    Walter Scott, *Redgauntlet*

To what extent, then, does Scott's novel participate in the Romantic attempt to remove Shakespeare from contemporary sociopolitical struggles? Edinburgh and Abbotsford might be far from the London stage, but the im-

---

79. Joyce Green MacDonald highlights another dimension of Kean's actions: "The perhaps unexpectedly contradictory result of Kean's racial strategy of whitening Othello points to a similar resistance of black signs to seamless incorporation within narratives of white superiority" ("Acting Black," 243); Scott exploits such "resistance" in the service of Celtic identity.

pact of performances and reviews was not, at least not for Walter Scott. He
was trebly "interested" in the theater: as business, as art, and as a political
vehicle. He was an active playgoer, critic, would-be playwright—and tireless investor, campaigner, and trustee for the Edinburgh Theatre Royal.[80]
For Scott, London productions provided an important part of the cultural
context in which one might imagine transposing Othello's domestic tragedy
to befit a powerful white man without believing this to be an utter contradiction. But to do so still necessitated major changes that would have been
visible to the Shake-shifter. For while Scott might not conceive of Othello's
racial otherness as essential to his character, he was obviously aware of the
play's reiterated reference to Othello's blackness and its stereotypical associations.

Scott's heraldic crest attests that he participated to an extent in the debas-
ing symbology that marks a common ground between Iago's perspective and
the nineteenth-century critics' views of blackness: one of the "supporters" is
a minimally clothed black man (the other, the exoticized half-human figure of
a mermaid).[81] In *Ivanhoe*, the villain Brian de Bois-Guilbert is "burnt almost
to Negro blackness" and anachronistically has Negro attendants; Sutherland
considers that novel "largely responsible for injecting consciousness of race
(and a sizeable dose of racism) into the popular British mind" (*Life*, 229). The
conventionally negative use of blackness as a metaphor creeps into the 1831

80. Scott was an avid (weekly) theatergoer in Edinburgh. Sutherland posits that Scott was
looking toward a career writing for the London stage (*Life*, 69–70). In 1799, he translated
Goethe's *Götz von Berlichingen*, and while in London submitted his gothic drama *The House of
Aspen* to Kemble (who turned it down). Later he acquired the lease for the Edinburgh Theatre
Royal, which he wished to elevate above "the garbage of melodrama and pantomime" into a
Scottish national theater performing the works of John Home and Joanna Baillie—and, with
apparent incongruity, Shakespeare (Scott, *Letters*, 2:118). He tried to lure the Kembles by making Henry Siddons manager, after whose death (1815) the theater "limped along" for another
fifteen years. In 1817–18 Scott composed a "goblin drama" for his actor friend Daniel Terry,
but Terry turned it down; it was published in 1830 as *The Doom of Devorgoil* along with a later attempt, *Auchindrane*. The year 1817 was also that in which Kemble retired from the stage, having
visited Scott and performed *Coriolanus* as his Edinburgh farewell. See also Alasdair Cameron,
"Scottish Drama in the Nineteenth Century," in *History of Scottish Literature*, ed. Gifford, 3:429–
35; Brewer (17, 30–35); and the article by Christopher Worth.

81. Such use of servants to attest to rank is not necessarily a sign of intentional racism, nor
need the symbolic use register in the user's mind as connected with exceptional figures such as
Othello. Nevertheless it testifies to a cultural "blindness" that is not in fact blind to race but simply presumes that inferior positionality for the black man is apt and uninsulting. Although we
do not know exactly why Walter cut off contact with his brother Daniel, Sutherland speculates
that the disgrace may have involved the failure of colonials (including Daniel) to put down effectively the 1805 slave uprising in Jamaica (*Life*, 114); if true, it suggests Scott's active, specific
endorsement of racist policies (beyond general support for the empire and its armies), but one
must be cautious in attributing motives, for Scott feared all forms of insurrection (as his response to Peterloo unfortunately attests).

74   introduction to *Kenilworth*, where Scott remarks on his choice to make the
Earl more dupe than villain, in order to rescue him for the fiction's purposes
from the most scathing reports that "may have blackened the character of
Leicester with darker shades than really belonged to it."[82] Figuratively,
Leicester too must be "whitened" to be a worthy subject of romance.

Yet Scott's relationship to issues of race and nationhood within the British
Isles was different from that of Lamb and Coleridge. As the "Minstrel of the
Scottish Borders," Scott had gained fame by enunciating his own border position between Celtic and English culture. And while the stage shift from
blackness to Arabian Moorishness provided impetus for an aesthetic that
would disconnect the "essence" of Othello from his ethnicity, it also provided the precedent for a logic of ethnic replacement. In other words, Scott
does not participate exclusively in that universalizing move whereby substituting white for black is interpreted as the erasure of race—the white blindness to its own ethnic particularity that is part of the Romantic legacy of
self-universalizing subjectivity. Instead, Scott retains some of Shakespeare's
attention to ethnic difference, but in the form of Celticness, obliquely addressing a "racial" struggle within Britain of direct concern to him. *Kenilworth* thereby encourages a strategic rather than essentialist understanding
of "race" as a social position, with specific historical origins and consequences. Thus too *Kenilworth* transmutes *Othello*'s unconventional use of ethnic otherness as both a symbol of transcendent love and a means by which
an "insider" can unjustly defame and undo a cultural border figure. Such
otherness is resituated, aptly enough for Scott, at the borders of the narrative: not in the figure of the jealous husband but rather in the rejected suitor,
the Cornishman Tressilian.

When we first learn the name of Tressilian, "the silent guest" at Gosling's
Inn, his host immediately associates him with a Celtic ancestry.[83] While
tempering the literalness of Gosling's identification, Tressilian continues to

82. Cited in Lang ed., *Kenilworth*, xxvii–iii.
83. "Tressilian?" answered my host of the Bear, "a worthy name; and, as I think, of Cornish
lineage; for what says the sooth proverb—
> By Pol, Tre, and Pen,
> You may know the Cornish men.
Shall I say the worthy Mr. Tressilian of Cornwall?"
"Say no more than I have given you warrant for, mine host, and so shall you be sure you
speak no more than is true. A man may have one of these honourable prefixes to his name,
yet be born far from Saint Michael's Mount." (11)
The name seems to derive from a list of *extinct* Cornish families, and the character is Scott's creation, one of the novel's few noncomic parts not derived from Elizabethan sources (however
loosely); see Alexander's note in Scott, *Kenilworth*, 478. Scott would also have known of a similarly named character in the Elizabethan play *Woodstock*.

be viewed as Cornish throughout. Michael Lambourne chastises his rash-
ness (linking it, not incidentally, with the colonized foreign): "But hark ye,
my Cornish comrade, you have brought a Cornish flaw with you hither, a
hurricanoe as they call it in the Indies—make yourself scarce—depart—
vanish—or we'll have you summoned before the Mayor of Halgaver, and
that before Dudman and Ramhead meet."[84] Varney identifies Tressilian negatively as "the very Cornish chough, to whom old Sir Hugh Robsart destined his pretty Amy" (39). The narrator, by contrast, reinforces the connection in laudatory terms (35–36). And Tressilian himself eventually owns
the ancestry.

With it, he must acknowledge a history of defeat. Indeed, *Kenilworth* is ultimately as much Tressilian's tragedy as Leicester's—a tragedy of inaction
and loss resulting from competing loyalties and rootedness in the past. That
irrecoverable personal past is repeatedly associated with Celtic culture,
complete with angry ghosts. The Kenilworth jailor, for instance, recalls the
ghost of a Welsh lord, killed when held prisoner during the border wars that
established English sovereignty: "*that* raises you a ghost that will render
your prisonhouse untenable by any decent captive for some hundred
years—" (280). Aptly, the ghost's room is assigned to Tressilian, whom Varney has already called a "spectre." Since Scottish Enlightenment thinkers associated Celts with the Goths and gothic as part of their suppressed past,
such representations are particularly (and historically) weighted. Through
the invented story of Tressilian, the man of Celtic descent who is both marginalized and a victim of political evils, Scott thus resurrects other historical
ghosts. Injustices involving the Celtic "race," confronted more directly elsewhere in the Waverley series, lurk in the shadows of *Kenilworth*.

Tressilian's Cornishness affiliates him with a rebellion by his grandfather's
generation against the English throne, a tellingly similar historical position
to that of Scott with respect to the Jacobite risings of 1715 and 1745—rebellions his Scottish emotions lauded despite his having rationalized their
defeat as politically beneficial.[85] Like Scott's own great-grandfather

84. Scott's first footnote, one of the rare notes in the original edition, explains that these are
two Cornish headlands that could not meet, and Alexander elaborates on the story of the myth-
ical Cornish mayor (Scott, *Kenilworth*, 34). Tressilian also uses Cornwall as a point of reference
when he compares Wayland's smithy at the standing stones (themselves reminders, like Wayland's name, of ancient forebears) to a "Cornish barrow" (96). Cornwall was of course the first
"Celtic fringe" area of Britain to be subdued, and was eventually assimilated most completely
into England.
85. In the Ashetiel fragment, Scott took pride in his familial heritage of rebelliousness, particularly the marauder Auld Wat (Walter Scott) of Harden, and Beardie, who fought for the
Old Pretender. See Scott's letter of 17 December 1806: "My great-grandfather was *out*, as the
phrase goes, in Dundee's wars and in 1715, and had nearly the honour to be hanged for his

"Beardie" (and akin to his romanticized sixteenth-century ancestor "Auld Wat"), Tressilian's grandfather fought gallantly in a losing cause for a "Pretender" to the English throne. Tressilian explains that his "grandfather, like some other Cornish-men, kept a warm affection to the House of York, and espoused the quarrel of [Lambert] Simnel," fighting on his behalf "at Stoke, where most of the leaders of that unhappy army were slain in their harness. The good knight, to whom [Tressilian's grandfather] rendered himself, Sir Roger Robsart, protected him from the immediate vengeance of the King" (80), although the family was impoverished as a result. For York, think Stuart; for Simnel, read Bonnie Prince Charlie; and the story would have had tragic resonance for many Scottish readers. So too the thwarted marriage contract between this younger Tressilian and Amy Robsart, which would have confirmed the union of Celt and Norman in blood as well as friendship "on the frontiers of Devonshire" (112). In a masque presented at Kenilworth, Merlin's intervention magically resolves battles between the "four races" of England—the "aboriginal Britons" (a phrase Scott used to describe Celtic Scots as well), Romans, Saxons, and Normans. But Scott conjures no good wizard to appear in Devon.[86] Instead, the happiness of that projected union in the border territory is thwarted by the intrusion of Richard Varney, acting on Leicester's behalf. Varney thus becomes the double villain of the piece, disrupting a match akin to an idealized relationship between Celtic Scotland and England (versus the contentious legacy of the 1707 Union), as well as corrupting the courtly center itself. Here again one discerns *Othello*'s usefulness as ur-text. *Kenilworth* recollects the play's similar

---

pains. . . . [M]y father, although a Borderer, transacted business for my Highland lairds. . . . I became a violent Jacobite at the age of 10 years, and ever since reason and reading came to my assistance, I have never quite got rid of the impression which the gallantry of Prince Charles made on my imagination." In his letter of July 1813, Scott adds: "I am very glad I did not live in 1745 for though as a lawyer I could not have pleaded Charles's right and as a clergyman I could not have prayed for him yet as a soldier I would I am sure against the conviction of my better reason have fought for him even to the bottom of the gallows" (in Henderson Scott, *Walter Scott*, 20; see also Sutherland and David Hewitt's edited volume). From *Waverley* through the *Legend of Montrose* and beyond, Scott had an interest in those who change sides: another might call them traitors—or collaborators. Tressilian, of Cornish blood but raised in Devon, shares the assimilated position of Scott himself (and recalls Othello's tenuous assimilation into Venetian culture). In accepting the first baronetcy awarded during George IV's reign, Scott aggravated his conflicted position: while he might like to think of it as a chivalric award, the title was, he knew, created (and sold) by James I to raise revenues. Thus Scott's title was a product of emergent (by his time dominant) market relationships.

86. In the masque, the Britons get the most attention, though the piece is laudatory about the "progress" of Britain; such progress, the Queen points out in "gracious answer" to Merlin, relies on all groups' combining their positive traits; 350–52.

villainy acted out at the borders of empire (Cyprus being a Venetian imperial "frontier") and upon a man "naturalized" into the culture.[87]

Should this figuration of Celtic history sound far afield, it is worth recalling a crucial scene that directly confronts Scottish affairs, in the person of Mary, Queen of Scots. Tellingly, Tressilian's mentor Sussex supports freedom for the Stuart monarch, whereas Leicester successfully opposes it. The privy council is

> agitated touching the affairs of the unfortunate Mary, the seventh year of whose captivity in England was now in doleful currency. There had been opinions in favour of this unhappy princess laid before Elizabeth's council, and supported with much strength of argument by Sussex and others, who dwelt more upon the law of nations and the breach of hospitality, than, however softened or qualified, was agreeable to the Queen's ear. Leicester adopted the contrary opinion with great animation and eloquence, and described the necessity of continuing the severe restraint of the Queen of Scots, as a measure essential to the safety of the kingdom, and particularly of Elizabeth's sacred person. (167)

Leicester's position favoring national security over international law pleases the Queen, although the narrator clearly sympathizes with the losing side.[88]

Given that Scott was already involved in racial alteration when reconceiving Othello's part to fit Leicester, it is less surprising that other questions involving nationality and ethnicity sidle in to replace blackness as a site of difference in *Kenilworth*. To comprehend this displaced association of blackness and Celtic culture, one must remember not only the political struggles involved in the creation of the United Kingdom but also the way in which

87. In a further parallelism with Scott's emphasis on a lost ideal union, Venice had lost Cyprus to the Turks some thirty years before *Othello* was written, making the play's representation a fantasy state or past prefiguring the harsh realities of a major Christian military defeat.

88. Less than a year after writing *The Abbot*, Scott may have temporarily exhausted his deep interest (he had established his fame through a series of narrative poems set in Scotland during the period, including *Marmion* and *The Lady of the Lake*). Nevertheless, both Scottish affairs and Mary Stuart are discussed, as when Leicester reveals a jewel that "was bestowed on me when it was thought the young widow of France and Scotland would gladly have wedded an English baron," leading his wife to pause "as if what he has said had excited some painful but interesting train of thought" (59). Amy's unspecified thoughts might prompt an early nineteenth-century reader to remember the alleged relationship involving Stuart and Dudley (culminating in secret offspring) popularized in Lee's *The Recess*. Later Leicester and Varney discuss the fate of Mary's second husband, Lord Darnley (184). The only dialect in the novel comes from a Cumberland border guard, one of Lord Hunsdon's "northern retainers" now "protecting" Amy rather than Mary (329). Scotland thus remains beyond the pale of representation, but the relationship between what Scott regarded as "aboriginal" Celtic groups allows symbolic connection.

78   this history mingled with the developing discourses of race. The "Norman Yoke" theory that regarded Celts as a "darker" race suggested a pseudo-biological rationale for the association. That theory certainly factored in Scott's thinking, but ambivalently: he both felt the cultural appeal and nobility of archaic values associated with the Celts, and believed that lighter races represented more advanced, "enlightened" civilizations.[89] Yet he lived at a time when the ill effects of British Union upon the "Celtic fringe" in Scotland were most evident. During the later eighteenth century, Scotland had for the most part managed its own affairs without interference from the British central government and "not only prospered but had reached a great peak of intellectual achievement," the Scottish Enlightenment.[90] But in the early nineteenth century things changed, with increasing parliamentary and fiscal interference from London, plus the Highlands clearances wrought by those policies and the greed of Scottish lairds and landowners.[91]

    Through starvation, intimidation, and acts of violence, much of the Highlands population was driven from their land, onto boats or into graves. Celtic speech and traditions were banned, ignored, or berated. Scott witnessed the horrific consequences of the clearances firsthand during the "year of the burnings," 1809, on a trip to the Highlands.[92] As early as 1802, he had written that he wished to "contribute something to the history of my

89. For Scott, "The Borderers and Highlanders represented pockets of Scottish aboriginality squeezed to either end of the country's habitable territory. They were partners in persecution" (Sutherland, *Life*, 141; see also 92, 134). On the resistance of the "Celtic fringe" to assimilation within British national development, see Hechter. Although Robert Knox was similarly a product of an Edinburgh education, I do not think Scott's views can be lumped together with Knox's 1830s racism so neatly as Sutherland implies in discussing *Ivanhoe* (*Life*, 229). Nevertheless, Scott's mixed feelings about the Celts as a "race" do accord with the ambiguous liminal position of Othello as a racially "other" border figure choosing to serve a more sophisticated empire. Moreover, Stocking attributes British interest in racial thinking to antiquaries "following the lead of Sir Walter Scott," culminating in the elevation of the Saxon who, having long "been juxtaposed against the impulsive, imaginative, violent, and somewhat childish Celt, was now on a broader stage contrasted with the savages of the non-Western world, in whom the Celtic character was painted with a darker brush" (*Victorian Anthropology*, 55). Prichard made an explicit analogy between Africans and Celts (Stocking, 62–63; see also Stepan, and Elsie Michie's discussion of this racial conflation with respect to *Jane Eyre*). Stocking discusses the ambivalence among Scottish Enlightenment thinkers "lest the manly virtues be sacrificed to the development of commercial and industrial society," in contrast to the primitive ancestral Scots "whose manner were 'so pure and refined as scarce to be paralleled in the most cultivated nations'" (17).

90. Henderson Scott, *Walter Scott*, 21.

91. Henderson Scott elaborates, "If Jacobitism was a dead issue, the effects of the Union on Scotland, the creeping anglicisation, were not. In fact they only began to be felt from about the beginning of the nineteenth century" (*Walter Scott*, 21).

92. "1809 was . . . the overture to ten years of ruthless persecution. Scott made serious visits to the Highlands in 1809–10. His celebration of the clan way of life was given poignant force by the coffin boats leaving every week for the New World, crammed with uprooted Highlanders"

native country, the peculiar features of whose manners and character are daily melting and dissolving into those of her sister ally."[93] Even without emphasizing Scotland in *Kenilworth*, Scott raises the question of British ethnicities and border identities repeatedly, especially in connection with Tressilian. The displaced Cornishman intends, upon returning Amy to her father, to emigrate to Virginia, a more distant outpost of the nascent British Empire where the internally colonized could (and did) become colonizers (82).[94] After Amy's death Tressilian pursues that course and dies prematurely — proleptically figuring the many Scots forced to emigrate by the clearances that peaked in the decade before *Kenilworth*'s publication. In this context, the ghost of the defeated Welsh prisoner haunting Tressilian's room and the allusion to Tressilian as "spectre" take on another layer of tragic meaning.[95]

Several aspects of Scott's veiled allegory deserve comment and connection. The fate of Tressilian, ill used but uncomplaining, captures Scott's own position regarding British rule of Scotland. He was writing after the immediate threats posed by the French Revolution and Napoleon had receded and before further English attempts to erode Scotland's prerogatives prompted him briefly (and effectively) to turn pamphleteer in the later 1820s.[96] Tressilian's loyalty — though exploited by others, including his puta-

---

(Sutherland, *Life*, 134). Moved by the sufferings caused by economic "progress," he recorded that response in personal writings and *Guy Mannering*.

93. Cited in Henderson Scott, *Walter Scott*, 69.

94. Again Scott's anachronism signals the importance of his symbolic point, since it would be another decade before Raleigh's first abortive attempts and another generation before there would be an enduring Virginia colony.

95. See Sutherland, *Life*, 182, and Duncan, *Modern Romance*, 9, on the premodern as a "cultural uncanny" for Scott. A specific biographical link may also be figured in Tressilian's romantic loss. The narrator reflects: "Nothing is perhaps more dangerous to the future happiness of men of deep thought and retired habits, than the entertaining [of] an early, long, and unfortunate attachment. . . . This aching of the heart, this languishing after a shadow which has lost all the gaiety of its colouring, this dwelling on the remembrance of a dream from which we have been long roughly awakened, is the weakness of a gentle and generous heart, and it was that of Tressilian" (268–69). It seems also to have been that of Scott in regard to Williamina Belsches. Though biographers debate the extent of Scott's devastation when she married another, Scott (and Lockhart) felt it to be the heartbreak of his life.

96. Scott was far from indifferent to political struggles of the day: in the most rigid of his Tory stances, he defended the Peterloo Massacre as a necessary police action and feared even moderate workers' movements. However, Scott in 1820 was less gripped by the war panic that earlier in his life had justified Union above all. Nor was he yet impelled to overt criticism by the banking crisis of 1825–26, which he would see as an unjust punishment of Scotland for English mistakes (his distress aggravated by his own ruin, deriving ultimately from his London publishers' overextensions). He lamented the destruction of Celtic culture but attributed it — at least on a conscious political level — not solely to English domination but rather to economic "progress" enacted by lairds in concert with government policy. Scott was of course aware that London was pulling capital and power south, and wrote repeatedly of English arrogance with regard to Scottish members of the armed forces (see Sutherland, *Life*, 280, 305–47, on Scott's

tive benefactor Sussex and his beloved Amy—might be a better figure, in fact, for Scott's attitude to the British nation than is conveyed by portraying him solely as imperial cheerleader. No rebel he, but Scott was increasingly ambivalent about the Union's inequity. Ferris observes that Scott's work generally was "instrumental in initiating the historically significant process of authorizing cultural margins in nineteenth-century Europe, a process that depended on but was not always congruent with the nationalist drive. Admittedly, the early national novel typically sought recognition for colonized groups within the current imperial arrangement of things"; but they also "challenged assumptions of cultural homogeneity and superiority."[97] Tressilian's demise recalls the cost of nation building. As such, it creates an allegory consonant with the lamentations in *The Heart of Midlothian* and (especially) *Redgauntlet*, and functions as the return of what Scott's Tory politics repressed. It gives *Kenilworth* greater kinship with those Waverley novels now considered his serious achievements.

The doubled impulses at work in this Celtic subtext also bear upon the novel's patriarchalism, which thereby assumes a more textured political meaning. Although Scott gives the women in his story as much affective sympathy and more awareness of evil than did Shakespeare, the righteousness with which he invests Tressilian and Robsart has gendered consequences. One is left with the impression that had Amy simply followed her father's arrangements and ignored her lack of passion for Tressilian, she would have thrived. By contrast, the Elizabethan court lacks father figures and Amy suffers as a result. Scott does compare Leicester to Oberon as an overseeing eye, but this Oberon fails to institute the more "progressive" version of patriarchy found in Shakespeare's comedy, in which romanticized marital choices are integrated into an overarching system that still upholds male political control.[98]

---

increasingly resentful portrayal of England and what Robert Gordon calls *The Bride of Lammermoor's* "Tory pessimism," as well as Henderson Scott, passim). Duncan's argument that "all romance is sentimental, purposeful, allegorical, local in the sense that it speaks to and from particular positions" pertains (*Modern Romance*, 7). Mary Lascelles emphasizes the "tragic" dimensions of Scott's historical vision, a "fundamental insight . . . not (so far as I can ascertain) derived from contemporary historians. It was his own." However, she thinks he "kept the sombre vision to himself, at least when he was writing the novels"; *The Story-Teller Retrieves the Past* (Oxford, 1980), 78–79. Tellingly, she makes no mention of *Kenilworth*.

97. Ferris, *Achievement*, 107–8.

98. The narrator remarks of Leicester: "He had the Fairy King's superiority over his friends and dependants, and saw much which they could not" (210). See Raman's discussion of the shift from feudal paternal to modern fraternal patriarchy founded on social contract theory as figured in *A Midsummer Night's Dream*. Scott's representation thus allows interpretations such as Marshall Walker's: "The Queen's absolute power moderates romance by inversion: because of Elizabeth, Amy is a damsel who needs rescuing from her prince, and Leicester is finally responsible for her death"; *Scottish Literature since 1707* (London, 1996), 131.

What we see instead is a world of confusion and subterfuge as regards sexual relations. Amy protests to her husband that he at least has the right to assert his marital choice. She is appalled that he should fear for his life "because you used the freedom and liberty of an English subject in chusing a wife? — for shame"; she concludes that his "distrust of the Queen's justice, this apprehension of dangers . . . cannot but be imaginary." But Dudley rejoins, "'Ah, Amy, thou little knowest!'" (333). And indeed, she shows a sheltered idealism as naive as is Desdemona's concerning marital infidelity. Amy's vision of proper order matches Shakespeare's comic vision, in which free choice of marriage, and loyalty therein, allows political patriarchy to thrive. But Leicester is closer to Scott's understanding of the Elizabethan world, in which the Earl's secrecy is partially justified by the Queen's behavior. As long as this untamed Fairy Queen continues to inhibit the amorous desires of her court, enmeshing domesticity and politics, Leicester cannot instate his male authority in either sphere.

Thus Elizabeth too is made to bear some share of the blame for domestic disruption. Attributing her moments of irrationality to her gender helps justify Scott's nostalgic yearning for an already antiquated model of feudal patriarchalism, emblematized by old Sir Hugh Robsart. This once vital squire now sits weeping for his lost daughter, a sentimentalized representation of the abandoned father as the retainer of lost virtues, both domestic and martial. Presented as a sinless King Lear, a feeling Egeus, a righteous Brabantio, Robsart laments, "I have cause to weep, for she was my daughter" (115), but concludes, "'Let her go,' he said; 'she is but a hawk that goes down the wind; I would not bestow even a whistle to reclaim her'" (121).[99] He perceives himself as vestigial: "I were wrong to name broadly the base thing she is become — there is some new court name for it, I warrant me" (115). Amy has in fact become a Countess, but her father is justified nevertheless: her legal elevation means nothing when kept secret from a tempestuous female ruler by dishonest, fearful men. To the extent that these traditional gendered representations deflect attention from the opposition between England's corrupt core and honest periphery, they mute the contemporary resonance of that more provocative critique of the state.

In another sense, though, Scott's longing for a purer past ruled by benign fathers similarly derives from his border critique of English policy toward the Celts. For in the author's mind, at least, a robust form of patriarchy was affiliated with the Celtic past. Scott overtly connects them in an 1806 letter to Anna Seward. Imagining his next poem (*The Lady of the Lake*), he writes that he intends to give "as far as I can a real picture of what that enthusias-

99. See *Othello* 3.3.266.

82   tic race actually were before the destruction of their patriarchal government."[100] Likewise, Robsart, the Devon patriarch defiantly aligned with defeated Cornish rebels, suggests an alternative historical model to England's
devastation of Celtic culture. But he, like Tressilian, is destroyed by the feminized court's intrusion into his borderland. Ultimately what is being "romanticized" here is not, as in *Othello*, the marital choice of two lovers from
different backgrounds crossing boundaries that prove more impenetrable
than they had imagined. Rather, in *Kenilworth* it is a nostalgic version of
Celtic/English alliance and premarket patriarchy that is the site of purity,
and of tragic defeat.

    Which is not to say that Scott is advocating a political return to the feudal
world. Rather, Scott turns back the clock in a way analogous to Shakespeare's manner in the *Henriad*: to lament and celebrate an idealized order
"lost" prior to the moment of representation.[101] As with Shakespeare's histories, how we are to interpret the ideal's present applicability remains debatable. Potential ironies abound, given Scott's active participation in precisely
those dimensions of modernity seen as sources of corruption within his
tragic romance: symbolic alliance with the English court, independent marital choice, and, as we shall see, the market.[102] That Tressilian witnesses but
cannot change the course of events testifies to Scott's split feelings about the
world he honors and the world he inhabits: a romantic's nostalgia for a lost
nation colliding with (and ultimately ennobling by "justifying") the collaborator's pragmatism.

    Should we then read *Kenilworth* as a doubled act of bad faith—first erasing
the cultural quandaries that a black hero would evoke during the heyday of
slavery, and then evading even the thorny political consequences suggested
by the substitution of other "racial" conflicts? If Scott still wielded the cultural authority of his dramatic source, there would be a more obvious purpose in harsh critique. In its collaboration with the erasure of (a rare case
of) black humanity in British literature, *Kenilworth* arguably helped consoli-
date an imperialist, racist worldview internalized by thousands of Euro-
peans, North Americans, and Commonwealth colonizers. More emblemati-
cally, even in Scott's inclusion of a Celtic twilight on the borders of his
domestic tragedy, one might still see a more complicated form of the es-

---

    100. Cited in Buzard, "Translation," 32.
    101. The echo is made consciously, in discussion of Shakespeare's "Chronicles" (see below)
and the epigraph from *Richard II* initiating vol. 2, chap. 4. Sussex and Leicester's appearance before Elizabeth thus refers back to the Bolingbroke/Mowbray confrontation in which corruption extends to the sovereign.
    102. Scott married Charlotte Carpenter (possibly illegitimate, definitely French) despite his
father's opposition.

capism endemic to much modern art. By subtly acknowledging the dilem- mas and mixed responses caused by belatedness, a writer can be deluded into believing either that intervention is pointless or that the act of represen- tation has itself been a concrete political achievement. Furthermore, in lo- cating positive difference in a particular ethnicity at the very moment when that ethnic group no longer has political potency, Scott eerily forecasts the hollowness some now perceive in identity politics. That is, the nostalgic, ro- manticized veneration of a "culture" separable from the particulars of his- tory and power relations becomes a consoling substitute for challenging the material and political conditions that have led to the group's marginalization and that continue to uphold structural inequities.[103]

All this may be true. But a more charitable reading of Scott's Celtic sub- text would not reduce him to a cautionary tale for anxious postmoderns. Rather, it would stress that he did inject some consciousness of the Union's cost into his "romance," presenting a muted protest or at least tragic testi- mony regarding the destruction of the Celtic fringe. He did so knowing this might not help his novel's popularity. With *The Lord of the Isles* Scott had learned that open, or nearly open, defiance of the English was neither prof- itable nor successful: "English readers—who made up the bulk of Scott's contemporary readers—have never liked to be reminded of Bannockburn. Nor do they like militant—as opposed to picturesque—Scottishness" (Sutherland, *Life*, 179). A subtler means of criticism was required.[104] In the case of *Kenilworth*, the allegory may have been too subtle. As later nineteenth-century commentary indicates, Scott was perceived to have been a spokesperson for Scottish interests in the Waverley novels as a whole—but *Kenilworth* was never specifically mentioned in this regard. Of course, for most of the same century *Henry V* was likewise regarded as an unambiguous celebration of Englishness, by ignoring the script's more disturbing mo- ments. And by surviving as a writer in a confusing, nascent industrial world and increasing his remarkable popularity, Scott would be licensed to pro- duce more overtly haunting and critical works, such as *Redgauntlet* and the Malagrowther letters.

103. For a related discussion of *Waverley*'s translation of traditional (nearly extinct) Scottish culture into an aestheticized imaginary domain, see Buzard, "Translation," 33ff.

104. Reviewers discounted potential critique in Scott's novels by stressing their fictionality rather than historicity; see Ferris, *Achievement*, 139, 154. James Kerr argues that ideology is at issue and that "Scott's novels are fictive reconstructions of a historical subtext of which Eng- lish colonialism is a central pattern." As regards the anglicization of Scotland, "While Scott could not have conceived of himself as an agent of 'internal colonialism,' at some level he knew what he was writing against"; *Fiction against History: Scott as Storyteller* (Cambridge, UK, 1989), 3. On the broader issues of internal colonialism, Scottish support of Britain (as distinct from England), and Bardic nationalism, see Buzard, Colley, Hechter, and Katie Trumpener's book.

84   Ultimately, the best way to reinforce the novel's more challenging stance may be to return to the stage—the stage that reproduced Scott's stories alongside Shakespeare's. For even a brief glance at the theatrical adaptations of *Kenilworth* makes apparent their process of simplification. In their erasure of the novel's troubling aspects and tragic ending, they provide a negative proof of Scott's more ambiguous, liminal position. Thus, by comparison, they confirm Scott's greater political subtlety and the functional resemblance between his Shake-shifting art and that of his diachronic collaborator.

Adapting *Kenilworth* for stage production streamlined its narrative back even closer to its dramatic ur-text.[105] Most of the passages of Shakespearean derivation cited earlier are transposed verbatim from the novel into the stage versions.[106] Yet for all the echoes and generic resemblance, the stage *Kenilworth*s are further removed from the political and ethnic complexities of *Othello*. In these simpler costume melodramas, the women's roles were the prized ones. William Oxberry's dramatic text regards simplification as a purely formal issue, noting that "[w]here so many characters are brought into action it was found impossible to render all of them conspicuous—and the chief display of it, as well as the interest dependant upon it, has been confined to that of the Queen and Amy—no other plea can be urged for this apparent dereliction." By focusing on sentimentalized and heroic femininity, he displaces state corruption: "The character of Queen Elizabeth will be found more fully displayed than any other—and necessarily so—it stands in history so distinguished that it would be impossible to pass it over slightly." Thus begins the movement that culminates in current scholarly dismissal of *Kenilworth* itself as a jingoistic tribute.[107] Purged of Scott's critical ambiva-

105. The exceptions to this generalization are those theater pieces that used the novel's popularity as an excuse for spectacle, focusing on the pageants almost entirely.

106. See for example W. Oxberry, *Kenilworth, A Melo-drama*, in *The New English Drama*, vol. 19 (London, 1824), 16, 21–23, 28–29, 49, 50; and Alfred Bunn, *Kenilworth: An Historical Drama, in Two Acts* (London, [1832]), 8–13, 18–22. The tragedy *Leicester* also intensified "the resemblance between the protagonists of this novel and those of *Othello*," according to Richard Ford, who remarks that "Hugh Robsart took on the function of Brabantio and died midway through the play"; *Dramatizations of Scott's Novels* (Oxford, 1979), 33.

107. Oxberry, *Kenilworth*, iii. The version performed on Shakespeare's birthday 1821 at the Adelphi Theatre was subtitled "the Days of Queen Bess" (and "Good Queen Bess" at Drury Lane in January 1824; see Ford, *Dramatizations*, 28). In competition, however, was the subtitle at the Surrey Theatre—"the Countess of Leicester"—perhaps because the manager, describing another show on the bill about the daughters of Danaus, was "fully aware that Marriage and Murder are now regarded as the most successful features of modern melodrama" (Playbill, Surrey, 1821, from the Folger Shakespeare Library collection). Some later versions were performed as *Amy Robsart*, returning closer to Scott's emphasis. But Elizabeth sold tickets, especially in English towns such as (ironically) Leicester, where a playbill rhapsodized: "*Queen Elizabeth* will be found to be more fully displayed than any other [character], combining the dignity, yet familiarity—passion, yet gentleness—refinement, yet vulgarity—the acuteness, discern-

lence, scenes such as the Queen's discovery of Amy in Kenilworth gardens take center stage in a monumental version of history (as evidenced in the published editions by the choice of frontispiece; see Bunn's from 1832, figure 2).

What disappears is precisely the dimension of Scott's work that would earn him praise from Georg Lukács: that he "never explains the age from the position of its great representatives. . . . Hence they can never be central figures of the action. For the being of the age can only appear as a broad and many-sided picture if the everyday life of the people are portrayed."[108] Whereas Scott presented schoolmasters and servants as well as noblemen, the plays focus on the elite, and especially on a more esteemed version of Good Queen Bess. Crucially, the shift mutes the already veiled allegory of internal colonialism suggested by Tressilian's story. In an all too familiar manner, a nuanced narrative built upon multiple social categories is simplified into a single opposition—here, that of gender. Like many nineteenth-century and twentieth-century *Othello*s, the stage versions of *Kenilworth* efface "race" by emphasizing gender difference, instead of considering both the kinship and distinction between these two forms of "otherness."

Kenilworth thus staged can be seen as a collective nineteenth-century fantasy solution to the most troubling aspects of *Othello* as a play—going the novel one better. In Scott's version of the *Othello* plot he at least retained the murder of Amy. Moreover, as in *Othello*, the remorseless villain seems to control his own fate; others do not kill him. This last point, distinguishing Iago among Shakespeare's tragic villains, has always disturbed audiences, and Varney's self-determination evoked similar distress. As a solution, almost all the many stagings based on *Kenilworth* simply (and, given the book's currency, rather astonishingly) changed the ending, allowing Amy to live and altering Varney's death. James Robinson Planché's version, which debuted at the Adelphi on 8 February 1821, reportedly was faithful to the novel's ending, though (tellingly?) no text survives. But on 14 February, Thomas Dibdin's production at the Surrey concluded with Varney—in an uncharacteristically stupid moment—charging onto his own trapdoor in an unsuccessful attempt to prevent Leicester from rescuing Amy.

> *Var. (Seeing he does not stop)* Nay, then, thus I rush on thee, and destroy thee and thy hopes for ever!

---

ment, quaintness, and general peculiarities that distinguished the mind and manners of that extraordinary woman" (Bolton, *Scott Dramatized*, 403).

108. [sic] Cited in Richard Waswo, "Scott and the Really Great Tradition," in Alexander and Hewitt, *Scott and His Influence*, 63.

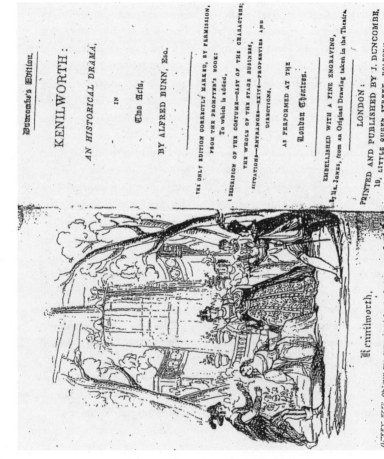

Figure 2. The Queen and Amy take center stage: frontispiece from *Kenilworth: An Historical Drama*

As Leicester nearly reaches the top of the stairs, Varney runs towards him,
the trap gives way, and he is hurled down.—The Countess is seen at the door
of the chamber.—Tressilian is on another part of the stairs, and Janet rushes
into her father's arms.—Servants &c. fill up the tableau, R. & L.
THE CURTAIN DROPS

Dibdin's version, staged within weeks of the novel's publication, began to
circulate almost simultaneously and played an important role in shaping
contemporary interpretation of the much longer work.[109] The reviewer of
this production's 1832 revival notes the major plot change but directs his attention to the larger question of dramatizing novels (echoing the Romantic
preference for the reader's imagination, in terms that have become clichéd in
our era of movie adaptations):

> In adapting the novels of Sir Walter Scott for the stage, the Dramatist labours
> under the disadvantage of being sure to fall short of the expectations of the au-
> dience, for in reading the story the imagination inevitably does much more to-
> wards the filling up of the picture, than can be accomplished by the best actors
> and machinists. Dibdin has closely adhered to his original, in all the incidents
> of his Play, except the catastrophe, where he has with poetical justice made
> the villain Varney become the victim of his own stratagem, instead of Amy
> Robsart. Miss Phillips looked the virgin Queen to the life.[110]

Despite the utter departure from Scott's tragic vision and final mood, the
changed conclusion is presented matter-of-factly, with poetic justice a self-
evident explanation. One is almost surprised that the same solution was not
deployed at the Theatres Royal for saving Desdemona and killing Iago—but
not quite. That, after all, would preclude the melodramatic thrill of witnessing the husband's intolerable act of murder (which had already been mediated and purged of miscegenetic sensationalism in Scott's version) and
would forfeit Othello's poetic lamentation (the actor's payoff). It would also
directly challenge the choices of the one writer more esteemed than Scott—
who, after all, was not even the named author of the stage versions. In
changing *Kenilworth*'s ending, there was less to be lost, and the crowds were
pleased.[111]

109. Bunn, *Kenilworth*, 18. Versions were produced at the Olympic and Covent Garden in
February–March 1821; see Ford, *Dramatizations*, 27–28; Bolton, *Scott Dramatized*, 394, Henry
Adelbert White, *Sir Walter Scott's Novels on the Stage* (New Haven, 1927), 124–43.

110. Review [unsigned] of *Kenilworth*, *Theatrical Observer*, 26 October 1832.

111. The movement toward (claiming) fidelity and accuracy in Shakespeare productions increased in the wake of Kemble. Scott was in theory still the anonymous author of *Waverley*, having publicly acknowledged only his poetry. The dramatizations were a step further dissociated,
bearing the names of their stage adapters. Dibdin and Bunn feuded over "the" authorship of the
version ultimately published under Bunn's name. (Thomas was the son of comic actor Charles

88   These dramas in one sense simply extend Scott's own freedom in Shake-shifting, but they do so in a manner that effaces the signs of political and "racial" conflict that balance and qualify the novel's elements of romance escapism. No less than in the case of Kean's *Othello*, the price of *Kenilworth's* popularity onstage seems to have been the dilution of the material's challenging political potential. Oxberry's 1824 version has an even happier ending that reorders the book's major events: after Varney "*is precipitated down the abyss,*" word arrives that Leicester is pardoned and the Kenilworth pageants will go on. And in a fin-de-siècle staging by J. S. Blythe in Glasgow, the Othello figure finally succeeds in killing the villain. Rather than allow Varney's equivalent to Iago's taunting rejoinder, "I bleed, sir, but not killed" (*Othello* 5.2.289), Blythe reworks the plot so that "Foster fell through the trap door at Cumnor rather than Amy, and Leicester killed Varney." *Kenilworth* so revised could and did become a piece of British propaganda to cheer colonizers as far away as India.[112] Clearly the changes contributed to the perception of Scott as a simple storyteller and to his eventual decline in reputation. The alterations themselves became the object of burlesque, as in Andrew Halliday's delightful 1858 lampoon where, after Amy appears to have died, Wayland Smith reenters carrying her on his back and announces grandly (with an added dig at women's fashion): "Tis false. She's saved— saved for the last grand scene— / Her feet went through but not her crinoline." Nevertheless, the revised dramatic productions endured right into the twentieth century.[113] Any trace of Scott's ironic conclusion regarding Leicester disappeared. Such Anglophilic alterations help account for the fact that stage productions of *Kenilworth* were far more popular in England than in Scotland.[114]

Dibdin who famously played the black slave Mungo in *The Padlock*; on which see MacDonald, "Acting Black," 239).

112. Oxberry, *Kenilworth*, 59. Blythe's 1899–1900 version cited from Bolton, *Scott Dramatized*, 419–20. Noting Scott's popularity among Anglo-Indians from the 1820s onward, Trumpener concludes: "The Waverley novels both entertain colonial administrators and educate them for their new duties; when Anglo-Indians plan to act out Scott's *Kenilworth*, they do so primarily for amusement—but the novel's elaboration of pageantry and court life will also provide a model for their imperial role in England" (*Bardic Nationalism*, 258–59).

113. Halliday cited from White, *Sir Walter Scott's Novels*, 138. In Abbott's version dramatized for school use (1925), Amy is saved and Varney kills himself; Bolton, *Scott Dramatized*, 420.

114. Bolton observes, "Scarcely do the data of theatrical history so distinctly illustrate the regional nature of dramatic taste"; *Scott Dramatized*, 395. This pattern accords with Peter Thomson's observation about the general relationship between English and Scottish theater: "The theatrical taste and repertoire of British regional centres, with only rare exceptions throughout the period [1715–1965], were determined in London. . . . Just occasionally, the traffic was reversed, most notably with John Home's *Douglas* (1756) and with the innumerable adaptations of Scott's Waverley novels, but only on condition that the distinctively Scottish voice was muted"; "What Scots Say," *Times Literary Supplement*, 13 December 1996, 20.

One might argue that *Kenilworth* onstage still served to circulate the domestic side of the Othello story to a wider theatrical audience in the 1820s and 1830s: those outside London's two Theatres Royal, which held the licensed monopoly on "legitimate" drama, including the production of Shakespeare.[115] By billing *Kenilworth* as a "melodrama," it could be—and was—performed at the Surrey as well as Covent Garden. Thus it straddled the legally sanctioned divide between serious art and mass entertainment in the theatrical medium, just as Scott's writing straddled a similar, albeit informally policed divide in the world of reading. Perhaps this also accounts for the greater popularity of *Kenilworth* dramatizations outside the legitimate theaters, where it was not in direct competition with *Othello*.

Scott, characteristically, saw the theater's general problem in terms of modernity's debasement of taste. In an April 1819 letter to Robert Southey, Scott criticized modern actors, playing spaces, and audiences as well. They provided reasons not to write (any longer) for the theater: "To write for low, ill-informed, and conceited actors" such as Kean, a "copper-laced, twopenny tearmouth, rendered mad by conceit and success"—he breaks off—"I do not think the character of the audience in London is such that one could have the least pleasure in pleasing them."[116] But while he might not like to dwell on their character, some members of that audience were among the readership making Scott a (temporarily) rich man. Scott's readers also played their role in shaping the possibilities and limits for *Kenilworth*, determining whether or not his political subtext and subtleties were perceived, much less consequential. His retreat into the study at Abbotsford, like the Romantic critics' retreat into their studies to read Shakespeare, acted as a mediating shield helping to distance "art"—though for Scott, only partially—from the crass realities of race and money that marked his cultural moment.

The vexed, collaborative status of theater as artistic medium and business found its analogue in the production and reception of Scott's novels. For *Kenilworth* and its spinoffs were not the work of Scott's mind alone. As he noted in his edition of Dryden, "He whose bread depends on the success of his vol-

115. On the patent theaters' control and *Kenilworth*'s theatrical fortunes, see White, *Sir Walter Scott's Novels*, 2–3, 124–28. Of course other theaters did find ways to modify "Shakespeare" and circumvent the law.

116. Claire McGlinchee, "Sir Walter Scott: A Man of the Theatre," in Alexander and Hewitt, *Scott and His Influence*, 507. Writing novels for the London public allowed one to profit without seeing them, the authorial correlate to the Romantic critics' reading plays; this may have been sour grapes, given Scott's bad luck as a would-be playwright. See Bate, *Shakespearean Constitutions*, 131 ff., who like Watson associates Scott with the Romantics' privatization of the Bard. On the dwarfing proportions of the new patent theaters, see Taylor, *Reinventing Shakespeare*, 139. For all his insults, Scott may have been involved in the Oxberry dramatization, along with numerous others; as White remarks, "Here is collaboration for you!" (*Sir Walter Scott's Novels*, 129).

ume is compelled to study popularity."[117] The nineteenth-century popularity of *Kenilworth* ultimately rested on the cultural collaboration not only of Scott and Shakespeare but also of Scott and the publishers, readers, and adapters who would reproduce *Kenilworth* in the popular imaginary throughout the century. To understand the cultural work of *Kenilworth* fully, we must finally attend to a few more of these collaborators.

Bard for Sale

> We do not know that Scott was *the* author of *Waverley*; what we know is that he was *an* author of *Waverley*. To prove that Scott was *the* author, we should have to survey the universe and find that everything in it either did not write *Waverley* or was Scott. This is beyond our powers.
>
> Bertrand Russell, *An Inquiry into Meaning and Truth*

> [Constable] used to stalk up and down his room and exclaim, "By G—, I am all but the author of the Waverley Novels."
>
> J. G. Lockhart, *Life of Scott*

Within *Kenilworth*, art is already involved with politics and commerce. Shakespeare's cameo appearance points to the entanglement of aesthetic legitimation with the pressures of a commodified world: pleading a suit against the bear baiters, he calls special attention to the theater's location within a marketplace of competing interests. Moreover, the book harps on the vocabulary of "interest" throughout, whether the topic be drama, political advancement, or love. Against the world of Sir Hugh Robsart's old-fashioned hospitality stands the corruption of a new moneyed culture in which loyalties are for sale. The unprincipled mercenary Lambourne exploits those less jaded: "I spoke to yonder gulls of Eldorado. By Saint Anthony, there is no Eldorado for men of our stamp equal to bonny old England" (37). Despite this recognition, in money matters as in its invocations of a Celtic-inflected past, *Kenilworth* expresses a nostalgic desire to commemorate values already outmoded by the market economy developing during the sixteenth century. The narrator confirms the "embarrassing" truth that Tressilian would have forgotten: "To prosecute a suit at court, ready money was as indispensable even in the golden days of Elizabeth as at any succeeding period" (121). The distance between the problems of Elizabethan En-

---

117. Scott, cited in Sutherland, *Life*, 128.

gland and Regency Britain evaporates, and with it much of the escapism often attributed to Scott's romance.[118]

Kenilworth's representation of tensions between authority and modernity, traditional loyalties and market values, resounds in the novel's own history. Although Scott's 1831 introduction implies he was "naturally" drawn to represent Elizabeth after Mary Stuart, in fact it was his publisher, Archibald Constable, who pushed Scott south of the border. The more one knows of this negotiating process, the more obvious becomes Scott's aversion to composing a simple celebration of Elizabeth's reign. Constable first suggested the topic and contracted for the book to be entitled *Kenilworth*. But Scott rejected the further suggestion that it focus on the Armada, instead researching the death of Amy Robsart.[119] While agreeing to include the Kenilworth pageants, Scott preferred the title "Cumnor Hall," which would have emphasized his Scottish poetic source and Amy's tragic story rather than English royal spectacle. Constable refused, and the title stood. One thus begins to comprehend the publisher's boldness in asserting of Scott's novels: "I am sometimes half tempted to believe that of those books I am myself all but the author." David Hewitt, noting Constable's role in encouraging Scott's translation across media, observes that "[w]ithout Constable's marketing flair, it may be argued, Scott's novels would not have been the first best-sellers."[120] Indeed, Scott often expressed his resentment about Constable's role, feeling "uncomfortably as if the publisher owned him";[121] the desire of "the" author of *Waverley* for control and profit had earlier led him to break with Constable and publish his own work (via the Ballantyne brothers), until inexperience and mismanagement forced a reconciliation.

And here too the figure of the Bard came to Scott's aid. As market forces and pragmatism led him to compromise, Scott found in Shakespeare a model who welded together indisputable artistic authority with professional success. No wonder that he shows up in the novel upholding his business interests rather than composing, reciting, or even acting.[122] (Scott similarly re-

118. In a hopeful moment, the requisite sum is provided by Master Mumblazon, a faithful recipient of Sir Hugh's generosity who donates his life savings to Tressilian's effort to recover Amy (and hence, symbolically, the old uncorrupted order). But the attempt fails and the money goes out into circulation among court retainers and hired hands, while Robsart Hall loses its master and the bloodline ends.

119. Lang ed., *Kenilworth*, ix; Scott, *Kenilworth*, 395–96.

120. Constable to Robert Cadell, dated 14 June 1822; see also David Hewitt, "Walter Scott," in Gifford, *History of Scottish Literature*, 3:66.

121. Sutherland, *Life*, 135.

122. At about the time he was composing *Kenilworth*, "Scott's relations with his publishers continued to be vexed—a vexation arising principally from the author's resolute disinclination to be anyone's sole property" (ibid., 237).

92   garded his other poetic source, Mickle, as a figure successfully uniting art
and commerce.)[123] The inclusion of Amy Robsart, the creation of the Celtic
Tressilian, and the reiterated allusion to Shakespeare are all Scott's—with
Othello providing a literary rather than historical lever to connect them.
Shakespeare is thus enlisted, paradoxically, in Scott's attempt to stave off
unwelcome commercial pressures and preserve his Scottish border position.
By collaborating with Shakespeare, Scott creates a romanticized British tradition of authorship based on elective affinities. As Scott journeyed back
northward from George IV's coronation later in the year of *Kenilworth*'s publication, he stopped in Stratford-upon-Avon and, on the bedroom wall at
Shakespeare's birthplace, inscribed his own name. The return to Shakespeare as aesthetic source, figured within *Kenilworth*, became a biographical
gesture as well, signifying kinship between the Minstrel of the Scottish Borders and the Swan of Avon.[124]

    Sir Walter thereby succeeded in selling not only his many novels but him-
self as Shakespeare's heir. Nor, one suspects, has any novelist ever been so
repeatedly compared to Shakespeare. Thomas Carlyle, in an unsigned but oft-
quoted essay in the *London and Westminster Review* (1838), stresses their
shared "naturalness," building on a venerable tradition in Shakespeare criticism (traceable back to Ben Jonson and Milton):[125]

> surely since Shakspeare's time there has been no great speaker so unconscious
> of an aim in speaking as Walter Scott. Equally unconscious these two utter-

---

123. Julius Mickle was among the eighteenth-century "Scottish (or pro-Scot) poets who
combined the muse with trade and professional career"; ibid., 35–36. Linda Colley, noting the
north's comparative poverty at this time, invokes Scott: "'I was born a Scotsman and a bare
one,' Sir Walter Scott would write, 'Therefore I was born to fight my way in the world,' and this
gets the connexion between economics and aggression exactly right." She links this with imperialism: "A British imperium . . . enabled Scots to feel themselves peers of the English in a way
still denied them in an island kingdom"; *Britons: Forging the Nation, 1707–1837* (New Haven,
1992), 127, 130.

124. Authorial comparisons with Shakespeare, as Jeffrey noted in 1820, were a standard
critical move, but the Waverley novels "save it, for the first time for two hundred years, from
being altogether ridiculous"; cited in Ferris, *Achievement*, 241. Granted, Scott's derivativeness is
also recognized through this authorial comparison, as in the *Monthly Repository* of November
1832, soon after his death: "Many a character which Shakspeare drew *was* an original: every
character which Scott drew *had* an original. But if he could not create like Shakspeare, he was
only second to Shakspeare for presenting the vivid portraiture of what nature had created"; in
Hayden, *Walter Scott*, 332–33. This sense of imitative familiarity may actually have contributed
to Sir Walter's immediate and extraordinary popularity. For in this regard Scott outshone even
Shakespeare: as Hayden observes, "[N]o writer before him had been so well received by his
contemporaries—*ever*" (1).

125. See the tribute poems in the Shakespeare First and Second Folios, and Douglas
Lanier's article. Robertson, *Legitimate Histories*, 3, observes: "From the earliest reviews onward . . . critics have tended to view Scott as a 'natural' rather than as a 'literary' writer, and
have been correspondingly distrustful of the heavily stylized parts of Scott's writing."

ances: equally the sincere complete products of the minds they came from: and now if they were equally *deep*? . . . It will depend on the relative worth of the minds.[126]

It was Carlyle who praised Scott for his "healthy" sensibility, rescuing the novel from gothic morbidity. All the border conflicts have disappeared, as disposable as Othello's blackness.

Yet Carlyle's universalizing rhetoric binds Scott with Shakespeare at the cost of turning him into a political naïf. The desire to venerate Scott as a comforting presence grew more powerful as time passed, even if it involved simplifying his works—like those of Shakespeare—to fit the needs of the moment. In 1871, an *Atheneum* reviewer effused: "It will be a hundred years ago next August since this wonderful man was born into the world to exercise an influence literary, social, and political not inferior in the aggregate to that of Shakspeare. Shakspeare's influence was almost exclusively literary, and in this of course he was even to Sir Walter Scott as the sun is to the moon. But Scott's influence in another sphere was greater than Shakspeare's by as much as Shakspeare's in that sphere was greater than his."[127] Citing *Kenilworth* to exemplify this social power, the essay praises Tressilian as a perfect gentleman and Amy Robsart as among the "simply well-bred unaffected English girls" in Scott who though "merely soft, warm lovable pets . . . are thorough ladies: all are girls whose natures would have recoiled with a shiver from the modern idea of 'fastness.' "[128] Briefly citing the *Othello* parallel to judge Scott less successful at "the scheming, intriguing, Iago style of villain," this essay indicates how directly Scott's Shake-shifting was understood to befit the manners and politics of his century—though, through the century's selective interpretation, his politics were being reduced to a matter of manners and gender conventions alone.[129]

126. Hayden, *Walter Scott*, 357.

127. Ibid., 460–61.

128. Ibid., 463–64. The comment about "fastness" echoes contemporary worries about the representation of women in the "sensation" novels, such as Mary Elizabeth Braddon's *Aurora Floyd* (which, in a fascinating parallel to *Kenilworth*, presents a woman with a loyal Cornish ex-fiancé within a tortured domestic near-tragedy).

129. Ibid., 465. This essay provides valuable information about *Kenilworth*'s enduring appeal and the shaping role of a predominantly English readership: "We are informed by the booksellers that the novels which sell most readily in the cheap modern editions are those of which the scenes are laid in England—*Kenilworth* and *The Fortunes of Nigel*, *Woodstock* and *Ivanhoe*; and that of the Scotch ones, the popular favourites are *Waverley*, *The Abbot*, and *The Bride of Lammermoor*. . . . This was not the verdict of Scott's contemporaries; for though *Waverley* and *Kenilworth* were always in the front, *Guy Mannering* and *Old Mortality* were thought to be the foremost. . . . The fact we have quoted shows a marked preference for those in which there is a strong tragic element" (467).

Not all critics, however, dismissed Scott's political subtlety so quickly. Walter Bagehot, foreshadowing Georg Lukács's rare twentieth-century praise for Scott as the "originating consciousness of historical realism," uses the same bardic comparison to stress a social vision. Bagehot finds that in the imaginations of both Shakespeare and Scott, "the principal form and object were the structure—that is a hard word—the undulation and diversified composition of human society."[130] Thirty years later, R. H. Hutton agreed: "The most striking feature of Scott's romances is that, for the most part, they are pivoted on publick rather than mere private interests and passions. . . . Indeed," he avers with epigrammatic clarity, "no man can read Scott without being more of a public man, whereas the ordinary novel tends to make its readers rather less of one than before." Turning to *Kenilworth*, Hutton concludes that "whether Scott draws truly or falsely, he draws with such genius that his pictures of . . . Elizabeth Tudor, of Sussex and of Leicester . . . will live in literature beside Shakespeare's pictures—probably less faithful if more imaginative—of John and Richard and the later Henries."[131]

This historical comparison is the fruit of Scott's own construction within *Kenilworth*, which includes direct reference to the chronicle plays within a debate about the political impact of art. Leicester "defends" the theater by arguing for literature as a form of quietism, effectively distracting the masses:

> On behalf of the players, I must needs say they are witty knaves whose rants and whose jests keep the minds of the commons from busying themselves with state affairs, and listening to traitorous speeches, idle rumours, and disloyal insinuations. When men are agape to see how Marlow, Shakespeare, and others, work out their fanciful plots as they call them, the mind of the spectators is withdrawn from the conduct of their rulers. (175)

Scott, always one to put the "serious" matters of state and business above literature in his nonfictional pronouncements, might well be accused of similar distraction in composing historical romances disconnected from the issues (such as racial slavery) that constituted major political dilemmas for his century. Read superficially, *Kenilworth*'s use of history might also serve to keep his middle-class readership distracted by the past, dreaming of royal pageants or going to theatrical recreations of them, rather than fomenting revolution, seeding Chartism, or merely backing Whiggish reforms.

---

130. Lukács's honored interpretation is marred by misreadings, while the terms of his praise work least well for romances such as *Kenilworth*. On Lukács, see Kerr, *Fiction*, 2, and John Mac-Queen, *The Rise of the Historical Novel* (Edinburgh, 1989), 7. Bagehot is cited from the *National Review* 1858, in Hayden, *Walter Scott*, 402.

131. Hayden, *Walter Scott*, 489, 496.

But two vehement respondents belie a cynical reading of Scott's novel as simply escapist. The first, Mark Twain, bitingly observes in his famously heretical attack on Scott's popularity (in *Life on the Mississippi* [1883]) that even "fanciful plots" can have political consequences. Twain laments that after the social progress initiated by the French Revolution and Napoleon,

> comes Sir Walter Scott with his enchantments, and by his single might checks this wave of progress, and even turns it back; sets the world in love with dreams and phantoms . . . with decayed and degraded systems of government; with the sillinesses and emptinesses, sham grandeurs, sham gauds, and sham chivalries of a brainless and worthless long-vanished society. He did measureless harm; more real and lasting harm, perhaps than any other individual that ever wrote. . . . [I]n our South [the harms] flourish pretty forcefully still.

While Scott would have been humbler about his impact, he probably would have been pleased to believe that his historical romances had countered French revolutionary forces. He might not even have objected to Twain's claim that, "[b]ut for the Sir Walter disease, the character of the Southerner . . . would be wholly modern." The grounds and associations for these charges, though, would have rankled: "it was he that created rank and caste down there, and also reverence for rank and caste, and pride and pleasure in them. Enough is laid on slavery, without fathering upon it these creations and contributions of Sir Walter." Considering *Ivanhoe* to have undone all the debunking good of *Don Quixote*, Twain concludes with a hyperbolic flourish: "Sir Walter had so large a hand in making Southern character, as it existed before the war, that he is in great measure responsible for the war."[132] All this, without even addressing explicitly the issue of blackness we have seen (effaced) in *Kenilworth*. While Twain certainly considers Scott to have impeded progress, it is not through mere distraction but rather through the active politics produced by the specific nature of the fantasy itself.

What Twain omits entirely, of course, is the Scottishness of Scott's fantasies and their potential to spark a nationalist challenge to the British status quo—even, perhaps, when presented obliquely. This would not have been Scott's aim at the time, any more than it was his aim to "cause" the Civil War. Nonetheless, his representation of discontent and tragedy still fostered remembrance of Celtic woes, which others could turn to their own ends or carry as a form of resistance. We are not so many worlds apart from the celluloid fantasy of *Braveheart* and the political reality of 1990s Scottish devolution.

---

132. Ibid., 537–38.

And indeed, *Kenilworth* itself recognizes this other view of literature, not as a separate aesthetic world but as a shadow representation involved with political realities. There the vehement response to Leicester's complacent view comes from the Puritan Dean of St. Asaph's, who retorts that "these players are wont . . . even to bellow out such reflections on government, its origin and its object, as tend to render the subject discontented, and shake the solid foundation of civil society" (175). Scott would not align himself with insurrection, of course—except in moments of reflection upon a romanticized version of the Scottish past (and given the impact of his writings, a big exception it is). *Kenilworth* makes no critiques to shake the state, but in its quieter key mourns a lost past and exposes a presently corrupted court— a combination of moods that align it less with Southern pseudo-chivalry than with those other plays to which R. H. Hutton compared it and to which Scott calls attention in text and epigraph alike: Shakespeare's English historical "Chronicles."

It is therefore fitting that Queen Elizabeth's cheerful anticipation of those plays serves formally as the synthetic conclusion to *Kenilworth*'s internal debate on art and politics. Elizabeth (associated with Richard II so often, and aligned with him in the novel through an epigraph) proclaims: "it is ill arguing against the use of any thing from its abuse. And touching this Shakespeare, we think there is that in his plays that is worth twenty Bear-gardens; and that this new undertaking of his Chronicles, as he calls them, may entertain, with honest mirth, mingled with useful instruction, not only our subjects, but even the generation which may succeed to us.'" To this, Leicester replies: "'Your Majesty's reign will need no such feeble aid to make it remembered to the latest posterity'" (175–76).[133] But with courtiers like this Earl, she will indeed need some spin-doctoring assistance from the artists—or so Scott's retelling of Leicester's life, interwoven with the invocations and echoes of Shakespeare, might have us believe. Fiction again trumps "history." This dialogue about the role of art can be read—like *Kenilworth* as a whole, and like Shakespeare's history plays—either as ultimately celebratory or as heavily tinged with irony. We come back to the future, to the same debates of interpretation that still shape criticism of Shakespeare. The question remains as to what precisely *Kenilworth* "instructs" us to believe about a world as morally and monetarily corrupt as is shadowed by this Elizabethan court. Especially given the novel's unhappy ending, complacency seems far-fetched.

133. Scott anticipates his review essay of the *Life of Kemble*, where he regards drama as "an engine possessing the most powerful effect on the manners of society," which can be used for "evil as for good. In this respect it is like the printing press, or rather like literature itself" ("*Life of Kemble*," 14–15).

Nevertheless, whereas in his own day Scott was prized for his epic sweep and historical care, his "Big Bow Wow" as distinct from the ladylike comedy of manners,[134] concern about his becoming quaint gradually emerges. The figure of Shakespeare (now safely enthroned with the gods immortal, thanks to Lamb, Coleridge, and in a measure Scott himself) returns in defense of the newly beleaguered Wizard of the North. Thus, also writing at the centenary, Leslie Stephen discerns faint signs that perhaps "the great 'Wizard' has lost some of his magic power, and that the warmth of our first love is departed"; yet "[i]f Scott is to be called dull, what reputation is to be pronounced safe?" The oblique egocentrism of Stephen's fears accords perfectly with his daughter's portrait of Mr. Ramsay in *To the Lighthouse*, a character who likewise worries about the fate of Scott among the moderns.[135]

Both in fact and in fiction, Stephen epitomizes the increasing anxiety within late Victorian culture about its own impermanence; forty years after Samuel Colman's *The Edge of Doom*, art, the Bard, and the Wizard are all enlisted to shore up an Englishman's fragmenting sense of universalized importance. Despite praise for *Waverley*, Stephen cannot himself save Scott's novels of earlier England, among them *Kenilworth*, *Ivanhoe*, and other "stucco-work of a highly crumbling and unstable tendency"; they have become antiquated, gothic fantasies bound up with a particular historical moment. In this critique, Stephen disputes Carlyle and anticipates Ruskin, who placed *Kenilworth* among the works "composed in the three years subsequent to illness all but mortal," evincing "the marks of broken health . . . prevailing melancholy, and fantastic improbability."[136] But Stephen does not despair. He instead seeks solace by asking rhetorically, "How many English authors between Shakespeare and Scott are still alive, in the sense of being familiar, not merely to students, but to the ordinary bulk of conventionally 'educated persons'?" Like Shakespeare, Scott remains widely read, and that is a comfort.

Yet mass popularity in the modern era implies the same monetary corruption that so vexed Scott. Responding to Carlyle's criticism on this point, Stephen observes that "the name of Shakespeare occurs several times . . .

---

134. The phrase is Scott's endearing journal comment (differentiating his art from Jane Austen's comedies of manners), here cited from David Hewitt, ed., *Scott on Himself: A Selection of the Autobiographical Writings of Sir Walter Scott* (Edinburgh, 1981), 210.

135. From *Cornhill Magazine* 1871, cited in Hayden, *Walter Scott*, 440. See the following chapter for more on this aspect of the novel and Woolf's relationship to nineteenth-century authors as well as Shakespeare.

136. Stephen and John Ruskin's *Nineteenth Century* (1880) both cited from Hayden, *Walter Scott*, 457, 529–30. Reiterating Carlyle's vocabulary, Ruskin connects this atmosphere with modern decadence and unhealthiness, versus the heroic Scott he likes. See Ferris on Henry James's overt feminization of Scott (*Achievement*, 237–38).

98   and suggests to us that we can hardly condemn Scott whilst acquitting the greatest name in our literature. Scott, it seems wrote for money. . . . Well, and did not Shakespeare do pretty much the same?"[137] Whereas Scott represented Shakespeare precisely as a man of business, here the stain of the market must be countered, or at least neutralized, by appeal to that same author. In the wake of the Romantics' success in apotheosizing Shakespeare, the playwright is so clearly the very epitome of aesthetic value that even the marketplace cannot taint his work.

More difficult for Stephen is Carlyle's charge that Scott stood for nothing, a position he can neither fully defend (given his own strong feelings and the evidence of Scott's celebration of Scotland) nor attack (given that the aesthetic, by his day, is deemed "above" the merely local or political). Again the Bard comes to the rescue: "Scott did not believe in anything in particular. Yet once more, did Shakespeare?" Gilding the lily with a pseudohistorical explanation, Stephen generalizes: "Scott could but share the intellectual atmosphere in which he was born, and at that day . . . few people had any strong faith to boast of." This jaw-dropping variation on Carlyle's theme of an apolitical, unbelieving Scott would seem to contradict not only the historical record but Stephen's own assertion that Scott must be held accountable for a romanticized version of the Highlander and "the strange perversion of facts which induces a good Lowland Scot to fancy himself more nearly allied to the semi-barbarous wearers of the tartan than to his English blood-relations." While Stephen does not pursue the importance of such reconstructed allegiances in the formation of (a clearly threatening) Scottish nationalism, his awareness of it appears in one of the essay's more effusive passages:

> Scott is one of the last great English writers whose influence extended beyond his island. . . . We cannot afford to surrender our faith in one to whom, whatever his permanent merits, we must trace so much that is characteristic of the mind of the nineteenth century. Whilst, finally, if we have any Scotch blood in our veins, we must be more or less than men to turn a deaf ear to the promptings of patriotism. When Shakspeare's fame decays everywhere else, the inhabitants of Stratford-on-Avon, if it still exist, should still revere their tutelary saint; and the old town of Edinburgh should tremble in its foundations when a sacrilegious hand is laid upon the glory of Scott.[138]

Although he begins with Scott's international influence, Stephen ironically responds precisely to the nationalism implicit in the vision of Scott as Edin-

137. Hayden, *Walter Scott*, 440, 445.
138. Ibid., 447, 452, 442.

burgh's saint. Yet even as he recognizes this political potential, Stephen shies away: he quickly shifts back to his late Victorian emphasis on the need to uphold what is honorable in the face of decay and modern sacrilege (the elegiac "Dover Beach" mode). This rhetoric certainly captures part of Scott—his romanticization of the past, his nostalgia for simpler codes of honor than the modern market and imperial relations allowed—but it leaves out the vigor, the mockery, and, one might even say, the authorial mind. This is Scott without either the lightness of touch or the awareness of political ironies that made him aptly turn to Shakespeare as ancestor and collaborator.[139] No wonder Stephen is worried.

Ironically and perhaps unwittingly, Stephen's imagined scene in Edinburgh hearkens back to a funerary tribute to Scott, a spectacular pageant staged repeatedly during the year of his death. In 1832 at Covent Garden, Sheridan Knowles's *Visions of the Bard* presented an elaborate series of tableaux from Scott's greatest hits, including *Kenilworth*, framed by a scene in which an ancient Bard comes to honor the new grave of Scott. After the first performance, the *Theatrical Observer* reported that the pageant

> met with the most brilliant and well deserved success. It opens with a view of the burial place of Sir Walter Scott, Dryburg Abbey . . . whither the Bard . . . comes to place a wreath on the tomb of the poet. . . . The Bard then falls asleep, and fancy conjures up a vision, in which the Geniuses of England, Ireland, and Scotland, mourn the loss of the Scottish Poet, when Immortality appears, and tells them the fame of him they mourn shall last forever. Eight beautiful scenes or living pictures from his principal works are then exhibited, and nothing can surpass their beauty . . . unless it be the last scene, where by a pretty conceit . . . posterity are supposed to be engaged, in 3364, paying a tribute to the still cherished memory of Scott, by celebrating a jubilee at his mouldered tomb. The most tumultuous applause burst forth.[140]

Like Mark Twain's vitriol, the effusion here for Scott as great author would not last into the twentieth century, nor can one imagine any author except Shakespeare easily sparking this degree of adulation and condemnation today. And indeed, what is most striking here is the year chosen for the jubilee. Rather than a round-number anniversary year of Scott's death or birth, Knowles places the gathering almost two millennia hence upon a (multi)centenary of *Shakespeare's* birth. While a contemporary playbill con-

139. Contrast this with Scott's playfulness with fake sources and anachronism when composing *Woodstock*, *The Heart of Midlothian*, and so on.

140. Review, *Theatrical Observer*, 23 October 1832. A second viewing did not diminish the *Theatrical Observer*'s enthusiasm, as the *Vision*'s power "renders it absolutely necessary that every person of taste should set [*sic*] it" (review, 25 October 1832). Wales has given up the ghost.

100 fuses the record as to the tribute's location, it makes explicit the comparison to Garrick's (belated) 1769 Shakespeare tribute at Stratford:

> Scene 1—A View of Abbotsford (the residence of the lately deceased Poet) Painted expressly by Mr. Stanfield, to which celebrated place will be introduced in commemoration of Scotland's Immortal Bard, a Pilgrimage of the principal dramatic characters his genius has created by the whole company, in imitation of the honours paid to Shakespeare in the celebrated Jubilee.[141]

The ghostly presence of that other Bard captures both Scott's novelistic practice in *Kenilworth* and the entire century's slightly anxious practice of linking the two authors. In so doing, the tribute captures what becomes one typical relationship between Shakespeare and his modern artistic collaborators: while the pageant producers and commentators alike love and want to remember their beloved modern, when they imagine a tribute as far into the future as Christ's life was in their past, it is still Shakespeare who determines the calendar.

Great Walter's Ghost

Though *Visions of the Bard* may in retrospect seem pathetic or ludicrous, Scott has not disappeared entirely, even now. When the British Museum's famed Round Reading Room closed in 1997, the BBC evening news reported that such notable writers as "Sir Walter Scott and Karl Marx" had worked there—despite that particular version of the library having been built twenty-five years after Scott's demise.[142] The anachronism might have amused the granddaddy of historical fiction, no purist himself; it certainly attests to the perceived gravitas and historical importance of Scott still, whether or not we actually read him. And while the academic fortune of *Kenilworth* has dimmed, the legacy of its vision likewise persists in the popular

141. Playbill, inserted between 24–25 October 1932, *Theatrical Observer*. Scott was buried at Dryburgh, whereas the playbill describes his famous home. As Garrick's jubilee missed the actual bicentennial by five years, this imaginary tribute goes his one better in historical pseudo-accuracy, an irony Scott might have appreciated.

142. BBC 1, 24 October 1997; no doubt someone found that Scott had read at the British Library and checked no further—despite the 1858 construction date inscribed on the wall being televised. The BBC cited no female authors—not even Virginia Woolf, who in *A Room of One's Own* memorably lampooned the domed room as a great brain in which she felt an outsider. Her self-appraisal of her status was confirmed (in the BBC's worldview) despite her popularity, while Scott was transported inside, even if unread.

imagination in appropriately veiled ways—indeed, masquerading as historical truth. The "Kenilworth buffet" at Warwick Castle, for example, was created by local woodcarvers for the Great Exhibition of 1851 as an historical
tribute: it says "1575" and the central panel shows Queen Elizabeth riding in
progress. But its two largest panels, at lower left and right, present Amy
Robsart and Leicester respectively, pleading before the Queen, in scenes derived from Scott's novel rather than history (see figure 3).

And so it goes. In the summer of 1996 within the central courtyard of the
ruined castle at Kenilworth, an "historical" pageant was being staged for
tourists. The place is rich in history, as Scott's novel recounts: it was home to
Roger Mortimer and John of Gaunt, a site for Edward II's imprisonment
and Leicester's pageantry. But the story being told on that stage was again
none other than the encounter of Amy Robsart and Queen Elizabeth in Kenilworth gardens, Scott's historically impossible fiction. Echoing Sir Walter's description of the castle, in which he mixes quotation from Shakespeare
with historical fact, Kenilworth itself now mixes history and Scott's Shake-
shifting.[143] The truth will out in this untrue form. While Lukács and other
critics might wish to portray Scott as an historical realist, it is in fact through
the privileging of fiction over archival accuracy that the novel both gained a
readership and commented upon larger political forces. For those purposes,
one volume of Shakespeare's plays was more useful than a shelf load of antiquarian texts.

Scott's achievement in *Kenilworth* was to combine the resources of history
and fiction effectively: to create a vivid retelling of *Othello* and a vision of
Elizabethan England—corrupt and tragic as well as spectacular—that,
while effacing some of the boundaries and conflicts found in Shakespeare's
play, re-places those conflicts and Shakespeare himself in a landscape of political imbroglios in tension with art and feeling. If we see only the superficial celebration of the past now, we reiterate that act of erasing the political
of which one might accuse Scott in regard to Othello's blackness; we may
even seem to duplicate the more egregious forms of whitewashing enacted
by the nineteenth-century theater and critics. And while the tensions among
British peoples that Scott instead figured within *Kenilworth* produced injustices less horrific in scope than those of the international slave trade, nevertheless these struggles also have a history, a cost, and a legacy worth re-

---

143. When the narrator describes Kenilworth, he notes how "Edward II., languished in its
dungeons. Old John of Gaunt, 'time-honoured Lancaster,' had widely extended the Castle . . ."
(254), thus mingling *Richard II* with his antiquarian sources.

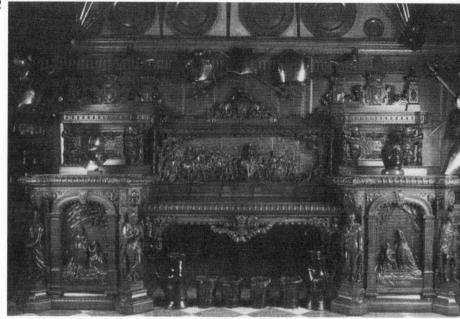

Figure 3. Scott's fiction becomes history: the Kenilworth buffet

membering. At the same time, as Scott's work reminds us, romanticizing that remembrance will avert neither change nor tragedy.

Although Scott reanimated Amy Robsart and created Tressilian only to record their decline and fall, he served his artistic collaborator, William Shakespeare, more "kindly." Others would complete the separation of a transcendent Shakespeare from the politics of his or their day, but Scott kept him, though "immortal" in retrospect, historically vital within his messy picture of an emergent market economy. He figured Shakespeare (self-servingly, no doubt) as an author concerned with his sales as well as his verse. In that anachronistic fictional representation locating Shakespeare on the borders between art and business as well as aesthetics and politics, neither hovering in the skies nor musing by bardic lakes, Scott, ironically and prophetically, was truer to history—and to the continuing uses of Shakespeare in practice (if not theory) within our own culture.

Scott's own location, however, has proven more precarious. Like the border figure Tressilian, vexed by competing codes and a changing society as he attempts to remain faithful to an adopted English father, Scott has played the role of Shakespeare's fortunate, and then not so fortunate, son. In the company of the Celtic and English ghosts he created, Scott and his Shake-shifting novel now hover on the borders of literary history, in shadowlands.

2

A Fine Romance

Cymbeline, [Jane Eyre], and *Mrs. Dalloway*

We must then have a theory as to what this influence is. But let us always
remember—influences are infinitely numerous; writers are infinitely sensitive; each writer has a different sensibility. That is why literature is always
changing, like the weather, like clouds in the sky. . . . We can only hope
therefore to single out the most obvious influences that have formed writers into groups. Yet there are groups. Books descend from books as families from families.

Virginia Woolf, "The Leaning Tower"

Family Trees: Scott, Brontë, Woolf—and Shakespeare

When, after an orphan's long wandering, Jane Eyre finally inherits a fortune and discovers her family, it is to the accompanying strains of Sir Walter
Scott's poetry: St. John Rivers gives her a copy of "Marmion" (1808) on the
evening when he deciphers her true name, and she is reading it when he returns the next day to reveal that she is his cousin and is rich. Charlotte
Brontë goes so far as to transcribe a stanza of Scott's "music" into her novel
of a woman's progress, and his "bright pages" inspire, even at this critical
point in her narrative, a characteristic excursus—an excursus of the kind
that would so annoy Virginia Woolf. Thinking back, Jane rapturously lauds
the gift as

a poem: one of those genuine productions so often vouchsafed to the fortunate
public of those days—the golden age of modern literature. Alas! the readers of
our era are less favoured. But, courage! I will not pause either to accuse or re-
pine. I know poetry is not dead, nor genius lost; nor has Mammon gained
power over either, to bind or slay: they will both assert their existence, their
presence, their liberty, and strength again one day. Powerful angels, safe in

104

heaven! they smile when sordid souls triumph, and feeble ones weep over their destruction. Poetry destroyed? Genius banished? No! Mediocrity, no: do not let envy prompt you to the thought. No; they not only live, but reign, and redeem: and without their divine influence spread everywhere, you would be in hell—the hell of your own meanness.

While I was eagerly glancing at the bright pages of "Marmion" (for "Marmion" it was), St. John stooped to examine my drawing.

For Charlotte Brontë as for her enthusiastic first-person narrator, Scott stands supreme among moderns, possessing the "poetry" she finds lacking in female novelists such as Jane Austen.[1] As we have seen, Brontë was not alone in her veneration of Sir Walter—or in echoing his romance of literary history. His eager protégé Jane similarly locates genius in the past (that is, his present) and expresses mixed messages about the modern age: Mammon and Mediocrity try but fail to destroy the virtuous literary spirit, which still aspires to "reign, and redeem." Just as Scott's Shake-shifting tried to maintain the model he found in Shakespeare despite marketplace and political corruption, so too Brontë's words imply a benignly substitutional mode of diachronic collaboration, in which adaptations befit changing times but do not thereby criticize or feel the need to "correct" the earlier author. For Virginia Woolf, however, inheritance from the male—or female—would not be so simple.

Nor, for all Jane's rapture, was Charlotte Brontë's own writing without its implicit difficulties and signs of critique—if not of Sir Walter, at least of the conventions of a gendered narrative tradition. In *Jane Eyre*, Brontë attempts to meld poetry, romance, and mythic tale-telling with the life and voice of a socially ordinary woman, creating in the process one of the most influential and compelling of Victorian novels. Its innovation resides in great part in presenting a woman who speaks her mind forcefully and directly, who journeys, and who survives to tell her own story. Although it is St. John who gives "Marmion" to Jane, he himself renounces the world of earthly romance and—like a number of the book's other patriarchs—dies. But both materially and spiritually, he helps Jane on her path to self-knowledge and a social identity. Her male relatives (Mr. Reed, St. John, and her uncle in Madeira) provide aid and exemplary lessons, which Jane then adapts to fit her own priorities as a woman; so too for Brontë, the writings of Scott and,

---

1. Charlotte Brontë, *Jane Eyre*, ed. Beth Newman (Boston, 1996), 369, 363. All subsequent citations refer to this edition. In a letter to G. H. Lewes, Brontë asserts one cannot be a "great artist without poetry."

more subtly, Shakespeare provide a romance tradition, which she must nevertheless modify in order to create a female bildungsroman.[2]

And yet, reflecting upon this novel in chapter 4 of *A Room of One's Own*, Virginia Woolf's own female narrator would not remark upon any of this. Instead, vaunting artistic "impersonality," Woolf criticized Victorian women writers such as Brontë for failing to keep their personal voice and social grievances from intruding upon their fictions. There is without doubt a strategic utility in Woolf's positioning earlier women writers as victims for the purposes of the progressive feminist argument developed in *Room*. Nevertheless, mere reflection on their plight does not explain her repeated diminution of *Jane Eyre*'s achievement. In an essay published the same year as *Mrs. Dalloway*—the novel of Woolf's to which I shall be turning—she misrepresents *Jane Eyre* as revealing what it is "always to be a governess and always to be in love." Furthermore, she professes, "Charlotte Brontë, at least, owed nothing to the reading of many books. She never learnt the smoothness of the professional writer, or acquired his ability to stuff and sway his language as he chooses."[3] Woolf thus underplays the ways in which Brontë consciously altered (elegantly or no) both her received literary tradition and the representation of female experience. In other words, through a strategy that likewise bears upon her Shake-shifting in *Mrs. Dalloway*, Woolf effaces those aspects of Brontë's writing that anticipate her own.

Once one sees *Jane Eyre*'s indignation, *Room*'s narrator concludes, one realizes that Brontë's "books will be deformed and twisted. She will write in a rage where she should write calmly. She will write foolishly where she

2. There are of course less positive feminist readings of *Jane Eyre* besides Woolf's; see, for example, Bette London, "The Pleasures of Submission: *Jane Eyre* and the Production of the Text," *ELH* 58, no. 1 (1991), who regards it as being "as much a study in subjection as in subjecthood" (199). My comments do not discount such critiques but aim to locate the obvious strengths of the novel that might pertain for a later Englishwoman attempting to rewrite the romance, in relationship to her Shake-shifting.

3. "*Jane Eyre* and *Wuthering Heights*" (1925) revised Woolf's 1916 essay on Brontë, with additions that abet the argument for anxiety, although not in a straightforward sense; that is, many of the stylistic criticisms are well-grounded and could "objectively" support Woolf's confident belief in her own writing's superiority. Nevertheless, her blindness to Brontë's extensive use of book learning to illuminate Jane Eyre's sentimental education—including the rich series of allusions to Bewick, *Rasselas*, Scott, Milton, the Bible, and Schiller, most obviously—undermines Woolf's critical perspicacity. Woolf was thinking about Charlotte from the very beginning of her writing career: "Haworth, November 1904" is usually regarded as Virginia Stephen's first essay, even though her review of William Dean Howells was published a week prior. Patricia Laurence, *The Reading of Silence: Virginia Woolf in the English Tradition* (Stanford, 1991), 65–77, constructing a "female tradition" based on techniques of interiority and silence linking Brontë and Woolf (and Austen), tellingly ignores Woolf's negative comments.

should write wisely. She will write of herself where she should write of her characters. She is at war with her lot. How could she help but die young, cramped and thwarted?"[4] Leaving aside the biographical cheap shot at Charlotte for dying after childbirth (at an older age than any of her five siblings, and after having achieved remarkable literary success), the key point is that Jane Eyre—like Woolf's Lily Briscoe and Clarissa Dalloway—most assuredly survives. And so does *Jane Eyre*, the foremother of both feminist novels and Harlequin romances. In Woolf's indifference to that success (even if more obvious now than in the 1920s), clearly more was at stake than the line of her essay's argument. For Woolf too was interested in female survival as a writer, and the threats to it. She worried about the potential to be "cramped and thwarted" not only by patriarchy but also by literary tradition, even as she wished to adapt and benefit from it.

Woolf's own invocation of Scott within *To the Lighthouse* becomes all the more suggestive in this literary historical context. While she, like Brontë, strove to make the novel a more poetic form, it was assuredly not to Scott that she turned in that endeavor. Rather, Woolf identifies Scott's historical romances with the taste of the older generation—that of demanding patriarchs in particular. When Charles Tansley denounces the Waverley novels, Mrs. Ramsay perceives that Mr. Ramsay "showed his uneasiness quite clearly now by saying, with some irritation, that, anyhow, Scott (or was it Shakespeare?) would last him his lifetime. He said it irritably." Deftly satirizing Mr. Ramsay's ego-based fears for Sir Walter's reputation, Woolf uses them as a means of defusing more general authorial anxieties. Woolf has Mrs. Ramsay (after characteristically blurring her bards) locate the true source of her husband's irritation: "Tansley . . . had been saying that people don't read Scott any more. Then her husband thought, 'That's what they'll say of me.' . . . He was always uneasy about himself." Taking a swipe at Scott's fading glory also allows Woolf to diminish the critical legacy of her own father, Leslie Stephen, whose defensive praise of Scott ("Well, and did not Shakespeare do pretty much the same?")[5] she resurrects here with stinging accuracy. One imagines old Sir Leslie's ghost crying out, *Et tu, Virginia?* And yet Woolf herself enjoyed a good Waverley read and repeatedly reiterates his pattern of association between Scott and Shakespeare; indeed, at the conclusion of a *Vogue* essay about writers one loves, she places Scott

4. Virginia Woolf, *A Room of One's Own* (New York, 1989), 70.
5. Virginia Woolf, *To the Lighthouse* (New York, 1955), 162, 177. Mrs. Ramsay's interpretation is borne out by her husband's private meditations (180–81). See the previous chapter for discussion of Stephen's remark in context.

(alongside that radically different poet, Donne) just below the all-nourishing Shakespeare in her "indiscreet" affections:[6]

> But all these preferences . . . pale, as the flirtations of a summer compared with the consuming passions of a lifetime, when we consider the great devotions which one, or at most two, names in the whole of literature inspire. Of Shakespeare we need not speak. The nimble little birds of field and hedge, lizards, shrews and dormice, do not pause in their dallying and sportings to thank the sun for warming them; nor need we, the light of whose literature comes from Shakespeare, seek to praise him. But there are other names, more retired, less central, less universally gazed upon than his. . . . one cannot help but love John Donne. With him is associated a man of the very opposite sort—large, lame, simple-minded; a scribbler of innumerable novels not a line of which is harsh, obscure or anything but propriety itself; a landed gentleman with a passion for Gothic architecture; a man who, if he had lived today, would have been the upholder of all the most detestable institutions of his country, but for all that a great writer—no woman can read the life of this man and his diary and his novels without being head over ears in love with Walter Scott.[7]

As her letter to Hugh Walpole (cited in the previous chapter's epigraph) registers, this warm regard for Scott and his novels was also enmeshed with her happier recollections of life with father: Sir Walter Scott's affiliation with the father in *To the Lighthouse* illuminates her uncanny ability to transform biographical material into literary allegory. Scott may be falling out of fashion, but his work (aptly *The Antiquary*, a novel about history, rather than Jane Eyre's Romantic poem "Marmion") still provides consolation to Mr. Ramsay after the younger generation's barbs at the dinner of *boeuf en daube*. Rereading the passages about Mucklebackit's cottage and his sorrow while Mrs. Ramsay (by contrast) peruses Shakespeare's sonnets, Mr. Ramsay realizes "the astonishing delight and feeling of vigour that it gave him" and concludes triumphantly: "Well, let them improve upon that" (180). Woolf

---

6. In 1921, Woolf records, "I am reading the Bride of Lammermoor—by that great man Scott" before proceeding to skewer D. H. Lawrence's *Women in Love*; *The Letters of Virginia Woolf*, ed. Nigel Nicolson and Joanne Trautmann (New York, 1977), 2:474. She read *The Antiquary* (Mr. Ramsay's choice) soon after her 1912 marriage, and in 1928 bought the Waverley set (see previous chapter epigraph). Days earlier she playfully signed off a letter to Saxon Sydney-Turner: "no one reads the Waverley Novels now except / Virginia Woolf." While Scott played no part in her modernist aesthetics, there is one tantalizing connection beyond Mr. Ramsay's citation: back in 1902, when Leslie Stephen was in decline, his daughter found Scott's "diary of a voyage to the lighthouses on the Scotch coast" in a borrowed copy of Lockhart's *Life* (*Letters*, 1:49). One wonders whether she consciously recalled it when designing her Hebridean novel.
7. Virginia Woolf, *Women and Writing*, ed. Michèle Barrett (New York, 1979), 76.

would try. She would do so, moreover, by returning repeatedly to Shakespeare rather than Scott as her diachronic collaborator.

That Scott did not loom larger as the locus for either collaboration or competition in her own authorial attempts (or personal comments) says much about Woolf's literary project and psyche as well as the changing fortunes of Sir Walter. Or rather, precisely because of his historical distance and dwindling prestige, "large, lame, simple-minded" Scott can be relegated with ease to a past honored by Eminent Victorians, the time of her childhood. Certainly modernism accentuated the difference between pre- and post-world-war realities, and in numerous ways Woolf put the nineteenth-century novel behind her. But whereas Sir Walter's antiquarian delights went gently into that good night, other Victorian ghosts still haunted this female writer's elegiac imagination, despite her conscious gesturing back beyond them to the ever-vital sunlight of the worthier Bard.

Crucially, it is not Mr. but Mrs. Ramsay whom Woolf kills off during the course of *To the Lighthouse*. With that death, Woolf felt she had represented both her mother's sad fate and her own need to do away with the nineteenth century's oppressive roles for women, "killing the angel of the house." Mrs. Ramsay dies, then, that the artist Lily Briscoe might live and initiate a differently gendered community. Analogously, in presenting Brontë as a victim of patriarchy who died young, Woolf makes her into a figure bearing all the obstacles a Victorian woman writer faced, in contradistinction to the modernist Virginia who becomes the successful novelist by revising masculine traditions. Reversing her novelistic transformation of the personal into the literary, here she makes literary history personal, treating writers as ancestors. And the difference in tone between her love of Scott and frustration with Brontë suggests that, as with the Ramsays, it was easier to diagnose the flaws of the father than the complex legacy of the mother.

At the most overt level, Woolf leaves Brontë as far behind as Scott. Discarding the assertive first-person narrator that Brontë had adopted so boldly to tell a woman's story, Woolf instead makes an art of connection: moving among the minds of many characters, among internal meditations, memories, and sensory experiences, and between past and present. And for these purposes, she turns back to the "unrealistic," less personality-driven world of Shakespearean romance. Woolf repeatedly structures her work to make the present moment the one of feminine completion, the omega to Shakespeare's alpha male—most explicitly in *Orlando* and *A Room of One's Own*, more subtly within the romance logic of *Mrs. Dalloway*. She revised an untitled story about women's erasure from history originally set in the fif-

110 teenth century, publishing instead the fiction of Judith Shakespeare's doom as part of *A Room of One's Own*; the temporal shift more conveniently shapes history to suggest the possibility of Woolf's being herself the female fulfillment (not just any old surrogate sister) of Shakespeare.[8] Despite her slyly hesitant peroration to *Room* and her assertions elsewhere that the female Shakespeare has not yet arrived, her fictions often belie such tentativeness. They also show, however, that her literary self-positioning is a fully conscious construction, neither a natural nor an inevitable inheritance. And in the case of *Mrs. Dalloway*, closer attention to Woolf's writing reveals the extent to which this artistic connection with Shakespeare allowed her to suppress another relationship, with *Jane Eyre*, that might seem more consistent with her feminist politics. One form of diachronic collaboration supplants another.

Thus it is not "Marmion" or *Jane Eyre* but the dirge from *Cymbeline* that echoes in Woolf's modern London, encouraging Clarissa Dalloway and Septimus Smith to "Fear no more the heat o' the sun." Woolf's repeated reiteration of the allusion recalls more of *Cymbeline* than just the lyrics to its famous pastoral dirge: its quotation (like that of *Othello* and *Antony and Cleopatra* as well) is only the starting point for her Shake-shifting. Woolf's dynamic resetting of Shakespeare's tropes and structures from this late romance serves as an allegory both for the transformation of Clarissa Dalloway into the narrative fulcrum of an innovative representation of female experience, and for Woolf's own establishment of literary and personal authority as a woman writer. While an earlier story, "Mrs. Dalloway in Bond Street," primarily satirized the class insularity and superficiality of its protagonist as an embodiment of society ladies whom Woolf knew, the novel complicates that image by interspersing romance elements of a remembered, recovered past for Clarissa as well as by adding a dying male double.[9] In this process of re-

8. Louise De Salvo unearthed and analyzes the previously unpublished story. On Woolf's relation to other forebears, see Beth Rosenberg, Juliet Dusinberre, Laurence, Alice Fox, and Sally Greene. As Maria DiBattista's book attests, the ties to Shakespeare overshadow other lines of inheritance. Beth C. Schwartz argues that Woolf sees Shakespeare himself as a "Mother," but Woolf does not so absolutely efface her predecessor's masculinity.

9. In creating Clarissa, Woolf thought of her distant cousin and chaperone Kitty Maxse most specifically, but also Lady Ottoline Morrell: "I want to bring in the despicableness of people like Ott [Morrell]. I want to give the slipperiness of the soul. I have been too tolerant often. The truth is people scarcely care for each other. They have this insane instinct for life. But they never become attached to anything outside themselves." 4 June 1923, *The Diary of Virginia Woolf*, ed. Anne Olivier Bell and Andrew McNeillie (New York, 1977–1984), 2:244. This early attitude matches the representation of the Dalloways in Woolf's first novel, *The Voyage Out*; but as *Mrs. Dalloway* developed, Woolf's "tolerance" again emerged to temper the representation. For example, the type of unwanted sexual advances Richard made in *The Voyage Out* are transferred to the character of "the admirable" Hugh Whitbread in *Mrs. Dalloway*. She instead

claiming romance from Scott's nostalgic borderlands or Brontë's barren moors and transporting it into the twentieth-century metropolitan center, Shakespeare's play provides far more than a song.

As is true of the heroine Imogen in *Cymbeline*, Clarissa journeys through a symbolic death to rediscover at last her lost "siblings." In Shakespeare's play, "Fear no more" is chanted over Imogen's apparently dead (but only drugged) body by the men whom the audience knows to be her brothers. Although Imogen's ultimate reunion with those blood brothers displaces her as royal heir, she celebrates it. Restoration of the male line of inheritance removes the impediment to her marriage with Posthumus Leonatus; that marriage is always her primary concern. By contrast, the return of Clarissa's sibling surrogates (her youthful loves Peter Walsh and Sally Seton) challenges the centrality of the conventional marriage plot that led Clarissa away from those friends to become Mrs. Richard Dalloway. Despite *Cymbeline*'s self-conscious ironies about representation and its attentiveness to the paradoxes inherent in mystifying aristocratic blood, the play nevertheless dramatizes several aspects of the romance genre seen as compatible during the Renaissance: the love-and-marriage plot and the ancient motif of lost and recovered siblings, linked as familial concerns; the subordination of individuated characterization to formal or thematic patterns; and (to some extent subsuming these particulars) a vision of a providential cosmos in which certain social relations are privileged as being natural as well as conventional.[10] *Mrs. Dalloway* draws on Shakespeare in order to combine similar elements (which Shakespeare after all adapted from narrative fiction himself), but more clearly queries and blurs the relationships among them and the naturalness of each.

In so doing, however, Woolf curiously bypasses the intermediary text that similarly reworked romance tropes in the service of a female narrative of self-discovery and social relocation. Charlotte Brontë provided Woolf with an alternative ur-text in *Jane Eyre*, mixing romance and social satire to tell

---

worried about making Clarissa too "glittery" and sterile a figure, hence the additions. Those interested in Woolf/Shakespeare bibliography and my departures from other Woolf criticism should consult the citations in Diana E. Henderson, "Rewriting Family Ties: Woolf's Renaissance Romance," in *Virginia Woolf: Reading the Renaissance*, ed. Sally Greene (Columbus, OH, 1999), 155–60.

10. Shakespeare's narrative sources included the tale *Frederycke of Jennen* as well as the *Decameron*, but he was also influenced by the neochivalric romances and hybrids popular in his day; for more on these relationships, *Cymbeline*, and romance as a genre, see the bibliography to Henderson, "Rewriting," 155–60. Subsequent citations from *Cymbeline* refer to *The Norton Shakespeare*, ed. Greenblatt et al., 2965–3046, although I retain the First Folio spellings of the title and characters' names.

112   the tale of a woman's wandering journey through suffering, leading to the
        recovery of a more benign family and the realization of her own desires. Nor
        was the connection merely one of general intention or a shared interest in
        matters of gender and narrative. For an attentive reader such as Virginia
        Woolf—who at the time of *Mrs. Dalloway*'s composition was thinking con-
        sciously about *Cymbeline* and had written repeatedly about *Jane Eyre* (includ-
        ing that revised essay published the same year as *Mrs. Dalloway*)—a striking
        set of parallels between their stories would have been hard to miss. In *Jane
        Eyre*, as in *Cymbeline*, after being betrayed by a would-be husband, the ex-
        hausted heroine wanders alone in the wilderness before collapsing, close to
        starvation, at the threshold of unknown relatives. The discovery of these
        "lost" family members turns out to be, in each case, a crucial step leading to
        the heroine's recovery of social position and marital love. Moreover, Jane
        Eyre's refiliation does not involve sacrificing social position or wealth but
        rather brings financial independence, a key concern in Woolf's feminist writ-
        ings but a possibility never entertained by Imogen. Nevertheless, Woolf de-
        nies any specific debt to *Jane Eyre* in (or outside) her novel, instead quoting
        only *Cymbeline*.

        In *A Room of One's Own*, Woolf's interpretive and rhetorical stretches in
        representing *Jane Eyre* as an unmediated testament of frustration strain cred-
        ibility, ironically redirecting attention back to the "impersonal" critic. In her
        vexed relationship to Brontë, the difficulties of reconceiving authorship be-
        yond the Romantic parameters of individual genius come to the fore, com-
        plicating her feminist ideals of collaboration and "think[ing] back through
        our mothers." Even in *Orlando*, where the galloping entrance of her hero/ine's
        Byronic mate recalls Rochester's arrival in *Jane Eyre*, it is nevertheless
        Shakespeare who gets the accolades and indeed (as in Scott's *Kenilworth*) a
        cameo role as a character. In *Lighthouse*, retelling the mother's story left a
        dead angel in the house. And in *Mrs. Dalloway*, *Jane Eyre*'s rewriting of the re-
        covered siblings trope from the perspective of a female narrator signifies a
        striking absent presence.

        Citing *Cymbeline* exclusively, Woolf simplifies her genealogy. She re-
        places the vexatious nineteenth-century foremother, whose realist conven-
        tions and stylistic breaks she deplores, with an earlier poetic sensibility—
        but one that requires her twentieth-century perspective to render female
        subjectivity in a more satisfying fashion. Whereas the once immortal Scott
        and willfully diminished Brontë become signs of their age, Shakespeare
        (with Woolf as gendered supplement) remains for all time. In rejecting an
        eminent Victorian, Woolf was more in tune with her Bloomsbury peers, the
        living brothers who sometimes vexed her as well. Shakespeare serves as

her kindred spirit, the dead brother whose elegy she sings. Yet as in *Mrs. Dalloway*, where loved ones blur the boundaries of familial and erotic romance, so too in Woolf's literary relations a certain useful fluidity abides. After all, she grew up in a crowded house. Shakespeare — the enabling sun of British literature — is presented in *Room* as "androgynous" of mind, yet still does not allow Chloe to love Olivia. Thus the need for a Shake-shifting model less continuous than that represented by Sir Walter's Elizabethan romance. In the diachronic collaboration that is *Mrs. Dalloway*, Woolf accentuates formal change rather than narrative homage: it makes a world of difference.

Shakespeare/Woolf: Elegy and Resurrection

Within Woolf's narrative, the distancing perspective of Shakespearean romance serves as a means of muting the more oppressive aspects of both blood and marital ties for Clarissa Parry Dalloway. For Virginia Stephen Woolf, whose beloved older brother died of typhoid in 1906, the romance tropes also negotiate the difficulties of writing about the death of an actual sibling (her biographical connection with Clarissa, who has lost a sister in an accident long before the action of the novel begins). At the same time, Woolf's creative adaptation of romance conventions allows her to assert her complex identity as a woman writer. This mixed claim of inheritance and innovation remains interwoven with Woolf's sense of familial identity, differentiating her position from Clarissa's and, more important, from the post-Renaissance tradition of masculine authorial singularity.

In Woolf's first recorded "writerly" response to Shakespeare, a letter composed at age nineteen and sent to her admired brother Thoby at Cambridge, two levels of fraternal concern converge in her reading of *Cymbeline*. Her authorial claim to criticize and appreciate Shakespeare as a brother craftsman intersects with her claim to an intuitive literary understanding despite (or because of) her status as an outsider, denied her actual brother's access to formal education. Virginia Stephen — very tentatively indeed — challenges both the interpretive ability and the masculine prerogative of her university-educated, analytical brother. She announces that she "read Cymbeline just to see if there mightnt be more in the great William than I supposed," and she does indeed find it, in the poetry, though she feels "a little oppressed by his — greatness I suppose. I shall want a lecture when I see you; to clear up some points about the Plays . . . I mean about the characters . . . I find them beyond me. Is this my feminine weakness in the upper region? . . . Of course

114   they talk divinely. I have spotted the best lines in the play—almost in any play I should think." Christine Froula concludes that the letter as a whole

> acts out a covert sibling rivalry . . . thrilling to Shakespeare's "best" lines, she paints herself his true inheritor. . . . [T]he Shakespeare she makes her own is . . . associated with male cultural privilege, yet not inseparable from it—on the contrary, admitting of appropriation by the daughter-writer, even from her position outside the line of succession.

Perhaps the nineteen-year-old was not quite so confident or aware as this implies. She was, after all, retracting "a whole cartload of *goatisms*" she had earlier made regarding "a certain great English writer—the greatest" ("goat" being the young Virginia's family nickname).[11] Nevertheless, the letter certainly does foreshadow the trajectory of her own voyage out toward authorship. Inverting Imogen's journey in *Cymbeline* (which transforms her from being her father's sole heir into a politically marginalized but contented sibling), Virginia Stephen first defers to her esteemed brother but gradually comes to assert her own perception. And in fact she was fated to outlive Thoby, ultimately becoming the Stephen family's primary bearer of the word. She would one day write that she could not have become a writer had her father remained alive; whether the death of her older brother similarly played a part in allowing her to take up the literary mantle is a moot point. But certainly fraternal substitution, rather than father-daughter inheritance, best captures Woolf's attitude in negotiating between two stances toward Shakespeare, claiming a less oppressive kinship while acknowledging the masculine gaps that in part license her addition of another authorial perspective. Thoby's premature death of course devastated Virginia, and his absent presence informs many of her works, from the obvious elegy of *Jacob's Room* to the more ambiguous recollections about the fallen hero Percival in *The Waves*. But in *Mrs. Dalloway*, a turn to romance provides the most oblique mode of remembrance, one that allows Woolf to transmute some of the pain of personal loss into a poetic narrative of female survival.

Thus on a biographical level as well as a characterological one, it seems particularly apt that *Cymbeline* should haunt the Woolf novel in which the shadow double to the titular character is a doomed, Shakespeare-loving young man. As Woolf reveals explicitly in her preface to the 1928 edition,

11. Woolf, *Letters*, 1:45. The lines Virginia praised include Posthumus's famed simile, "Hang there like fruit, my soul, / Till the tree die" (5.6.263–64). Christine Froula, "Virginia Woolf as Shakespeare's Sister: Chapters in a Woman Writer's Autobiography," in *Women's Re-Visions of Shakespeare*, ed. Marianne Novy (Urbana, IL, 1990), 125.

Septimus dies so that Clarissa may live: "in the first version Septimus, who later is intended to be her double, had no existence; . . . Mrs. Dalloway was originally to kill herself, or perhaps merely to die at the end of the party."[12] Septimus Smith's role in the narrative concludes with the now-surviving woman reciting words from the dirge that he recalled just before his death earlier in the evening—"Fear no more"—words "originally" chanted by Imogen's brothers over her "corpse." The novel's scene of gendered inversion could hardly avoid evoking for its author the memory of Thoby, by then Woolf's own dead sibling.

And indeed, Thoby's specter returns explicitly in a diary entry for 15 August 1924, as she approaches her "last lap" in composing *Mrs. Dalloway*. Woolf recalls him as she contemplates the greater understanding of poetry she has acquired over the years: "When I was twenty, in spite of Thoby who used to be so pressing and exacting, I could not for the life of me read Shakespeare for pleasure; . . . [whereas i]t is poetry that I want now—long poems."[13] She is either forgetting that her youthful letter to Thoby hinged precisely upon her poetic appreciation, or revealing just how much her earlier perception had been crafted to please him, how much of his "pressing" she had felt. As a mature writer, Woolf has come to see herself encompassing and longing for the poetic tradition that had once seemed, if not entirely masculine and alien, at least a source of anxiety for Virginia Stephen. Her authority has come in part through the act of collaborative fiction making, drawing upon her surrogate brother Shakespeare to help craft a story in which the death of an actual sibling recedes into the background; familial bonds and losses are played out through less personal sorrows, such as Clarissa's feelings for Septimus, the young man she never meets. Despite the obvious differences between Woolf and her female protagonist in *Mrs. Dalloway*, both come to terms with loss and exclusion through identification with and lamentation for a young man whose elective affinity is with Shakespeare. Under the sign of romance, in Virginia Woolf's Shake-shifting death brings renewed life, and inheritance from the male brings female authority.

Yet for all the sympathy and androgyny Woolf applauds in Shakespeare, he remains a father figure in his comic solutions.[14] Here was a potential

---

12. Woolf, introduction, *Mrs. Dalloway* (New York, 1928), vi.
13. Woolf, *Diary*, 2:310.
14. In *A Room of One's Own*, 82, Woolf remarks on the dearth of female friendships in Shakespeare; aptly, *Dalloway's* conclusion brings back Clarissa's female friend and beloved, Sally Seton, although the encounter is presented in a mediated fashion. Carol Thomas Neely observes that "unlike other chaste heroines [in late Shakespeare] . . . Imogen has no female friend

116   problem for Woolf as his diachronic collaborator. In the final act of *Cymbe-line*, he restores a male British monarchic line along with a happily mother-less family (sons returned, wicked stepmother dead) and celebrates a mar-riage in which Imogen remains subordinate and faithful even after "dis-covered" of her emblematic identity (though not her garb) as the ser-vant Fidele.[15] The reappearance of Cymbeline's two lost sons licenses Imo-gen's secret marriage to her commoner love as an exchange for sacrificing her entitlement to sovereignty—a power in which she never expresses inter-est.[16] Given the ideological import of the last act, then, it is not surprising that (despite her recognition of its beautiful lines) Woolf turns instead to *Cymbeline*'s pastoral interlude for her quoted refrain. In so doing, she turns to a scene within the sibling-recovery rather than marriage plot. Further-more, she selects one of the most radical scenes of play with "character," bodily identity, and recognition in all of Shakespeare, a scene far from the normative social roles of the soon-to-be revivified British court.

    In act 3 of *Cymbeline*, Imogen dons the disguise of a pageboy. She does so in desperation, after Posthumus's servant Pisanio reveals to her that his mas-ter, misled by Iachimo's claims to have lain with her, has commissioned her murder. Her husband's ravings about "the woman's part" (2.5.20, 22)—and specifically inheritance from the female, a focal Shakespearean theme that will return later in this book—have thus forced Imogen to discard its trap-pings in favor of a boy's. Shakespeare here unsettles gender within his fic-tion, a blurring always implicit in "her" theatrical representation by a boy actor but now made doubly significant, as disguise leads to truth. Imogen/Fidele, an outsider driven from court to Wales and the world of out-laws, simultaneously crosses over the borders of gender, class, and nation. Indeed, the perilous process soon forces her to address one truly universal "essence" of the human condition, the need for bodily sustenance. Yet in the

---

and double"; *Broken Nuptials in Shakespeare's Plays* (New Haven, 1985), 182. This is perhaps an-other reason her story appealed as one in particular need of revision.

    15. Given the extensive attention recently to the androgynous "otherness" of the cross-dressed boy heroine, and particularly the significance accorded to Viola's remaining clothed as the master-mistress Caesario at the end of *Twelfth Night*, it is worth noting that Imogen too re-mains in her pageboy outfit until the end—even as she "hangs like fruit" on Posthumus and greets her brothers as a "sister."

    16. See especially Imogen's comments at 1.7.1–9, 3.4.130–36, 3.7.48–51, and 5.5.374–79. Lynda E. Boose observes that in the romances, "the shattered human world, through obsessive reenactments of broken rituals, strives to recapture what has been lost and thus to reconnect it-self with the sacred world of its origins"; "The Father and the Bride in Shakespeare," *PMLA* 97 (1982): 338. Woolf revises the gendered and familial dimensions of this attempt to recapture what has been lost.

magical way of pastoral romance, at the point of utter abjection s/he is
driven by hunger to enter the very cave that houses her long-lost brothers.
Without knowing their relationship, the siblings become deeply devoted to
one another. But then, while the brothers hunt and behead her stepbrother
Cloten, s/he seems to die, poisoned by a drug Pisanio gave her as a cordial.
The pageboy Imogen/Fidele thus crosses the ultimate boundary, becoming
the living corpse over which her brothers chant the dirge whose first words
return repeatedly in Woolf's novel:

> *Guiderius* Fear no more the heat o' th' sun,
> Nor the furious winter's rages.
> Thou thy worldly task hast done,
> Home art gone and ta'en thy wages.
> Golden lads and girls all must,
> As chimney-sweepers, come to dust.
>
> *Arviragus* Fear no more the frown o' th' great,
> Thou art past the tyrant's stroke.
> Care no more to clothe and eat,
> To thee the reed is as the oak.
> The sceptre, learning, physic, must
> All follow this and come to dust.
> (4.2.259–70)

Although scholars have (appropriately) attended to Imogen's gender blurring and resurrection following this scene, the dirge itself focuses not on the
specificity of Imogen but on the universal leveling of death; since the brothers do not know their own, much less their addressee's, direct relation to the
"sceptre" they mention, the piece makes sense for them primarily as a lyrical
moment bringing peace. For the audience it also serves as such; yet while
moving beyond narrative specificity, it can simultaneously appeal to our
greater (and more sardonic) awareness of the play's layerings of identity,
tone, and its issues of governance. Shakespeare's song works by self-
consciously stepping back from the plot even as it elaborates upon its
themes, obliquely justifying the play's notable disregard for mimetic plausibility through a richer meditation on last things.[17]

As if to reiterate the point as farce, directly after the dirge the boys bring

17. Woolf's essays "Modern Fiction" and "Mr. Bennett and Mrs. Brown" famously discuss
her desire to reconceive characterization, as do many diary comments; see, e.g., *Diary,* 2:265 (5
September 1923): "Characters are to be merely views: personality must be avoided at all costs."
Frank D. McConnell notes the "sublime and self-sufficient *un*humanity which finds articulation
in the dirge from *Cymbeline*" as "an important 'hidden theme' for both *Mrs. Dalloway* and *The*

118   on the headless corpse of the "truly" dead Cloten (wearing Posthumus's clothes), laying him beside Imogen. Setting the stage for her mistaken horror upon awaking next to "Posthumus," the moments after the dirge further emblematize not only the erasure of difference in death but the arbitrariness of the physical signifiers of social status and identity itself. This layering of fictions and truths ultimately recalls us to the level of performance, to the recognition that all death is a fiction onstage: in this regard, even the doltish Cloten and our heroine Imogen could be subject to confusion—another motivation for differentiating "his" body through its beheading. Yet Imogen's misidentification of the headless corpse as her husband makes obvious that to clarify one difference is to blur another: the body makes a dubious sign. Some (perhaps predisposed by hearing the dirge's zeugmatic "chimney-sweepers" pun) discern satire here, with bodily confusion serving to remind us how little distance there is, after all, between the misogynous anger of Posthumus and that of the would-be rapist Cloten. Others find tragic poignance in Imogen's mistake, a response evoked by Geraldine James's performance in the RSC production directed by Peter Hall.[18] The interpretive complexities of Imogen/Fidele's punning address to the corpse's "martial thigh" and "jovial head" continue to baffle, disturb, and delight diverse viewers. All that remains clear is that all "come to dust."

The terms of the dirge's eschatological meditation, though not precisely linked to Imogen as a character, remain specific in a different sense: in emphasizing material disintegration. The words draw attention not to the traditional Christian consolation of an afterlife but rather to obliteration, the silver lining of which is the erasure of class, gender, and all other forms of hierarchical social power. In this respect, the dirge might seem less elegiac than nihilistic.[19] But the dramatic ironies of the scene preclude the audience's resting with this lyric reading alone. Within the fiction, the brothers who recite the dirge are in truth those great ones whose frowns—the second stanza suggests—may soon induce fears; their putative father, Morgan (Belarius), has already suffered from courtly treachery and "the tyrant's stroke" of their true father, Cymbeline. What might seem a facile or self-destructive

Waves"; "'Death Among the Apple Trees': *The Waves* and the World of Things," in *Virginia Woolf*, ed. Harold Bloom (New York, 1986), 63.

18. See Roger Warren's detailed description of this rendition; *Staging Shakespeare's Late Plays* (Oxford, 1990), 32ff. I quarrel only with his leap from this production's success to a judgment about the right textual reading.

19. Bloom levels this accusation of nihilism at *Mrs. Dalloway*, before qualifying it with acknowledgment of Woolf's writerly craft as a positive value of sorts (*Virginia Woolf*, 2). The mood certainly accords with that of Mrs. Dalloway (and *Lighthouse*'s Mrs. Ramsay too) in key moments of solitude.

dismissal of social distinctions, were the brothers aware of their own elite status, here becomes a reminder of the sheer arbitrariness and whimsical shifting of British royal power, whether lost or gained. Furthermore, we are told that the dirge was "originally" sung to mourn the actual death of the boys' (seeming) mother, whereas now their chanting laments (what they cannot know is) the seeming death of their actual sister. In other words, even within *Cymbeline* the dirge functions as an allusion demonstrating that verbal repetition is never simply that. What the boys intend as a simple gesture of homage (like "mother," like "brother") instead signals the complexities and limitations of blood inheritance and the dubious status of discrete bodily identity, the performance context involving an inversion as well as a quotation. Until one comes to dust, the bonds of family and state remain powerful if elusive, even illusive, constructs. Here they shape the significance of the lyrics, making them into an "interlude" (a temporal break, a Tudor entertainment) rather than the last words of a last rite. Even at a moment of ritual closure, the performers cannot know and control all the meanings of "their" words.

Akin to Woolf's overarching project of supplanting characterological individuation with "views" and interconnectedness among those views, *Cymbeline* does more than give airy nothing a local habitation and a name. It makes the local multiple, linking many people, countries, and times without denying social distinctions. In Shakespeare and Woolf's shared logic of connections, identity itself involves social collaboration. Thus the first time Clarissa Dalloway recites lines from this dirge, she is thinking of all those who suffered in the Great War (she sees the words in a book displayed in a shop window during her morning errands). The last time, she thinks specifically of Septimus Smith, the young war veteran who has died, his name unknown to her though his mouth echoed the same Shakespearean phrase. The dirge echoes in each of their minds during their respective final scenes, creating a quasi-magical connection between the society lady and her less privileged "double." Citing Shakespeare provides the occasion for Septimus's "resurrection" in her—and the reader's—thoughts. The context of the scene in *Cymbeline* recalls the complexities always attendant upon interpretation; at the very least, Clarissa has sensitively fastened upon lines particularly appropriate to her endeavor to cross class as well as gender boundaries—and (like young Virginia Stephen) some of the "best lines" in *Cymbeline* at that. Gender identity, tyranny, death: all are crucially at stake in *Mrs. Dalloway*. Moreover, the link with this romance underscores the generic choices Woolf makes in rethinking the novel form, choices that prevent the characters from having unqualified agency or control over their actions' import. In both

120   Shakespearean romance and Woolf's novel, order comes—if it comes—
through the mysterious threads stretched between figures, figures who
(sometimes) gain momentary access to a symbolic system more potent than
is the knowledge of individuals.

So a reading of romance would have it. In both play and novel, however,
the mystical moment passes and the (always present) specifics of gender and
social status reappear: because politics too are at stake. Indeed, they constitute another reason why *Cymbeline* of all Shakespeare's romances is the one
most appropriate for Woolf's revision in *Mrs. Dalloway*. For Shakespeare remains true to the convention of historical and tragical drama in naming the
play after its sovereign, even as the romance narrative centers on a woman
who has made her own marital choice.[20] To the extent that the play should
thus be known as *Cymbeline*, it is because it locates the love-and-marriage
and sibling-recovery plots within a larger struggle between political states
whose hierarchies likewise come under scrutiny. Knee-jerk audience identification with a British nation fighting Roman domination is subverted by the
wickedness of that nation's queen and the imbecility of her son Cloten, who
are the most animated proponents of war; Cymbeline's bad judgment in re-
lying on corrupt courtiers and his second wife undermines his sovereign authority and has caused both his family's disintegration and his country's
peril.

The extremity of corruption reached under the auspices of nationalism,
patriarchy, and aristocratic privilege is precisely what requires *Cymbeline*'s
turn to the conjurations of romance in order to achieve a social and familial
solution. Among the many "miraculous" discoveries and reversals of the
final act, perhaps the most unexpected is Cymbeline's decision to undo the
consequences of his military victory over Rome, agreeing to free his prison-
ers and pay the tribute that has occasioned violence. The romance topos of
forgiveness after suffering here displaces—without logically resolving—the
complex power struggles involving sovereignty. But familial and erotic reconciliation among individuals remains easier to effect and accept than does
this odd rapprochement between a defiant island kingdom and a cosmopolitan international empire. Shakespeare can ultimately finesse gender and
class tensions through the acts of individuated characters, but the weak, er-
ratic Cymbeline cannot easily bear the weight of this political "solution," this
Pax Romana. He whose "tyrant stroke" banished first Belarius and later

20. The First Folio contains only three genres: comedy, history, and tragedy. *Cymbeline* is the
final play and classified as a tragedy, making two plays now usually referred to as romances the
volume's bookends (*The Tempest* begins the comedies). Edward Dowden's 1893 *Introduction to
Shakespeare* first added the fourth category explicitly.

Posthumus, to his royal family's cost, now attempts to vindicate himself by transferring responsibility for his most recent belligerent choice onto "our wicked queen."[21] This ancient Briton in no way embodies the myth of a robustly benign Celtic patriarchy, the myth that would be reanimated by Sir Walter Scott; instead, Cymbeline's court is more like *Kenilworth*'s Elizabethan center of "modern" corruption. The drama ends with the king shifting the focus from human agency to cosmic fate, lauding the gods — though not without recognizing that "[n]ever was a war did cease, / Ere bloody hands were wash'd, with such a peace" (5.6.484–85). Indeed, those who bled on Cymbeline's behalf would seem to be left wondering why they did so, their bloody hands and sacrifices made inconsequential by his sleight of hand. Had it been written in a lighter key, the play might be entitled *Much Ado About Blood*. But *Cymbeline* displays throughout the scars of tragic history, written for an emergent nation-state bloodily achieved in part through the displacement and slaughter of that ancient Briton's inheritors, a nation-state in which clarity about "race," social status, and geographical boundaries always involved historical suppression and lies.

Like *Cymbeline*, Woolf's postwar novel hovers between the logics of romance and historically specific satire, with traces of tragedy in its midst.[22] *Mrs. Dalloway* exposes the particular social structures that limit the lives of women and nonelite men, associating oppression with the workings of empire and patriarchy. At the same time, excursions into a myth-inflected landscape (Peter Walsh's dream of the solitary traveler, the ancient woman singing her song of love by the tube station) qualify that focus on the particular ills of 1923 Britain. In the treatment of social inequities and problems

---

21. Cymbeline has one reflective moment when he recalls his love for his dead Queen, now revealed to him as evil:

> Mine eyes
> Were not in fault, for she was beautiful;
> Mine ears, that heard her flattery; nor my heart
> That thought her like her seeming. It had been vicious
> To have mistrusted her. Yet, O my daughter,
> That it was folly in me, thou mayst say,
> And prove it in thy feeling. Heaven mend all!
> (5.6.62–68)

Like Posthumus's remarkable fifth-act repentance in which he recognizes the evil he has done *prior* to learning of Imogen's innocence, Cymbeline's words deny the easy "solution" of universal distrust in a world where some (but only some) appearances are false. Of course, one can also read the speech as inadequate and evasive for a king who has repeatedly been misled. In each case, the sufferer Imogen is not present to hear the men in her life recognize her maltreatment.

22. My reading counters Avrom Fleishman's premise that *Mrs. Dalloway* lacks "the mixture of genres which was to enrich her later fiction"; *Virginia Woolf: A Critical Reading* (Baltimore, 1975), 69.

122   inherited from Shakespearean romance—a woman's place in marriage, erotic and sociopolitical possessiveness, and the analogy between state and domestic tyranny—the two generic impulses of romance and satire effectively combine in a specific yet generalizable critique of Britain's dominant ideology.

For example, Woolf repeatedly shifts tone and vantage to comment on those who do or would tyrannize; this strategy becomes especially notable when the narrative perspective dissociates from that of any particular character or group of characters. Thus we learn of the fur-wrapped Lady Bradshaw's slowly "going under" (like an etherized patient), her sense of identity obliterated by her doctor-husband's "reasonable" dominance. Overtly connecting this domestic tyranny with the Enlightenment thinking that undergirds British colonialism (Sir William Bradshaw's "goddesses" of Proportion and Conversion), Woolf's description of Lady Bradshaw's submission serves as a foil to the stories of both Septimus and Clarissa. Giving in to Sir William's authority long before Septimus refuses to do so, Lady Bradshaw loses the potential for a life or a narrative presence independent of her husband.[23] Granted, Lady Bradshaw has a son at Eton and "interests" in child welfare and especially photography, we are first told; but then we learn that "quick to minister to the craving which lit her husband's eye so oilily for dominion, for power, she cramped, squeezed, pared, pruned, drew back, peeped through," victimized by the "slow sinking, water-logged, of her will into his" (143, 152). *Cymbeline*'s Imogen may wear her husband's "manacle of love" on her arm (until it is stolen and she roams as a boy); but here Lady Bradshaw's entire being has been manacled and then drowned. She is reduced to a cautionary tale, a reminder of the ideology that threatens to reduce all wives to appendages—a subordination that Peter and Sally fear has similarly transformed Clarissa into a mindless society hostess. They are indeed correct in surmising that she has replaced her youthful radicalism with knee-jerk support for her husband's political views; now consciously indifferent to world affairs, she has diverted her intense love of "life" into diversion itself, hosting parties.

But Clarissa has only partially succumbed, and the Bradshaw model

23. As part of her construction of a congenial ancestry, Woolf traces the genealogy of the sociopolitical structures she criticizes most forcefully in *Mrs. Dalloway* back to the Enlightenment rather than the Renaissance. Patriarchal empire building is allegorically personified by Sir William Bradshaw (whose Proportion and Conversion spur Septimus to suicide) and, in an ironic gender twist, the emigration-obsessed, military-minded Lady Bruton (who, Peter Walsh observes approvingly, "derived from the eighteenth century"); Virginia Woolf, *Mrs. Dalloway* (New York, 1953), 264. Subsequent citations refer to this edition.

helps explain why: Clarissa's marital choice of mild, independence-allowing 123
Richard Dalloway. Lacking the force of personality that leads others in that
culture to preach and convert, to seek "power" and "dominion," Dalloway
allows Clarissa that which he cannot understand, allows her to retain her
tenacious hold on her own notions of "life." Septimus leaps to his death
rather than let the doctors gain control over his body; Richard encourages
Clarissa's recovery from influenza and heart damage by granting her the
private bedroom she prefers. Her journey (like Imogen's, like Jane Eyre's)
beyond symbolic death is in this case enabled in part by class privilege, but
also in part by Richard's not fully inhabiting the dominant—indeed, domineering—gender position of husband that the social order endorses (indeed,
his domestic consideration may have limited his political career, the martial
Lady Bruton laments). The darkly satirical representation of the Bradshaws' marriage, then, contrasts with the romantic compromise that allows
Clarissa to survive.

The remembered death of Clarissa's own blood sibling, Sylvia Parry, also
epitomizes Woolf's use of romance mingled with satire to suggest a multilay-
ered social critique. As in *Cymbeline*, the mode of romance tempers (or di-
lutes, depending on one's investment in the political) commentary on the
given order's corruption—the thoughtless inheritance of British patriarchs.
Sylvia's death is recalled elliptically, through the memory of Peter Walsh,
who thereby accounts for Clarissa's fatalistic view of the cosmos:

> Those ruffians, the Gods, shan't have it all their own way,—her notion being
> that the Gods, who never lost a chance of hurting, thwarting and spoiling
> human lives were seriously put out if, all the same, you behaved like a lady.
> That phase came directly after Sylvia's death—that horrible affair. To see your
> own sister killed by a falling tree (all Justin Parry's fault—all his carelessness)
> before your very eyes, a girl too on the verge of life, the most gifted of them,
> Clarissa always said, was enough to turn one bitter. Later she wasn't so posi-
> tive perhaps; she thought there were no Gods; no one was to blame; and so
> she evolved this atheist's religion of doing good for the sake of goodness.
> (117–18)[24]

---

24. David Dowling sees a potential link between Sylvia's death and the prophecy in *Cymbeline* involving a cedar's revival; he also asks whether Septimus might be "the diseased branch,
lopped off for the sake of Britain's health?"; *Mrs. Dalloway: Mapping Streams of Consciousness*
(Boston, 1991), 63. If so, the point must be deeply ironic, since Septimus has become "diseased"
precisely by serving Britain in battle; the implicit antinationalism of this critique goes well beyond anything in Shakespeare, as if to satirize *Cymbeline*'s presentation of the princes as natural
warriors.

124   Transmuted into a gendered allegory with the temporal remoteness and symbolic consequence characteristic of romance, the death of Clarissa's sister provides a distanced though parallel case to Septimus's suicide. Both are victims of violent daylight forces, those phallic pillars of society associated with an insensitive patriarchy. Whereas Septimus reluctantly leaps to his death (impaled on iron fence spikes) to avoid capture by the doctors, Sylvia is struck down by that falling tree, the responsibility for which Peter Walsh attributes entirely—if parenthetically—to Clarissa's father, the family patriarch.

Here again, *Cymbeline* illuminates Woolf's technique and tone and provides an episode ripe for Woolf's Shake-shifting. Turning from the Latin-monikered "seventh son" to the posthumous last chance of the Leonati family, one encounters nearly as grim a representation of the gods' role in human affairs. In act 5's masquelike sequence, as their imprisoned, repentant son sleeps, the bitter ghosts of the Job-like Leonati appear, complaining to the biggest daddy of them all about their "harsh / and potent injuries" (5.5.177–78). Asking repeatedly why the incomprehensible Jupiter, like Clarissa's Gods, has "never lost a chance of hurting, thwarting and spoiling" their son's life, they plead that the god cease to "show / thy spite on mortal flies" (5.5.124–25). At this point, however, the parallelism ends, as a peremptory Jupiter confirms his providential plan—albeit in essence merely an early modern version of no pain, no gain ("Whom best I love I cross, to make my gift, / The more delayed, delighted" [5.5.195–96]).[25] Whereas Jupiter appears, Clarissa's Gods disappear: Woolf's Shake-shifting here corresponds with her own atheistic refusal to join Cymbeline in prayer and foreshadows her more extensive recasting of the play's terms of resolution. Unlike Shakespeare, she will not accept or endorse the hierarchical status quo, be it sociopolitical or cosmic.

Who is Sylvia? For Woolf, creating this fiction of the traumatizing loss of a venerated older sister must surely have recalled, in addition to the death of Thoby, that of her half-sister, Stella Duckworth, ill used and worn down to an early grave (as Virginia saw it) by Leslie Stephen. In Clarissa's memories of adolescence, however, Sylvia is supplanted by her passionate love for a surrogate sister, Sally Seton, and her vexed but formative relationship with Peter. Surrogate siblings, in Clarissa's case, allowed her to begin to integrate sexuality with friendship, albeit imperfectly and temporarily. Moreover,

---

25. Sarah Wall-Randell's 2005 Harvard dissertation, "Imagining the Book in Early Modern England," includes an excellent analysis of the ambiguous tablets/book that Posthumus receives from Jupiter.

they encouraged her to form radical new intellectual and political affilia-
tions, breaking from oppressive family and class allegiances. And her desire
for distance from actual blood ties persists. Even when as an adult she is
brought back to political conservatism by her husband, Clarissa still wishes
she could have resisted inviting her relative Ellie Henderson to her party; it
is Peter Walsh rather than Clarissa who attends to her aging Aunt Parry.
Clarissa's desire for distance—albeit snobbish or selfishly motivated—resists both the fatalism of birth and the inevitability of death. It is in this regard akin to Woolf's own acts of veiling in her representations of lost siblings: through class difference, in Septimus's case; through mediated
narrative, in Sylvia's case; through the mode of romance throughout,
whereby relations and social positions become symbolically laden and for-
malized. As in *Cymbeline*, filial distance—if not ingratitude—is necessary for
survival.

Finally, Woolf draws upon Shakespeare's romance model of miraculous
restorations at the close—though again with a Shake-shifting twist. Clarissa's
party imports figures from her Bourton youth to mingle with many of the
novel's London characters, countering the separations and irreversibility of
time. It also allows her "discovery" of a dead spiritual brother in Septimus—
even as, crucially, it brings the return of her two dearest living friends.[26]
With Peter and Sally, she finally acknowledges, "(more even than with
Richard) she shared her past. . . . A part of this Sally must always be; Peter
must always be" (277). Putting her husband in parentheses as the past flows
into a willed perpetual present, the reunion of this triad from Clarissa's
young adulthood constitutes the novel's final event; Woolf thus borrows yet
alters the hierarchical balance between sibling and marital love that resolved
Shakespeare's play so differently.

As the examples of the Bradshaws and Sylvia Parry have demonstrated,
the deployment of romance motifs does not entirely erase anger at the forces
that oppress and destroy. Indeed, in her final thoughts Clarissa also decides
that hatred is more useful than love at her stage of life. Nevertheless, her hatred of "tyranny" is not easily interpreted as a feminist statement, a recognition that women must turn from self-criticism to action against oppressive
social structures; nor, more arguably, is Woolf's. In this respect, *Mrs. Dalloway* not only represents but also participates in a more conservative social
order than do several of Woolf's subsequent writings. And the place where
this becomes most clear is in the representation of an unhappy woman

---

26. These two arrive unexpectedly during the day—Sally's appearance at the party without
a formal invitation in particular adding to the scene's magical quality.

126   within its story, a figure in some measure analogous to what I shall dub
"Brontë's bogey" (that angry, cramped authorial figure to whom I shall return). Despite her explicit desire to avoid anger, the narrator of *A Room of
One's Own* curses an Oxbridge beadle and savagely cartoons a misogynous
professor. By contrast, Clarissa's most intense hatred is directed at the allegorically monikered Miss Kilman, who has suffered from both anti-German
nationalist "patriotism" and the limitations of a rigid class and gender hierarchy: it is she whom Clarissa thinks of when concluding that "i[i]t was enemies one wanted, not friends" (266).

   Nor does Woolf's representation of Kilman encourage us to read
Clarissa's response simply as a delusion or object of satire.[27] As in the case of
her connection with Septimus, Mrs. Dalloway's class differences and limitations remain obvious, yet the narrative at least partially endorses Clarissa's
perception of Kilman. Indeed, it is precisely because this figure should be a
political ally or at least a cause for progressive change that she poses such a
threat to Woolf (as distinct from Clarissa): Kilman becomes a projection of
the humorless, aggrieved personae Woolf perceived among some dedicated
social reformers with whom she could sympathize only ideologically. To
claim that Woolf's creation of this unhappy, limited woman is part of a progressive politics, one must emphasize the author's recognition of the systemic consequences of gender inequities (as her naming of Kilman implies)
and her refusal to essentialize behavior by fitting all members of a class or
gender into a politically congenial grid, as much socialist realism would soon
do. But the larger case is difficult to make when Woolf renders Kilman's vo-
racious éclair eating with enough grotesque energy to repel not only her
young protégé Elizabeth but the reader as well.

   The alternative is to acknowledge that both Clarissa and Woolf make
judgments founded on what they would consider aesthetic and personal
grounds. From their perspectives, those grounds cannot be wholly discounted as epiphenomena of social hierarchies.[28] In this regard, *Mrs. Dal-*

----

27. Emily Jensen's romanticized reading of homosexual love leads her to venerate Miss Kilman's "power . . . to love women"; "Clarissa Dalloway's Respectable Suicide," in *Virginia Woolf:
A Feminist Slant*, ed. Jane Marcus (Lincoln, NE, 1983), 175. But this hardly captures the tone of
Woolf's representation. Greedily wolfing down eclairs in a way that leads Elizabeth to flee, desperately praying for relief in the Abbey, Kilman is portrayed as a pathetic when not fearsome
creature. At the other extreme, see Jean M. Wyatt's overly laudatory reading of Clarissa's
laughter at Kilman as the triumph of "the comic spirit of civilized society"; "*Mrs. Dalloway*: Literary Allusion as Structural Metaphor," *PMLA* 88 (1973): 447. Elizabeth Abel, "Narrative
Structure(s) and Female Development: The Case of *Mrs. Dalloway*," in Bloom, *Virginia Woolf*,
263) adds that Kilman's desires to "grasp" and "clasp" Elizabeth parody the line from *Othello*
that Clarissa applies to her love of Sally (discussed below).
   28. While Woolf clearly sketches the wounding effects of social categorization here, it remains debatable whether she would acknowledge the dynamic of blaming the victim at work in

loway as much as *Cymbeline* collaborates with its culture's categorizations: not with the ones that subordinate groups of people because of gender or birth (class remains a thorny issue), but rather with those paradigms that deem personal identity and behavior to involve something more fundamental than social construction. Here indeed is the domain of "taste," of aesthetic — and moral — distinctions that undermine obvious political alliances. Despite the criticism of certain social inequities in each work, beauty and kindness, of appearance and of behavior, remain virtues presented in some measure as if transcendent of the possessor's social position. Clarissa ultimately transcends; Miss Kilman does not.

In this regard, it is likewise telling that the dirge from *Cymbeline* is not the only line of Shakespeare's to echo through the pages of Woolf's novel. The other repeated quotation concerns a moment of socially unconventional transcendent love, also extending the novel's concern with possessive desire and its political as well as emotional consequences. The line is from *Othello*, a play directly related to *Cymbeline* through its similar emphasis on a husband's deluded sexual jealousy provoked by an artful Italian villain.[29] "If it were now to die, / 'Twere now to be most happy," says Othello as he is reunited in Cyprus with his new bride (2.1.186–87). Although some scholars interpret this statement as a death wish, the dramatic situation is layered and ironic, for the words are spoken at what is indeed a nearly miraculous moment of celebration that life can afford such "perfect happiness." So Woolf herself cited the line in her diary a little over a month before the publication of *Mrs. Dalloway*, to describe the joyous moments in her unconventional marriage to Leonard:

> But L. and I were too too happy, as they say; if it were now to die etc. Nobody shall say of me that I have not known perfect happiness, but few could put their finger on the moment, or say what made it. Even I myself, stirring occasionally in the pool of content, could only say But this is all I want; could not think of anything better; and had only my half superstitious feeling at the Gods who must when they have created happiness, grudge it. Not if you get it in unexpected ways, though.[30]

---

her unappealing portrait of Miss Kilman. Clarissa certainly does not recognize her hatred as symptomatic of social conditions but rather considers it personality-driven, viewing Kilman as both an unpleasant rival for her daughter's affection and a would-be tyrant like Bradshaw.

29. In her attentive study of the circulation of material objects in *Cymbeline*, Valerie Wayne also calls attention to the "bloody cloth" that links *Cymbeline* to *Othello* (with its red-patterned handkerchief), signs of the absent woman's body on the Renaissance stage; "The Woman's Parts in *Cymbeline*," in *Staged Properties in Early Modern Drama*, ed. Jonathan Gil Harris and Natasha Korda (Cambridge, UK, 2002), 288–315.

30. Entry for 8 April 1925; Woolf, *Diary*, 3:8–9.

128   Her words share a kinship with the cosmic skepticism Peter Walsh attributes to Clarissa within the novel. Woolf imagines the sorts of grudging classical gods whom Shakespeare transmutes into (ultimately) providential figures in his romances—such as the gruff Jupiter who allows unexpected
happiness to Posthumus and Imogen only after great suffering. (Certainly
that couple find happiness "in unexpected ways.") But in contrast to Woolf's
location of Othello-like moments of great joy within her marriage, her fiction uses the Shakespearean citation to describe a less socially acceptable
form of romance. Its referent is Clarissa's passionate love for Sally Seton,
potentially as challenging to typical representations of romance in the novel
as was the interracial marriage of Othello and Desdemona to Elizabethan
dramatic conventions: "she could remember going cold with excitement . . .
feeling as she crossed the hall 'if it were now to die 'twere now to be most
happy.' That was her feeling—Othello's feeling, and she felt it, she was con-
vinced, as strongly as Shakespeare meant Othello to feel it, all because she
was coming down to dinner in a white frock to meet Sally Seton!" (51).[31]

Along with the poetic imagery of "an illumination, a match burning in a
crocus" (47), the Shakespearean line makes more explicit those same-sex
desires that Mrs. Dalloway herself acknowledges but shies away from. It
gives the relationship with Sally an intensity as charged as was Peter Walsh's
passionate, possessive, and thwarted love for Clarissa at the same time in
their lives. Thus the youthful friends become overdetermined figures of both
"true love" and sibling-like affinity, mediating between the marital romance
plot and the familial, and offsetting the satiric venom of Clarissa's unsisterly
feelings about Miss Kilman. Kilman's intense devotions to Elizabeth and to
God are still represented as incongruous and pathetic, but these youthful
passions, once challenging the norms of "polite society," are bathed in the
amber light of a transcendent moment poignantly recalled from a great distance in time. Both of Clarissa's youthful relationships remain crucially distinct from the milder, appreciative affection between the Dalloways—the
marriage she chose in order to sustain her (comparative) independence, her
"virginal" sense of self, but also the relationship through which she is further
interpellated into the privileged, sterile society of Westminster (70–71).[32]

Mrs. Dalloway does see the compromise she has made in having distanced herself from Sally and Peter. She remembers the "purity, the integrity, of her feeling for Sally. It was not like one's feeling for a man." But

---

31. It is hard not to think of Woolf's immanent infatuation with Vita Sackville-West as well.
32. My use of interpellation draws upon the analysis of ideology by Louis Althusser, adapted
by Teresa de Lauretis (among others) to address questions of gender specifically.

she in part rationalizes its sacrifice by locating it within a particular, irrecoverable stage of life (one thinks of Helena and Hermia in Shakespeare's *A Midsummer Night's Dream*): "it had a quality which could only exist between women, between women just grown up. It . . . sprang from a sense of being in league together, a presentiment of something that was bound to part them (they spoke of marriage always as a catastrophe)" (50). For this female friendship, Clarissa's marriage to Dalloway is indeed a catastrophe, not dramatic yet as heartbreaking in its way as that same event had been for Peter Walsh. It is the cost of the socially normative plot of female development. But the passion of that youth, the love Clarissa tries to embalm in the past, is not so easily entombed—not for Clarissa, and certainly not for Peter Walsh. Clarissa still has memories and imagines alternatives to her conventional "maturation." And Woolf will not allow those alternatives to become frozen in amber, instead ordering her story to bring them back to life.

Even Peter, whom she never loved so passionately as she loved Sally, arouses feelings that challenge Clarissa's decision to become Mrs. Dalloway, allowing her past to haunt and ultimately revivify her present. At midday when Peter barges into her quiet hour of mending (his knife aborts her needle's work), she imagines that their marriage would have been the stuff of a five-act drama. In part because such drama has already been written by Shakespeare, it need not be lived to be understood: "Take me with you, Clarissa thought impulsively, as if he were starting directly upon some great voyage; and then, next moment, it was as if the five acts of a play that had been very exciting and moving were now over and she had lived a lifetime in them and had run away, had lived with Peter, and it was now over" (70–71). What Clarissa need not live through is the traditional romance material that Woolf wants to reconceive, to revive in a way that does not subdue female subjectivity.[33] For this, the author needs the distance of a late Shakespeare play, but with the conclusion for its heroine modified. While Imogen may be satisfied, *Cymbeline* itself ends with reminders of how fragile and even artificial its resolutions are, and the king's final resort to the gods can be read as both structurally necessary and socially inadequate: the audience is given space to reflect upon the costs of achieving a "happy ending." Woolf builds on that distancing effect and reminds us of the difference in the story she wishes to tell. The solution would not be to return to the old bourgeois, one-

---

33. As Reuben Brower notes, Walsh is an "interrupter" and "destroyer," though he too experiences "life"; "Something Central Which Permeated: 'Mrs. Dalloway,'" in Bloom, *Virginia Woolf*, 13–14. I see a broader parallelism between the figures of Walsh and Posthumus. Woolf gives Peter a major narrative role and energizing force in Clarissa's life, without allowing him to dominate or marry her.

130   and-only, love-and-marriage plot (itself in great measure derived from
Shakespeare's earlier drama), as both Clarissa and Peter realize at later moments in the novel. Instead, the problem of how to reintegrate intensity of
emotion and a social practice is left hovering, not to be solved simply through
the intentional actions or awareness of these represented characters.

For them to find resolution would be for Woolf to erase her social critique
of the Dalloway world too absolutely, to empty the novel of too much of its
satiric power. It would remove the blinders and restrictions created by class
and gender ideologies, which limit even the more thoughtful characters. And
it would also blunt Woolf's interwoven insight about nationalist ideologies:
Britain's imperial projects carry an ideological force that shapes the thinking
even of those who rationally would resist their logic and from which there is
no escape through particular personal relationships. The contradictory attitudes of reforming, domineering Peter Walsh toward his participation in the
colonization of India most richly represent this latter mental bind. Clarissa's
collaboration with social conventions (choosing heterosexual marriage to
the most unexceptionable man while recognizing and enshrining other
loves) conveys the matching domestic dilemma, as does Sally's exchange of
active socialism for a husband who earned rather than inherited his title.

Nevertheless, though they do not find answers, these characters are allowed to recognize their dilemmas and ultimately are given moments of
romance-like, even mystical, connection. Clarissa is shown struggling with
the taint of her choices when she repeats Othello's line again during her
party, while meditating upon Septimus Smith's death:

> They went on living (she would have to go back; the rooms were still crowded;
> people kept on coming). They (all day she had been thinking of Bourton, of
> Peter, of Sally), they would grow old. A thing there was that mattered; a thing,
> wreathed about with chatter, defaced, obscured in her own life, let drop every
> day in corruption, lies, chatter. This he had preserved. Death was defiance.
> Death was an attempt to communicate; people feeling the impossibility of
> reaching the centre which, mystically, evaded them; closeness drew apart; rap-
> ture faded; one was alone. There was an embrace in death.
>   But this young man who had killed himself—had he plunged holding his
> treasure? "If it were now to die, 'twere now to be most happy," she had said to
> herself once, coming down, in white. (280–81)

Read satirically, her "use" of Septimus Smith to sustain her own spirit replicates the nation's recent use of many such naively patriotic young clerks in
the war—destroying them to sustain an idealized image of English duty
and nationhood. But read under the aegis of romance, it also signals a
reawakening of sorts for Clarissa, if only to the recognition of her moral

failure in sustaining a status quo that squelches passion and compromises integrity. Thus her quotation of Othello leads Mrs. Dalloway both back to Sally and forward to overt criticism of Sir William Bradshaw. Earlier she reluctantly left Sally and Peter because she felt she "must" go to the Bradshaws "whom she disliked" (277), thus subordinating her own affections and bonds again to sustain the most superficial definition of "polite" society. Now she correctly imagines and identifies with the feelings of Bradshaw's victim: "forcing your soul, that was it—if this young man had gone to him, and Sir William had impressed him, like that, with his power, might he not then have said (indeed she felt it now), Life is made intolerable; they make life intolerable, men like that?" (280).Finally, this associative process leads her back to *Cymbeline*. Through authorial "magic," she repeats the line from the dirge that Septimus recalled in his last moments before leaping to his death:

> The young man had killed himself; but she did not pity him; with the clock striking the hour, one, two, three, she did not pity him, with all this going on. There! the old lady had put out her light! the whole house was dark now with this going on, she repeated, and the words came to her, Fear no more the heat of the sun. She must go back to them. But what an extraordinary night! She felt somehow very like him—the young man who had killed himself. She felt glad that he had done it; thrown it away. The clock was striking. The leaden circles dissolved in the air. He made her feel the beauty; made her feel the fun. But she must go back. She must assemble. She must find Sally and Peter. And she came in from the little room.

Having seen "the old lady" across the street "put out her light," Clarissa refuses to follow Othello's tragic lead and "put out the light." Instead, after this passage—the last in the book from Clarissa's perspective—she enters the room to find Sally and Peter. Thus she carries a version of Septimus and the past into the present, into the fictional moment at which the book will end when re-presented from Peter's perspective (283–84).[34] On this "extraordinary night," Clarissa like Septimus will "fear no more the heat of the sun"— or the daylight structures of the British Empire upon which the sun never sets. And as Woolf again cites the dirge, she now deploys Shakespeare's elegiac ironies within the play—sung for a seeming dead man, it leads to the

---

34. Woolf edited out the sentence "He made her feel the beauty; made her feel the fun" from the British edition (issued soon after the American); see the Vintage edition, 165. This could be her recognition that "fun" might seem to trivialize his death. A stronger reading of "fun"—especially as aligned with "beauty"—might argue that it captures those life-affirming values so lacking in Kilman. Woolf's worries about being too much seduced by "beauty" imply why for her both words had to go in revision.

132   resurrection of that figure as female survivor—for all they are worth: she will conjure with their (and her own added) allegorical power. Unlike Shakespeare (and like Clarissa), Woolf will not allow even a formal "lauding" of "the Gods," but she will allow a final celebration of being alive, of symbolic resurrection. Clarissa has been perilously ill in her recent past; one would not be altogether surprised (especially given Woolf's opinion of doctors) if she were now to echo Imogen's stark response when asked whether she had taken Dr. Cornelius's drug: "Most like I did, for I was dead" (5.6.259).[35] The charged citations from Shakespeare again reinforce the double-edged perspective Woolf brings to the representation of Clarissa Dalloway as female survivor and social collaborator. Simultaneously, they illuminate her own authorial mode of "re-naissance," transforming Shakespearean fragments and topics in order to revise gendered assumptions about authorship and narrative. "For there she was" (296).

Brontë/Woolf: Are You My Mother?

With the layered collaboration of *Mrs. Dalloway* in mind, then, let us return to the question of Woolf's relationship to Charlotte Brontë. This requires a closer look at her analysis of *Jane Eyre*'s stylistic technique. In *A Room of One's Own*, Woolf's narrator makes a judgment after citing the famous "Anyone may blame me" passage from *Jane Eyre*, in which Jane shifts abruptly from a meditation upon women's constraints to the report of Grace

---

35. My reading here departs from that of J. Hillis Miller, "*Mrs. Dalloway*: Repetition as the Raising of the Dead," in Bloom, *Virginia Woolf*, 185–89, 187. Already Woolf has staged one resurrection during the party, having had Peter Walsh believe Clarissa's Aunt Parry dead and then presenting her otherwise: "For Miss Helena Parry was not dead: Miss Parry was alive. She was past eighty" (271). Embracing but also subsuming Clarissa (who was once herself "Miss Parry") in a romance pattern of rebirth after suffering, these motifs undo linear temporality in a book whose working title was *The Hours*; they signal the allegorical complexity of any narrative conclusion for Clarissa or the social milieu she animates. It is apt, then, that Michael Cunningham's *The Hours* revivifies this, of all Woolf's novels, in later times and places; its characters and social milieu again refuse to stay dead, even if the author resorts to a frame that highlights the death of the female author (and even if the Stephen Daldry/David Hare film adaptation stresses depression to the detriment of *The Hours*'s emphasis on creative energy). The romance trope of sibling recovery in *Dalloway* informs the final scene's rhetorical movement to the present tense ("It is Clarissa"), reviving a link between Clarissa and her past within the representation as well as for the reader. Sally has gotten up, preparing to leave a "moment" before Peter becomes conscious of Clarissa's return; nevertheless, the narrative links the three figures in the final paragraphs, and it remains suitably ambiguous whether the "moment" is long enough to have allowed the now portly Lady Rosseter to reach Richard to say her farewells. For Clarissa certainly, "Sally and Peter" remain the unit to which she is planning to return, and the book seems to confirm that intention in its close.

Poole's laughter: "That is an awkward break, I thought. . . . The continuity
is disturbed" (69). Woolf goes on to attribute the stylistic "jerk" between
first-person pronouncements and fictional action throughout *Jane Eyre* to
Brontë's socially disadvantaged position as a woman writer and her resulting "indignation" and "anger": here is Brontë's bogey, seeming to block
Woolf's path to success as a Shakespeare-like androgynous author. In a way
that seems warranted by the passage from Brontë's novel with which I
began this chapter (perhaps more legitimately than by the passage Woolf
herself chooses), Woolf conflates the voices of Jane and Charlotte; she thus
presumes we hear Charlotte's lamentation when Jane protests the limits of
women's lives.

One must acknowledge the perceptiveness of Woolf's ear regarding such
"jerks"—or, to put it less negatively, Jane's tendency to go off on animated
(seeming) digressions before being recalled to her narrative line. This does
not, however, make Woolf's explanation sufficient for passages such as the
one extolling "Marmion." Given the abysmal fortune of the Brontë sisters'
volume of poetry—all the more glaring when contrasted with that of Scott's
best-seller—Charlotte might well lament the contemporary publishing
scene in 1846–47 as she composed *Jane Eyre*. Furthermore, the stark contrast between Scott's "golden age" and "our era" makes more sense coming
from one of Charlotte's generation, rather than her fictional heroine's (theo-
retically alive during the Regency and writing her story a decade after the
events she narrates).[36] Yet Jane's impassioned defense of poetry here comes
from a reader's rather than a frustrated author's perspective, and the mis-
treated females and morally dubious "hero" of "Marmion" would certainly
resonate with particular force for the long-suffering Miss Eyre. Even granting Woolf's point about authorial intrusiveness, then, one must in fairness
balance her tonal judgment by acknowledging both the characterological
aptness of Jane's enthusiasm and the celebration of art itself in "Charlotte's"
interjection: the passage expresses delight in the male tradition she is now
supplementing. Thus, the narrative discontinuity remains, but cannot so unequivocally be attributed to Woolf's own bogeyman of anger (which she felt
would interfere with her assuming an "impersonal" modernist stance, and
hence displaces onto the safely dead Charlotte—and the safely fictional Miss
Kilman in *Mrs. Dalloway*). In fact, Brontë's break signals gender in a different way, as a self-consciously marked alteration and play of perspective.

36. Given that Jane is eighteen at Thornfield, and receives "Marmion" (1808) from St. John
as a gift of new poetry, she seems to be born of the French Revolution in a more specific way
than just having a rebellious spirit.

134   Even in the instance Woolf cites, a clear rationale motivates the "abrupt" shift from Jane's frustrated sense of confinement while stalking the roof of Thornfield to the intrusive laugh of "Grace Poole": as second-time readers of the novel know, that laugh is actually issuing from the truly confined Bertha Mason, the other would-be Mrs. Rochester who serves as Jane's shadowy doppelganger throughout her courtship with Edward.[37] This juxtaposition, then, is richly symbolic within the fable-like structure of *Jane Eyre*. More generally, such shifts capture Jane's delightfully inconsistent discursive personality. She often blurts out rude truths (to Brocklehurst, Mrs. Reed, Rochester, and St. John) and then attempts to cover her tracks or—to adapt the image from her childhood outburst—extinguish the heathfire she has set ablaze. Much of the humor and enjoyment of reading Jane Eyre (and *Jane Eyre*) depends on appreciating such "jerks," of sympathizing with the romantic soul who learns to adopt an air of extreme propriety, the correcting governess attempting to govern her own emotions only to be exposed by her pupil's attention to a revealing blush. The danger for modern readers is to take the comedy too far and to lose the nineteenth-century sense of struggle and moral integrity that both the heroine and her author vociferously upheld even when accused of insolence or unladylike behavior; the shifts in perspective convey that delicate (and difficult) balancing act. It is Septimus-like Bertha who will lose her balance and leap from a burning building while Jane learns early on to smother and put out fires, leading her finally to tend to one scarred by the flames. While Jane's own road to social acceptability is never easy, her narrative reflections remind us of the ongoing vitality and struggle within. Hers are the jerks of invention.

       From the animated first-person perspective to its narrative shape, it was arguably the assertion of gendered difference in *Jane Eyre*, manifest in representation and style alike, that made it innovative. In moving energetically between Jane's story and her retrospective narrative reflections, Brontë presents a woman rewriting the romance tradition as well as the events of a fictional life. Moreover, she spends major portions of her novel on youthful female friendship within the confines of a limiting social institution at Lowood, and on Jane's postcourtship discovery of self-sufficiency and social position, surprisingly intertwined. Here are the portions of the novel one might expect to receive more laudatory comment from the author of *Mrs. Dalloway* and *A Room of One's Own*. Even if one concedes that many read-

---

37. On Woolf's possible misprision in that passage, see the now classic essays by Adrienne Rich and Sandra M. Gilbert (the latter reprinted in the Bedford *Jane Eyre*); see also Mary Jacobus's discussion of Woolf's concern with anger.

ers find the stay at Marsh End and the figure of St. John a disappointment, for a novelist with *Cymbeline* on her mind and with more than a passing interest in telling women's stories, the latter part of *Jane Eyre* would be very hard to ignore.[38] In other words, if one is seeking a case of fictionally useful misprision in Woolf's criticism, comparable to Milton's "misremembrance" of Spenser's Cave of Mammon episode, here it is.

The numerous resemblances between Jane's story and Imogen's suggest that Brontë anticipated Woolf in the practice of gendered Shake-shifting. The connections gain more potency the more one attends to the sequence and specifics of volume 3: Jane's sense of betrayal by and estrangement from the man she would marry, balanced by her ongoing love for him; her "escape" into the wilderness, where she wanders for three days in despair until nearly famished; her fortuitous collapse at the home of kind strangers, who intuitively love her and turn out to be her close relatives; her return to "civilization" in part through the agency of, and in company with, these siblings (as Jane names them); the replacement of a wicked stepfamily, led by a mother and her boorish son, with virtuous blood relations; and Jane's ultimate reintegration of family and romantic love, enacted with the help of supernatural forces and good fortune as well as through her own tenacity and devotion. In each instance, one could substitute Imogen's name for Jane's and accurately describe *Cymbeline*. It is precisely the unrealistic, overtly symbolic dimension of these key developments in Jane's story—a far cry from the social reportage of, say, the typhus outbreak at Lowood—that calls attention to their literary heritage. Furthermore, Jane's mystical attraction to the right doorstep, her immediate affection for Mary and Diana, her resurrection to a new identity all hearken back to Shakespearean romance rather than the gothic novel conventions haunting volume 2. Like "Fidele," Jane hides her identity (in a manner) when asked her name: "'My name is Jane Elliott.' Anxious as ever to avoid discovery, I had before resolved to assume an *alias*." Like Guiderius and Arviragus, Jane's unknown relatives express their love for this pitiful little being almost immediately: before Jane is even well enough recovered to speak, Diana declares, "To speak truth, St. John, my heart rather warms to the poor little soul. I wish we may be able to benefit her permanently" (342). Once able to tell them that "[n]ot a tie links me to any living thing: not a claim do I possess to admittance under any roof in England" (344), she—again like Imogen/Fidele—soon finds the beginnings of a route out of personal despair.

---

38. Jasper Fforde's postmodern frolic *The Eyre Affair* riffs on readerly dissatisfaction with St. John.

And like *Mrs. Dalloway's* Shake-shifting, *Jane Eyre's* protofeminist departures from romance norms become more pronounced when the book is compared with *Cymbeline*. Perhaps the most telling local difference between
Brontë's representation and that of her Shakespearean pre-text involves the
sex of the recovered siblings. Long before Woolf penned Sally Seton and
Peter Walsh's return, Jane importantly discovers "sisters" as well as a
brother figure, first in the sense of metaphorical kindred spirits, then confirmed as blood cousins. Jane is closest in temperament to Diana, the cousin
named for a Roman deity rather than a biblical holy person. (Shakespeare's
Imogen is "adopted" by the Roman general Lucius after her corpse-side resurrection.) While Jane continues to struggle with St. John's coldness and
self-abnegation, she overflows with warmth and love—and eventually financial support—for her two "sisters": "Our natures dovetailed: mutual affection—of the strongest kind—was the result" (355). Whereas Imogen ends
by stepping into the dynastic shadow, Jane supports her sisters and the
novel must instead send away the "brother," to India and death. The narrative differences reiterate Jane's greater emphasis on her own integrity and
female self-sufficiency.

As to whether Brontë consciously thought of herself as rewriting *Cymbeline* in the third volume of *Jane Eyre*, no direct testimony remains. Brontë was
certainly conversant with Shakespeare's plays, and she wrote with his work
in mind. She incorporates lines from *The Merchant of Venice, Much Ado About
Nothing, 1 Henry VI, Richard II, 1 Henry IV, Julius Caesar, Hamlet,* and *King Lear*
into her familiar letters, sometimes signing herself "Caliban" (as well as
other *C* words such as *Charivari*). In her memorable reading list for Ellen
Nussey (whose "characteristic and naïve manner" of reading *Kenilworth*
amused her the year prior), Charlotte anticipates moral worries but still rec-
ommends the Bard: "Now Ellen don't be startled at the names of Shakespeare and Byron. Both these were great Men and their works are like
themselves. You will know how to chuse the good and avoid the evil."[39]
Shakespeare is worth the risk. As regards *Cymbeline*, Hazlitt and Anna
Jameson had found Imogen the most perfect woman in Shakespeare, a compliment hardly forgotten by writers in the 1830s and 1840s. And more perti-
nently still as regards his admirer Brontë, Sir Walter Scott himself cites the
lines of *Cymbeline's* heroine simply by invoking her name, without feeling the
need for further identification, in *The Heart of Midlothian*.[40] For the nineteenth century, Imogen's was a name to conjure with.

---

39. Brontë, *Letters*, 1:121, 131.
40. The would-be legal expert Saddletree arrives at poor Reuben Butler's door as "that additional vexation, of which Imogen complains so feelingly, when she says, 'I'm sprighted with a

Cymbeline had been a popular play in Garrick's repertory for a time in the late eighteenth century and remained "a staple part of the repertory" for provincial companies into the early nineteenth century; it was performed occasionally by stars such as John Philip Kemble, Charles Kemble, and William Charles Macready.[41] Most notably, Macready staged an 1843 production with Helen Faucit in the role that soon became a centerpiece of her acting career. Faucit too would call Imogen "Shakespeare's masterpiece." The Macready *Cymbeline*, "despite its short life, was long remembered" and much admired by George Fletcher (at the time, and in a volume issued in 1847, when Brontë was composing her novel).[42] He described Faucit's Imogen as (in Carol Carlisle's paraphrase) a "dignified, intelligent woman with noble ideals, her strength of character gave additional effectiveness to her normal gentleness of manner and explained her occasional abandonment of that manner." That would do nicely to describe Jane Eyre. The year Brontë finished composing her novel also saw Samuel Phelps producing *Cymbeline* "with much success at Sadler's Wells."[43]

During Brontë's London visit in the wake of *Jane Eyre*'s success, she saw the great Macready perform in *Macbeth* and *Othello*—and felt confident enough about her understanding of Shakespeare to dismiss his acting as "false and artificial."[44] Charlotte knew full well that she was upsetting the applecart of received opinion in saying so, as she mischievously reports in a letter to her former teacher Margaret Wooler: "I astounded a dinner party by honestly saying I did not like him." Moreover, she proceeds (with far more confidence than the youthful Virginia Stephen) to claim a discernment superior to that of the entire theatrical community: "The fact is the stage-system altogether is hollow nonsense—they act farces well enough—the ac-

fool—Sprighted and anger'd worse.'" Scott, *Heart of Midlothian* (Oxford, 1999), 263. The opening epigraph of volume 4 (chapter 38) of the same novel invokes the play by name.

41. See Carol Carlisle, "Macready's Production of *Cymbeline*," in Foulkes, *Shakespeare and the Victorian Stage*. Juliet Barker points out the falsity of the myth of the Brontës' cultural isolation: they were avid book borrowers at the Keighley Mechanics' Institute Library and had extensive knowledge of newspapers and magazines; "The Haworth Context," in *The Cambridge Companion to the Brontës*, ed. Heather Glen (Cambridge, UK, 2002), 23–24. On *Cymbeline* in the Bath-Bristol provincial company repertory between 1750 and 1805 and "revived regularly" until mid-century, see Arnold Hare, "Shakespeare in a Victorian Provincial Stock Company," in Foulkes, *Shakespeare and the Victorian Stage*, 259. During Macready's tenure as manager at Covent Garden (1837–39) and Drury Lane (1841–43), he produced *Cymbeline* six times. Some reviewers, says Carlisle, "pointed out such impediments to theatrical success as its improbability, indelicacy, and lack of 'dramatic coherence'" (139)—accusations soon to be leveled at *Jane Eyre* (see for example Barker, 13–14). The Brontës' juvenilia show they were already familiar with reviews of contemporary theatrical production; Carol Bock, "'Our plays': The Brontë Juvenilia," in Glen, *Cambridge Companion to the Brontës*, 35.

42. Carlisle, "Macready's Production," 138.

43. Ibid., 144, 151.

44. See Brontë, *Letters*, 2:318–19, 344.

138   tors comprehend their parts and do them justice—they comprehend nothing about tragedy or Shakespeare and it is a failure. I said so—and by so saying produced a blank silence—a mute consternation."[45] If there is a coincidence in the voices of Jane and Charlotte, perhaps it is better revealed here, in this mixture of self-assertion and wry amusement, than in Woolf's critical interpretation. As for being angry and cramped by conditions and tradition, one could do no better than cite the "true" Charlotte in her letter to her publisher, W. S. Williams: "Were I obliged to copy any former novelist, even the greatest, even Scott, in anything, I would not write—Unless I have something of my own to say, and a way of my own to say it in, I have no business to publish; unless I can look beyond the greatest Masters, and study Nature herself, I have no right to paint; unless I have the courage to use the language of Truth in preference to the jargon of Conventionality, I ought to be silent."[46] Silent—be it in judging Shakespeare productions or composing novels—she was not. But neither was she by any stretch of the imagination naïve and unaware of those "Masters" and precedents (as Woolf would have her be) as she wrote her own female "Nature"-based "Truth."

It would be odd indeed if this Charlotte Brontë never meditated upon *Cymbeline*. But even if my claims for her Shake-shifting must perforce remain based on circumstantial evidence and close reading, her use of the same romance tropes conclusively locates her novel in the same generic "family" as *Cymbeline*, with very particular echoes and variations. This in turn places *Jane Eyre* in the line of ancestral relations that lead to *Mrs. Dalloway*. "Books descend from books as families from families," writes Woolf in "The Leaning Tower."[47] Or, to put it more pointedly, it is remarkably uncharacteristic that as perceptive a reader as Virginia Woolf, writing about Brontë's novel and citing Shakespeare's play repeatedly, at virtually the same time, would not have noticed any family resemblance that would merit her attention or positive comment.

As one familiar with the subsequent biography of the Brontës, Woolf also knew that the novelist who concludes by sending Jane's male cousin to India (and premature death) would soon after lose all her surviving siblings— with hideous irony, one brother and two sisters. The autobiographical parallel of adult sibling loss obviously did not affect *Jane Eyre*, although it did interfere with Brontë's composition of *Shirley* and *Villette*, far more than did any perceived "cramping" by male prerogative. While her brother Branwell

45. Ibid., 344. The letter is dated 14 February 1850.
46. Ibid., 118.
47. For the full essay, see Virginia Woolf, "The Leaning Tower," in *The Moment and Other Essays* (New York: Harcourt Brace, 1948), 128–54.

was no longer Charlotte's closest ally, as when they were children writing of
the imaginary land of Angria, she was devastated by his sudden demise. In
the seasons following, first Emily then Anne would die of tuberculosis, leaving Charlotte alone with her father. To the clever Miss Stephen who lost
(like Charlotte, after a mother's death) first her brother, then her half-sister,
a bond of suffering—and endurance—would be hard to avoid.

Most strikingly, right within volume 1 of *Jane Eyre* lies the disease that
killed Thoby Stephen: typhoid fever. The epidemic at Lowood, based on
that at Cowan Bridge school which killed Charlotte's two elder sisters in
1825, becomes transformed into the literary occasion for the death of Helen
Burns—a surrogate sibling, if ever there was one.[48] Here indeed was a
precedent for symbolic distancing of autobiographical loss, in precisely the
form Woolf would employ in *Mrs. Dalloway*. Perhaps it was all too close for
comfort: silence can speak volumes. Brontë almost becomes Woolf's own
Bertha Mason, the one who came before but whose story did not bring reassurance. Brontë was a woman writer and suffering sibling who managed
to produce a successful poetic novel but whose very success led to a barrage
of artistic and gender-based attacks by the end of the century, howls of
wounded male vanity mixing with benignly patronizing domestication of the
family's story to diminish Charlotte's status as a major novelist. And even if
she and her book were not locked away in attics, for the modernist experi-
menter the style was all wrong.

Woolf's eagle eye for jerks and authorial intrusion, then, ultimately reflects back upon her own worries more aptly than it captures Brontë's. Can
a similar explanation be found for Woolf's (very few) narrative breaks and
signs of anger in *Mrs. Dalloway*? Putting aside the almost too obviously parallel episodes involving Miss Kilman and the hate-rationalizing Clarissa, one
is left with the extensive passage from which my earlier discussion of Lady
Bradshaw was drawn. Her "going under" is just one illustration in a lengthy
excursus upon the imperial unpleasantness of Sir William, a discussion that
wanders far from the knowledge and stylistic perspective of the only possible character briefly "connected" with the words, Rezia Warren Smith.
Within a segment that describes the past lives and beliefs of the Bradshaws
with scathing contempt, Woolf makes only a perfunctory gesture to link
Rezia with the narrator's perspective:

---

48. After Charlotte's two elder sisters died, she and Emily were withdrawn from Cowan
Bridge. Ellen Nussey recalled of Charlotte, "whenever she was certain of being quite alone with
her friend, she would talk much of her two dead sisters, Maria and Elizabeth. Her love for them
was most intense"; Thomas James Wise, ed., *The Brontës: Their Lives, Friendships and Correspondence* (Oxford, 1980), 97.

140   But Proportion has a sister, less smiling, more formidable, a Goddess even
now engaged—in the heat and sands of India, the mud and swamp of Africa,
the purlieus of London, wherever in short the climate or the devil tempts men
to fall from the true belief which is her own—is even now engaged in dashing
down shrines, smashing idols, and setting up in their place her own stern
countenance. Conversion is her name and she feasts on the wills of the weakly,
loving to impress, to impose, adoring her own features stamped on the face of
the populace. . . . This lady too (Rezia Warren Smith divined it) had her
dwelling in Sir William's heart, though concealed, as she mostly is, under some
plausible disguise. . . . But Conversion, fastidious Goddess, loves blood better
than brick, and feasts most subtly on the human will. For example, Lady
Bradshaw. . . . (151–52)

For all the incisiveness of Woolf's rhetoric, it would indeed take an act of "divine" intervention for Rezia—the Italian shopgirl baffled by England—not
only to divine the life of a woman she never meets but to meditate in the (urgent and unusual) present tense on what "is" being done in the name of the
British Empire. The condemnation of Bradshaw's will, his goddess, and his
logic of imperial domination enacted through the practice of medicine—all
come only from the pen and attitude of Woolf herself. Unlike the neutral
wanderings through the park early in the day, or the allegorical fantasy of
the Solitary Traveler, which derives from and returns to Peter Walsh's view-
point, here the commentary seems perilously close (given Woolf's own aesthetics) to a personal expression.

Connecting state imperialism and medical practice, Woolf would seem to
have been drawing on her own painful experience; her understandable disdain for the rest cure and arrogant doctors derived from her treatment during her mental breakdowns. However, one can argue that she finds an appropriate occasion to express that emotion through the figure of a soldier,
and in doing so melds her personal frustration with that of a "lost" generation. The definition and proper treatment of shellshock was very much at
issue as Woolf wrote, in both parliamentary reports and medical debates. Indeed, a surprisingly specific connection with a contemporary *Cymbeline* production reinforces the topicality of her linking the worlds of High Street
medicine and imperial war.

In its 21 April review of H. K. Ayliff's 1923 Birmingham Repertory Company modern-dress staging, the *Birmingham Gazette* explicitly describes the
character of Dr. Cornelius "as a smooth Harley Street doctor," while Cymbeline wore a field marshal's uniform adorned with the Victoria Cross and
DSO. Whether Woolf knew of this remarkable analogue mixing *Cymbeline*
and Harley Street is not certain—albeit the production was also favorably

reviewed in the *Times* on 24 April 1923, as she composed her novel.[49] The *Times*'s response certainly resonates with Woolf's project, observing "that poetry prevails over costume . . . such a lyric as 'Fear no more the heat of the sun' suffers nothing from being said by two young men in tweed coats and football shorts"; furthermore, it concludes that this was an important production because a "living dramatist who is also a poet, may know now that he can write in verse on modern themes if he can write well enough. It opens a new possibility not only to Shakespeare producers but to the contemporary theatre."[50] And perhaps to contemporary poetic novelists, as well.

Yet even if we cite this production to suggest that more than personal topicality is involved in Woolf's portrait of a Harley Street doctor and a veteran, the tonal and narrative shifts remain. She breaks no rules in wandering away from the putative "event" of Septimus Warren Smith's visit in order to discuss the abstractions that underlie Bradshaw's complacent bullying: this is a novel of movements and multiple perspectives. The only "fault" here is the resemblance to precisely what she attacks in *Jane Eyre*: the seeming intrusion of an urgent (even if generalizable) autobiographical concern into the supposedly impersonal palace of art, and a stretch when trying to reconnect the author's vehement opinions with the ongoing fiction— "(Rezia Warren Smith divined it)." This is a matter of literary pots and kettles, whether rendered in the first or the third person. Indeed, without the potential inherent in *Jane Eyre*'s first-person narration, which encourages one to "fit" the voice to the writing character, the passage in *Dalloway* stands out all the more.

Ultimately, acknowledged or not, Woolf's achievement in *Mrs. Dalloway* builds on foundations already there in jerky, passionate *Jane Eyre*, which likewise rewrites Shakespearean romance as a woman's survival story. And not just as a return from the dead as in *Cymbeline*, from crossed boundaries to a restored social order built on the old model. Rather, from start to finish, Jane controls the narrative, speaking her mind in the present; and Brontë concludes with major changes within the social system of her represented world—with the master reliant on his former employee, the female leading the chastened man, the orphan endowed with social position and her own

---

49. Claire Cochrane, *Shakespeare and the Birmingham Repertory Theatre, 1913–1929* (London, 1993), 101; similarly, the jailer appeared as a World War I military policeman. Ayliff was not deterred by Granville Barker's preface in the fall 1923 *Player's Shakespeare*, which argued the play should be staged as a masque. The same autumn, Lewis Casson toured in another production with futurist designs, making this (like Brontë's 1840s) a comparatively rich time for *Cymbeline* onstage. Woolf might agree with Ayliff's 1928 statement that "*Cymbeline* taught us more than anything else that Shakespeare was a modern author"; Cochrane, 103.

50. Ibid.

142   disposable wealth.[51] Woolf may create a cartoon Charlotte, but Brontë's final moves for her Imogen figure are far more interesting. Having escaped becoming the madwoman in the attic through self-reliance, Jane—who loves Mary and Diana, if not Chloe's Olivia—manages to attain a room of her own. Only after this stint as an independent working woman (and reader of "Marmion") will she return to the now marriageable Rochester, leading her shaggy Samson out of his darkness. Of course she remains constrained, or rather participates in her own subjection, in this journey toward Victorian social acceptance; to expect otherwise would be utopian indeed.[52] But attending to the divergences between her journey and that of the Shakespearean romance heroine who traveled before her allows Brontë's particular achievement in cultural collaboration to become, or remain, more vivid. And doing so also fills in an intermediate step between *Cymbeline*'s elaborate act 5 restoration of familial hierarchy and marriage and *Mrs. Dalloway*'s final nonlinear scene of non-blood-"sibling" recovery. Supporting her female cousins and continuing to make her own choices, Jane concludes her saga by both achieving and displacing the love-and-marriage ending, as she imagines the note from her male cousin-double who will soon cross the final border. St. John dies, one could argue by analogy with Septimus Smith, that Jane Eyre/Elliot/Rochester might live.

In fact, the "mystical" episodes toward the end of both *Jane Eyre* and *Mrs. Dalloway* bear a further kinship that distinguishes them from the masculine-centered revelation of *Cymbeline*'s fifth act. There, it is Posthumus's "dream" that allows the revival of his dead family, which then turns into a scene of divine revelation with Jupiter's thunderous arrival and presentation of the prophetic tablet. Although Posthumus lies down announcing, "O Imogen, / I'll speak to thee in silence" (5.5.122–23), the focus shifts to his own familial inheritance and the justice of the ultimate cosmic patriarch. By contrast, both *Jane Eyre* and *Mrs. Dalloway* approach their resolutions through mystical connections received by their female protagonists. Jane, having "entreated of Heaven" to show her the right path as she confronts St. John, feels her senses "forced to wake" and then hears a voice "where, or whence, for ever impossible to know!": it is of course the disembodied voice of

---

51. The novel ends with Jane married with a son and Rochester recovering his sight, while St. John gets the last word; but those final few paragraphs complicate rather than negate the achievements and drama of the final volume.

52. See London's Foucauldian critique of those who ignore her bondage *"through* increasingly powerful and interiorized forms of discipline" ("Pleasures," 201). Although an apt corrective to earlier feminist readings, this does not account for the full experience of reading Jane's story and discounts its literary innovations.

Rochester calling from afar, "and it spoke in pain and woe wildly, eerily, urgently." Denying the "black" "spectre" of superstition or witchcraft in this "work of nature," she nevertheless pursues the voice and thereby regains her will: "It was *my* time to assume ascendancy. *My* powers were in play, and in force." Finally, she prays ("a different way to St. John's, but effective in its own fashion"), realizing she has "seemed to penetrate very near a Mighty Spirit" (410). In consequence, she leaves Moor House and finds her happy ending with a newly marriageable and manageable Rochester. Clarissa's quasi-mystical connection with Septimus's thoughts, while less flamboyant and overtly telepathic, nevertheless crosses an even more remarkable boundary between the living and the dead; though never meeting him, Clarissa accurately perceives what his devoted wife could not comprehend, feeling "somehow very like him" and hearing, if not "his" voice, then the "voice" of Shakespeare he too had heard—as close to a "Mighty Spirit" as an atheist skeptical of "the Gods" might allow. In contrast to the baffled Posthumus, who finds the prophecy a "senseless speaking, or a speaking such / As sense cannot untie" and must await enlightenment by others (5.5.240–41), the two eponymous women realize a new point of departure as a result of their mystical receptivity.

One border that Jane does not cross, however, cannot remain unspoken: she does not directly challenge the logic of imperial subjugation and conversion that will lead St. John to India and death. And while Clarissa Dalloway may only abstractly abhor Conversion, Woolf clearly portrays Septimus Smith as a martyr of empire at its worst. Jane stays firmly fixed in England: Imogen at least went to Wales. Charlotte Brontë herself came from Celtic stock (Cornish and Irish), studied in Belgium, and would love Scotland once she got there: as she wrote to W. S. Williams in 1850, "I always liked Scotland as an idea, but now, as a reality, I like it far better." She praised Edinburgh's "poetry" and (of course) the Scott monument, whereas of England and London in particular she remarked, "above all you have not the Scotch National Character—and it is that grand character after all which gives the land its true charm, its true greatness."[53] As Virginia Woolf knew, Mrs. Humphry Ward had described "the Celtic nature of the Brontë genius," and G. K. Chesterton remarked upon her "more sensitive Irish temper."[54] Nevertheless, Brontë's Jane is all English, with the moral smugness about her national superiority that characterizes the imperial core. Her wealth as well as

---

53. Brontë, *Letters*, 2:427–28.
54. Woolf cites these remarks in her 1917 review of a centennial celebration volume, both being entitled "Charlotte Brontë"; in Virginia Woolf, *Essays*, vol. 2, ed. Andrew McNeillie (New York, 1987), 192–95.

144   her monstrous rival comes from the West Indies, overtly implicating Jane in the colonial systems of domination that Jean Rhys would render with excruciating vividness in her "prequel" novel, *Wide Sargasso Sea*. To argue that Brontë saw her work as a conscious critique of the exploitation of periphery by core requires even more stretching than a feminist defense of Woolf's portraiture of Miss Kilman. Elsie Michie, noting the "Africanoid celt" rhetoric developing at the Victorian mid-century (a connection deployed to very different ends than in *Kenilworth*), makes the case for Rochester as an orientalized/darker figure for both a colonizer's fears and desires, and thereby suggests a more complicated layering of the domestic/foreign binary within *Jane Eyre*; even she, however, distinguishes between sympathy for the internally colonized (Irish) and endorsement of comparable domination in more distant lands (India, the West Indies).[55] At least in Charlotte Brontë's letters, juvenilia, and other personal writing, it is hard to find signs of critical doubts about the overseas imperial project. Even within the British Isles, with respect to the land to the north, political resentment does not arise. For Brontë, the remembrance of her beloved Sir Walter is connected not to border disputes (despite Jane Eyre's specific praise for a poem about the battle of Flodden Field, so disastrous for an independent Scotland) but only to a "golden age" of poetry and romance.

    If, as Woolf argues in *Room*, the woman writer can reveal that bald spot at the back of a man's head which he cannot see (thereby enriching his vision), Rhys and subsequent critics such as Gayatri Spivak would reveal the white spot in the British woman's brain. India, the site where St. John attempts to save souls through self-mortification, becomes for Woolf the land where Peter Walsh engages in extramarital affairs; likewise, the journey from unironic messianic missions to William Bradshaw's nightmare goddess Conversion is a long one, the gulf between perhaps enough to displace any sense of political kinship with Brontë on Woolf's part. Where Shakespeare restored gender and class hierarchies, both Brontë and Woolf at least challenge them. But the struggle to balance blood and nation, to venerate a green and pleasant land, remains a sticking point. What Shakespeare labors to create, Brontë takes for granted—and Woolf (only) begins to unravel. Not just the jerks of narrative but the confident pieties of Victorian thinking estranged Woolf from her artistic foremother. They encouraged a step back even further, to the dramatic, confused Britain of *Cymbeline*, reinterpreted through a woman's mind and with that degree of cosmic detachment crucial to Shakespeare's—but not Brontë's—version of poetic romance.

---

55. Elsie Michie, *Outside the Pale: Cultural Exclusion, Gender Difference, and the Victorian Woman Writer* (Ithaca, 1993); essay reprinted in the Bedford *Jane Eyre*.

To which, a coda: for all the harshness of stylistic judgment and seeming
misprision in Woolf's reading of Brontë, one further comment in her 1925
essay on *Jane Eyre* and *Wuthering Heights* cannot go unnoted. The tribute may
not be acknowledged elsewhere, nor does it undo the larger dynamic of gendered displacement and erasure I have traced. Still, it seems more just to the
full portrait of Woolf as an artist to conclude by stressing not just her strategic collaboration with tradition but also her perspicacity: the attentiveness
that allows a writer sometimes to break out of her own frame, to find pleasure (at least momentarily) in that which will not serve. Despite *Jane Eyre's*
limitations, Woolf concludes, Charlotte Brontë still powerfully conveys the
heart's fire, and hence one should read her "for her poetry." Coming from the
woman who had recently told her diary, "it is poetry that I want now—long
poems," this might be the best private compliment she could give.

Shape-Shifting Shakespeare

> *Antony* Eros, thou yet behold'st me?
>
> *Eros* Ay, noble lord.
>
> *Antony* Sometime we see a cloud that's dragonish,
>   A vapor sometime like a bear or lion,
>   A towered citadel, a pendant rock,
>   A forked mountain, or blue promontory
>   With trees upon't that nod unto the world,
>   And mock our eyes with air. Thou hast seen these signs,
>   They are black vesper's pageants.
>
> *Eros* Ay, my lord.
>
> *Antony* That which is now a horse, even with a thought
>   The rack dislimns, and makes it indistinct
>   As water is in water.
>
> *Eros* It does, my lord.
>
> *Antony* My good knave Eros, now thy captain is
>   Even such a body.
>   *Antony and Cleopatra* 4.14.1–13

What one chooses to adapt from Shakespeare's text is ultimately what
serves the interpreter. Woolf says as much, using Septimus's response to
Antony and Cleopatra—that most shape-shifting of plays—as her example.
Before the war, when Septimus first came to London, the experience "made
him anxious to improve himself, made him fall in love with Miss Isabel Pole,
lecturing in the Waterloo Road upon Shakespeare"; it had been she who "reflected how she might give him a taste of *Antony and Cleopatra* and the rest;
lent him books; wrote him scraps of letters; and lit in him such a fire as

146   burns only once in a lifetime, without heat, flickering a red gold flame infinitely ethereal and insubstantial over Miss Pole; *Antony and Cleopatra*; and the Waterloo Road" (128). But the same cluster of associations also leads Septimus to war and his destruction, as he "went to France to save an England which consisted almost entirely of Shakespeare's plays and Miss Isabel Pole in a green dress [echoing the color of Clarissa's party dress] walking in a square" (130). The education that began as a romanticized way out of the anonymity and uniformity of being born into a certain class and absorbed into the city's masses of clerks (Woolf's narration presents this unlucky seventh son as one of the "many millions of young men called Smith" whom "London had swallowed up" [127]) now itself becomes another means of interpellation into the machinery of empire. For Woolf too, resistant to educational institutions yet eager to be respected as part of a great British literary tradition, there were comparable spiritual and political risks inherent in collaborating with Shakespeare. Hers would be a working relationship, not starstruck infatuation.

After the war, an emotionally traumatized Septimus "opened Shakespeare once more. That boy's business of the intoxication of language—*Antony and Cleopatra*—had shrivelled utterly. How Shakespeare loathed humanity—the putting on of clothes, the getting of children"; even "[l]ove between man and woman was repulsive to Shakespeare. The business of copulation was filth to him before the end" (133–34). Obviously Septimus "discovers" in Shakespeare exactly what his own situation brings to the reading. The aftershock of the Great War overshadows the pleasurable warmth of nature's sun; indeed, the sun itself has been refigured by that symbolic system, proclaimed never to set upon the British Empire. Septimus's interpretation of Shakespeare is correspondingly transformed. Moreover, he feels disgust at the idea that others may read without sharing his sensibility: one of his most painful thoughts, for him exemplary of human cruelty and horror, is the image of his constraining doctor "Holmes reading Shakespeare" (213). On the verge of parodying her own novelistic interest in Shakespearean romance, Woolf presents the attempt to commune with or claim a particular authority from the Bard as a sign of possessive madness.[56] This is Shakeshifting run amok.

Septimus's illness is characterized by his writings of "how the dead sing behind rhododendron bushes; odes to Time; conversations with Shake-

---

56. Alice Fox stresses Septimus's postwar reading as "a badly distorted view"; *Virginia Woolf and the Literature of the English Renaissance* (Oxford, UK, 1990), 132. My point is stronger: Woolf's presentation shows the interested, distorting effect of *all* readings, not merely the unpleasant ones.

speare" along with "messages from the dead" (224). Given the specifics, it   147
seems Septimus is trapped in late Shakespeare—or Woolf's version thereof.
Septimus's sense of affinity contributes to his dysfunctionality, even as *Cymbeline*'s words echo consolation in his final hours:

> Fear no more, says the heart in the body; fear no more.
>   He was not afraid. At every moment Nature signified by some laughing hint like that gold spot which went round the wall—there, there, there—her determination to show, by brandishing her plumes, shaking her tresses, flinging her mantle this way and that, beautifully, always beautifully, and standing close up to breathe through her hollowed hands Shakespeare's words, her meaning. (211–12)

Within this desperate search for authorial meaning in the world, the figure of the Bard becomes, for shell-shocked Septimus as for his female creator, both an alternative source of British authority and a fluid construct destined to reflect his interpreter's needs, perhaps illusory but ultimately keeping the imperial patriarchs at bay.

To seek "her meaning," the clarity of an answer, in Woolf's or Brontë's metamorphic collaboration with Shakespeare (and Woolf's effacement of Brontë) may not be a madness as extreme as Septimus's, but it is at least as delusive as is his proclamation of "the" meaning of *Antony and Cleopatra*. In each case, changes wrought upon the interpreter by time and history become enmeshed with the "original" words. As Woolf wrote in this chapter's epigraph, "literature is always changing, like the weather, like clouds in the sky"—which, noble Antony might add, can be as "indistinct / As water is in water."

Nevertheless, after attending to this intertextual play, one does gain a fuller sense of Woolf's narrative logic in revivifying the past and reformulating the present at Clarissa's party. Perhaps softening though certainly not erasing the novel's satiric stabs at the British imperial project, Woolf's transformation of *Cymbeline* suggests as well the redemptive possibilities in reconceiving female experience outside traditional plots premised on aristocratic blood ties or the bourgeois equation of love and marriage. For Woolf as, arguably, for Charlotte Brontë, it was Shakespearean romance that provided a model worth revising to account for gendered experience differently. They imply the importance of recovering that which conventionally must be displaced or discarded in a search for "maturity" and social stability. In the final reunion of Sally and Peter with Clarissa ("For there she was"), Woolf goes further than Brontë's "Reader, I married him" would allow (even if that fa-

148   mous ending is not the end, and the last words of St. John are as defiantly complicating for interpretation as anything in *Mrs. Dalloway*). Woolf subordinates Shakespeare's interest in sexual jealousy while exploiting the analogical systems of thought that encourage us to see parallelism between domestic and imperial domination. Rewriting romance in *Mrs. Dalloway* thus becomes her particularly "corrective" mode of diachronic collaboration with, rather than simple rejection or perpetuation of, the Shakespearean literary tradition and the social categories it represents; it is also her means of evading spectral mothers and her own "dark ages" inhabited by oppressively close Victorian kin. Ultimately Woolf's revisionist mode of Shakeshifting helped her revivify the past as the necessary prologue, requiring the supplement of her own modernity.

That modernity is now our increasingly misty past, disappearing like the vapor writing of the airplane that *Mrs. Dalloway*'s Londoners regard with wonder. Seeking to decipher the sky's runic mystery long after Antony's demise, they find instead a brand name: GLAXO. Yet at such sardonic moments of satire no less than in her characters' deepest meditations, Woolf's writing continues to defy time passing, providing varied consolations while bodies grow "indistinct" and "come to dust." Nearly as far from us as Sir Walter was from her modernist heyday, Woolf's novels have managed to maintain their vitality as other, new screen forms have gained narrative ascendancy. Like Shakespeare (and *Jane Eyre*) in this regard as well, her works have now become material for cross-media adaptation and diachronic collaboration. The reverberations can startle: when one hears Winnie in Samuel Beckett's *Happy Days*, for example, buried up to her waist, beginning to recite "Fear no more the heat o' the sun"—"the old style"—in that shatteringly chirpy portrait of a modern marriage (her reward comes when an irritated Willie echoes her "Fear no more").[57] Such moments also serve as reminders of the increasing difficulty of determining stable lines of connection as words recirculate in new forms and economies, as more voices join in the cultural collaboration. The power of Shakespeare's dirge, echoing in *Mrs. Dalloway*, now makes it a frequent part of memorial services, leading to new modes of Shakespearean (and modernist) "back-formation": in the 2002 television remake of John Galsworthy's *The Forsythe Saga* (books Woolf famously criticized), *Cymbeline*'s dirge was recited at the memorial service for young Jolyon, even though it did not originally appear in the volume *To Let*. The fact that actor Rupert Graves had played not only Jolyon but Septimus

57. Samuel Beckett, *Happy Days* (New York, 1961), 26.

Smith in the 1997 film of *Mrs. Dalloway* created a layered moment of elegiac screen performance worthy of the ur-text. In these fluid group collaborations, as in Antony's lamentation at his loss of self-identity, the signs metamorphose and meaning "dislimns," mocking our eyes with air.

When *Mrs. Dalloway* was transformed for film, its final scene of sibling recovery was muted with a dance: Richard Dalloway was not "bracketed" but partnered, while Peter held Clarissa. As a result, the import of the novel's romance rewriting must have been lost on some. The hint of a more radical ending came instead through a freeze-frame added by the director, Marlene Gorris, known for her "feminist" film *Antonio's Line*: the final still, a visual tableau, aptly returns to the youthful trio of Peter, Sally, and Clarissa on the lawn at Bourton—the less conventional lost possibility.[58] The feminist tradition that Woolf helped create textually here returns, in a suitably indirect way, via the contribution of a visual artist. But this image remains frozen in time, in an idyllic lost past, and so even its ultimate presence does not convey the force of Woolf's radical departure. Moreover, despite admirably capturing Peter's heartbreak and Clarissa's love for Sally, the film repeatedly implies that Clarissa's "fear" kept her from marrying Peter, whom she loved more than Richard, and it presents Septimus's suicide as impetus for her finally to seek and dance with Peter, specifically. In other words, it implies the lost alternative was another heterosexual marriage plot, and "the heat of the sun" is reduced to sexual passion alone.

Ideas collide, saturate, and become even harder to account for when turning from novels to films, but this subtle reshaping of Clarissa's narrative is true to form, to the generic expectations and dominant use of the commercial film medium. In these larger-scale collaborations, material conditions and pressures play a much greater role in shaping the artistic product. Certainly a common complaint about screen adaptations of literary texts has been their conformity, visual and narrative, to the norms of realist Hollywood cinema. Even this film, with a British all-star cast and the screenplay by Eileen Atkins, had a very difficult time finding a distributor; the material weight of cultural collaboration plays a much more overt role in shaping artistic vision within mass market entertainment.

Attempting a film of *Mrs. Dalloway* was indeed a bold choice artistically as well as financially. Given the nonrealist dimensions of the text, and its focus on interior mental states and reflections, it is a wonder it was done at all.

---

58. In conversation following the London Film Festival screening, 14 November 1997, Gorris acknowledged that this was her directorial addition.

150   And poor Peter Walsh waited and suffered a long time before he got to that
dance. Like the stage versions of *Kenilworth* and spinoff novels like *The Eyre
Affair* and *The Hours*, film adaptations can serve as our wish fulfillments
when source texts seem recalcitrant, already written, "dead" on the page; a
new film can change an ending or add an erotic moment. Such recontextualizing strategies were already modeled within the novels themselves, of
course, in Scott's and Woolf's very differently toned collaborations with
Shakespeare. The operative distinction here, in other words, is not so much
the medium as the temporality of a given past and a pliable present, as one
works within material conditions that either constrain or license change.
Similarly, the strategies of Shake-shifting are not necessarily prescribed by
medium. In moving from the printed word to screen or live performance, we
shall see that moviemakers can be as respectfully confident of "continuing"
Shakespeare as was Scott, or as consciously "corrective" as Woolf. In the
genres of comedy and history, however, the need to address societal changes
since Shakespeare's day becomes even more urgent than in tragedy or romance. Some artists have extended Woolf's mode of critique in the representation of gender and nation, whereas others take refuge in the pretense that
they are merely representing "Shakespeare"—despite changes in time, despite medium, despite cultural context. To investigate such claims and decisions, the following chapters will thus also extend the closer textual analysis
of Shakespearean playscripts begun here with *Cymbeline*.

In "Novel Transformations," while gesturing at larger cultural frames and
the novels' and plays' recirculation, I have focused in depth on a few particular works with Shakespearean subtexts as exemplary and influential instances of Shake-shifting. As we have seen, even when one honors the specific agency of the writers, no diachronic collaboration is ever just a
two-person dialogue. Now, in turning to the group process of performance
art, I take advantage of this medial shift to widen my screen as well, moving
among multiple versions of Shake-shifting. But as before, a single play will
anchor each chapter, chosen for its particular importance in Shakespeare's
film career and in his mainstream modern reception. The chapters in "Media
Crossings" focus on an ideological problematic within the Shakespearean
text itself (shrew taming in a comedy, the ambiguities of national and gendered "others" in a history), which is then traced through several adaptations. This allows comparison of the ways in which different directors and
actors artistically engage with (or efface) the problematic at hand, and it
also emphasizes the breadth of Shake-shifting possibilities. No less than in
written compositions, these artists have labored and made choices to create
"meaning" through interpretation, and these chapters will again recognize

their consequential decisions as much as possible. When more hands, eyes, and minds are involved, attribution becomes even trickier, but no less important. Indeed, arguably more so, as these screen transformations now reach larger audiences than can ever see the same Shakespeare production "live." They may have become the primary bearers of Shakespeare. To understand modern Shake-shifting more broadly, then, it is time to refocus.

Part Two

Media Crossings

3

The Return of the Shrew

New Media, Old Stories, and Shakespearean Comedy

Now child, a lesson new you shall begin to spell:
Sweet babes must babies have, but shrewd girls must be beaten.
Sir Philip Sidney, "Astrophil and Stella"

Let her laugh at that . . .

Shakespeare, *Hamlet*

A shrew is being beaten.

Or is she? The frisson of uncertainty about the answer to this question helps account, perhaps, for the remarkably frequent representation of *The Taming of the Shrew* on stage and screen.[1] But collaborating with this old text is a dangerous game, and requires an exceptional amount of ingenuity, rationalization, or willful blindness: this is, after all, at least superficially a play with a plot that does what it says and strikes many audience members and scholars (including myself) as archaic and benighted in its social assumptions. So one may well ask why we still study and perform *Shrew*, investing considerable energies in order to understand it and make it "work,"

---

1. The play is a crowd-pleasing staple of regional theater and summer Shakespeare festivals. The Royal Shakespeare Company's 2003 iteration reminded audiences of the play's contentiousness even in Shakespeare's day by staging it in repertory with John Fletcher's 1611 companion play/rebuttal, *The Tamer Tamed* (both directed by Gregory Doran). More than twenty film and video versions have been produced in Europe and North America, at a conservative estimate. This number excludes spinoffs such as the musical *Kiss Me, Kate*, a 1986 episode of the television series *Moonlighting*, and — one of my favorites — "Mr. I. Magination," an early television show for children in which a little boy (Donny Harris) plays Petruchio's part opposite a grown-up woman (Ruth Enders). Mr. I. (Paul Tripp, Enders's husband) explains that a shrew is a "gal with a hot temper who's always scolding and nagging"; for a more historically informed definition of the word, see Lynda E. Boose, "Scolding Brides and Bridling Scolds: Taming the Woman's Unruly Member," *Shakespeare Quarterly* 42, no. 2 (1991): 179–213.

156   rather than concentrating on Shakespeare's later, seemingly more amenable comedies such as *Much Ado About Nothing* and *Twelfth Night*.[2]

Of course one woman's insult is another man's joke: from simply calling an adult "babe" to laughing at sadomasochism, somebody's sign of comedy or even affection will strike someone else as threatening or disgusting. Nowhere are the limits of "common sense" more evident than in appraising comedy—but perhaps nowhere are the stakes higher.[3] Long ago Freud called attention to aggression in our jests and violence in our fantasies; frequent public battles over "misunderstood" religious and political satire remind us that jokes can be no laughing matter. While differing tastes in tragedy may bring a sigh or dismissive shrug, acknowledging a diametrically opposite response to comedy seems to test the boundaries of civility and our shared everyday world. This is particularly true when a comedy (such as *Shrew*) reiterates rather than inverts the inequities of power that still make some people socially acceptable objects of ridicule and others off-limits. Collaborating here, as an artist or an audience member, has a social and psychic cost.[4]

After four hundred years and the kinds of complex collaborations explored in the previous chapters, one might think Shakespeare's comedies were safe from the passions of the present, that his stings could no longer carry any poison. Certainly many scholars, artists, and audience members believe this, mocking or dismissing those who would take offense.[5] But precisely because Shakespeare remains *the* name to conjure with, those attuned

2. The screen versions by Trevor Nunn (*Twelfth Night*) and Kenneth Branagh (both plays) may signal a shift to the comedies that include gender confusion, inversions of power, and more sustained poetic craft. However, *Midsummer* is still the other contender for frequency of film/video replication among the comedies.

3. See Alexander Leggatt, ed., *The Cambridge Companion to Shakespearean Comedy* (Cambridge, UK, 2002); Wylie Sypher, ed., *Comedy* (Garden City, NY, 1956); and Simon Critchley, *On Humour* (New York, 2002), for classic and recent philosophical reflections on comedy and humor.

4. Shirley Nelson Garner, "*The Taming of the Shrew*: Inside or Outside the Joke?" in "*Bad*" *Shakespeare: Revaluations of the Shakespearean Canon*, ed. Maurice Charney (Rutherford, NJ, 1988); Barbara Hodgdon, "Katherina Bound: or, Play(K)ating the Strictures of Everyday Life," *PMLA* 107, no. 3 (1992): 538–53; Barbara Freedman, *Staging the Gaze: Postmodernism, Psychoanalysis, and Shakespearean Comedy* (Ithaca, 1991), chap. 4; and Laurie E. Maguire, "Cultural Control in *The Taming of the Shrew*," *Renaissance Drama* 26 (1995): 83–104, are especially clear about the perceived costs of enjoying *Shrew*.

5. Two common evasive tactics are comparison to other shrew-taming stories of Shakespeare's day (to show they are worse) and appeal to the frame story. Frames of course can ironize an action, but if the frame and the inset narratives share the same ideological disposition, then they become mutually reinforcing. Essentialist thinking about gender, despite the optimism of some in the academy, is not yet passé.

to certain social inequities are inclined to disagree: if his works still have power, they still have power to hurt. As Sir Walter Scott himself noted, drama is "an engine possessing the most powerful effect on the manners of society" and can be used for "evil as for good."[6] The amount of energy devoted to avoiding what clearly does go on in theaters and cinema—especially in scenes where strong women and "foreigners" are humiliated for laughs—might better be employed in looking hard at the sources of friction, the reasons for misunderstanding, and what's at stake in "taking" a joke. In the case of *The Taming of the Shrew* onscreen, the medium itself may aggravate such tensions: as Barbara Hodgdon has effectively argued, film tends to confirm a voyeuristic and consumerist logic already present in the play's representation of sexuality. We are well trained to view Kate as a spectacle, bound by an economy in which her pleasure derives from placating "her" man; but the female spectator who identifies with Kate, not wishing to deprive herself of what is represented as the means to heterosexual pleasure, thereby participates in her double bind.[7]

At the same time, we all need our pleasures, and the task of criticism surely is not just to spoil others' fun. Elsewhere I have correlated *Shrew*'s filmic replication with eras of backlash against feminism and examined the investment of mass cultural producers of Shakespeare in a dominantly conservative, if not reactionary, project.[8] While valid, this account does not address the nature of the play's multiple sources of pleasure with enough nuance to explain why it continues to entertain insightful audiences, or why so many filmmakers (like scholars and theatrical artists) continue to return to *Shrew*. In this chapter, therefore, I build on my earlier analysis of the role of the camera and reconsider several screen *Shrew*s with a new emphasis—on the fascination of what's difficult.

Too often discussions of colliding sensibility and changing ideologies devolve into a pleasure/pain binary, with those who advocate social awareness being viewed as disruptive or lacking a sense of humor. (Arguably this binary, more than any disproportionate preponderance of dour advocates, has led to the shibboleth that feminism isn't fun.) Implicit here is another false opposition, between pleasure and work, one that permeates much of contemporary culture and undermines, if not denies, the actual experience of pleasure within certain forms of labor—the kind of pleasure, surely, that

6. Walter Scott, *Critical and Miscellaneous Essays*, 3:14–15.
7. See Barbara Hodgdon (both "Katherina" and *Shakespeare Trade*), to whom I am greatly indebted even when our interpretations diverge.
8. See Henderson, "Shrew," 120–39.

158   sustains most artistic and scholarly production.[9] In addition to the interpretive work of discovering ironic layers within a shrew-taming plot, or discovering true love in a financially motivated and farcically derived male lead, adapting *The Taming of the Shrew* for the screen also involves the work of the camera, using the apparatus to reinforce or alter what textual analysis suggests. Just as *Shrew* demands more shrewd scholarly work to become a source of modern pleasure for those who believe in gender equity, so too the camera gets to do more work in representing the story because it *needs* to do more: sometimes by filling in silences with "speaking" images, sometimes by redirecting attention, sometimes by providing framing commentaries or supplements. In both the production and the response to some screen *Shrew*s, then, forms of laborious, even "critical" pleasure emerge that suggest something more active than nostalgic (or masochistic) seduction. As a result, criticism, like feminism, cannot simply open eyes to the inherited problems and expect a "click" that leaves old stories and habits in the dust; rather, one confronts the more difficult task of understanding why we keep coming back, and what keeps the comedy current.

This is not to say that all engagements with *Shrew* manifest such energetic collaboration, or that the process is always conscious. Comparatively few artists appear to want to address the problems raised by importing very "early" modern gender relations into our present moment, or by their role and responsibility in that process; those who do often express discomfort and dismay.[10] Many appeal to the comic genre and the authority of Shakespeare, working desperately to discount or evade the text's recalcitrant historicity.[11] Yet by casting women rather than boys as Katherina and disposing of the play's initial frame story, screen *Shrew*s make the taming story being represented appear far more realistic, more like normative domestic relations, than the play ever did in Shakespeare's day.[12] Usually these ver-

9. Obviously there is a massive amount of alienated labor, and I am not denying Marx's analysis of the plight of the proletariat; but even in that instance, part of the difficulty for post-Communist class analysis has derived from overgeneralizing the dichotomy between work and pleasure, broadly conceived.

10. Among the most thoughtful responses, see the RSC actresses interviewed in Carol Rutter, *Clamorous Voices: Shakespeare's Women Today*, ed. Faith Evans (New York, 1989).

11. On performers using Shakespeare as the ultimate authority, see Worthen, *Shakespeare and the Authority of Performance*; for historicist feminist readings of *Shrew*, see Boose, "Scolding Brides"; Karen Newman, *Fashioning Femininity and English Renaissance Drama* (Chicago, 1991); Leah Marcus, "The Shakespearean Editor as Shrew-Tamer," *ELR* 22, no. 2 (1992): 177–200; and Coppélia Kahn, "*The Taming of the Shrew*: Shakespeare's Mirror of Marriage," *Modern Language Studies* 5 (1975): 88–102. Jonathan Miller is exceptional among screen directors in his invocation and use of historicism, as I discuss below.

12. Much work has been done on cross-dressing and the frame story as Elizabethan forms of irony and distancing; see among them Joel Fineman, "The Turning of the Shrew," in *Shakespeare*

sions "work," in part because Shakespeare wrote one foolproof farcical scene between Petruchio and Katherine to win us over (2.1.178–273); also, a good proportion of any audience these days appears almost desperately eager for confirmation of marital love.[13] Nevertheless—and sometimes despite the stated intentions of the filmmakers and actors—the process of transformation across media does bring new perspectives to an old story: the camera reveals another angle, psychological and farcical modes of acting collide, and modern collaborators uncover spaces of play within an always-already fractured narrative. Moreover, screen versions of one era may look quite different to later viewers. And in all these gaps, audiences may find another form of pleasure, in their own critical interpretations.

Kate Becomes a Movie Star

During the years when Virginia Woolf was conceiving and composing *Mrs. Dalloway*, a young film industry was already producing multiple silent film versions of *The Taming of the Shrew* (including a 1908 short directed by D. W. Griffiths); a year after *A Room of One's Own* appeared, so did the first Shakespeare talkie—and as if to rebuff Woolf's progressive feminism, the text chosen was again *Shrew*.[14] But forestalling conspiracy theories about misogynist moguls enforcing the subjugation of women is the presence of one key studio executive and star of the 1929 film: Mary Pickford. Her narrative of the experience as first an eager and then an uneasy collaborator captures in a nutshell the gendered power games that performing *Shrew* seems to provoke as well as represent. Her case also illustrates how the space between a character and the "star" inhabiting it can sometimes produce a double take comparable to that spurred by the cross-dressed boy

---

and the Question of Theory, ed. Patricia Parker and Geoffrey Hartman (New York, 1985), 138–59; Barbara Hodgdon, "Sexual Disguise and the Theatre of Gender," in Leggatt, *Cambridge Companion to Shakespearean Comedy*, 179–97; and Howard, *Stage*. See also Freedman's consideration of psychoanalytic and deconstructive double binds set in relationship to *Shrew* and theatricality. Uniquely among screen *Shrew*s, the CBC video recorded before a live audience in Stratford, Ontario, includes the Christopher Sly scenes (as well as the closing Sly scene from the contemporaneous Elizabethan play, *The Taming of a Shrew*). Although the Punch-and-Judy show at the start of the PickFair production and the university celebrations at the start of Zeffirelli's *Shrew* have been considered alternative "frames," neither breaks location.

13. All citations refer to William Shakespeare, *The Taming of the Shrew: Texts and Contexts*, ed. Frances E. Dolan (Boston, 1996).

14. On silent *Shrew*s, see Robert Hamilton Ball, *Shakespeare on Silent Film* (New York, 1968), and Henderson, "Shrew."

160   heroine of the Elizabethan stage—or, more immediately, by this chapter's
opening question ("Or is she?").

Pickford began the project believing it could help transform her image as
"America's Sweetheart," allowing her to play more adult roles; it also gave
her an opportunity to co-star with her husband, Douglas Fairbanks Sr., in a
"PickFair" production. Instead, the process undermined both her confidence as an actress and the marriage behind United Artists. According to
her autobiography, Pickford struggled with director and husband alike.
Sam Taylor nixed her attempts to embody Katherina as a serious grown
woman ("We don't want any of this heavy stage drama; we want the old
Pickford tricks"), with the result that "Instead of being a forceful tiger-cat, I
was a spitting little kitten." Meanwhile,

> The strange new Douglas acting opposite me was being another Petruchio in
> real life. . . . I would be waiting on the set for him till nearly noon [*as Kate waits
> for a belated Petruchio on her wedding day, "No shame but mine"*]. . . . When Douglas
> finally showed up, he wouldn't know his lines [*Petruchio refuses to dress or act like
> a proper groom*]. They had to be chalked on enormous blackboards, and I had to
> move my head so he could read them [*indulging his impropriety, leaving before the
> marriage feast*]. . . . With dozens of eyes focused on us every minute of the day
> I couldn't afford to let my real feelings be seen [*like the tamed Kate of act 5?*].[15]

Sam Taylor may have been right in his appraisal of what audiences wanted
from Pickford—nor can we know whether, working with another director
under different circumstances, she could have given a markedly more compelling performance. Later, Pickford's memories would themselves become
suspect.[16] But whether her self-taming narrative be regarded as fact or ex-
aggeration, her very manner of retelling it illustrates the power of that
story.

Without doubt, these were not the conditions to inspire great acting.
Pickford was already at a disadvantage in holding her own opposite the
swashbuckling Fairbanks. In the midst of an affair with the woman who
would become his next wife, Fairbanks/Petruchio was humiliating Pick-
ford/Kate off as well as on the set—this from a man who had been notoriously possessive, controlling his wife's movements. Pickford was not an im-

15. Mary Pickford, *Sunshine and Shadow* (Garden City, NY, 1955), 311–12; italicized annota-
tions mine.
16. The 2005 *American Experience* biography of Pickford, broadcast on PBS, emphasized her
family's fondness for alcohol and her increasing reclusiveness, while omitting any reference to
Fairbanks's marital shortcomings. Other accounts do give credence to many of Pickford's
claims.

partial observer, but even if read skeptically her tale of the traumas of playing Kate (and, to invoke Hodgdon's pun, play[K]ating Fairbanks in "real life") resonates with other actresses' accounts of performing in *Shrew*.[17] When she says the "set was tense with unspoken thoughts" and her opinions were dismissed, one thinks of Kate's textual silences. Recalling her own performance with the Royal Shakespeare Company, actress Fiona Shaw remarks, "Along comes a man to tame the noisy one. And for almost five acts we never hear her speak."[18] Pickford concludes: "The making of that film was my finish. My confidence was completely shattered, and I was never again at ease before the camera or microphone. All the assurance of *Coquette* was gone." The explicit contrast with her first talkie, for which she won an Academy Award, confirms that Pickford was not simply a victim of the technological change in her chosen medium, as were so many other silent stars; rather, her demise was involved (at least in her own mind) with *The Taming of the Shrew* in particular.[19] Internalizing the play's dynamics of female conformity, Pickford gave up on her unpopular attempt to be something other than America's Sweetheart, soon abandoning her career as an actress.

Yet this is not the entire story. When Pickford retired from the screen, she went on to become a successful behind-the-scenes businesswoman. She was even involved in the 1966 reissue of this film. Nor does the film itself carry traces of her abjection (although it does reveal Fairbanks's casualness with lines).[20] Indeed, it is notable precisely for the unusual equity in screen time and importance allowed Kate and Petruchio, unlike the silents that preceded it and many versions to follow. Instead of telling the story primarily from Petruchio's perspective, this film provides a precedent for later film alterations and additions that "fill in" Kate's perspective, from Zeffirelli's sixties *Shrew* to Gil Junger's *10 Things I Hate About You*. And while credit was given

17. Fiona Shaw remarks upon her parallelism with Kate as an actress alone among men in rehearsal, a gendered isolation that men don't (often) experience: "the sense of the terribly clouded confusion that overwhelms you when you are the only woman around. That was Kate's position, and it was mine: she in that mad marriage, me in rehearsal. Men, together, sometimes speak a funny language"; Rutter, *Clamorous Voices*, xvii. Pickford's portrait of marriage to Fairbanks includes obsessive jealousy, inequity, and confinement; see especially 216, 308.

18. Rutter, *Clamorous Voices*, 1.

19. Pickford made two more films, *Kiki* and *Secrets*, before retiring from acting.

20. Fairbanks's most memorably bungled line: "I come to wive in Padua—wealthily." The rerelease (with seven minutes edited out by Matty Kemp) tries to re-pair the stars through the editor's introductory captions; while conceding Pickford's difficulties during filming, the commentary claims that "in retrospect [she] has said that Fairbanks was magnificent in the final version." The laserdisc version attributes the 1966 copyright to Mary Pickford, Corp. and Douglas Fairbanks Jr. On the importance of female spectators and male performing bodies in early cinema (including reference to Fairbanks), see the article by Gaylyn Studlar.

162   to Sam Taylor (and should have gone to David Garrick as well) for "additional dialogue,"[21] clearly it was Pickford's star power that encouraged and allowed her to play a more knowing, in-control Kate during the last scenes of the film.

Pickford's equal time came through added speeches and close-ups creating a sense of her ongoing agency, albeit in solitude and often in silence. Kate and Petruchio have dueling whips, dueling dialogues, and dueling eavesdropping scenes. Katherine gets the last lines of the 2.1 "wooing scene" as a soliloquy (a form she lacks in Shakespeare), echoing Garrick's eighteenth-century *Catharine and Petruchio*—a tamed text that, in Michael Dobson's words, mutes "the outright feudal masculinism of *The Taming of the Shrew* in favour of guardedly egalitarian, and specifically private, contemporary versions of sympathy and domestic virtue":[22]

> Look to your seat, Petruchio, or I'll throw you.
> Katherine shall tame this haggard or if she fails,
> I'll tie up her tongue and pare down her nails.

The animal-taming metaphors that Shakespeare gave to Petruchio are now balanced, referring both to Katherine and her rider/falcon. Though the scene begins with a phallic parody in which Katherine visually assesses their respective whips—and retreats upon discovering Petruchio's length—here and elsewhere Pickford challenges the Fairbanks mystique. Rather than claim "shame" alone while she waits on her wedding day, she also claims his body movements: she mocks his arm gestures, swaggering, and incessant "ha ha." Crucially, she sustains her confidence even at Petruchio's "taming school." Rather than being thoroughly entrapped and policed once in his home (as the play's relocation suggests), this Kate has the freedom to overhear her husband's "rehearsal" of his taming method—a soliloquy made to appear all the sillier by being addressed to his dog. Watching from the landing above, she gains the superior position mentally as well as physically and is ready for him. The result? A man who began by leaping over walls ends up reeling in pain from her blow to his head with a joint stool.

Yet, although speech and visuals collude in deconstructing Petruchio's dominance, they nonetheless confirm one anxiety basic to *Shrew* that has not

---

21. The rerelease does not include the supposedly notorious credit "with additional dialogue by Sam Taylor," instead announcing "Adaptation and Direction by Sam Taylor." Although line cuts and variation from "pure" Shakespeare aroused criticism in 1929, the development of film theory and practice would confirm the necessity of true screen adaptation—including line cuts, of course, but also the discovery of visual equivalences and distinctly filmic motifs.

22. Dobson, *Making*, 190.

gone away: fear, masked as mockery, of "a woman's tongue." And while it is   163
indisputable that in Elizabethan England such mockery of female speech
signified a deeper anxiety about independent female sexuality, on the basis
of filmed *Shrews* we may well wonder whether the twentieth century hasn't
inverted priorities. At least on the silver screen, sexuality is just fine (so long
as the games eventually lead to heterosexual union and marriage) — but the
tongue is another matter. Katherina as embodied by Pickford (and later,
Elizabeth Taylor) has a voice ranging far from King Lear's ideal of
"soft, / Gentle, and low," and it is the implacability of that organ that inspires
true bemusement and fear among the men who surround her (as Sam Taylor's vocal coaching likewise attests).

Thus Petruchio's initial speech of braggadocio experience, emphasizing
sound as well as threat ("Have I not heard lions roar?" [1.2.191ff.]), becomes the frame for his own corollary "taming." At his initial announcement
of fearlessness, Bianca's suitors Gremio and Hortensio begin exchanging
winks behind his back, and the scene reaches its climax of skeptical detach-
ment from Petruchio/Fairbanks when he breaks down in near hysteria at the
prospect of fearing "a woman's tongue." While the others humor him, his
weary servant Grumio shakes his head sadly, knowingly. Then, in a remarkable dissolve shot, we continue to hear Fairbanks' laughing reiteration of "a
woman's tongue" as the scene shifts to the unhappy face of Baptista, being
chastised by Katherina in her first abrasive speech of the film (earlier we
only saw her, and briefly). The director's edit thus mocks Petruchio's confident dismissiveness even as it upholds the narrative's logical implication that
he plays a necessary role in taming Katherina's dangerous tongue.

The next sequence confirms Katherina's threatening power when (bor-
rowing a line from Gremio's part) she curses and thereby silences her father:
"you may go to the devil's dam." Granted, this is a comic threat, and Pickford's established image and vocal quality undermine its force: a knowing
movie audience could find in the disjunction between this angry character
and their beloved Mary another source of humor. It remains true, however,
that Taylor's direction repeatedly calls particular attention to the distress
this female speaker causes men, giving an edge (and hence more interest) to
the comedy. Moreover, the potential of the star's persona to "tame" her own
voice befits the film's larger trajectory and representation of Kate's agency.
For this *Shrew*'s narrative solution comes not through Petruchio's superior
bravery, cunning, or strength, a point made obvious when he again mur-
murs, "Have I not heard lions' roar?" while Kate cradles his wounded head:
it is her own tenderness of heart, spurred by having hurt him and revealed
his vulnerability, that ultimately tames her speech. Thus ironizing and then

164   undoing the harsh control of Shakespeare's Petruchio, the film moves directly to her notorious public speech in medias res—with her standing above Petruchio's wounded pate—and culminates in a visual rather than verbal form of insubordination: her famous wink.

That wink is clearly directed to her sister: with an openness that will not return onscreen until the teen spinoff *10 Things I Hate About You,* this Katherine's final assertion of ("proper") voice does not require the disappearance or rejection of Bianca but instead signals their alliance.[23] Bianca acknowledges it as such: behind patriarchal ventriloquizing remains a conspiracy of those "unspoken thoughts," a female subculture whose bond is confirmed rather than broken. Katherina may have changed the content of her speech, but she still sees more than her husband, sustaining a silent connection between her perspective and the filmmaker's own. In concert with the shift from an invulnerable Petruchio (current onstage and in the previous silent short films of *Shrew*) to a wounded one, the changes here preserve some space for female agency and suggest the grounds for a more fundamental change in what constitutes masculine attractiveness. This hardly presents a challenge to the social hierarchies of "Padua"—any more than Pickford's retreat to an off-screen career challenged the public's developmentally-arrested nubile image of her—but it does evade complete closure or "capture." It does so, moreover, in quite a different manner from that of the Shakespearean text, in which irony comes (if it comes) through deferral of any female presence at all, the absence of closure for the (male-dominated) frame story, or a "private" subtext that involves Katherina with her husband solely and completely. Instead, this first major screen Kate eludes the relentlessness of her narrative by playing with the visual apparatus, making the camera her much-needed friend.

Although this filmic conclusion may present only an illusion of self-creation from a subaltern position within the story (Kate the sneaky servant rather than Stepford wife of patriarchy), the representation nevertheless conveys a change in modernity's order of things that embraces yet goes beyond the new technologies of sound and film alone. This *Shrew* hints that

---

23. This crucial distinction is lost when Pickford's wink is conflated with the more common stage and screen habit: see, for example the conclusions of the 1950 Westinghouse and 1956 Hallmark Hall of Fame *Shrew*s, each of which ends with a wink at the television viewer (see my "Shrew," 125–26). Jonathan Miller, who is dismissive of such winks, presumes all are so aimed. Russell Jackson, "Shakespeare's Comedies on Film," in *Shakespeare and the Moving Image: The Plays on Film and Television,* ed. Anthony Davies and Stanley Wells (Cambridge, UK, 1994), 112, and more recently Carol Rutter, "Looking at Shakespeare's Women on Film," in *The Cambridge Companion to Shakespeare on Film,* ed. Russell Jackson (Cambridge, UK, 2000), have noted the distinctive Pickford wink and its importance; my reading follows Jackson's at several points.

there is no longer sufficient pleasure to be had in watching a simply obedient puppet-wife; indeed, it acknowledges that its target audience will want the feisty woman to win. Being a "kitten" and taming the voice are the costs, but the benefit is the last look and the position of superior knowledge. Like the five hundred pounds a year and room of her own that Woolf's narrator confesses to be of more immediate benefit to her than was winning the vote, here the political remains only personal—but given the shaping role of such personal relations in women's lives, it is no less pleasurable for that. Perhaps it is not quite so surprising to find Pickford herself overseeing the rerelease of this once-painful collaboration at the moment when another star couple was following in her footsteps. Even if the actress/wife experienced and recollected playing the shrew as a rite of abjection, her Kate remains distant from that reality. The performance remains a testimonial to Pickford's star power, her own choices and (ironically) limitations as an actress, and—strained as their relations might have been—the writing, shooting, and editing of her United Artists collaborators.

The 1929 *Taming of the Shrew* works by keeping things light and "comic" in the classic sense: characters are presented as caricatures and are cheerfully resilient rather than scarred by painful experiences en route to their happy ending. In this regard, the PickFair version of a private triumph thus excludes another—perhaps the key—dimension of twentieth-century Western modernity: the perception of depth and disturbing contradictions within the human psyche. To find pleasure in that murky element, we must turn elsewhere.

A Shrew Is Being Beaten: Fantasizing Pain as Pleasure

In 1918, the British Parliament passed the Representation of the People Act granting the vote to married women, women householders, and women university graduates aged thirty and over;[24] in 1920, the Nineteenth Amendment to the United States Constitution was ratified and became law. During the year between them, Sigmund Freud wrote "A Child Is Being Beaten." British and American women were well on their way toward being regarded as full-fledged adults, both as citizens and complicated subjects. Yet centuries of infantilization and violent subjugation would not disappear

---

24. Full equality with male voters came to Britain in 1928, the year before the PickFair *Shrew*.

166   overnight, and old assumptions continue to manifest themselves in fact and fantasy, on celluloid and inside brains. In beginning this chapter by juxtaposing Sir Philip Sidney's "comic" 1580s poem of babes and shrews with an allusion to Freud's clinical essay, I want to suggest the way in which these texts of symbolic violence elude simple definition and placement, be it historical, psychological, or artistic, even as those frameworks create and illuminate them. Is Kate to be regarded as a rebellious adult, an unruly child, a female-boy fantasy object, or all three at once? Is physical violence or psychic reprogramming more disturbing, and what pleasures can be derived from witnessing either? In the interplay between a seemingly timeless thematic (a shrew is being beaten) and its specific temporal manifestations, spaces of possibility or closure, of questioning or necessity, emerge.

And in this regard, Freud's "A Child Is Being Beaten" provides a fascinating heuristic document—illustrating both the psychological vocabulary used by moderns in analyzing *The Taming of the Shrew* and also the way we transform events into meaningful narratives. This essay is indeed the comedy's uncanny double. For Freud too creates a tripartite story implicated within its historical moment of composition while gesturing beyond it. Moreover, in aspiring to understand his patients' socially aberrant forms of pleasurable fantasy as a deterministic narrative, Freud anticipates many modern directors and actors who labor to mold Shakespeare's playscript into a similarly plausible and satisfying whole. By contrast, other modern collaborators emphasize the potential for disruption and dynamic change in *Shrew* even as they too attempt to register psychological depth. The disposition of viewers toward these structural and motivational choices has much to do with whether they in turn will take pleasure from the narrative dimension of diverse screen *Shrew*s.

Freud begins by remarking on the surprising frequency of patients who "have indulged in the phantasy: 'A child is being beaten'" and proceeds to transform this image or vignette into his tripartite developmental narrative.[25] Focusing on data derived from four female patients (although he

---

25. Sigmund Freud, "'A Child Is Being Beaten': A Contribution to the Study of the Origin of Sexual Perversions" (1919), in *The Standard Edition of the Complete Psychological Works of Sigmund Freud*, trans. and ed. James Strachey, vol. 17 (London, 1955), 179: all citations refer to this edition. This essay was written the same year as "The 'Uncanny.'" I do not attempt to address the clinical usefulness of (or massive bibliography on) this essay and Freud's theories of masochism more generally, being interested primarily in its rhetoric, narrative structure, and resemblances to *Shrew*. Nevertheless, remarks of Gilles Deleuze and Félix Guattari overlap with my own in finding a "disquieting strangeness" in Freud's essay: "Never was the paternal theme less visible, and yet never was it affirmed with as much passion and resolution. The imperialism of Oedipus is founded here on an absence"; *Anti-Oedipus: Capitalism and Schizophrenia* (Minneapolis, 1983), 56. Laura Mulvey, Studlar, and many other feminist film scholars have been interested in the masochistic representation of females in film more generally, and Hodg-

draws on two male cases as well at times), he quickly clarifies that this fantasy with "feelings of pleasure attached to it" in no way carried over into enjoyment of actual beatings of children at school, and that it prompted feelings of shame and guilt as well (179–80). He then generates a theory to account for this disjunction and to integrate the fantasy within his normative model of oedipal desire. Freud sketches three stages through which his patient has passed, emphasizing what his analysis adds to the fantasizer's otherwise quite limited vision. Whereas the analysand enters with no image of the beater, in dialogue with Freud "this indeterminate grown-up person becomes recognizable clearly and unambiguously as the (girl's) *father*" (nowhere in the essay does Freud reveal that his own daughter Anna is one of the four patients under discussion; she would later describe the fantasy in her own words). Soon he adds—with the coy concession that he is "betraying a great deal" in advance—that in stage 1 "My father is beating the child *whom I hate*" (185).

This initial stage being translated easily into sibling rivalry, Freud moves to what is *not* the next stage from the analysand's perspective (that will be stage 3, in which other children are being beaten by a teacher or other adult, interpreted by Freud as a father-surrogate). Here is the centerpiece for the analyst:

> It is true that the person beating remains the same (that is, the father); but the child who is beaten has been changed into another one and is now invariably the child producing the phantasy. . . . Now, therefore, the wording runs: "*I am being beaten by my father.*" It is of an unmistakably masochistic character.
>
> This second phase is the most important and the most momentous of all. But we may say of it in a certain sense that it has never had a real existence. It is never remembered, it has never succeeded in becoming conscious. It is a construction of analysis, but it is no less a necessity on that account. (185)

As a result of this "construction," Freud is able to modify what might look like a simply aggressive movement from sibling rivalry to schoolyard competition and substitute for it a complicated oedipal drama complete with recognitions and reversals from (potential) sadism to masochism and then to a complicated synthesis. Now the third phase which "seems to have become sadistic once more" (190) can be reconceived: "only the *form* of the phantasy is sadistic; the satisfaction which is derived from it is masochistic" (191).

Although gender does not provide clear evidence early on, the constructed second phase allows Freud to interpret stage 3 as enacting a gen-

---

don draws on their work, but I am unaware of any direct connection having been made between this essay and *Shrew*.

168   dered, sex-based drama: now the "unspecified children who are being beaten by the teacher are, after all, nothing more than substitutes for the child itself," and as these children are "almost invariably boys," the fantasy testifies to a post-oedipal "masculinity complex" among the female fantasizers; they want to be boys and "for that reason the whipping-boys who represent them are boys too" (191; given the sample of four, that modifier "almost" accompanying "invariably" might give one pause). Later in the essay it turns out that the only "evidence" for the masochistic phase 2 derives from a male patient: thus what "as a rule" remains unconscious in females has been extrapolated from one male case. Explaining this requires Freud to make another gendered distinction: the male must exert more labor in repressing masochism (since he has had to change his sexuality from active to passive, whereas the female's sexuality by this point is presumed to be passive), hence his repressions are less successful and more easily recalled to consciousness. The result is to stress latent masochism and passivity even among females who appear to take pleasure in fantasies of active violence.

What is striking about this essay is less the internal inconsistency than the remarkable transparency of Freud's own desire to make the data "fit" his model. Perhaps paradoxically, this very transparency creates a more compelling account. Freud early on concedes several limits to the analysis. The "discovery of some constant relation between the sex of the child producing the phantasy and that of the child that was being beaten, was never established" (181). Nor was the person doing the beating ever identifiable for the analysand without analytic prompting. Most disturbing for Freud is his awareness that he cannot even correlate this fantasy with other symptoms (it accompanies cases of hysteria and obsessional neurosis—but also mere indecisiveness and possibly no clinical problems at all): "In the mind of the analytic physician, it is true, there remains an uneasy suspicion that this is not a final solution of the problem. He is obliged to admit to himself that to a great extent these phantasies subsist apart from the rest of the content of a neurosis, and find no proper place in its structure." Yet he adds, with breathtaking frankness, that he "only too willingly" puts "to one side" such impressions (183).

Seemingly more damaging still is the gap between what he defines as his method and what he goes on to describe: "strictly considered," Freud declares therapy to be "genuine psycho-analysis only when it has succeeded in removing the amnesia which conceals from the adult his knowledge of his childhood from its beginning (that is, from about the second to the fifth year)" (183)—and yet he proceeds to posit a masochistic middle stage of this fantasy that none the female patients recall, and further asserts that it is the crucial stage. He justifies the exception to his own rule (obliquely and in advance) by appealing to the youth of his scientific field and the greater need for theory than therapeutic success at his own historical moment. Such winning tentativeness will of course not be characteristic of some of Freud's more avid followers or indeed of himself elsewhere and on other points, his theories often being presented as dehistoricized truths and as a result becoming more vulnerable to accusations of cultural blindness and inaccuracy. Even here, he moves swiftly from arguing in one sentence that the fantasy "may quite well" have an "earlier history" to claiming in the next that "[t]his suspicion is confirmed by analysis" (184). Little wonder, then, that the masochistic stage 2, a stage that does not exist "in a certain sense"—that is, in Freud's own sense of psychoanalysis "strictly considered"—can quickly become "a necessity."

"A Child Is Being Beaten" brilliantly captures the struggle between openness and necessity involved in creating a narrative, even if Freud's authorial admissions make the ultimate shape of his interpretation no less deterministic. By the end of the essay, he confidently uses his account as a means of discrediting his own professional competitors (Wilhelm Fliess, Alfred Adler) and as a potentially plausible sociological explanation for litigiousness ("People who harbour phantasies of this kind develop a special sensitiveness and irritability towards anyone they can include in the class of fathers" [195]). The essay demonstrates the power of developmental narrative to transform—not merely connect—images and anecdotes, thereby making discrete analysis of anecdotes (that chestnut of New Historicist methodology) seem, if not trivial, then misleading. It also calls attention to the gaps between (a disturbingly) pleasurable fantasy and everyday violence and to the complexity of distinguishing agency from victimization within the desiring mind.

In the process, Freud produces and grounds a method of interpretation and a set of assumptions that reappear in certain twentieth-century iterations of *The Taming of the Shrew* with surprising exactitude. Once recognized, this resemblance is not hard to explain. Arguably, both "A Child Is Being Beaten" and *The Taming of the Shrew* focus on females who may or may not need help; present a three-stage narrative that brings them into conformity; and represent a male protagonist able to transform a potentially sadistic—and at least aggressively violent—female subject into a fundamentally masochistic one. But also like Petruchio (and many modern artistic and scholarly collaborators), Freud shows remarkable assurance—or presumption—in filling in the blanks of women's silences and reinterpreting their words as befits his desires.

To clarify what is at issue, let me substantiate my claim that *The Taming of the Shrew* shares with Freud's essay a tripartite narrative. For the resemblance is not obvious at the surface level: Freud is not here interpreting psychology directly through the lens of Shakespeare (arguably the case in his relation to *Hamlet* or *The Merchant of Venice*, for example). The three-stage design is in fact less adequate to describe Shakespeare's play in its entirety (considering its induction scenes and multiple unspecified locales) than to describe its modern screen representations. But the combination of Freud and film brings out what is certainly implicit in the main plot of Katherina and Petruchio and its involvement with the rest of the play. In simplest form, Kate's story can be summarized as a shrew farce (acts 1–3, in Padua), followed by wife taming (act 4, at Petruchio's home and on the road), culminating in the public performance of obedience (act 5, again in Padua). Kate's journey out from and back to Padua, then, serves to "re-move" her geographically and, more important, tonally, with the undefined space and location of her journey allowing two breaks between.

That space of the "in-between" can be glossed over in the interest of various binaries, in a manner comparable to interpretation of other dual-locale Shakespearean comedies such as *A Midsummer Night's Dream* or *The Merchant of Venice*: thus one can see Padua/Petruchio's house as representing town/country, mercantile/domestic, female/male (that last unconventional twist on conventional hierarchies being "corrected," at least conceptually, by the conclusion). But the "in-between"—signified above in familiar deconstructive mode by the slash mark—can also suggest a gap in and of performance, calling attention to the disjunctiveness and arbitrariness with which one narrative segment is made to follow from another. It thereby throws into question, like a Brechtian rejoinder to Aristotle, the cause-and-effect "necessity" of this five-act drama. Nor does such questioning seem far-fetched in a play that allows a solitary Petruchio to query the audience and thus this very plot (in a conscious parody of the wedding ceremony he earlier disordered): "He that knows better how to tame a shrew, / Now let him speak. Tis charity to show" (4.1.180). The audience is challenged to contemplate (even as its presumed silence implicates it in) the transformation of distinct and varied acts of aggression into a seamless teleological sequence. The labor and artifice involved in such linear constructions, and the possibility of alternative choices or sequences, all hover in the air.

If one comes to *The Taming of the Shrew* fresh from Freud, however, minding the gaps can only mean filling them in and justifying them—like a realist actor, changing silence into subtext. The farcical violence of Shakespeare's story likewise lends itself to modern reinterpretation as a symptom

of more consistent characterological troubles, simmering below the surface
throughout: indeed, the play now looks very much like a tripartite beating
fantasy, shifting with Kate's location. Her first violent outburst, for instance,
resonates elegantly with "A Child Is Being Beaten": she turns against the
younger sister who has supplanted her not only in the eyes of suitors but in
her own father's affections. Thus when Baptista rescues a bound and abused
Bianca from Katherine, the elder daughter complains that "[s]he is your
treasure" and vows revenge (most immediately exacted offstage upon suitor
Hortensio, over whose head she breaks a lute [2.1.32]). Her next act of violence takes place within the larger struggle of her first encounter with Petruchio (which I shall henceforth call the "wooing" scene without the quotation
marks that should be understood to surround that word). Criticism has
made the most of Kate's slap; even Frances E. Dolan's recent introduction
represents this as the only definitive act of violence between them that we
view.[26] While it is true that Petruchio withholds himself from a "cuff" in ret-
ribution (2.1.216), it nevertheless seems overly literal to ignore his other
forms of physical restraint — of her, not toward her. For example, stage performers often motivate his line "Why does the world report that Kate doth
limp?" (2.1.245) with some form of foot stomping or injury prior — although
films tend to "tame" that too.[27] More to the point, Petruchio works indi-
rectly, using horses or (as Dolan notes) intimidating Kate as a witness to his
violence against other subordinates (4.1). To the extent that the wooing
scene contains a fantasy, then, it is of an "equal" tussle rather than of an
even temporary gendered reversal of power: Kate's slap is outdone by
Petruchio's various forms of bravado but neither emerges fully "tamed" of
their wild ways or words. Hence the scene's enduring delightfulness as a
fantasy performance.

Stage 2 of *Shrew*'s narrative, considered in terms of this type of indirect violence, accords well with Freud's fantasy shift to masochism. At Petruchio's

26. Shakespeare, *Taming*, 14–19.
27. Kate injures herself in the PickFair and Zeffirelli films, while Petruchio grabs and retains
one shoe in *Kiss Me, Petruchio*. By contrast, the CBC video of a Stratford, Ontario, stage production has Petruchio kick Kate in the shins and then grin as he recites the line. To notice only
Kate's violence collaborates with the play's representational sexism, since only Kate's violence
is regarded as demanding "correction" through taming. Two "gentlemen" (Petruchio, Vincen-
tio) physically attack their unruly servants (Grumio, Biondello) in the first and last acts respectively, and Gremio, Curtis, and Grumio all remark that Petruchio is "more shrew than she" in
this regard, not only beating his own servants but also knocking down a priest at the altar and
throwing sops at the sexton (4.1.61–62; see also 3.2.145ff.). Granting this, Kate's explosions of
violence onstage are the ones perceived as a challenge to the status quo, and are therefore unlike the "normative" background violence of servant beating or (in Freud's essay) corporal punishment by teachers.

172   house, Kate becomes the beaten child of Freud's construction. The transitional scene comes on her wedding day, just prior to leaving Padua: after her angry "No shame but mine" speech (consistent with her shrew-farce indignation at indignity—and Freudian primary narcissism), she changes gear and exits weeping, "Would Katherine had never seen him though!" (3.2.8, 26). Although her father mixes sympathy with a reminder to all that she is still a "shrew," her tears signal the beginning of a vulnerable Katherine, weakened by affection itself. As if to confirm the change, her next onstage humiliation, after the absurd wedding ceremony, results from her attempt to "entreat" rather than threaten her husband. She soon learns that showing love is trickier and riskier than showing pride. "Content" to accept her pleading, Petruchio nevertheless proceeds to re-move her hence:

> *Katherina* Now if you love me, stay.
>
> *Petruchio*   Grumio, my horse.
>
>   (3.2.204)

Setting the pattern for the next act of the drama in his own home, Petruchio now overrides her wishes and gentler requests; he will continue thus, long after her "sadistic" stage is over. As in Freud's construction, if Kate has any agency or desire to be treated this way, it must be deeply repressed indeed. As Kate is taunted for showing concern for servants as well as traces of her own will, the "pleasure" of section 2 demands audience collusion with Petruchio, premised on the idea that Kate is "getting her own back" for her earlier behavior—the kind of reversed punishment Freud imagines his female patients inflicting upon themselves out of shame and guilt. Her only act of staged violence at Petruchio's occurs in 4.3, when she lashes out at Grumio's mockery as he withholds food; it is a pathetic last gasp of Kate-as-beater though, and even symbolically makes her a shadow not of her former self but of her servant-beating "master."

    Given the murkiness of Kate's "pleasure" and agency in stage 2, it makes sense that the final stage of *Shrew* involves only symbolic forms of beating—the interpretation of which remains a source of great debate. If the metaphorical beating victims in the wager scene are the men who lose their money, Kate is not taking pleasure in their pain (as the Freudian scenario would posit). Rather, she focuses on a new version of her oft-reiterated "shame," directed no longer at male neglect or mistreatment but rather at her own sex, for being irrationally blind to their own "weakness."[28] Rhetorically, Kate is now beating a larger category of "women" including but no

---

28. One may in fact interpret her repeated professions of "shame" as a transitional signal at the conclusion of each stage, her "shame" at apparently being jilted (3.2.8) and being

longer limited to her sister Bianca, and in so doing she might be deemed to fit both a sixteenth-century and a Freudian definition of healthy maturity (though she talks more than ever). She claims a space that is not overtly masochistic by appearing to act obediently of her own volition and at the expense of her female rivals; but here one might well echo Freud that "only the *form* of the phantasy is sadistic; the satisfaction which is derived from it is masochistic."

The Doctor Is In: Pathologizing Kate

Whether Jonathan Miller ever thought consciously about "A Child Is Being Beaten" when directing *The Taming of the Shrew*, I cannot say—but his version for the BBC-Time/Life television series provides the example par excellence of a production informed by the interpretative method of Dr. Freud. Miller certainly thought of Kate as a patient in a developmental narrative and justified Petruchio's treatment of her through analogies with child therapy. Fiona Shaw, who played Katherina in the stage production Miller subsequently directed along some of the same conceptual lines as his BBC *Shrew*, makes it explicit: of Petruchio's disorienting Kate and denying her words during what I have dubbed "stage 2," she reports, "Jonathan says that's what doctors do with aggressive children. I think he's translating the 'taming' of the shrew into 'therapy.' "[29] For the well-trained, highly learned (and once very funny) Dr. Miller, Kate becomes the object of clinical inquiry, a diseased mind. And through analogies with a Freudian analyst, Shakespeare's farcical shrew tamer gets a new lease on life—and a new, modern authority—as "Dr. Petruchio." Yet this director's comments also betray the problems of attempting to combine such a psychoanalytic conception with historicism when reproducing *The Taming of the Shrew*—of trying both to acknowledge and gloss over the centuries that have intervened since Philip Sidney could sardonically "joke" that "shrewd girls must be beaten." The result is an interpretation in which both the (timeless) psyche and (Reformation) history are enlisted in the services of a deterministic master-narrative, sacrificing the more obvious pleasures of playing and the play-text's own gaps in order to create a paean to social control, sixteenth- and twentieth-century style.

"ashamed" to kiss in the street (5.1.118) climaxing in her grand "stage 3" speech of socially "proper" shame ("I am ashamed that women are so simple" [5.2.165]).

29. Shaw conveys Miller's view that Kate is "like many children who are unloved. I have a slight problem with that because I don't think Kate is a child"; Rutter, *Clamorous Voices*, 6.

174   Miller begins taming Shakespeare's disorderly text by removing the Sly frame and presenting Petruchio as Kate's analyst as well as her destined husband, deliberate throughout the three stages and always with a consistent goal in mind. In this, the director could build on a theatrical tradition that goes back to Garrick, who made Petruchio more thoughtful than the Shakespearean blusterer who arrives in Padua knocking his servant soundly as he comes to "wive it wealthily" ("if wealthily then happily" to "one rich enough to be Petruchio's wife," should we need reminding [1.2.62, 70–71]). However, such character alterations are usually designed to emphasize greater similarity and equity between the leading couple: by imagining Petruchio to be more "eligible" from the start, and then altering or ironizing the latter two segments of the narrative, a modified *Shrew* can become a semifarcical, semiromantic comedy. What distinguishes Miller's version, by contrast, is his overt willingness to emphasize gender *in*equity and use the Shakespearean text and its historical times as justification for doing so. At the same time, he draws on — indeed, needs — psychoanalytic schemas to make the taming of Kate seem something other than a simple replication or restoration of reactionary misogyny. Therefore, he argues, Petruchio sees Kate's "symptoms of unhappiness, and, by behaving badly, he gives Kate back an image of herself" — that is, she is taught to see an objectification of her inadequate, improper self.[30] Ironically, Miller represents this emphasis on a "serious" Petruchio and the domestication of a psychologically troubled Kate as itself unruly, an act of his own rebellion against what he deems stale and inappropriate theatrical traditions. These supposedly dominant practices can be contained in two words: farce and feminism.

     At first glance, farce seems an odd target for a director who came to fame through the rollicking revue *Beyond the Fringe* and who cast John Cleese as Petruchio on the basis of his work with *Monty Python*. But of course those shows combined the dead parrot with the Proustian reference, "saucy Worcester" with G. E. Moore's philosophy: it is the reduction of farcical British stagings to a "mandarin," eyebrow-raised distance from anything of substance that galls Miller.[31] That, plus the desire to surprise and claim this *Shrew* as his own. Thus even Cleese, fresh from *Fawlty Towers* and famous for silly walks, performs for the most part naturalistically, understatedly, and

30. Jonathan Miller, *Subsequent Performances* (New York, 1986), 122. Meryl Streep also internalizes this logic: "I think he's mad . . . then I see what he's doing . . . he's being me, as I was" (this, despite his being "mad" from the moment he meets her, and violent even before). See Fineman ("Turning") on this mirroring position of women in patriarchy.

31. The "mandarin" reference hearkens back to John Barton's 1960 *Shrew* with Peter O'Toole and Peggy Ashcroft, though it could also describe the 1956 U.S. televised version with Maurice Evans and Lilli Palmer.

sometimes almost inaudibly (albeit letting out the occasional chicken cluck).
To counter expectations is a basic element of comedy, of course—and what
could be more unexpected than that? Cleese's rendering of Petruchio as a
man thoughtfully bemused by the follies of this world did indeed win critical
praise, and the difference of Miller's production (while by no means so well
received) made it memorable.[32] For two men accustomed to getting laughs,
perhaps a greater pleasure came in being taken seriously—even if doffing
their comic straitjackets came at the expense of putting Sarah Badel (as
Kate) into a not so comic one.[33]

Which leads to the trickier of Miller's f-words. Although he might seem
prescient in dismissing what would later be called "p.c." (as distinct from
politically conservative) concerns, Miller's stated argument against contemporary productions that rethink gender roles was that they overvalue our
own time. In his 1986 volume *Subsequent Performances,* he associates this de-
based form of "relevant" theater with Joseph Papp specifically and Papp's
country more generally: "The American vice is seen most clearly in a play
like *The Taming of the Shrew* which suddenly becomes a test case for feminism. Petruchio is portrayed as a typical male chauvinist pig, and Katherina
as a bullied victim."[34] With dazzling sleight of hand, Miller turns any acknowledgment that Shakespeare's Katherine is indeed "bullied" (even if
confirmed by John Fletcher's 1611 companion play *The Tamer Tamed*) into
an anachronistic sign of modern self-indulgence (even as Miller himself employs the modern discourse of therapy). Perhaps Miller's displacement of
feminism to America was an act of wishful thinking—or professional com-
petitiveness worthy of Freud—given that the RSC's theatrical versions directed by Michael Bogdanov (1978) and Di Trevis (1985) were far more
"feminist" than the one Papp produced for television (*Kiss Me, Petruchio,* discussed below). Still, Miller's remarks would appeal to those who enjoy confirming their intellectual superiority through contrasts with a homogenized
United States. Even more usefully for his purposes, he invokes a general-
ized model of historicism: attributing a dominant, if not uniform, ideology to
a particular time and place. It is this way of reading history—as a control-

---

32. On Miller's production, see also J. C. Bulman and H. R. Coursen, eds., *Shakespeare on
Television* (Hanover, NH, 1988), 76–81, 266 ff.; Graham Holderness, ed., *The Shakespeare Myth*
(Manchester, UK, 1988), 195–202; Irene Dash, review, *Shakespeare on Film Newsletter* 5, no. 2
(1981): 7 ff.; Worthen, *Shakespeare and the Authority of Performance,* 58; and Stanley Wells, "Television Shakespeare," *Shakespeare Quarterly* 33 (1982): 261–77. Susan Willis's imputation that U.S.
boredom with the BBC series derived from ignorance of British conventions is not persuasive;
The BBC Shakespeare Plays: Making the Televised Canon (Chapel Hill, 1991). The show was broadcast on the BBC in June 1980 and in the United States in January 1981.
33. In light of the previous chapter's analysis of *Mrs. Dalloway,* it is consoling to see Sarah
Badel's "resurrection" as Sally Seton, Lady Rosseter in the 1997 film.
34. Miller, *Subsequent Performances,* 119.

176   ling narrative determining the parameters of (in)appropriate thought, rather than as a contentious space of debate among interested parties—that informs Miller's understanding of the sixteenth century as well as the twentieth; and it in turn provides the other guiding principle for his screen *Shrew*.[35]

When the program was originally broadcast on the BBC in 1980, the gendered implications of Miller's choices extended beyond the fiction into the postperformance discussion. It excluded the leading actress and instead presented Miller and Cleese, emphasizing the male bond between director/doctor and actor/protégé: like the production itself, this interview obliterates Katherine's shrew/d perspective on events.[36] Avoiding a debate between the sexes, Miller instead invokes the historical studies of Michael Walzer and Lawrence Stone to connect *Shrew* with the rise of (radical) Protestantism and its household effects. As he would later write, "If you represent Petruchio as a serious man, you can take and develop the implications of lines such as 'To me she's married, not unto my clothes' and 'tis the mind that makes the body rich' and see how consistent these are with a Puritan view. The alternative is to present Petruchio as a flamboyant bully."[37] To acknowledge bullying is again out of the question for Miller: therefore, on the basis of two of Petruchio's most sententious lines—decontextualized from the social humiliation of Kate that each involves—he constructs an unironic identification throughout between Petruchio and the growing Puritan squirearchy of Shakespeare's day. Even granting the questionable specifics chosen to ground an entire narrative, the "fit" here between text and historical context depends on a vast simplification of the times. As Herbert Coursen points out, sixteenth-century commonplaces did not function as unchallenged doctrine, especially when transferred to that locus of unusual "liberty" and license, the public playhouse; and if one group was anathema and antithetical to the culture that sustained professional theater, it was the Puritans.[38] Moreover, Scott McMillin remarks, "This is a skimpy version of the Puritan doctrine of marriage. . . . There is nothing about starving them

35. Miller's chastisement appears inconsistent if this "American vice" is indeed a symptom of its historical moment, when the dominant ideology is self-absorption; his own manner of applying history would seem to make the desire to be relevant less a vice than a necessary evil.
36. The U.S. video of the BBC/Time-Life TV production does not contain this interview, so I rely on the accounts by Dash, Coursen, Holderness (*Shakespeare in Performance*) and others, as well as Miller's own book.
37. Miller, *Subsequent Performances*, 121.
38. Herbert Coursen, *Shakespearean Performance as Interpretation* (Wilmington, 1990), 57–58. The Puritans were the butt of jokes in Ben Jonson's and Thomas Middleton's comedies—and Shakespeare's own *Twelfth Night* as well.

into submission."[39] And most importantly, adds Graham Holderness, Miller's understanding of the family unit itself is not historicized but rather "applied retrospectively to dramatization of Renaissance values."[40] Ultimately, Miller's selective application of historicism appears more of a learned license or "cover" for a psychoanalytic interpretation very much rooted in twentieth-century male subjectivity: it allows him to sustain his self-image as a "socialist liberal" whose art avoids "politics" even as he dramatizes a celebration of benign patriarchalism.[41]

Miller's practice in directing *Shrew* nevertheless contradicts his own theory of theatrical vitality, the more subtle and flexible hermeneutics he puts forth generally in writing about director's theater. In the introduction to *Subsequent Performances*, he argues that an artistic work must be allowed a changing "afterlife," adaptable to its times. He criticizes those who believe "the text has some sort of quantum of intrinsic meaning that can be identified with something elusive called 'the intention' of the author which can be discovered and restored in an ideal performance. . . . [T]his critical notion is fraught with contradictions." Such a view would ossify the text and lead to moribund productions; if we were "bound by the one canonical production" from Shakespeare's time, theater would become a museum or church, and "audiences would be subtly changed into congregations, witnesses of a rite rather than spectators of a play."[42] All the more ironic, then, that the BBC *Shrew* ends by not so subtly transforming its cast into a psalm-singing congregation, the tableau resembling a museum diorama of sixteenth-century life.[43] Tellingly, this is the sole instance when Miller's scholarly research on Puritanism directly intrudes, the rest of the production being set within an artist's version of the Renaissance (using designs from Vermeer and Serlio) but in no obvious way representing that sect. Unlike his consistently applied psychoanalytic model, then, the director's historical concept becomes obvi-

39. Scott McMillin, "The Moon in the Morning and the Sun at Night: Perversity and the BBC Shakespeare," in Bulman and Coursen, *Shakespeare on Television*, 76–81.

40. Graham Holderness, *Shakespeare in Performance: The Taming of the Shrew* (New York, 1989), 106.

41. In other words, gender trouble undoes the "logic" of historical difference. In an interview with Holderness (*Shakespeare Myth*, 200ff.), Miller asserts that his emphasis on the family and the domestic supplants a political interpretation—a position that would barely be plausible in a nineteenth-century world of separate spheres, much less the twentieth (or sixteenth) century. It is utterly at odds with the Puritan ideology he purports to be reproducing. On the ideological contentiousness of *Shrew* in its own day, see also the article by Thomas Moisan.

42. Miller, *Subsequent Performances*, 20, 54.

43. Willis (*BBC Shakespeare Plays*, 110–11) suggests that Miller's intellectual historicism was a strategy for coping with an unconducive philosophy of timeless productions imposed by Time-Life and the BBC; however, his book six years later confirms these opinions.

178   ous only during stage 3, its impact being simply to distance the tricky politics of the conclusion by making us "witnesses of a rite." And in this distancing, Miller's method is ultimately not very different from that "mandarin"
theatrical tradition he castigates: he just identifies with Petruchio's perspective, and indeed with the position of the patriarch, more overtly and less
playfully than usual.

   Keeping gender trouble at bay by pathologizing the shrew certainly removes much of the active pleasure of the stage 1 shrew farce: Sarah Badel's
Katherina looks positively nauseous during her first scene, screams and sobs
violently with Bianca (so much for the pleasures of beating a sibling), and
hyperventilates during the wooing sequence. What in early modern terms
would have been conceived of as social and behavioral rebellion, common
enough to warrant the dismissive label of "shrew" (if one wishes to be historicist), becomes developmental and attitudinal deviancy, with the further
implication that Katherine should not only accept but be grateful for her
reinterpellation into the system that disciplines her.[44] By replacing the textual motivation for Petruchio (money) with a moral one that makes him
more nobly disinterested, it also becomes possible for Miller to say that
Katherine "begins to realize that someone who is prepared to devote so
much time to her must be prompted by affection." In this production where
maturity and personhood are gifts from the male analyst to the female patient, any claim to distinctive subjectivity that Kate might be making
through her disorderly behavior disappears, invisible to both the director
and the societal order he "restores" onstage (narratologically and historically). Badel's laughter is hysterical, her anger uncontrollable. True to
Miller's vision, her Katherine becomes attractive only when the "fountain
moved" is reduced to still waters: "Kate's final speech is rather moving as it
is an agreement to abide by the rules within a framework in which it is possible to enjoy close affection."[45] One may assume it is we in the modern audience who are being "moved" here, despite Miller's earlier claim to be viewing a different time as if it were a "foreign country." When pleasure derives
from a narrative line so unequivocally moralized and uncontested, however,

44. This description is obviously indebted to the theoretical work of de Lauretis and Foucault's *Discipline and Punish*.
   45. Miller, *Subsequent Performances*, 122. For one not admitting he has constructed a paean to
male privilege, Miller's judgment of Bianca in the last scene is particularly jarring: "In contrast
to Kate's rather graceful submission, the disagreeable behavior of her sister Bianca [pointing
out her husband's folly in betting on her obedience] becomes repugnant and you can see that
the real shrew is Bianca and not Katherine at all" (ibid.). While the need of commentators to
find "the real shrew" somewhere is not (alas) unusual, this comment certainly undermines the
credibility of Miller's psychiatric model for "diagnosing" shrews: so it's really about female obedience, after all.

shrews are not the only ones who may find themselves resisting such disciplinary education. Even Miller's unconventional camera work for television, emphasizing spatial depth by presenting action "behind" the familiar close-ups and half-body shots, adds to the sense of tunnel vision. His filming accords with his belief that only through Petruchio's "tuition" (versus "taming") has Kate "become spiritually and morally visible in a way that she was not when simply perceived as a scold."[46] Midway through her big speech, Badel's Kate sits down. Thus, in her moment of social triumph, she is still physically confined, now literally "by" her husband, on a bench at table in a fairly humble interior; if she moves us, it is not by moving. Those less enamored of normative social hierarchy—who might imagine a female subject resisting paternalistic affection for reasons other than arrested development—may find this small-screen version more claustrophobic than comic. Time to think outside the box.

The Pleasures of Petruchio

While Jonathan Miller's production appears "content" with its conclusion, few other screen *Shrew*s rest here. Realizing at some level that either Petruchio or the patriarchal social organization is still beating Kate even as she ventriloquizes their desires, filmmakers do tend to ironize or modify stage 3 somehow. Among the favorite strategies is the reconception of Kate as part of a still unconventional—for which read "exceptionally sexy"—couple, so that Kate-and-Petruchio can beat the normative culture in a happy ending that does not appear to hinge on gendered self-loathing. This solution, like Miller's, remains embedded in a psychologically realist idea of character and narrative coherence. But for it to work with the script as given, modern actors must use the gaps, the "in-between" spaces in Shakespeare's story a bit more imaginatively: within the shifts and silences that disrupt textual ideology, Kate must get "her" man.

The most creative use of video simultaneously to dramatize and finesse these tensions between continuity and disruption may be *Kiss Me, Petruchio*, a 1981 pastiche of scenes, backstage moments, and audience responses from the New York Shakespeare Festival's summer production in Central Park, originally broadcast on PBS.[47] Although Miller associates feminism with the United States, this nearly contemporary Papp production shows no such signs; indeed, in their interspersed commentary, the stars Meryl Streep and

46. Ibid., 119, 122.
47. The show aired on 7 January 1981; I work from the 1982 Films Incorporated Video release.

180   Raúl Juliá share Miller's desire to deny that the play is or should be about feminism.[48] But the video makers (led by director Christopher Dixon) know the matter is not so simple and use jump cuts and the words of audience members to "frame" the actors, even as the actors get to provide a frame for bits of their *Shrew*. Not only do the camerawork and editing disrupt the linear narrative but they also undermine the leads' Stanislavskian method of character justification. At the same time, much of the editing serves to "contain" objections to the shrew-taming story by demonstrating the pleasure *The Taming of the Shrew* provides for its actors and audience, outdoors on a summer night. And after the self-conscious visual and narrative containment of Miller's *Shrew*, *Kiss Me, Petruchio* can indeed seem like a breath of fresh air. The video's pleasures emanate from maniacal energy on the stage and the fractious debates created beyond it—all concentrated on the boastful, erotic body of Juliá's Petruchio.

And what better body could there be? Juliá says as much of himself/Petruchio in comments shifting between the third and first person: Petruchio "is very self-confident . . . [and] feels he can make the best husband in the world, and he *can*, too. . . . I'm here to make money . . . and any father [with the money for a dowry], he's getting a good bargain." Refreshingly frank about following the text's given motivation for his courtship, Juliá is utterly comfortable in his role, effectively creating a sexual Svengali whose behavior is credited as fully reasonable. That "a good husband" means a good sexual partner seems fairly self-evident: erotic desire, leading automatically to true love, provides the quick fix to explain away the societal dynamics of power. His body becomes both the rationale and the compensation for Kate's taming, offsetting the potential offensiveness of his words from the start. Thus the video begins with Petruchio performing his post-wedding assertion of ownership ("she is my goods, my chattel . . . my ox, my ass [pun performed], my anything" [3.2.219ff.])—the only speech presented twice, out of and in context. The actors soon reveal that we should not have been identifying with the audience members who boo (Streep, patronizing in her anguished sincerity: "They boo because they don't *see* it")—or if we do, our protest has already been as domesticated as Katherine herself (Juliá, more compelling because cheerfully unabashed: "I love it when they boo and hiss Petruchio, because that means Petruchio is making them feel something"). By showing the actors' backstage solidarity with one an-

---

48. Wilford Leach directed this *Taming of the Shrew*, but Papp's Public Theater produced it, and Papp introduces the video, which emphasizes his proprietary control; Leach is not mentioned or interviewed.

other, these offstage cuts consistently try to deflect potential criticism, as do many camera pans of a happy audience: we are shown women laughing at the end of the wooing scene as Petruchio sits on Katherine announcing that she will become as "conformable as other household Kates." Still, the boos are there, and a few audience exchanges confirm that the play can divide as well as amuse—one smug would-be Petruchio, for instance, making the cartooning onstage seem a little less funny:

> *She* I think that it's such a silly subject, I mean nowadays anyway . . . who can believe that?
>
> *He* But it's not silly.
>
> *She* [*exasperated*] Well, it *is* silly. I can't believe how many people were applauding when he did that "my horse, my ass" bit.
>
> *He* [*smiling to the interviewer*] That scene is a good representation of what our relationship strives to be. [*He chuckles; she glances at him with disgust.*]

It is Juliá's particular physicality and panache that must paper over such gender gaps.

Hence the emphasis on the act 2 wooing scene as well, presented in a manner that allows Petruchio to dominate playfully and seductively rather than with overt violence. He tickles, carries, and encloses Katherine, but only she actually slaps, hits, and spits; nevertheless, she is the one left breathless lying on the stage, whereas he retains his poise and humor. When Kate strikes Petruchio to "try" whether he is a gentleman, he does not flinch. When she spits in his face in response to his request to "kiss me, Kate," he pauses and then delightedly licks his lips to ingest her spittle. Although Streep parries with bawdry of her own (looking into his lap to "see a crab" [2.1.225]), she is clearly outmatched by a superior force whose apparent invulnerability to abuse or opposition matches that of Douglas Fairbanks in the corresponding PickFair scene. The tide of inevitability that Petruchio predicts is thus fulfilled through Juliá's gleeful embodiment, and Kate's resistance seems not only doomed but counterintuitive.

Where this version differs crucially from PickFair's, however, is in keeping Petruchio as invulnerable as the text created him in the latter acts. And because the two leading actors are commenting during their performance run, they try to make sense of this narrative line. As a result, *Kiss Me, Petruchio* shares with Jonathan Miller's BBC *Shrew* the project of justifying Petruchio to a modern world—though here, less as intellectual therapist than as perfect hunk. Despite Miller's comments, it is not in the overarching gender ideology but in the particulars of desirable masculinity—what will bring

182   Kate (and the audience) pleasure—that these two television shows diverge. In physical style more generally, Papp's production likewise announces its distance from Miller's British broadcast. The New York cast rejects British accents, rhythms, and bodily constraint for a looser, brasher, characteristically "American" style, as does the camera. Thus Raúl Juliá recalls his own stylistic development: "Some people think that the only way to do Shakespeare is to do it like the British do it because the British have the answer to Shakespeare, so I would imitate [them] [and he does]"; but then he realized that "I could bring myself to it, I could bring my own culture, my own Puerto Rican background, my own Spanish culture, my own rhythms, my own feelings to Shakespeare; because Shakespeare is too big, Shakespeare is too big to put into one little way of doing him." Unlike the English Romantic model of a transcendent Bard, this is a multicultural, Whitmanesque Shakespeare, containing multitudes—albeit the immediate consequence here may just be to assert that celebrations of male dominance can be transnational and transhistorical.

    Adopting the character's perspective adds another layer of comedy to Juliá's backstage remarks: this model of modern machismo never appears to doubt himself. But Streep's replication of Katherina's "conversion"—seeing the world through the eyes of patriarchy—is more bizarre. Her backstage comments are almost desperate in tone, frustrated that others don't understand the simple goodness of her story and Petruchio's love. The usually intelligent actress appears willfully obtuse about the unequal power relations and asymmetrical changes that the plot demands.[49] Nor can this be explained entirely as consistent Method acting or the attempt to create an authentic throughline, since she never exerts equivalent energy or imagination to understand Katherine's identity as "shrew." Instead, in the early scenes she performs a cartoon catalogue of "masculine" antisocial behavior (stomping on flowers, "pumping up" for a fight), without any of the nuanced psychological realism she accords to the reformed Katherine. She therein collaborates not only with her Petruchio but with the inherited logic of patriarchy. In a way, Streep's Kate fits Freud's "A Child Is Being Beaten" even better than does Miller's *Shrew*, since her stage 1 captures the simplicity of a child's anger, whereas her later scenes, interspersed with her back-

---

49. One moment she compares her sacrifice to maternal love for a baby, the next he is her master. When Juliá good-naturedly tries to mimic her words and assert he too shows such love, he gets caught up by language: "she is my master—but not my master." She laughingly suggests "mistress" without noting the modern ironies or the play's comparable lack of parallelism regarding power relations. Streep does have a few more assured ripostes, as when she points out that Kate did not "choose to fast" (Juliá having tried to diminish his stage 2 domination by remarking that some people fast for their health!).

stage comments, convey a tortuous mixture of righteousness and distur-
bance. Stylistically, this is another way to finesse the narrative fracture, the
"in-between" that changes shrew farce into wife taming: because (on the
video, at least) she has no developed "self" early on to sacrifice, her transformation into obedient wife arguably involves more overt gain, at less cost,
than were she to imagine the untamed Kate as a multidimensional adult. Yet
the Method too exacts a political price.

The video accentuates the shift by allowing Streep's voiceovers to explain
the latter part of the play, whereas Juliá's comments dominate earlier: as in
Shrew, she "earns" a voice worth listening to through her taming. During the
tailor scene, as we watch Kate sitting with torn gown in hand, Streep asserts,
"Really what matters is that they have an incredible passion and love; it's not
something that Katherine admits to right away but it does provide the source
of her change." The visual image might seem to mock her motivation, but if
so it will not be reinforced through framing commentary: the sequence
merely records the gap between what the playtext shows and what modern
psychologically trained actors create as a worthy subtext, leaving interpretation to the audience's discretion. As Katherine then gives the tattered dress
to Petruchio in silence, Streep's voiceover makes the leap to his perspective:
"What Petruchio does is say I'm going to take responsibility for you, and I'm
going to try to change you *for your better*, make you as great as you can be."
She thereby legitimates what she never directly confronts, the inequity of
behavioral reformation and her infantilization within this putatively mutual
scene of "incredible" passion and love. Both actors seem to presume
throughout that Petruchio does not need to be (could not be?) improved.

Streep's exasperated attempts to portray the later stages of the narrative
as consistent romantic growth hearken back to the deterministic reading
method of Freud and Miller, even as her earlier shift from silly to serious in
acting style reminds us of the gaps in that reading method. Despite her obvious labors, *Kiss Me, Petruchio* instead leaves one wondering about the
downside of certain forms of actor training, and agreeing with Ann Thompson that "we can no longer treat *The Shrew* as a straightforward comedy but
must redefine it as a problem play in Ernest Schanzer's sense: . . . 'so that
uncertain and divided responses to it in the minds of the audience are possible and even probable.' "[50] And indeed, the video's last word goes to such
an audience member, a woman who feels "very ambiguous" and who considers *Shrew* "a fantasy that is dangerous for men." Visually, however, the video
ends by emphasizing this production's "solution" to the problem: Petruchio
as sexual prize. As if to defuse the societal effects of her final speech, Kate

50. Shakespeare, *The Taming of the Shrew* (Cambridge, 1979), 41.

184 begins to drag him off to bed during the play's last lines, and he consents to exit in her direction during the curtain call. The last image is Streep patting Juliá's ass as they exit: she may be his "ass, my anything," but here "equality" means his ass is also hers. Just as his dynamism and the camera's location jumps have upstaged narrative determinism throughout the show, in the end erotic desire trumps psychological consistency as the name of (superficially depoliticized) pleasure.

This reverse pat does represent gender progress of a sort, at least when compared with another condensed *Shrew* once broadcast, courtesy of Westinghouse. In 1950, Charlton Heston was both a bottom slapper and smugly invincible:[51] three decades later, the sexual revolution allows Kate the sexual gesture, even as Petruchio remains triumphant. More importantly, here the language of love has another layer, captured by the documentary camera: when the actors say their story happens "all within a context of love," they are referring not just to the represented love story they discover in Shakespeare's text but to the theater in the park, performed for free by skillful and dedicated actors. As theater in the past two decades has become progressively more expensive and less successful in capturing young audiences (who have plenty of other media and distractions to choose from), this love has sometimes come to seem a rarified thing indeed. To the extent that *Kiss Me, Petruchio* (and PBS) recognized the need to "sell" theater to television viewers, and to the extent that the video captures the kinetic energy of live performance (more poignant after the early death of Juliá and of the stage director Wilford Leach), perhaps it does, after all, discover and preserve a bit of transcendent love. There's life in the old story yet.

Camera Knows Best

What if, returning to the gaps and slippages within both Freud's essay and *Shrew*, a director reconsidered Kate's story more as a dynamically changing multistage fantasy rather than as a simple linear narrative? While the handheld documentary style of *Kiss Me, Petruchio* adds to the show's summery air of improvisatory playfulness, its openness makes all the more jarring its leading actress's committed collaboration with a self-sacrificial plot. But more successfully and on a grander scale, the most famous screen version of *The Taming of the Shrew* used the camera to reveal new possibilities in

51. Broadcast date June 5, 1950, as Westinghouse Studio One Theater, directed by Paul Nickell. Available through USA Yesteryear video (1987).

disjunctions and silences, ones that would complicate the narrative more fundamentally—and qualify another remarkable self-taming attempt by its notoriously unruly female star.[52]

Director Franco Zeffirelli recalls Elizabeth Taylor's decision to perform Kate's final speech "straight," to the surprise of both himself and her co-star husband Richard Burton:

> The usual trick is for the actress to wink at the audience. . . . Amazingly, Liz did nothing of the kind; she played it straight . . . and she meant it.
>
> Full of that Welsh passion, Richard was deeply moved. I saw him wipe away a tear. "All right, my girl, I wish you'd put that into practice."
>
> She looked him straight in the eye. "Of course, I can't say it in words like that, but my heart is there."[53]

The sentimentality of the scene, complete with Taylor's professed inability to deploy the powers of language, epitomizes one facet of this *Shrew*, which presents Katherina with far more pathos—and agency—than most other "straight" *Shrew*s. On camera, she makes the speech not only without a wink but also without any lead-in request from Petruchio/Burton. Instead, she launches into her chastisement immediately upon reentering the banquet hall when called for, dragging along the other women on her own initiative. The result is to naturalize Katherine's assertions as her own spontaneous feelings, flamed by her newly internalized indignation at unruly wives and her empathy for her husband's unexpressed desires. And in a sense, this seems true to the actress's own wifely desires. It also presents yet one more instance in which an intelligent performer labors to fit herself into this difficult role, a collaborative process most disturbing to modern (or at least progressive) sensibilities precisely when it succeeds.

But Zeffirelli, willing to indulge the sentimental on so many occasions, ends the film with a visual twist that plays against the emotion that has characterized Kate's story: after finally achieving a much-delayed, uniquely passionate kiss, Petruchio turns to find his wife gone, and the farcical game to contain her is afoot once more. In this dynamic motion between emotional involvement and filmic distance, with the camera changing its perspective and sympathies repeatedly, Zeffirelli's *The Taming of the Shrew* (1967) manages to use rather than paper over narrative gaps and silences. More remarkable still, it does not abandon the Shakespearean text or idealize Petruchio in order to create its pleasures—pleasures that have grown rather than

52. Directed by Franco Zeffirelli, and produced by FAI/Royal Films/Columbia Pictures. 1967.

53. Franco Zeffirelli, *Zeffirelli* (New York, 1986), 216.

186   withered with age. As a result, it is not a film from which one can grab a
single scene, add an anecdote or two, and come to an adequate judgment of
the whole (as Deborah Cartmell does, dismissively).[54] Instead, like Freud's
essay considered critically, this is a work that both contains and overgoes its
narrative, in the process revealing more than first meets the eye.

Although most people assume this film was spurred by Richard Burton's
theatrical experience performing Shakespeare and by the tempestuous Bur-
ton/Taylor marriage, it was Zeffirelli's brainchild, born of his desire to film
"a stage classic. So Dennis [van Thal, his London agent] began to come up
with suggestions from Shakespeare and that triggered off the idea of remaking the Douglas Fairbanks/Mary Pickford version of *The Taming of the Shrew*,
which I thought could be done amusingly with a couple like Mastroianni
and Loren." One imagines it could, but a truly Italian *Shrew* was not what his
agent wanted: he "insisted I think about British actors if I really intended to
make my début in movies as a director of international stature."[55] Zeffirelli
was both delighted and surprised when Taylor and Burton were willing to
join (and co-produce). As both his thoughts on casting and his conscious desire to "remake" the PickFair *Shrew* attest, Zeffirelli entered the project with
more equitable visions of a fair fight in mind, rather than a defense of Petruchio's dominance. And indeed, the choice made by director and actor to
present a predominantly boorish, hard-drinking Petruchio caused many
male critics to protest when the film was released. Some also complained
about the busy sets and fast-paced camerawork—the latter, influenced by
'60s pop culture, now seeming merely a harbinger of things to come and one
reason the film continues to "work."[56] It was through this unexpected mix of
fresh elements with old farce that Zeffirelli managed to create what was undoubtedly a popular success as well as the most layered and lasting of cinematic *Shrew*s.

Perhaps most surprising, amidst the comic gaiety of Zeffirelli's Padua, is
his empathetic treatment of the socially isolated, which creates a close alliance between "the shrew" and the camera for much of the movie. Repeatedly, we watch Kate thinking in private moments, and in key instances the

54. Deborah Cartmell, "Franco Zeffirelli and Shakespeare," in Jackson, *Cambridge Companion to Shakespeare on Film*, 213–14. See also Robert Hapgood's more nuanced comments. Russell
Jackson anticipates my emphasis on Taylor's performance, noting that when in a locked room
her looks "suggest stiller, deeper waters"; "Shakespeare's Comedies," 114. For other perceptive
analyses, see Tori Haring-Smith; Jack J. Jorgens; and William Van Watson.
55. Zeffirelli, *Zeffirelli*, 200.
56. Zeffirelli's favorite film that year was *Help!* He hired disaffected Roman *capelloni* (long-
haired ones) as university students (Holderness, *Shakespeare in Performance*, 55–56) and cast
Beatles-film veteran Victor Spinetti as Hortensio.

camera even adopts her visual perspective. To regard this solely as a result of Taylor's stardom, her famed violet eyes, and her beauty as a screen image (important though they be) is inadequate; it fails to recognize the clarity and patterning of perspective play throughout the film, and—crucially—how it changes. I have discussed elsewhere the biographical contexts (including illegitimacy) that encouraged Zeffirelli's cross-gender identification with Kate:[57] here, I want to emphasize how his fundamentally filmic choices both sustain and revise *Shrew*'s narrative line.

This film truly fulfills actress Paola Dionosetti's observation that "Kate has eyes everywhere."[58] In the stage 1 shrew farce, the camerawork not only accentuates Taylor's feminine beauty but also mimics her positionality. We first "see" Kate as a single watchful eye, above the street action. We view her viewing, just as the camera will soon pause to contemplate her when she pauses to contemplate, and will conclude scenes when she concludes her sequence of emotions and decision making. Indeed, it is Bianca's usurpation of Katherine's one-eyed viewing position at the window that initiates Kate's violent attack on her sister: in an amusing parody of horror film technique, the camera's perspective actually unites with Kate's own gaze, and the next sequence shows a screaming, cowering Bianca unable to escape "us." But the vicarious thrills and potential sadism here have little to do with sibling rivalry: in this encounter between a pleasant young thing and the inimitable Miss Taylor, ingénues are put on warning not to compete with a movie star in her prime. She is very much an adult already, and a thinking one as well. The film's visual affinity with Taylor's Kate soon returns in a more meditative key, after the extended wooing scene. The camera joins her looking out from a darkened room, instead of moving on with the men (and the scripted narrative) exiting the hall: gone is their Bianca-bartering scene, leaving Katherine's solitary smile to complete this segment of the story. Thus the last word is an ambiguous image, leaving her "meaning" open to interpretation.

Before this smile, however, and even within one of the most energetic, over-the-(roof)top sequences in Shakespeare film history, the flip side of being a viewer/image begins to emerge: the lens reveals the isolation that characterizes Kate's position as a woman in Paduan society. Even if on occasion she manages to scream and lash out, her role as alienated watcher pro-

---

57. See my "Shrew," Zeffirelli's autobiography, and Peter S. Donaldson, *Shakespearean Films/Shakespearean Directors* (Boston, 1990), esp. 147–52, on the family dynamic in his other films. Zeffirelli found Taylor easier to direct than Burton, precisely because of her inexperience with Shakespeare and lack of established mannerisms; no doubt this working relationship also contributed to their thematic collaboration.

58. Rutter, *Clamorous Voices*, 1.

188   vides a dynamic counterpoint to the farcical energy surrounding it and a
critical perspective on the financial preoccupations of the men. And by presenting Petruchio as such a material creature from the start, Zeffirelli allows
these camera shots to establish Kate's difference from him, as the movie's superior thinker.

In this choice, Zeffirelli not only retains but exploits one dimension of
Shakespeare's text that most modern *Shrew*s suppress: the importance of
money. Money motivates Petruchio from the start, and Burton's scruffy, ill-
mannered entrance makes his need for financial support entirely plausible.
But here Michael Hordern's Baptista is similarly driven in his treatment of
Katherina. He shrugs in obvious ignorance when Petruchio mentions his father (making the line that he is "known throughout all Italy" into a joke), but
when the suitor offers all his leases and lands upon Katherina's widowhood,
Baptista perks up, "knows" the father, and initiates the frenzied activity
leading to the wooing scene. Nor does Burton's Petruchio forget money
even during that active encounter, as an interpolated comment makes clear;
when he sees Katherina leap through a window to escape him, he mumbles
his fear of what he might lose: "my twenty thousand crowns."

To achieve the dowry that has motivated his suit, Shakespeare's Petruchio
must obtain "the special thing. . . . That is, her love" which her father regards as "all in all." Nevertheless, as in the parallel wooing scene in *Henry V*,
it is not clear that Katherine's consent is actually required: Petruchio's reply,
"Why, that is nothing" (2.1.124–26), indicates not only his confidence that
he will make her yield but also how little evidence it takes for the men of
Padua to decide she has been won. (The sexual puns, in concert with Petruchio's subsequent "kidnapping" of the bride, might also remind those familiar with Elizabethan customs that sexual abductions did on not so rare occasions make a "special thing"—legal marriage—out of "nothing.") Both in the
play and in much scholarship, Katherine's own last words of the act, her refusal to marry ("I'll see thee hanged on Sunday first!" [2.1.292]), are dismissed and supplanted by Petruchio's brazen assertion, "'tis incredible to
believe / How much she loves me" (2.1.299–300)—directly contrary to what
he knows of her "private" behavior, and consistent with his decision to invert the truth verbally in order to get his way. Indeed, to transform *Shrew*
into a romantic comedy one needs to make Petruchio a truth teller in spite of
himself or else motivate an even more "incredible" reversal later (having
Katherine fall for him when he deprives her of all forms of ownership). Neither subtext is psychologically implausible in a world of contorted desires
and socially endorsed abjection, as the BBC and Papp productions demonstrate, but to say so removes much of the lightheartedness associated with

farcical comedy and may make a viewer feel like an uneasy collaborator. The
dominantly realist conventions of filmmaking with its close-up attention to
"real" women aggravates the difficulty in this regard. Once the complexities
of real-life psyches intrude, slapstick can look distressingly like domestic violence, and the problem of Kate's consent is not evaded but compounded.

Zeffirelli's wooing scene "solution" is twofold, at least: not only does he
add visual reflection and smiles to complicate (or compli[K]ate?) the textual
assertions of both leads, but he also creates an extended farcical chase to defuse the scene's focus. Thus he uses the distinctive resources of his newly
adopted medium (swift cuts linking multiple locations, the priority of images
over words) to "re-place" rather than deny the text. Petruchio's relentless
verbal enclosure of Katherine becomes an unpredictable game in which neither words nor rooms can effectively enclose them: both their bodies hurtle
precariously through space, walls, and ceilings. Petruchio does show his
bullish persistence, using his head to raise the trapdoor upon which Kate
heavily sits—thereby giving extra visual punch to the bawdry of his "tongue
in your tail" retort. But the camera's giddy tracking from room to courtyard
to barn to roof and back down through roof to wool bin conveys most effectively the film's ongoing message that an errant Kate may eventually be
trapped but not easily tamed. Indeed, reordering and supplementing the
text's repartee, Kate gets to rebut Petruchio's "Will you, nill you, I will marry
you" by yelling, "I'd rather die!" before appearing to jump out the window.[59]

Nevertheless, the concluding shots of the wooing also testify to the trickiness of interpreting this film in any simple way. The violence until now has
been presented as farce, in which bodies can fall through roofs and be
thwacked with sticks (as Kate pounds Petruchio's head) without much effect. At this point, however, another filmic allusion hints at a more disturbing vision and signals Katherine's diminishing power: as Petruchio pins her
down in the wool bin, the stick is forced across her throat, while the camera
angling down upon her head and heaving breast comes close to alignment
with Petruchio's perspective of dominance. This eroticized shot puts a struggling Katherina in the position of countless female victims in movie thrillers,
cowering with a knife at the throat. Whereas with Bianca, Kate took the unseen killer/monster position, her placement now shifts: she succumbs to the
superior force of Petruchio and in doing so becomes an eroticized object of
violence (see figure 4). As her tearful collapse on the floor and retreat on her

---

59. She thereby fills in a key moment of textual silence; Fiona Shaw has remarked that
Katherine's part is particularly difficult because of "moments when Kate's story simply isn't
tenable, because she doesn't have the lines" (Rutter, *Clamorous Voices*, xxv).

Figure 4. Kate (Elizabeth Taylor) as victim in Franco Zeffirelli's *The Taming of the Shrew*

wounded leg soon confirm, she has been revealed to be vulnerable in both body and spirit. Even this ungallant Petruchio seems abashed at the change, gently helping her to her feet. The private wooing thus concludes uneasily, signaling his slightly uncomfortable power and her abjection, rather than her consent. While he will still bluster his farewells in front of the other men, a wall—literally—stands between himself and Kate; thus at the line "kiss me, Kate" he can merely blow the farewell kiss to the isolated woman in her darkened retreat. Only after he is gone does she slowly smile, perhaps allowing an admission of pleasure in what has transpired, or anticipating new opportunities for wedded power or another battle, or simply appreciating that someone would address as well as contest her. One cannot be entirely sure how to read this woman's silence, but the sentimental music and lingering close-up imply that our sympathy and interest should remain with her— while her softened look, just as importantly, announces that she has not been (merely) beaten.

If her smile (and location) temporarily does encourage us to see Kate as a closet masochist or desperate desirer, the impression recedes in the subsequent sequence. On her wedding day, the material concerns of the men upstage romantic wishes, confirming not her deviancy but the crassness of societal norms. Zeffirelli imagines indignities beyond her announced "shame," including a trio of added sequences that leave her silenced and alone in the crowd. First Katherine, humiliated by Petruchio's loud, late arrival, tries to yell "I will *not*" at the altar in response to her wedding vows—yet another sign that she is not so desirous as to submit at any price. But Petruchio literally stops her mouth in an uneroticized kiss before the last word, at which point the entire congregation celebrates. Then in a second shot Katherine is shown half buried by the crowd congratulating Petruchio, as she desperately and vainly yells "no" and "father." As after the wooing, the last sequence shifts mood and appears to have moved on: while a musical consort plays, Katherine graciously thanks her guests at the reception. This, however, is merely the prelude to her witnessing, beyond another door frame, the handshake and transfer of dowry funds from father to new husband, an action confirming her isolation as well as her sale. She stands silently gazing from outside the space of a more orderly transaction than the one that took place in church. This aggregation of isolating moments, which highlight the culture's traffic in women, works in concert with that undercurrent of violence and the shifting camera perspective to create a more interesting reflection on the female subject. Even here she has a solo moment of thought and (limited) choice to complete the episode and signal the difference to come in stage 2. After Petruchio's blustering exit by horse, she pauses on her donkey's back at Padua's gate, the quintessential liminal location. Looking forward and backward, she recognizes that neither prospect—her father's home or Petruchio's home—holds much promise. Her pregnant pause before deciding to spur forward clearly marks the "in-between," challenging narrative necessity.

Having mixed farce and finesse in Padua, however, Zeffirelli must still confront stage 2, potentially all the more daunting given his earlier representation. Since the film has just confirmed that Kate is isolated and ill-treated rather than somehow desirous of ill-treatment, how can he make her stay in Petruchio's house a source of pleasure? At first, the patterns of the shrew farce continue: she strikes back at Petruchio and then appears angry or sad at the results. In this the camera remains her ally: she is seen last in the freshly dramatized travel sequence (in which Kate actively schemes to intercept the other riders, rather than merely suffering under a horse as in Grumio's textual account), and she gets both the nuptial bed and the last image on her wedding night. But the end of the bed scene, like the end of the wooing scene, signals a change to come—and this time the change will effectively "tame" Petruchio as well as her own anger. Pretending to be more inviting as they awkwardly get ready for bed, Katherine instead pulls out the warming pan and conks Petruchio on the head. Predictably, he rages and wrecks the bed before exiting, leaving Katherine alone again, sobbing in the unfamiliar space. As before, however, her expression begins to shift and a calculating smile slowly emerges. What is she thinking?

The answer comes next morning, and with it arrives new authority and control for Kate, even in the lion's den: she cleans house. It is easy enough to point out the limits of home improvement as a means to power, and to grant

192   that this is a patronizing as well as ideologically conservative "solution" (especially in the mid-1960s when the feminine mystique was being challenged).[60] Nevertheless, by drawing upon his own nostalgia and sense of al-
legiance to peasant life, Zeffirelli manages to make the change appear a
matter less of gender subordination than of social realignment, and hence
potentially more seductive; not only does Katherina remake herself as the
force of culture and domestic beauty in opposition to Petruchio's ruffian
masculinity but she does so through an alliance with the servants. She transforms the dusty barrenness of his bachelor farmhouse into a lively arcadian
villa, in which lady and grooms share featherdusters and wear similar home-
made clothes. Indeed, it is through this bond—this creation of a new social
order in which she appears benignly assured and he feels excluded—that
the film overturns the easy power politics of Shakespeare's act 4. Manual
labor brings un-Shakespearean pleasure, and images trump words. Shorn of
most of his soliloquy the night before, Burton's Petruchio has a rude awak-
ening that heralds the shift of control to, not from, Kate: *he* now becomes the
solitary watcher, left out or in the way. With the shift, moreover, he grows
more "real"; the buffoon becomes self-conscious and thoughtful in his Kate-
like silences. While Zeffirelli creates a domestic fantasy, his own idealized
vision of "home," sympathy goes to the latest outcast. Thus when Petruchio
destroys Kate's new clothes, he looks less like an assured taming master than
like a shrew himself, lashing out in desperation. The power of cinematic visuals and recontextualization contains the male dominance of his speeches,
even when he returns to Padua: uncomfortably isolated and focusing on his
drink at the banquet, he too waits anxiously, uncertainly, to see whether
Kate will come at his call.

   This pattern of sympathy for the vulnerable and excluded sentimentalizes
the story more thoroughly than does Taylor's particular, though consistent,
choice in the banquet scene. Her speech overtly boosts her husband's fragile
confidence and rewards him with social affirmation. At the same time, Kate's
early subjectivity, the will and mental energy that sustain her and bring her
a (politically suspect) form of social power, remains even as Zeffirelli's narrative shifts allow his empathy to embrace Petruchio as well (now quieter,
smarter, and sadder than before Kate started cleaning house). And because
we have already seen Katherina plotting, acting unexpectedly, and only afterward revealing her motives, Taylor's final "straight" delivery of her major
speech likewise benefits from that sense of anticipation and uncertainty:

   60. See my "Shrew" on the relationship with 1950s television *Shrew*s, as well as Zeffirelli's
autobiographical subtext here.

when Petruchio turns to find her gone, he experiences the surprise that we, filmically, have been trained to expect. The ironies are legion: the actress's unexpected choice of sincerity is overridden by the director, who sustains his own vision by crediting the character with more artfulness than the actress professes. Zeffirelli's perspective play, in and out of Kate's vantage point, makes obvious the shaping potential—and ironic open-endedness—of that other movie "subject," the camera. More socially progressive versions of *Shrew* struggle to equalize the battle of wills by showing Katherine in thought or by constructing visual matches. In Zeffirelli's film, the balance keeps shifting with his visual priorities and emotional sympathies, and these dynamic changes and contingent reversals avoid infantilizing or pathologizing Kate. Granted, there is none of the PickFair *Shrew*'s sisterly solidarity in this director's "remake": Taylor's Katherine is a woman interested in holding her own with the big boys, sharing their company. But like Pickford in her star power as well as in her love affairs with the camera and her co-star, Taylor takes command in Petruchio's private space and then makes the world her home.

The consequence is a far more radical remaking of masculinity than in *Kiss Me, Petruchio*: it is Petruchio's vulnerability, his likeness to the shrew herself not in violence but in abjection, that gains him favors. This is "equity" of a different color, reorienting the narrative not by ignoring its gendered power plays but by reevaluating the bases for a strong wedded bond. Revealing the moneyed boorishness of Padua's boys' world, Zeffirelli has Petruchio "grow up" (rather than regress à la Fairbanks) by becoming more vulnerable, more emotionally attuned, more quiet—dare I say it, more "feminine."[61] In desiring this Cleopatra, he becomes a very Antony. Queerer things have happened.

Thoroughly Modern Shrews

Shakespeare tamed his shrew, but the cinema brings her back alive and kicking. In classics such as *The Philadelphia Story* and *All About Eve*, two of

---

61. Infantilizing Petruchio (the husband as "just a boy") is not unusual, from Pickford cradling Fairbanks's bandaged head to the frame story of the *Moonlighting* parody (perhaps itself influenced by Mr. I. Magination). The American Conservatory Theater's (ACT) stage performance starring Marc Singer and Fredi Olster presents an even more emotionally vulnerable Petruchio combined with the physical strength and allure of Juliá: the result, within a broad *commedia dell'arte* production, is an energetic yet gently awkward performance unmatched before Heath Ledger (in *10 Things*). Because this is indeed a filmed staging, rather than a cinematic or designed-for-video *Shrew*, I do not discuss this (most easily enjoyed) *Shrew* recording.

194   Hollywood's strongest actresses in their strongest roles still get their stage 2 comeuppances—those masochistic moments in the middle that appear necessary in order to prove the bold woman is not in fact a monster. The true moral monsters like Eve Harrington do need a particularly odious man to recognize and tame them (and who better than a theater critic for that role?). But for the unruly heroines, the process has become a bit less obvious. When Margo Channing is "put in her place" (a stalled car instead of the Broadway stage), it happens through the guilty machinations of her putative best friend Karen—the revenge of the beaten sibling, one might say. Tracy Lord's nemesis is the heady Miss Pommery 1926 with an assist from almost all the men in her life: it takes a group effort to knock the goddess from her pedestal. Each learns her lesson and returns to the man she should have treated better all along.

     The pleasures of these films are manifold, and it is perhaps churlish to emphasize a few humiliating moments; or perhaps it is a reminder that the stories we grow up seeing one way often lose the simplicity of (some of) their pleasure with time and intertextual attention. Sometimes diachronic collaboration, be it with a particular Shakespeare text or with the ironic structures his works helped make conventional, can maintain attitudes we would prefer not to notice. To acknowledge the conservatism of class politics in *The Philadelphia Story* hardly erases the enjoyment of watching Cary Grant embody the suave ideal of manhood—though more and more students tell me they prefer Jimmy Stewart. A narrative logic that once seemed unimpeachable becomes open to question, its causal "necessity" arbitrary or even coercive. Thank goodness the men—always excepting the deliciously despicable Addison de Witt, as played by George Saunders—appear vulnerable too. (As Margo's eventual husband Bill concedes, "Everybody can't be Gregory Peck.") At the same time, perusing these familiar old tales with a critical eye on their narrative choices has its own pleasures: as with Zeffirelli's *Shrew*, a paradigm that once seemed more hegemonic and hence coercive (such as female power through housekeeping) becomes more amusing at a distance.

     The last cinematic version of *Shrew* released during the twentieth century knows times have changed and presents a modern world speaking its own rather than Shakespeare's language. *10 Things I Hate About You* (1999) also finds a new way to finesse the problems of collaborating with old gender roles: it makes its shrew neither an infant nor an adult woman but a teenager. Gaps and shifts in behavior, abnormal responses, and a wicked tongue all being the normal stuff of intelligent adolescence, Kat Stratford can look fearsome to her peers without intimidating a moviegoer too much. *10 Things* was one of the first attempts to use Shakespeare to make a movie popular with (even as it mocks popularity among) the high school crowd. Although only a loose spinoff, this jaunty little film, like its predecessor *Shrew*s, still grapples with the contrary impulses of reproducing Shakespeare (his story, his "spirit") and crafting a narrative amenable to its putatively enlightened postfeminist viewers.

On the one hand, Shakespeare has become a flexible enough figure to appeal to the rapping black English teacher and his feminist student nemesis as well as to the nerdy smart boy. Where the source story cannot be reformed adequately to fit this world, the film simply changes the story. Yet the female tongue of *Shrew* persists as a "terrorizing" threat even now, transforming the otherwise attractive, once popular Kat (Julia Stiles) into a "heinous bitch." Her insults and references to feminist literature are enough—along with reports of the occasional well-placed knee kick—to make the thought of a date with Kat a horror, inducing even the neediest high school misfits to scream, laugh, and flee. Like Petruchio, Patrick Verona is lured to court Kat by the offer of money, but new times require his reluctance in accepting the bribe, his ongoing discomfort, and finally his transformation of bribe into gift; thus he provides Kat with the guitar that can help her sustain her rebellious self-image even as she accepts interpellation into the traditional romance plot. Patrick's evolution from (seeming) bad boy to sensitive stud corresponds with the movement of the film as a whole, which gradually shifts perspective from lampooning its cartoonish caricatures (the a-v geek, the white Rastas, the Prada-loving Bianca) to humanizing them. Nor is this attitudinal shift, as in *Kiss Me, Petruchio*, a means to make inherited power hierarchies more palatable: in a generous, equitable extension of developmental narrative, Patrick, Bianca, Kat, and even the girls' father all "grow up" as the story progresses, as they learn to see (and reveal themselves) beyond farcical surfaces. To his own detriment, the Gremio/Hortensio surrogate, Joey—the male narcissist who works as a model and is thus rich enough to bribe Patrick—is the only major character left out of this re-viewing process.

The famous *Shrew* "wink" also returns in *10 Things*, but with gender-inverted hipness. Now it signals misguided sexual arrogance on the part of males: first Patrick tries winking at Kat (prior to his sentimental education), and Joey reiterates the gesture after inviting Bianca to a party—but at himself, in a hallway mirror. Joey's self-involved wink epitomizes his complacent delusion throughout the story, for it follows fast upon his unwitting rev-

196   elation of his limited vocabulary (not impressive to Bianca). However, the shift also reveals how thoroughly the causes for female subaltern behavior have been erased in this film, to the extent that Kat's anger at patriarchy can become a running joke. There are no white males in authority positions at the high school, and at home Mr. Stratford is a beleaguered overprotective dad whose wife left him three years prior. Indeed, along with Joey, the only potential "bad guys" of the film are this absent mother and Bianca's back-stabbing girlfriend Chastity. Joey becomes the scapegoat replacement for an erased social order, and is gradually revealed to be the cause for almost all the film's antisocial and conflicted behavior—including that between females. In the most ironic of these cases, Kat's feminism turns out to be a reaction to Joey's having rejected her because she would not continue their sexual relationship (Kat's uncharacteristic one-night stand occasioned by the combination of her mother's desertion and peer pressure). Like her "statement" of ripping down prom posters and lecturing Bianca about doing things for her own reasons, Kat's politics are reduced to predictable personal responses to emotional vulnerability.

Whether an internally driven critique of high school values would be possible, given the consumerist MTV world parodied here, remains a moot point; even Kat's supposedly radical stance of questioning what is "popular" has been incorporated into the English classroom as a banner slogan. *10 Things* certainly does not require its audience to pursue such thinking, instead substituting yet another gorgeous hunk as the reward for female acceptance of normative romance—but with a bit of Burtonesque uncertainty to temper his Julián machismo. As embodied by Heath Ledger, this Petruchio is both physically invulnerable and gentle, asking a drunken Kat to "open your eyes" and see the green in his as her reward. He may sing "Can't take my eyes off of you" to Kat, but as he does so he makes himself the real (disarmingly sweet, comic) spectacle. The camera endorses his increasing allure, at the same time revealing his anxiousness and bad judgment in hiding his original mercenary motive. When the Zeffirelli wooing scene is finally quoted by having Kat and Patrick play paintball among haystacks, all we get is a lingering kiss in the hay and acceptable romping, without a stick or a hint of the earlier film's symbolic violence.

But ultimately, the shrew must have her taming speech, and in this, *10 Things* remains true to the dynamics—that is, the jarring disjunction—of *Shrew*'s final scene.[62] Signaling its affiliation to Shakespeare as text, Kat's climactic public oration takes place in English class, a response to the assign-

---

62. Cartmell, "Franco Zeffirelli," 214, is inaccurate on this point.

ment to write "your own version of" Shakespeare's sonnet 141, "In faith I do not love thee with mine eyes." An ironic choice, given film's reliance on the eye to reveal rather than contest the heart's judgment—but this central conceit of the sonnet will have no bearing on Kat's "poem" anyway. Nor will poetic craft. Kat does query whether she should write in iambic pentameter (which results, absurdly, in her again being kicked out of class—as befits a teen film, in which all actions by adult authorities should appear ludicrous). Yet nothing could prepare one for the dreadful "poem" she voluntarily performs. While the film has earlier "detached" from Kat's perspective on occasion (when she is doctrinaire in her antiprom stance, for example), here the incongruity truly baffles. One wonders how this sharp-tongued reader of *The Bell Jar*, bright enough to gain admission to Sarah Lawrence despite spending much class time in the guidance counselor's office, could come up with the nursery doggerel that begins:

> I hate the way you talk to me
> And the way you cut your hair.
> I hate the way you drive my car.
> I hate it when you stare.

and concludes:

> But mostly I hate the way I don't hate you,
> Not even close,
> Not even a little bit,
> Not even at all.

Not even rhyme, not even rhythm, not even verse at all. Dr. Seuss would be abashed. Moreover, this act of "poetic" self-confession drives Kat to tears and yet another hasty exit from the classroom—and not for the reasons that would be obvious were she an English teacher herself. Rather, we are directed to see this performance, addressed to Patrick, as a sign of love, emotionally embarrassing but ultimately worthwhile, since the next sequence shows her approaching her car to discover the guitar gift and Patrick, in that order. Taming this shrew means temporarily erasing her intelligence and sarcasm and replacing them with emotional submission: we have been here before.

While the lovers' final exchange—without peers listening—confirms the value of the newly educated Patrick and allows Kat her chosen future, the oddity of her "sonnet" performance resembles the voluntary strangeness of Liz Taylor's and many an earlier shrew's final speech. Quickly moving out to frame the ending with Kat's favorite band improbably performing on the

198   school roof, the filmmakers of *10 Things* are arguably as tongue-in-cheek about this sentimental interpellation as anybody—or one might say, as Richard Burt does in the service of a quite different reading, that the music tracks "cover" not only earlier bands but also the film's own "cheap trick" in popularizing Shakespeare.[63] Certainly Kat became more attractive to Patrick in the traditional Hollywood manner as the object of his gaze, first when dancing at a club and then when (like Tracy Lord) vulnerably drunk. Sisterhood may be more powerful these days, allowing Bianca to be applauded rather than dubbed "the real shrew" when she learns to stand up and fight for her boyfriend and her sister (by punching Joey twice in the nose and then kneeing him in the groin for herself, à la big sister). But beyond the slapstick reversals, girls talking political rather than heterosexual remains uncool. The film creates the illusion of freedom by keeping the focus local, on a world purged of traditional white male authority; in so doing, it accurately replicates the perception of many middle-class teens, whose immediate subculture no longer betrays such overt signs of traditional sexism. But the adults who made the movie thereby perpetuate a very different kind of tunnel vision from Jonathan Miller's, making Kat's gender-consciousness epiphenomenal and the (proper) sex life of teens the material reality. In finding pleasure in this status quo with a patina of rebelliousness, *10 Things* does indeed capture the narrative shape and consequences of *The Taming of the Shrew*, becoming yet another in the long line of Shake-shifting film comedies sending mixed messages.

The Work of Comedy

Times do change. *10 Things* presents a shrew who is overprotective rather than jealous of her sister; from her window above, Kat watches Bianca with melancholy sympathy instead of Liz Taylor's fury. And Patrick's ultimate acknowledgment that he "screwed up" is, given both the text and most performance traditions of *Shrew*, a refreshing addition—prior to his more conventional move to stop her mouth by kissing. Of course, it is easier to Shake-shift *Shrew* in spinoff form, without the textual specifics, and the cleverness of *10 Things* resides primarily in enmeshing the generic conventions of a teen movie with a "literary" classic. In doing so, it testifies once more to the pleasures filmmakers continue to discover in retelling the shrew-taming

---

63. Richard Burt, "T(e)en Things I Hate about Girlene Shakesploitation Flicks in the Late 1990s, or, Not So Fast Times at Shakespeare High," in *Spectacular Shakespeare: Critical Theory and Popular Cinema*, ed. Courtney Lehmann and Lisa S. Starks (Madison, NJ, 2002), passim.

story; whether their interest lies more in the taming itself or in the excuse it provides for focusing on a bold, unconventional female, that is the question. The media may be new, but the Shakespearean inheritance lingers on.

Yet so does the labor of adapting cross-medium and cross-time, the difficult work that transforms the "given" into something more amenable to us. On the evidence of the cinematic versions discussed here, that "us" remains as divided and willful as *The Taming of the Shrew* itself. Clearly the task of diachronic collaboration is more difficult if one finds offense in the play's central narrative; somehow, one must uncover a way to discount, distance, or deny what Kate's final speech asserts, that "taming a shrew" means subordinating a woman to a man as the natural order of things. The means modern directors, actors, and filmmakers find are many and various—sometimes even within a single production. Jonathan Miller does not deny the taming itself (and dismisses those who would do so as evading the text): he turns to history and psychology to vindicate its video replication. The temporal collision between these two contexts and the questionable applicability to the text of either (as he interprets them) weaken the effect for many viewers, but the director found his solution potent enough to continue justifying it in print six years later. In almost all other cases, the taming is called into question: either Kate's speech itself, or its visual and narrative "surround," provides ironic counterevidence to the overt meaning of her words. Understandably, the actress who must mouth these words often works hardest to believe what she says is benign, whereas the men here (invariably) who direct the camera find it easier to acknowledge ambiguity. Through narrative fragmentation and competing commentaries in *Kiss Me, Petruchio,* and through additional story elements and visual patterns in Zeffirelli's film, the camera belies simple shows of sincerity. Realist modes of filmmaking and acting cannot capture the very idea of a "shrew," much less its comedy, sufficiently. Thus the whole conclusion may also be played with a wink, as in the PickFair film—arguably the only point at which the vision of director and actress truly come into alignment. Finally, the lead-up narrative and words themselves can be altered, as in the PickFair *Taming* and *10 Things I Hate About You.*

Nor is this only a matter of Kate and her speech: questions of power necessarily make Petruchio's role focal, and the modern screen versions here again display a variety of approaches. The addition of a developmental narrative for the leading man in the Zeffirelli *Shrew* and *10 Things* means Katherine is not the only one to "grow up": both are shown to be emotionally vulnerable, and they know it. By contrast, Douglas Fairbanks's Petruchio remains the dupe of his own triumph, exposed to the camera as less

200   knowing and not physically invulnerable after all. Only Raúl Juliá gets to preserve his male prerogative and strength unchallenged (except by those pesky audience members), but in an ironic twist he does so precisely by becoming an eroticized prize body—a film role usually occupied by females.

Finally, however, *The Taming of the Shrew* is not just its leading characters but a story, and the treatment of that tripartite narrative involves making fundamental decisions about that "whole." In the use of psychiatric and historical models, artists emphasize continuity and necessity, as does Freud (ultimately) when he transforms violent fantasies into something comprehensible in normative terms. But the comic spirit can also be about turning the conventional upside down, and while Shakespeare's text fails to invert gendered power norms, it may still elude linear "sense." There is nothing particularly logical about Kate's turn to housekeeping in the Zeffirelli *Shrew*, but it provides a satisfying reversal of control, at least temporarily, and thereby points out what is missing in the Shakespearean script. And this, like the very structure of *Kiss Me, Petruchio*, redirects our vision away from collaboration-as-endorsement to collaboration-as-performance: a dynamic reflection upon working with "Shakespeare."

During a live stage performance of *The Taming of the Shrew* directed by Andrei Serban at the American Repertory Theater (1998), the actress playing Kate stumbled over her last speech, lost concentration, and went back to regain her place: "I am ashamed that women are so simple," she said once again. Perhaps the most powerful moment in the drama, it captured a struggle over what was being performed: between Serban, whose "spiritual" interpretation attempted to disregard gender as an issue here at all, and the actress who had to make sense of the specific words her director wanted to ignore. That struggle in turn ended up appearing to many in the audience as part of the battle within the representation, as Kate attempted to tame herself and say what would naturally stick in her throat. For those who realized it was a line drop and those who didn't, the result was an authentically tense moment fracturing the necessity of Shakespeare's conclusion. Screen media tend not to replicate such awkwardly serendipitous events, nor can they capture their kinetic energy in a shared space of actors with audience, but in their own ways they can call attention to the elements that disrupt intellectual coherence: this is the very stuff of comedy.

Making the body matter, making the silence speak, these cinematic *Shrew*s bring us close up to its taming story, and thus take on an even more difficult challenge, to keep it amusing. Perhaps they do not always make us laugh, or laugh at the same things—or laugh the same way. Simon Critchley argues that the truest laughter is that which Freud himself emphasized, the laugh-

ter of finding oneself ridiculous. This is not the aggressive laughter of jokes
but rather the sardonic laughter of (disturbing) knowledge. It is the mirth-
less laugh of Samuel Beckett: "the laugh of laughs, the *risus purus*, the laugh
laughing at the laugh, the beholding, the saluting of the highest joke, in a
word the laugh that laughs—silence please—at that which is unhappy."[64] In
the most interesting of these *Shrew*s, we do not discover the easiest pleasures
of classic comic form or elevating "role models"; we do not necessarily feel
better about ourselves. But as we labor to explain this recalcitrant tale and
make it modern, the comic spirit in perhaps its most profoundly challenging
sense comes to life. Seizing pleasure from the jaws of despair (despair over
distance, over power, over violence and meanness), one may begin to appre-
hend why this so-dated text can still provide a strangely modern (not timeless) experience. Consenting and laboring for our own enjoyment, we see—
silence please—"we" are not of one mind.

Shall we laugh?

64. *Watt*, in Critchley, *On Humour*, v.

What's Past Is Prologue

Shakespeare's History
and the Modern Performance of Henry V

Histories, Plural

When Franco Zeffirelli arranged the Italian premiere of his *The Taming of the Shrew*, he insisted upon screening the English-language version: he wanted to please any of the surviving English ladies in Florence (later memorialized in his film *Tea with Mussolini*) who had shared in his youthful discovery of filmed Shakespeare. Theirs was the only audience response to his *Shrew* that the director valued enough to describe in his autobiography (otherwise just noting that the film "was an immense success"). He remembers: "as soon as the film had started I could sense that they were loving it. This was their Shakespeare."[1] Zeffirelli's reference to "their Shakespeare," however, hearkened back not to earlier *Shrew*s but to Laurence Olivier's *Henry*

---

1. Zeffirelli, *Zeffirelli*, 224.

V—the film that gave young Franco, when he first watched it in war-ravaged Florence, the confidence to choose the life of an artist.

Henry V has had a remarkable afterlife on screen, initiating the Shakespearean film careers of both Laurence Olivier and (in part as a result) Kenneth Branagh; their versions in turn prompted an upsurge in Shakespeare film production. Moreover, as was the case for Zeffirelli, *Henry V* has functioned or been perceived as a story of liberation. Perhaps surprisingly for an English history play set in the early fifteenth century, modern *Henry* performances often have as much to do with psychological or artistic freedom as with national politics. While Olivier certainly saw his Shake-shifting as a contribution to the British cause during World War II—and the play continues to be enlisted in both the service and the criticism of militarism—even this most historiographically self-conscious text appeals to many who have little interest in questions of state or history.

If comedy can divide moderns, history can bore them. Only a few of the plays categorized as histories in the First Folio are still among Shakespeare's most popular, and those remain so *not* because they confront events from the past. Rather, fascination with the characters of Falstaff, Richard III, and Prince Hal/Henry V motivates their revival on film and stage, at least overtly (as in *The Taming of the Shrew*) depoliticizing by repsychologizing history.[2] Consider Branagh's preparation for the role of Henry, during which he interviewed the current Prince Charles and was struck by his mental isolation. Disregarding the disconnect between a reigning feudal monarch and a constitutional figurehead—not to mention the utterly different political structures, events, and mentalities that surround each "Prince"—Branagh found his acting focus in the twentieth century. The result, as W. B. Worthen has observed, is to reduce "history" to set dressing, so that the design elements of Branagh's film constitute all we really see of "the past."[3] Olivier's film, with its shifts in temporal and stylistic location, self-consciously accentuates this tension between past and present, yet it too represents its emotional core (that "little touch of Harry in the night" as well as the battle of Agincourt itself) using twentieth-century cinematographic notions of realism: it's back to the future.

Even when they look past the leading character to consider the politics of war, these films encourage interpretation focused on twentieth-century atti-

2. By contrast, nineteenth-century Britain delighted in *King John*, a less character-driven history. A psychological focus, as the previous chapter shows, can of course have broadly "political" consequences.

3. See Worthen, *Shakespeare and the Force of Modern Performance*, 69. This is not to diminish the importance of design, instead indicating that sometimes it has too little effect upon acting style and other film elements.

204   tudes. Thus critics routinely chastise or defend Branagh's representation through reference to the Falklands war or the aftermath of Vietnam, while Olivier's prettied-up medievalism is understood as abetting Allied morale during World War II.[4] Although the directors adhere to the historical record for factual accuracy on selective points (Agincourt's bad weather and mud in Branagh, the crucial role of the archers in Olivier), the overarching rationale and effect of their battle scenes remain firmly rooted in modernity. The past is denuded of its difference from the time of performance in significant ways, most notably in the conceptual assumptions made about characters and war itself.

    If we are to believe much recent scholarship, this film practice may be far from Shakespeare in time and medium but not so different in historical method: focusing on contemporary events mentioned and potential allegories buried in *Henry V*, many argue that the feudal conflict with France represented therein is "really" about England's troubled attempts at colonizing Ireland. Henry thus serves as a wish fulfillment, a figure of imaginary union who compensates for the vexatious fractures within late Elizabethan nationhood. Certainly such references exist, and matter: greater attention to them is part of what late twentieth-century literary studies can add to current performances of *Henry V*.[5] Yet these readings also thereby participate in the effacement of other dimensions of the text that might qualify as more truly "historical" for those trained in that discipline rather than in Fluellen's "disciplines of the war": the play's signs of consciousness of the past as the past, its awareness of what data can be gleaned and comprehended about another, temporally distinct world. In other words, to the extent that Shakespeare's plays do attempt to represent a past, as well as shadow a present through that past, the tension created by a gap of two hundred years between Henry's day and Shakespeare's can be effaced by this more univocal modern reading of the political as contemporary allegory.

    4. See especially Donald Hedrick, Chris Fitter, Graham Holderness ("'What ish'"), Willy Maley.

    5. The much-discussed Harfleur encounter among representatives of the four territories eventually subsumed as the United Kingdom includes the Irish Captain, Macmorris, famously challenging the provocative Welshman, Fluellen, by crying, "What ish my nation?" On the Irish connection, see Joel B. Altman; David J. Baker and Willy Maley; Jonathan Baldo; W. F. Bolton; Christopher Highley; and Philip Edwards. Also on nationhood see Sinfield; Christopher Pye; Claire McEachern; and Terence Hawkes. Maley ("'This sceptred isle'") and Holderness ("'What ish'") make connections with Tory nationalism and RSC performance practices. Lisa Jardine argues that only some of these (UK) critics and recent ethnic warfare in the former Yugoslavia have made it possible for "us" "to recognise as sharply as we currently do the problems lurking within *Henry V*'s depiction of fervour for English nationalism" (*Reading Shakespeare Historically* [London, 1996], 7)—a blinkered overgeneralization from one reading "historically." As the fifth act Chorus makes explicit, the English victory at Agincourt is meant to prefigure a similar hoped-for triumph over the Irish.

However, another (sometimes related) method of scholarly inquiry now popular may remind us of the distance between Shakespeare's day and the time of his fictional/historical play: this is the work of recovering the obscure or marginalized from eras past. Familiar labor for historians of women and others of "subaltern" or colonized status, such explorations are usually presented in opposition to traditional "top-down" political history. But as a closer look at both the text and afterlife of *Henry V* will suggest, these approaches might better be seen as interdependent and importantly complementary. The terms of exclusion and power are dynamic and layered even within one playtext, and all the more so when modern artists mix aspects of that script with their own times and methods.

This chapter focuses on two cases of historically based political "collaborators." Queen Isabel of France and Davy Gam of the Agincourt dead are (marginally) included in *Henry V* at moments of plot resolution, but their "real" lives were far more contentious. Their representation in Shakespeare reveals historical change involving two basic categories, nation and gender, and suggests the difficulty of capturing such complexity in modern productions. Illuminating their shadowy histories (in fact, text, and performance) also illustrates how attention to the artistic process of diachronic collaboration moves us beyond any easy opposition—or impasse—between study of the past and action in the present.

Scholarship on *Henry V* divides fairly neatly among those who regard it as a typically Elizabethan celebration of English nationalism in formation; those who emphasize its subversive undoing of that epic enterprise through dialogic dramatization; and those who see this "rabbit/duck" perceptual oscillation as itself the play's dramatic core.[6] The difference between the Folio and Quarto texts further emphasizes the doubleness and potential for deception inherent in its representation of history for contemporary performance.[7] The textual and performance choices of Shakespeare and his modern collaborators thus encourage a range of aesthetic and political effects. At the same time, analysis of their specific use of—and changes to—received historical narratives confirms *Henry V*'s status as a diachronic collaboration

6. See the book by Phyllis Rackin and the article by Anthony B. Dawson on the implications of dramatizing history. In Henry's case, Shakespeare resurrects the dead "star of England," yet doing so only through an actor's impersonation makes the gap between performance and history more poignant. The differences between the Chorus's laudatory comments and the events as represented provide further ground for doubt about the past's recoverability (and for some, cynicism about the very notion of military heroism). On the "rabbit/duck" perceptual alternation within the text itself, see Norman Rabkin.

7. The roles of Chorus and Queen Isabel, crucial to the play's historiography, do not appear in the Quarto, only the Folio text. Almost all scholars consider the latter to be a superior document.

involved in particular forms of both ideological complication and simplification. The relationship between playtext and history prefigures (and is in part constitutive of) that between contemporary performances of *Henry V* and the Elizabethan playscript(s). And the tendency to reiterate certain patterns in representation reveals that a knowledge of historical conditions is crucial for understanding the present as well as the past. History helps shape modern productions, inflecting our current understanding of what gender, nationhood, and honor mean — or cost. Exploring the analogies between Shakespeare's palimpsest and those later versions of *Henry V*, we learn more about both twentieth-century Shake-shifting and Shakespeare himself as a "modern" collaborator with history.

Unburying the Dead

Let us begin with a dead man's name: Davy Gam, Esquire. Davy (*gam* means "squint-eyed") attains his place in Tudor historiography and hence in Shakespeare's play by dying at Agincourt, one of only four men "of name." Henry memorializes the "English dead" thus:

> Edward the Duke of York; the Earl of Suffolk;
> Sir Richard Keighley; Davy Gam, Esquire;
> None else of name, and of all other men
> But five-and-twenty.[8]

Davy joins his English social betters — not to mention a goodly portion of the French nobility, that "royal fellowship of death" (4.8.102) — as a human sacrifice enabling the most glorious victory of Henry's campaign. His name prefaces the mention of a mere twenty-five unnamed men whose "vile" birth makes them unworthy of historical record, despite Henry's prebattle profession of blood brotherhood with them all as the "happy few":

> For he that sheds his blood with me
> Shall be my brother; be he ne'er so vile,
> This day shall gentle his condition.
> (4.3.60, 61–63)

8. William Shakespeare, *King Henry V*, ed. T. W. Craik (New York, 1995), 4.8.104–7. All play citations refer to this Arden 3 edition, unless otherwise noted (I use the play's shorter title for convenience and consistency with the films).

Henry is not the only one with a short memory. Here Shakespeare must work within the obvious constraints of retelling old histories: common soldiers, living or dead, were listed as groups from geographical areas rather than as individuals. An esquire is as low as he could go. But thereby hangs a tale, and another minor miracle for Henry. For in naming Davy Gam among his blood brothers, Henry has made the unseen bloody corpse of a Welshman, Dafydd ap Llywelyn of Brecon, stand for England.

Wales had been a troubled territory for Shakespeare's Henry when he was its nominal prince. The set of four plays sometimes called (in the feudal familial mode) the Lancastrian tetralogy or (in the epic great-man mode) the Henriad focus upon the fall and rise of English princes, on the fracturing and repair of the "nation." In the process of constructing the mythology of Henry V and England, these plays travel to locales in two (and only two) other would-be nations: Wales and France.[9] Indeed, not only does *Henry IV, Part 1* directly represent Wales, it presents that Welsh struggle in ways that then echo in the representation of the French in *Henry V* — providing, as we shall see, a fictional analogue to the historical fact of Franco-Welsh alliance. For Shakespeare, the Welsh and the French serve as national others who must be domesticated as well as beaten, transformed from bloody enemies to kindred blood. Thus in the concluding triumph of *Henry V*, it is the Welshmen both living and dead, namely, Captain Fluellen and Davy Gam, who emblematize the comparative success of England's national expansion. Like the Frenchwomen of act 5 to whom I shall later turn, the Welshmen who become collaborators with Henry allow a comic resolution to the question of nationhood.

A mere name among the dead can but dimly illuminate the larger drama: Davy Gam, after all, does not appear onstage. Yet in a set of plays that sets the "word against the word" and makes much of language's role in constructing national identity, perhaps it is fitting that a name should turn out to be consequential indeed. Languages are lost and won along with battles, and

9. Terence Hawkes's "Bryn Glas" importantly suggested that we read things Welsh with reference to Wales; see also Patricia Parker ("Uncertain Unions"), Frederick J. Harries, and Arthur E. Hughes. I agree with Hawkes that given recent attention to Ireland, some "reordering of the priorities" is now in order; *Shakespeare in the Present* (London, 2002), 44. Yet as insightful and delightful as they are, Hawkes's essays seldom pursue the precise application of historical contexts within the narrative, i.e., how exactly the artwork transforms or thematizes the history (and hence how it could be recontextualized for present performance). Maley observes that "[t]o naturalise Britain while retaining Ireland as a colonial or semi-colonial other is to reproduce the post-1603 ideological reification of political relations in the British Isles," yet he too quickly concludes that "Ireland is the battlefield in *Henry V*"; "'This sceptred isle': Shakespeare and the British Problem," in *Shakespeare and National Culture*, ed. John J. Joughin (Manchester, UK, 1997), 86, 98.

208   the struggle "properly" to name this Welsh body epitomizes tensions involved throughout *Henry V* in the renaming of royals and subjects—and with
them, emergent states. Certainly by Shakespeare's day language was one of
the few and crucial indicators left for those who considered themselves
members of a Welsh rather than English nation. And still, the mute corpse of
the historical Davy/Dafydd might well cry out, what is(h) my nation?

The question arises from the historical rather than the dramatic record,
and suggests a larger query: what relationship does Shakespeare's representation bear to the known historical events and personages he resurrects for
the stage? Determining what "nationality" meant to this early fifteenth-
century Welshman was—and is—not easy. For starters, he fought against
the Welsh rebellion of Owain Glyn Dŵr (anglicized as Owen Glendower in
Henry IV), and at great cost. Dafydd ap Llywelyn's opposition was rooted in
his social position within late medieval Brecon, namely, his family's feudal
connection to the Bohun family, earls of Hereford and lords of Brecon—the
very family into which Henry Bolingbroke married fifteen years prior to his
usurpation of the English throne. Thus, it was through Henry V's maternal
line, his Anglo-Welsh mother, Mary Bohun, that the Lancastrians won
Dafydd's loyalty—yet another way in which Hal, whose bid to the French
throne derives from his French great-grandmother, may be said to be
"claiming from the female."

Nor was Dafydd merely one among many Lancastrian loyalists: modern
historian R. R. Davies dubs him "the most redoubtable and famous of
Owain's opponents." Early in Henry IV's reign, Dafydd was made an esquire and rewarded with confiscated rebel lands "specifically for his
prowess in opposing" the rising.[10] One account has him involved in a major
1405 victory over Glyn Dŵr's forces, the battle of Pwll Melyn near Usk.
Promoted to master servant of the lordship of Brecon in 1410, he was captured two years later by a remnant of Glyn Dŵr's now-dwindling army and
held for a goodly ransom—an action that "created a stir in distant St. Albans
and prompted [the English chronicler] Thomas Walsingham to renew his vituperative comments on the Welsh leader." This is the Walsingham who pro-

10. R. R. Davies, *The Revolt of Owain Glyn Dŵr* (Oxford, 1995), 226. I rely centrally on Davies
as a careful recent history but draw on a range of historical sources here. On medieval Wales
and the figure of Glyn Dŵr, see also J.E. Lloyd, Ralph A. Griffiths, Elissa R. Henken, A. G.
Bradley, H. T Evans, and J. D. Griffith Davies. On sixteenth-century Wales, see Gareth
Jones, Glanmor Williams, Fleney, and J. Gwynfor Jones. On English representations including Holinshed's *Chronicles of England, Scotland, and Ireland* (note the absence of Wales) and
Shakespeare's adaptation, see Matthew Wikander; Annabel Patterson; Rackin; and Jean E.
Howard and Phyllis Rackin.

vided Shakespeare's source stories about the barbarous Welsh treatment of English corpses;[11] thus one can say that Dafydd's life helped *shape* Shakespeare's vision of Glendower and the Welsh in the Lancastrian tetralogy. Finally, in 1415 Dafydd followed Henry V to Agincourt, where he was "sufficiently distinguished to be retained individually rather than with the men of Brecon as a group. He was one of the few men of esquire's rank on the English side to be killed in battle, and for that reason alone his death was recorded in several contemporary chronicles"—and in Shakespeare's play.[12]

To read backward from later ideas of nation-states and regard Dafydd as a "traitor" to Wales would simply be to mirror by inversion Shakespeare's Elizabethan perspective in casting Dafydd's opponent Glyn Dŵr as a "traitor" against England. The truth is that Gam and Glyn Dŵr shared much the same experience and social position; like the anachronistically unified "French" against whom Henry V fights, these Welshmen made decisions whether or not to fight England primarily on the basis of local, familial, and proprietary situations rather than any easy sense of "national" identification.[13] A sixteenth-century Welsh antiquarian memorialized Dafydd as "a great stickler for the Duke of Lancaster," and R. R. Davies concurs that this epitaph "identified correctly that in the test of convictions which all revolts eventually entail, Dafydd Gam, like many other prominent Welsh squires, decided that the ties of service to English lords were too important to be overridden by appeals to patriotism and mythology."[14]

Nevertheless, once Glyn Dŵr's rebellion took shape, it most certainly tapped into Welsh cultural memories and in turn became one of the great Welsh nationalist stories of resistance—in opposition to which English chronicle accounts were written. David Powel, in his 1584 *Historie of Cambria*, might regard Glyn Dŵr's assumption of the title Prince of Wales as a moment in "fool's paradise," but that was not the fifteenth-century political vision.[15] His 1404 coronation took place at Harlech in the presence of envoys from Spain and Scotland as well as France, and even after Glyn Dŵr's defeat and disappearance there was a plot (the same year as Agincourt) that envisaged his return in collaboration with the Lollard Oldcastle (whose

11. See Rackin's gender analysis of the stories of Welshwomen mutilating soldiers' bodies.

12. Davies, *Revolt*, 302.

13. Davies observes that Dafydd's "story and that of his family is in many respects a reverse image to that of Owain Glyn Dŵr and his family. The contrast between them explains some of the profound paradoxes of loyalty and contradictions of conviction in the Wales of their day" (*Revolt*, 225).

14. Ibid.

15. Glanmor Williams, *Renewal and Reformation Wales, c. 1415–1642* (Oxford, 1993), 3.

210   name Shakespeare initially chose for the character known as Falstaff). There had been five other rebellions since Edward I's conquest over Llewelyn the Great in 1282, and one could hardly know that Glyn Dŵr's would become the last major Welsh military challenge to English rule. As Glanmor Williams describes the century, "the incipient patriotism observable in countries like England, France, Scotland, Bohemia, and Hungary, could also be seen fermenting in Wales; much of it negative in character and vented in hatred of the traditional enemy." During the Wars of the Roses, Welsh leaders and poets often subordinated that dynastic rift to their own people's cause, with even a Lancastrian poet bemoaning the slaughter of Welsh Yorkists by "Saxons."[16] As the late feudal system unraveled and came to be enfolded within early modern nation-states, then, the motivations of a figure such as Dafydd would be recast and come to stand for loyalty to the Tudor-enforced Union of England and Wales.

      Shakespeare's renaming does not end Dafydd's story. In the seventeenth century, a legend accentuated the mirror antagonism of Gam and Glyn Dŵr. "So intrepid a spirit was Dafydd Gam and so deep was his hatred for Glyn Dŵr," it was said,

> that he infiltrated Glyn Dŵr's parliament . . . [to assassinate] the Welsh leader, but . . . was foiled . . . and only escaped with his life . . . in return for a promise to support the Welsh cause. The legend, as we have it, is late and is implausible and inaccurate in its details; but its very survival, or manufacture, indicates that Dafydd Gam had acquired a legendary status as one of the most implacable and daredevil Welsh opponents of Owain Glyn Dŵr.[17]

Could Shakespeare's mention of Davy and representation of Glendower have provided further impetus for this *mano a mano* mythologizing? We cannot know, though the legend certainly shares with *Henry V* a shift in attention from feudal fractions to individuals bound by their duty to king and (competing notions of) "country." It also recalls the tight linkage between the *Henry IV* and *Henry V* plays in which the names of these two men appear—and reinforces the parallelism in those plays between England's Welsh and French opponents, both of whom the historical Dafydd fought and whom Shakespeare represents first as Henry's antagonists but eventually as subdued allies.

16. Ibid., 8, 7; see also H. T. Evans, passim.
17. Davies, *Revolt*, 226–27; see also Henken.

Nor was this simply Shakespeare's neat dramatic connection: the alliance between Welsh and French leaders in opposition to England was an historical one, evidenced by Glyn Dŵr's treaty with Charles VI of France in 1404. French soldiers joined the Welsh in attacks on the English from 1403 on, and Charles formally acknowledged Glyn Dŵr as Prince of Wales—thus displacing Prince Henry Monmouth, just as the Dauphin blocked Henry's claim to inheritance of the French throne. In August 1405, approximately twenty-five hundred French troops landed at Milford Haven (familiar to us from *Cymbeline*), combined with the Welsh, and burnt their way across to Carmarthen—militarily vital, and symbolically crucial as Merlin's town. Glyn Dŵr negotiated the town's capture. Legend has it these troops later pushed as far as Worcestershire before unwisely retreating: Woodbury Hill was memorialized in Shakespeare's day as the spot where they stopped, and Camden's *Britannia* (1586) noted that it was "vulgarly called Owen Glendower's Camp."[18] The subsequent demise of the Franco-Welsh alliance, not Hotspur's earlier failure at Shrewsbury in 1403, led to Glyn Dŵr's loss of power. Shakespeare mutes this worrisome French connection, but its historical traces linger.

Clearly the status of the Welsh territory on England's "Celtic fringe" had changed between the time represented in *Henry V* and the time of its writing. Shakespeare could represent Glendower with a mixture of amusement and respect, knowing that the Tudor monarchy, and specifically Henry VIII's Acts of Union, had effectively put an end to Welsh aspirations for political independence. Yet at the same time, Welsh differences remained a source of English anxiety. To represent late feudal Welsh "others" was to do two things at once—to shadow present tensions as well as past victories. Fears of powerful Welsh gentry and Catholic insurrection remained strong throughout Henry VIII's reign, and foreign invasion through Wales persisted as a concern during Shakespeare's lifetime. A Privy Council letter of January 1584 reflects this, instructing county muster masters of Anglesey, Merioneth, and Caernarvon to assemble trained men in readiness to fight during "these dangerous times."[19] Coming much closer to home and Shakespeare's play, Essex had strong support in southwest Wales; according to Gwynfor

18. William Camden, *Britannia* (New York, 1971 [facsimile of 1695 ed.]), 339. The line between historical memory and legend is a fine one: R. R. Davies counters most earlier historians, including Lloyd, in doubting the veracity of this invasion story. On Milford Haven, see Hawkes's "Aberdangleddyf" (its Welsh name) in *Shakespeare in the Present*.

19. Gareth Jones, *A New History of Wales: The Gentry and the Elizabethan State* (Swansea, 1977), 55–56.

212   Jones, a "large contingent intended to join in a *coup d'état* in February 1601 but turned back."[20] And providing a reminder that the troubles rippled across from Ireland to other vestigially Celtic regions, Catholic resistance to military service across the Irish Sea continued to cause unrest in Wales after the death of Essex.

Nor, despite the Acts of Union, was the exact national status of Wales itself a resolved matter. The official language and common law had become English, but Welsh circuit courts still had some autonomy, and over 40 percent of the population continued to speak Welsh not just into the seventeenth century but well into the twentieth.[21] Monmouth, where Henry V was born, became an anomaly for a time during the sixteenth century, neither fully English nor Welsh but suspended between them. Despite the loyalty of many gentry families to the Tudors and hence to the new "English" dynasty, signs of Wales's foreignness persisted in English culture, evinced onstage by scenes such as Lady Mortimer's Welsh speech and song in *Henry IV, Part 1*.[22] It is not merely coincidental that the matching scene of foreign womanhood and linguistic exchange occurs in *Henry V* with a French princess: for Hal, the threats of the two nations are always intertwined. Like the French crown Henry claims by inheritance, the princedom of Wales might nevertheless seem his and not his—and even more disturbingly to the Elizabethan English audience, still theirs and not theirs. More remained of Wales than the successfully re-membered "English" dead man, Davy Gam.

Dafydd and the Franco-Welsh alliance are only spectral presences in *Henry V*, but they influence how one interprets its action set in France. They add another dimension to scenes often reduced to "comic relief" and mindless caricature—most notably, those involving Captain Fluellen.[23] Whereas the Irishman Macmorris and the Chorus who talks of Ireland stay distanced from Henry, the Welshman repeatedly inhabits the same historical-dramatic

20. J. Gwynfor Jones, *Early Modern Wales, c. 1525–1640* (New York, 1994), 191.

21. The real decline of Welsh speaking among the masses occurs only from the 1870s onward, after a parliamentary education act forced children to learn in English.

22. On this scene, see especially Barbara Hodgdon's *The End Crowns All*. If Glendower and his daughter "speak Welsh" as the text and scholars argue, it means that at least two actors in Shakespeare's company spoke Welsh on a London stage more than sixty years after English had been made the official language of Wales. Its very sound would testify to the ongoing presence of an "independent"—and potentially challenging—subculture, not confined to the territories fictionally represented. Calling special attention to the land by having a map onstage, Shakespeare's Welsh scene represents Glendower as more mature than Hotspur and loyal to natural geography when the "rebels" divide the territories. Some audience members might thereby be reminded that Glendower was only trying to reconstitute the centuries-old kingdom he claimed as Prince of Wales.

23. My reading overlaps here with Parker's fine linguistic foray into Welsh leeks and "leakage."

space as the King. At Harfleur, Fluellen comically (and/or belligerently) raises the issue of nationality, and as the campaign's self-proclaimed historian, he turns back to the authority of the chronicles—perhaps to counter his being (viewed from the English "core") "a little out of fashion" (4.1.84). By the time they reach Agincourt, Henry gets directly involved with both Fluellen and the fragmentation of "English" identity. As at Harfleur, the incident begins with a joke—one reinforcing the association between the Celtic fringe and France.

When Pistol—beginning his encounter with the mangled "Che vous là?" (4.1.35)—asks "Harry le Roy" his name, he mistakes it for a "Cornish name" (4.1.49); while the audience understands the French, Henry replies that he is in fact a Welshman (shifting between Celtic territories in a way that would make Sir Walter Scott proud). Pistol's inability to understand the French Monsieur Le Fer will be the first scene in the "battle" to come, but here his belligerence is turned instead upon the Welsh. Upon learning that "le Roy" is Fluellen's kinsman, the English blusterer threatens, "I'll knock his leek about his pate / Upon Saint Davy's day" (4.1.51–52). The time to fight independent Welshmen, however, is past. It is the disguised English King who in reply warns, "Do not you wear your dagger in your cap that day, lest he knock that about yours" (4.1.55–58). Thus the French-Welsh-English "Harry le Roy" foretells Pistol's fifth act fate, when Gower will reiterate a message that resonates beyond the stage, chastising all bombastic advocates of "Little England": "You thought because he could not speak English in the native garb he could not therefore handle an English cudgel. You find it otherwise, and henceforth let a Welsh correction teach you a good English condition" (5.1.75–79). Shakespeare's play is certainly not above mocking Fluellen's pronunciation (or glancing at Henry's imperial ambitions in the battlefield comparison between Harry Monmouth and "Alexander the Pig" [4.7.13]), but Agincourt culminates in Henry's double assertion of his own Welshness—first disguised as "le Roy," then after battle unveiled and victorious as King of England.

In the exchange with Fluellen that leads to this public announcement, the text explicitly involves historical memory with the intermingled fortunes of the Welsh, French, and English, acknowledging the multiple perspectives that accrue to events over time. Gary Taylor observes that the word *memorable* is used four times in Shakespeare, all in this play;[24] even more to the point, those four instances tighten the associations linking Henry's lineage, Wales, and defeat of the French. The first invocation comes from the French

24. Gary Taylor, ed., *Henry V*, by William Shakespeare (Oxford, 1982), 148.

214   King, haunted by his nation's famous defeat a generation earlier. Reading the past prophetically, Charles recalls

> our too much memorable shame
> When Cressy battle fatally was struck,
> And all our princes captived, by the hand
> Of that black *name*, Edward, Black Prince of Wales.
> (2.4.53–56; italics mine)

This historical memory — captured with startling force by using a "name" to signify the identity and power of the now-dead body — shapes the King's attitude toward Henry. Because he is perceived as "a stem / Of that victorious stock," Henry conjures the King's fears of "the native mightiness and fate of him" (2.4.62–64). Only moments later, Exeter extends the metaphor and reinforces that fear by presenting an historical document to Charles: "this most memorable line, / In every branch truly demonstrative" is the "pedigree" entitling this younger Prince of Wales likewise to claim the French crown (2.4.88–90). When Fluellen at Agincourt recalls Henry's "grandfather of famous memory . . . and your great-uncle Edward the Plack Prince of Wales, as I have read in the chronicles," he thus confirms the accuracy of the French King's method of reading history as prophecy (4.7.92–94).

Tellingly, Fluellen supplements the account by including the Welsh: not only did Crécy foreshadow Agincourt but "the Welshmen did good service" there. If one battle prefigures the other, then we may extrapolate from his "historical" anecdote that Fluellen wants Henry to realize that the Welsh did "good service" on *each* field. Historically some Welshmen may have recently allied themselves with the French, but here they are rewarded for fighting against the French. In his typically comic way, Fluellen is making a serious point about the importance of his own "nation" in shaping both English history and the present performance that is fast becoming history. The Welsh custom he recollects, that of "wearing leeks in their Monmouth caps," has endured "to this hour" as "an honourable badge of the service," one which Fluellen himself will uphold. This doubled remembrance of an earlier victory in France and of loyal Welshness leads to Henry's direct naming of himself as Fluellen's countryman, for like Fluellen he "takes no scorn to wear the leek upon Saint Tavy's day": "I wear it for a memorable honour / For I am Welsh, you know, good countryman" (4.7.97–104).

Ironically, Fluellen's account from the "chronicles" may be Shakespeare's fiction: "For the fact of service done by Welshmen in a garden of leeks, Fluellen remains our only authority," G. Blakemore Evans remarks.[25] Gary

25. Craik, ed., *King Henry V*, 318.

Taylor elaborates, "[W]hat editors describe as the 'traditional' explanation of the wearing of leeks—commemoration of a Welsh victory over the Saxons in AD 540—is not found till the late seventeenth century, and the leek is not associated with Cadwallader until the nineteenth."[26] As in the mythology surrounding Dafydd Gam and Glyn Dŵr's personal enmity, looking back to uncover Welsh history leads instead to post-Shakespearean texts: past, present, and future intermingle. In making Crécy the Eden of leek wearers, Shakespeare may have been drawing on oral tradition, having a little joke over the reliability of chronicles or Fluellen's reading of them, or creating his own mythic explanation. Whatever the case, written accounts make clear that the leek was worn in Elizabethan times—indeed, by the Queen herself—upon St. Davy's Day.[27] It is also historically undeniable that the Welsh lancers and archers played an important part in the battles of Crécy and Poitiers; Fluellen has memorialized that valiant behavior. In comic fashion, Fluellen will likewise maintain his country's honor when he confronts Pistol in the scene prompting the play's final invocation of the "memorable"—from the mouth of an Englishman in defense of Welsh custom. After Fluellen cudgels Pistol, Gower adds his own verbal assault (cited above, but worthy of fuller quotation):

> Go, go, you are a counterfeit cowardly knave. Will you mock at an ancient tradition, begun upon an honourable respect and worn as a memorable trophy of predeceased valour, and dare not avouch in your deeds any of your words? I have seen you gleeking and galling at this gentleman twice or thrice. You thought because he could not speak English in the native garb he could not therefore handle an English cudgel. You find it otherwise, and henceforth let a Welsh correction teach you a good English condition. Fare ye well. (5.1.70–80)

The cowardly Englishman stands (or lies) corrected.

It is Fluellen, moreover, who reminds Henry of the terms of his sovereignty over at least one Welsh constituent: "I need not to be ashamed of your majesty, praised be God, so long as your majesty is an honest man" (4.7.112–14). The Welsh will otherwise fight back, as Pistol soon learns to his pain. Perhaps it is the slight challenge to Henry's absolute authority in Fluellen's phrasing that prompts the King, directly following, to use the Welshman as his whipping boy in his quarrel with another potentially unruly subject, Williams. Ironically, Henry's first action after their Welsh exchange is *not* "honest": exploiting Fluellen's loyalty and willingness to fight the French, Henry plants Williams's glove on Fluellen, telling him it belonged to the

26. Taylor, ed., *Henry V*, 248.
27. Craik, ed., *King Henry V*, 318.

216   duke of Alençon. One can debate whether the comedy reflects upon Henry's manipulative humor and insecurity (he could hardly hope for more faithful subjects than Fluellen and Williams) or displays the playwright's identification with an aristocratic English perspective that now appears patronizing, mocking those of lower position or different ethnicities for their (threatening?) irascibility; but indubitably, the episode proves yet again Fluellen's devotion to Henry—a neat prelude to the renaming of another loyal Welshman among the list of English dead. The sequence of memorable naming and renaming after the battle thus moves from Agincourt back to Crécy, linking Crispin's and Davy's days in the process, before finally listing the French and English dead. Only after the English king asserts his Welshness does the Welshman become English, with the naming of Davy Gam.

Willy Maley stresses how opportunistically Henry changes his identity, being "Harry of England with Montjoy and when storming Harfleur, and present[ing] himself as classless and multi-national" elsewhere.[28] While the accusation is true, more is involved here than one man's chameleon expertise at domination, and the role of history—and Fluellen as a symbolic bearer of that history—demands a closer reading of the play's incorporation of Wales. Such reading tightens the connections between Fluellen and Williams as potential challengers—ethically and politically—to the trickster King and makes their scenes of fighting about signs in caps more important; it strengthens the political logic of the foreign language scenes, including those with the women that also make the Welsh/French connection explicit, and Pistol's "battling" with both Fluellen and Le Fer; and it may even account for the oddity of the Folio's mislabeling of acts (act 4 beginning and ending with Fluellen in dialogue, thereby giving him exceptional structural prominence in the Agincourt segment). Shakespeare clearly does "remember" the vexed relationship between Wales and England that *Henry V* both recalls and more vigorously attempts to submerge. Comedy and sentimental bonds make light of the feudal fighting that fractured ethnic identities and made the "purity" of any Englishman—certainly of Monmouth-born Henry and the Tudor monarchs that would succeed him—suspect.

Enter the Queen.

Mustn't Forget Mother

Welshmen are not the only allies who help Harry England become "le Roy." The act 5 appearance of Isabel, Queen of France, raises even more

---

28. Maley, "'This sceptred isle,'" 104.

complicated questions about the gendered and nationalist assumptions interwoven to create the fabric of Tudor "English" identity. Like Davy Gam
but scarier, this French Queen Consort crossed boundaries in legendary
fashion. Shakespeare repeatedly recreates late feudal factions as if they were
the emergent (or in the case of Wales, obliterated) nation-states of his own
day. But when he chooses to include the representation of this Frenchwoman, he also lets in the familial dynamics of that earlier system which
fractured the definition of countries. More particularly, in her roles as wife
and mother, she symbolizes the blood politics that mingled imagined nations
and wreaked havoc with easy definitions of English blood "brotherhood." A
reminder that the English, unlike those who follow the Salic Law, claim
from the female, she is a necessary collaborator aiding Henry's claim to
France; yet for Tudor audiences she and her daughter recall other tricky lineage questions involving Franco-Welsh alliances. Moreover, to the extent
they knew their history, this Queen could conjure all their worst fears.

The French Queen's dramatic role in the Folio text is small: she speaks
fewer than thirty lines. Like the Duke of Burgundy, she arrives in time to
participate in the peace accords ending the bloodshed produced by Henry's
campaign for the French throne. But in her first speech, she does not so
much supplement the ceremonial welcome between Kings Henry and
Charles as challenge it. The scene is one of treaty making; those military
events so humiliating to the French are being translated into dynastic power
and prestige for Henry. Speaking third, however, Isabel refuses to ignore —
as the men have done in their greetings — the violent history that led them
there:

> So happy be the issue, brother England,
> Of this good day and of this gracious meeting,
> As we are now glad to behold your eyes,
> Your eyes which hitherto have borne in them
> Against the French that met them in their bent
> The fatal balls of murdering basilisks.
> The venom of such looks we fairly hope
> Have lost their quality, and that this day
> Shall change all griefs and quarrels into love.
>   (5.2.12–20)

Had she stopped after three lines, her response would have exactly matched
her husband's in length and tone, a proper matron's echo. But Isabel's view
of Henry's eyes prompts a swerve in the rhetoric away from polite formality
to the language of war and mythology, culminating in the punning invocation of basilisks. Among the meanings of "basilisk" in Shakespeare's day, the
first listed by the *OED* is the "fabulous reptile" whose "hissing drove away all

218   other serpents"; its "breath, and even its look, was fatal." Its eyes were believed to project rather than receive light—light that killed.[29] By a common
sixteenth-century transference, using the names of venomous reptiles as
slang for ordnance, the word also came to signify a large cannon that threw
shot weighing about two hundred pounds—perhaps the sort imagined bat-
tering the walls of Harfleur in act 3.[30] Thus Isabel's recollection of the "fatal
balls of murdering basilisks" is a layered reminiscence of Henry's violent
deeds and intent, in terms extending his own figurative language. Her
speech confirms that Henry's threats have indeed transformed the
Dauphin's gift of tennis balls into "gunstones" (1.2.283) to make mothers
weep; the sun always associated with this English king has risen, though it
remains questionable whether his fatal look carries the sort of "glory" he declared would "dazzle all the eyes of France, / Yea, strike the Dauphin blind
to look on us" (1.2.279–81). Along with Burgundy's extended lamentation
for a feminized, conquered French landscape, Isabel's lines expose the false
dichotomy in Henry's initial speech, when he stated that "France being ours,
we'll bend it to our awe, / Or break it all to pieces" (1.2.225–26). Whether
willfully or reluctantly, Henry has instead bent it precisely *by* breaking it,
collapsing the primarily linguistic distinction between conquest and destruction.[31] The truly dazzled, Isabel reminds us, are the dead.

    The basilisk Isabel conjures is all the more suggestive given the conven-
tional gendering of fatal looks, dating back to Medusa's murderous gaze. In
the first act, Henry took on the position of dazzling blinder; he echoes Marlowe's Tamburlaine, another underestimated young man who transforms
himself into an epic figure of military terror and verbal mastery. Katherine
Eggert rightly associates Henry's self-presentation with the phallic power of
England. Yet it is also true that in Shakespeare's plays, the paralyzing gaze
is often associated with women as "anti-historians" (as Phyllis Rackin terms
them), who disrupt the male narrative of action.[32] Isabel's explicit attribu-

29. Taylor, ed., *Henry V,* 266.
30. English cannons (along with the longbow) contributed to the demise of chivalric feudalism, the system still grounding French warfare and social hierarchies in 1415. Jean Markale
links the development of cannons and archery with the rise of the bourgeoisie, who literally
made them: "il y a des profiteurs de la guerre, et paradoxalement, ce ne sont pas les grands nobles féodaux qui pourtant *font* cette guerre"; *Isabeau de Bavière* (Paris, 1982), 9.
31. Shakespeare modifies history to present Henry showing mercy at Harfleur (it was
sacked) and (arguably) with some grounds for his most violent actions. Craik's edition, favoring a positive reading of the King, has a single mention of Isabel, quickly concluding that she
"hopes that now quarrels are to be changed into love—a hope which he echoes" (63). Her name
appears in the First Folio stage directions as Queen Isabel. For the historical figure, I use this
instead of the standard French "Isabelle" (and later, for reasons that will be made evident, another moniker).
32. Katherine Eggert, "Nostalgia and the Not Yet Late Queen: Refusing Female Rule in
Henry V," *ELH* 61, no. 3 (1994): 529; Phyllis Rackin, *Stages of History: Shakespeare's English*

tion of the basilisk's killing look to Henry inverts that convention, revealing its gendering to be reliant on the speaker's perspective. For the French, Henry is the paralyzing disrupter of history and inheritance.

At the same time, in describing Henry's look, Isabel intrudes upon what until this point in the play has been an entirely male world of elite public speech. She momentarily claims the power to comment on the men's ritualization of war, their willingness to incorporate its chaotic violence into a teleological narrative. Without directly defying their logic or blocking the action, she emphasizes its cost, and prompts Henry's assent that his venomous looks have indeed "lost their quality" before she completes her ceremonial greeting. If not exactly an antihistorian, she is at least a revisionist of the official story.

Between her substantial speeches, Isabel makes two brief comments crucial to the political matters at hand. First she volunteers to join the treaty negotiations, observing: "Haply a woman's voice may do some good / When articles too nicely urged be stood on" (5.2.93–94). She then sanctions Henry's request that Katherine stay to be wooed ("She hath good leave" [5.2.98]). The lines signal both Isabel's unusual position of power and her willingness, despite dismay at Henry's destructiveness, to adopt him as her surrogate son: her primary goal is to end the conflict. In placing that goal above sovereignty and nationhood, she embodies one conventional female role as peacemaker, yet by speaking from a position of authority she challenges her marginalization within the emergent political domain of nation-states.[33]

The Queen's active participation recalls the play's political as well as military starting point: the (il)legitimacy of the Salic Law. Her appearance dramatizes the gap between French rhetoric and practice and neatly illus

---

Chronicles (Ithaca, 1990), passim. Such women include Margaret and La Pucelle in the *Henry VI* tetralogy. Jean E. Howard and Phyllis Rackin argue the shift in the second tetralogy signifies a transformed idea of the nation; *Engendering a Nation: A Feminist Account of Shakespeare's English Histories* (New York, 1997), 29–30. This is a claim my reading at least locally qualifies, though the queen's comparative domestication supports some of their broader observations; see especially 6, 10, 14–15, and 186–215. They overlook Isabel (the females at the French court other than Katherine "are not visible or prominent in the play" [4]); indeed, most discussions of the play's concerns with bloodlines and threats to nationalism pay scant attention to the woman voicing worries and hopes about international intermingling. On the woman's part in *Henry V*, see also Eggert's book; Juliet Fleming; Lisa Hopkins; Laurie E. Maguire ("'Household Kates'"); Newman; Alan Sinfield; Peter Erickson (*Patriarchal Structures in Shakespeare's Drama*); and Lance Wilcox. Jardine also suggests intersections of gender and nationalism, though without addressing the complexities the French Queen creates (which could strengthen as well as modify her conclusions).

33. Regarding these lines as reminders that Henry made Katherine a "capital demand," Gary Taylor remarks that when they are cut, it "makes the wooing seem innocent of political overtones" (Taylor, ed., *Henry V*, 315). Isabel's lines also glance at the larger questions of gender and politics that structure the play, of which the "wooing" is but one (crucial) manifestation.

trates the importance of maternity for those claiming the throne. By having Isabel appear only in the scene of diplomacy that endorses Henry's claim, after the English have "proven" their claim on the battlefield, Shakespeare bookends his play's concern with the lawfulness of inheritance through the female line and further differentiates the two nations. It shows that although the French ignore the mother's part when assigning sovereignty, their own queen is a vital agent in determining state policy. By contrast to this French hypocrisy, Henry's acknowledgment of this mother's role—even if grudging and opportunistic—is consistent with his claim to the throne through maternal inheritance. In theory he is not only marrying the French princess but also upholding his great-grandfather Edward III's claim to inherit through his mother, an earlier French princess who married an English king. As Henry thus undoes the Salic Law's prohibition on such inheritance, the cooperation of the French females is symbolically essential.

As the following pages will demonstrate, the historical queen's role in legitimating Henry was far more remarkable than in Shakespeare's play; but even here, she is structurally crucial in validating Henry as one who does not simply batter the weaker nation/sex into submission. Were he resisted—that is, if Katherine and her mother were to continue seeing him as "de enemy of France" (5.2.169–70), as the Dauphin surely would—Henry would be only one more male empowered by force. By replacing the Dauphin with his mother in the final reconciliation scene, Shakespeare achieves in the public domain what Henry's wooing accomplishes in the more intimate scene with Katherine: he enlists the females as collaborators, as if the charismatic Englishman were the chivalric champion of their rights, their means of access to sovereign power through acknowledgment of their reproductive power.

Shakespeare's celebration of this national victory is more subtle than in earlier Elizabethan plays, in part because he adds Isabel to the picture. Both *The Famous Victories of Henry V* and another work mentioned by Thomas Nashe present the Dauphin humbled before Henry in the final scene. Rather than revel in a French comeuppance, Shakespeare instead deletes the Dauphin and introduces his mother.[34] In thus reanimating the figure of

---

34. Those versions present the French Dauphin and/or King being forced to kneel before the conqueror and kiss Henry's sword. Thomas Nashe vaunted "what a glorious thing it is to have Henry the Fifth represented onto the stage, leading the French king prisoner, and forcing both him and the Dauphin to swear fealty"; *Pierce Penniless*, in *The Works of Thomas Nashe*, ed. Ronald B. McKerrow (Oxford, 1958), 213; also Taylor, ed., *Henry V*, 3. Historically, the Dauphin Louis's death provides the obvious explanation for his absence from Shakespeare's treaty scene, but as we shall see, there were other Dauphins and issues involved. The *Famous Victories* (1586) may be the first English history play (see Seymour M. Pitcher; Scott McMillan and Sally-Beth MacLean; Richard Helgerson, *Forms of Nationhood: The Elizabethan Writing of England* [Chicago, 1992], 203), and Shakespeare follows it in "Englishing" the French princess's name (Maguire aptly stresses his pattern of using "Kate," though here was direct precedent).

the French queen, he turned not to the stage but to the chronicle historians Edward Hall (1548) and Raphael Holinshed (1587, 2nd ed.). And with this turn, questions about national identity arise similar to those involving Davy Gam. For this Queen too might cry out (in one European language or another), what is my nation?

Daughter of Stephen II of Bavaria, Elizabeth of Wittelsbach began life as a German. She became a French queen for the same reasons her daughter Catherine would marry Henry V: to solidify feudal alliances and reproduce dynastic heirs. She likewise did not speak the language of her betrothed when, almost fifteen years old, she was brought to France in 1385. Although her sexuality would later become one cause for her vilification, it was also one reason she was made queen in the first place. As Peter Earle indelicately puts it, the Burgundian duke, Philip the Bold, "thought that this good-looking and voluptuous German wench would dominate Charles VI by her animal sensuality and fecundity." Writing during her lifetime, Jean Froissart by contrast stresses her youth and innocence: "she was graceful and sensible by nature and had received a good upbringing . . . [but t]he Duchess of Hainault could not leave her with the clothes and outfit she had come with, for they were too simple by French standards." The variance among historical accounts is par for the course: like Dafydd, she would become the stuff of legends informed by nationalist agendas—and in her case, attitudes toward women as well.[35] Certainly Elizabeth/Isabel did prove her "fecundity," producing twelve children.[36] The now-"French" Isabel thus fulfilled her primary responsibility as queen consort. Or so it seemed in her youth.

As queen consort, she was also pleased to serve as "reine des fêtes et des jeux" (as at the ill-fated Bal des Ardents), attempting on a small scale to

---

Especially given the evidence that the Folio text in which Isabel (like Chorus) appears is based on Shakespeare's own working manuscript, this departure regarding the Dauphin and Isabel appears to have been a conscious personal choice.

35. Peter Earle, *Henry V* (London, 1972), 182. Jean Froissart, *Chronicles*, ed. Geoffrey Brereton (New York, 1979), 256. Contemporary or near-contemporary accounts include Froissart, Christine de Pisan, le Chroniqueur de Saint-Denis, Jean Juvénal des Ursins, Enguerrand de Monstrelet, and the journal of "un Bourgeois de Paris." The English accounts most directly influential on Shakespeare were Hall and Holinshed, though he clearly knew, among others, Froissart (whom he names in *Henry VI, Part 1*, 1.2.29). To show the divergent views and biases regarding Isabel, I draw on a range of historical writings both popular and specialist, including Alice Buchan, Alfred H. Burne, Victor Duruy, Earle, Hopkins, Charles Lethbridge, Markale, Peter Saccio, Desmond Seward, Jules Viard, and the anonymously authored *An English Chronicle of the Reigns of Richard II., Henry IV., Henry V., and Henry VI.* and *England and France under the House of Lancaster*.

36. Among them were three sons who were successively heirs apparent to the French throne (the Dauphins Louis, Jean, and Charles) and two daughters who married English monarchs: Isabel, the second child-wife of Richard II, and Catherine, who married the son of Richard's deposer.

222   mimic Eleanor of Aquitaine's court of love; Christine de Pisan would be among the writers she patronized. But in 1392, after several happy if financially indulgent years of marriage, Charles VI had the first of his periodic fits of madness; on horseback near Mans, exhausted by his lords' factional feuding and provoked by a mysterious stranger warning of treachery, he murdered his attendants. A distraught Isabel sought remedies for his illness, but as the years wore on, "one of the features of his madness was to be an aversion to his Queen."[37] The fact that she eventually became the intimate companion, and likely the lover, of his brother Louis, Duc d'Orléans, did not help matters—or her reputation.[38] Nevertheless, under the king's orders she repeatedly acted as regent when Charles was incapacitated.

Her greater responsibility involved her more directly with the infighting among the nobility stoked by feudalism's slow decline. Even as poverty, plague, and popular uprisings signaled the structural failure of the feudal order, familial loyalties and suzerainties continued to determine "public" policy, and Isabel's advisers initially included the Burgundian Duke Philippe le Hardi and her German brother, Louis de Bavière. As a woman, she was expected (and needed) to rely on the male peerage for security as well as advice; thus political positions shifted when friends such as Philippe died. Without a strong monarch, the peers also turned to violence in jockeying for power, usually with success. The royal Louis's murder in 1407 by agents of the new Duke of Burgundy, Jean sans Peur (the Fearless), sparked years of civil war between the Burgundians and the Armagnacs (those relatives avenging Louis).[39] Historians have criticized Isabel's wanton behavior and her use of the regency to avenge the murder of her friends, attacks echoed by literary scholars.[40] But even if the claims are true, a tendency toward violence, selfishness, and profligacy would hardly distinguish

37. Earle, *Henry V*, 182.

38. Desmond Seward calls her Charles VI's "beautiful, sluttish wife"; *The Hundred Years War* (London, 1978), 138. The general shift in historical studies (from a focus on elites to broader examination of social and economic conditions) has not encouraged work reevaluating the queen's biography. Until recently, it was stated as fact that Isabel's close relationship with her brother-in-law was sexual; some historians and feminist authors have begun to question that presumption (see Hopkins, Markale, and Marina Warner).

39. The latter faction was led by Bernard, Comte d'Armagnac, father-in-law of Louis's son Charles d'Orléans.

40. Charles Kean's souvenir promptbook said the Queen "was equally remarkable for her beauty and her depravity" (promptbooks, *Henry V*, Folger Shakespeare Library Microfilm Collection, no. 6:37). These common accusations have made their way into the appraisals of Saccio and Gary Taylor; they can be found in almost any of the standard historical sources with the exception of Froissart, a Hainault partisan. However, the Restoration play *Henry V* by Roger Boyle, Earl of Orrery, indicates that accounts more sympathetic to Isabel—at least in her struggles with the Dauphin—were in English circulation c. 1660.

her in this chaotic landscape of baronial bloodshed. At least in part, the greater moral outrage induced by her actions can be attributed to her foreign origin and gender. All of which was compounded by her notorious collaboration with the King of England.

This civil unrest in France provided the occasion for Henry V's adventurism, yet Agincourt itself did not put an end to internecine violence among the (surviving) nobility. Rather, after two years of stalemate with the English, it was Isabel who changed the political landscape. In Peter Saccio's dismissive phrasing, "Charles's queen, the self-indulgent, licentious, and flighty Isabel of Bavaria, altered the balance of affairs by leaving the Armagnacs to join John [the Duke of Burgundy]."[41] She again declared herself regent and in alliance with Jean sans Peur established a government at Troyes. Following a popular rebellion against Armagnac's harsh rule, they won the support of Paris. But Isabel had not simply up and left the Armagnacs owing to fickle giddiness, as Saccio and others imply. She had in fact been imprisoned at Blois and then Tours during 1417 through the agency of the Constable and her son Charles (who became heir apparent when his two older brothers died). Rumors abounded that her older son Jean had been poisoned by the Armagnac camp.[42] Finally, Armagnac had reported to the king that she was having a love affair with her steward, Louis de Bosredon (or Boisbourdon), leading to his murder. This ignominy and the queen's resulting vulnerability added to the ample motivation for her shift back to the Burgundians, who had always been the territorial and blood allies of her birth family. It may have been the very desperation of her position that likewise led to her (in)famous attempt to regain power through maternity—but as queen mother to an English rather than a French son.

She had material motivation as well. A marginal summation in Holinshed puts it bluntly: "The yoong Dolphin fleeced his old moother of hir trasure, what mischeeferose upon it."[43] Nevertheless, even in this sixteenth-century work of English nation building, the chronicler sympathizes with the belligerent Dauphin rather than with his mother:

---

41. Peter Saccio, *Shakespeare's English Kings: History, Chronicle, and Drama* (New York, 1977), 85.

42. Contemporaries reported that the Dauphin Jean had been poisoned because of his Burgundian sympathies; thus Jean, like his older brother Louis represented in *Henry V*, died before attaining the throne. If the story is true, here was another reason for Isabel's anger at Armagnac and Charles. Moreover, her direct power diminished when her sons approached the age of majority, the peers caring less about obtaining either her or her husband's official consent.

43. The Victorian author of *England and France under the House of Lancaster* (London, 1852) more delicately observes that the Dauphin seized his mother's treasures to be "applied to the public service"—that is, the military campaigns (144–45).

Charles the Dolphin being of the age of sixteene or seaventeene yeares, bewailed the ruine and decaie of his countrie ... but having neither men nor monie, was greatlie troubled ... he found a meane to get all the treasure and riches which his moother queene Isabell had gotten and hoorded in diverse secret places: and for the common defense and profit of his countrie he wiselie bestowed it in waging souldiers, and preparing of things necessarie for the warre.

As Shakespeare's Henry also knows, war is a great fundraiser—at least among men. Isabel felt differently, and would be castigated for it: "The queen forgetting the great perill that the realme then stood in, remembring onelie the displeasure to hir by this act doone, upon a womanish malice, set hir husband John duke of Burgognie in the highest authoritie about the king, giving him the regiment and direction of the king and his realme."[44] Vitriol aimed at her "womanish" behavior leads to another slur, the labeling of Burgundy as her "husband."[45] While Annabel Patterson may be right that "most of the chroniclers [in Holinshed] show a precise interest in anecdotes revelatory of female resistance, which on the whole they rather seem to admire," these passages do not bear out the observation.[46] And this was the history with which Shakespeare was working.

In Isabel's case, a mad husband, several murdered lovers or friends, and a thieving son would seem sufficient grounds for "womanish malice." Castle arrest was simply icing on the poisoned cake.[47] Moreover, Isabel apparently feared the political chaos and violence caused by the disputes among the nobility (with good reason), and saw the English as the inevitable beneficiaries and victors. Better to negotiate an acceptable peace treaty than be conquered. Even if she was not acting directly on Christine de Pisan's gendered advice (cited in my chapter's second epigraph, from a 1405 volume written

44. Raphael Holinshed, *Holinshed's Chronicles*, ed. R. S. Wallace and Alma Hansen (Westport, CT, 1978), 57.

45. Gender becomes the fundamental source of contention, as the next episode in Holinshed confirms: it elaborates on the "malice" caused by wives, noting a 1418 slaughter at St. Dunstan's near London due to two "gentlewomen of evill disposition." The juxtaposition reinforces the cultural distinction between large-scale violence in battle (glorious and responsible) and the petty but consequential hatreds of vain women (the section ends with "the verdict of the poet concerning the said sex: *Fœmina lœtalis, fœmina plena malis*"; 62).

46. Annabel Patterson, *Reading Holinshed's Chronicles* (Chicago, 1994), 216.

47. Nor do her son's actions seem concerned with "the realm" and "public service" so much as with his own skin and interests. This same Charles later benefited from the services of Jeanne d'Arc and then allowed the Burgundians to give her to the English, who burned her. Even if one blames mother for the Dauphin's weakness of character (see Alice Buchan, *Joan of Arc and the Recovery of France* [London, 1948], 26), his behavior makes one understand Isabel's interest in her daughter's fortunes (see Markale, *Isabeau*, 213).

at the French court and presented to the Queen), Isabel had decided it was time for "pacifying men."

Thus it was she, accompanied by Burgundy and not the King, who led her preferred child, Catherine, to a meeting at Meulan in 1419. Shakespeare's source Edward Hall confirms Isabel's political centrality:

> [T]he French party thither came [led by] Isabel the French Queen because the King her husband was fallen into his old frenetical disease . . . and she had attending on her the fair Lady Katherine her daughter and twenty-five ladies and damsels, and had also for her furniture a thousand men of war. . . . The King of England . . . received humbly the French queen and her daughter and them honorably embraced and familiarly kissed.[48]

Much has been made of this kiss. *The First English Life of King Henry V* (1513) observes that nothing came of the meeting except the flame of love, and even a twentieth-century military historian concludes that "Henry kissed her and immediately fell in love with her." Holinshed elaborates on Isabel's role in bringing this to pass: "The said ladie Katherine was brought by hir mother, onelie to the intent that the king of England beholding hir excellent beautie, should be so inflamed and rapt in hir love, that he to obteine hir to his wife, should the sooner agree to a gentle peace and loving concord."[49]

These sentimental narratives motivate the exchange in Shakespeare's act 5 between Henry and Isabel, in which she sanctions Katherine's remaining with the King; they also help explain the larger shift of mood to romantic comedy in the scene following. A perennial stage favorite, the wooing scene culminates in a kiss that for Henry bears "witchcraft" (5.2.273). That old black magic blinds Henry, as he tells Burgundy afterward—in lines of swaggering machismo which, despite their completing a crucial pattern of imagery, are usually cut in performance. Invoking blind Cupid and the need for maidens not only to "wink" but be blind themselves in order for men to achieve their love, Henry concludes: "and you may some of you thank love for my blindness, who cannot see many a fair French city for one fair French maid that stands in my way" (5.2.297, 313–15). From dazzling destroyer to blind lover: a mother's words and her daughter's mouth have thus prompted the basilisk's eyes to "lose their quality" and allow peace.

    48. Hall, ff. HV, xxxiii verso–xxxiv recto, as cited in Seymour M. Pitcher, *The Case for Shakespeare's Authorship of "The Famous Victories," with the complete text of the anonymous play* (New York, 1961), 223.

    49. Charles Lethbridge, ed., *The First English Life of King Henry V* (Oxford, 1911), 145; Alfred H. Burne, *The Agincourt War* (London, 1991), 140; Holinshed, *Chronicles*, 85.

But not right away, historically. For despite the kiss and Shakespeare's dramaturgical condensation, Meulan did not produce a treaty. The Victorian author of *England and France under the House of Lancaster* makes this the occasion for another gendered barb at Isabel; he remarks that the Princess's beauty "made a tender impression upon the English monarch, insomuch that the Queen-mother, with the calculating and sanguine spirit of her sex, hoped for better terms. In this, however, she was disappointed." In fact, it was Burgundy who found the English monarch's territorial demands too extreme to countenance. Not incidentally, Burgundy's resistance coincided with the arrival of an embassy from the Dauphin, territories under Armagnac control also being involved in the negotiations.[50] The secret communications and triangulated diplomacy were byzantine; suffice it to say that Burgundy's negotiations with both the English and the Dauphin failed, and the following year brought more bloodshed. Henry took advantage of the infighting to complete his horrific siege of Rouen, which briefly reconciled Isabel and Burgundy with the young Dauphin for the sake of "France"—but then the Armagnacs had Burgundy murdered in an ambush.[51] This treacherous act drove Jean's son and heir, Philip the Good—the Burgundy who appears in Shakespeare's final act—back into an alliance with England. Thus in May 1420, all these machinations and reversals led to successful negotiations involving Burgundy, France, and England, culminating in the treaty at Troyes.

The two meetings at Meulan and Troyes (and the delay between) may account for a slight tonal difference when Shakespeare's Isabel returns after Katherine and Henry's private interview. Her second speech is more conciliatory and forward-looking, befitting this ceremony of treaty ratification. She marks a shift from French grieving to the (desperate) hope that the marriage contained among the treaty's conditions will prevent further violence.

> God, the best maker of marriages,
> Combine your hearts in one, your realms in one!
> As man and wife, being two, are one in love,
> So be there 'twixt your kingdoms such a spousal
> That never may ill office or fell jealousy,
> Which troubles oft the bed of blessed marriage,
> Thrust in between the paction of these kingdoms
> To make divorce of their incorporate league;
> That English may as French, French Englishmen,

50. *England and France under the House of Lancaster*, 174. Charles, who had survived the 1417 Paris rising that killed many Armagnacs (among them the Constable), set up a rival government at Poitiers.

51. Burgundy's murder occurred at Montereau, as he left a direct negotiation with the Dauphin.

Receive each other. God speak this amen.
All Amen.

(5.2.344–54)

Structurally, Isabel's prayer can contribute to a comedic, even utopian, sense of an ending, as if to endorse Henry's assertion that God fought for the English at Agincourt, that the spirit of Richard II and internal English dissension have been laid to rest by the King's rhetoric and military exploits, and that he and his "Kate" can indeed create a crusader to unite Western Europe, if not universalize Christendom. Of course, the epilogue will soon remind those not familiar with English history (or with the popular *Henry VI* plays Shakespeare had penned nearly a decade prior) that the hopes expressed in this prayer will promptly come to nothing.

Moreover, like the intrusion of the basilisk, the Queen's rhetoric again includes a negative swerve. Nearly half of Isabel's prayer attempts to ward off evil: jealousy, ill office, and consequent divorce threaten to wreck this tenuous vision.[52] God must indeed help if this marriage is to enclose France within England as neatly as does her penultimate line's compensatory chiasmus. For all Henry's (and Shakespeare's) effort to present this as a natural conclusion and national alliance, these lines mark an uneasy peace. As the discovered treason plot, thievery, and verbal battles amongst soldiers of various "nations" earlier attested, "England" itself is still far from an easily "incorporate[d] league." Katherine's bawdy English lesson and Henry's brief excursus into another tongue comically use linguistics to illustrate the distances yet to be overcome between kingdoms—and to remind us at whose expense.[53] From Katherine's first appearance directly after the surrender of

---

52. Hodgdon (*End*) notes the analogy with the fairies' concluding speeches in *A Midsummer Night's Dream*, which also name fearful possibilities to be forestalled. Kay Stanton suggests that "the brutalities of both English and French history depicted in [*Henry VI*] need not have arisen if King Harry had heeded the last female voice of Henry V"; "Nell Quickly, Doll Tearsheet, and the Sexual Politics of the Henriad's Subplot," *Proceedings of the Third Annual California State University Shakespeare Symposium*, ed. Edward L. Rocklin and Joseph H. Stodder (Pomona, 1993), cited from manuscript. While appreciating her attention to the symbolic logic of the women's roles, I do not find such utopian feminism supported by the play or the historical events. Craik's added exclamation point in Isabel's speech accords with his choice to accentuate the positive.

53. The parallel with the linguistically divided Mortimers in *Henry IV, Part 1*, 3.1, reinforces the power imbalance here: Mortimer says he will not rest until he has learned his wife's Welsh tongue, but Henry expresses no such eagerness, whereas Katherine has already begun to mix English with her French. Anthony Brennan reads the scene as simply "charming," but notes a resemblance between Henry's wooing and Pistol's stumbling battlefield French: "Henry's struggle with French reminds us that England's gain and Pistol's individual profit have something in common—the demand for submission to irresistible mastery"; *Henry V* (New York, 1992), 59–60, 91. In Pistol's case at least, this "mastery" is deeply ironic.

Harfleur to the play's final moments when Burgundy and Henry banter about her being a siege substitute, Shakespeare makes clear that it is the Frenchwoman (and the territory she symbolizes) who must be "incorporated" into England.

Isabel's fragile prayer befits what must have seemed a tenuous occasion for peace at the historical Troyes. There, Hall reports, Henry "went to visit the King, the Queen, and the Lady Katherine . . . where was a joyous meeting, honorable receiving and a loving embracing on both parties." But most remarkable was the consequence for Dauphin Charles: he was disinherited. As Saccio explains it, "Isabel herself declared him a bastard, borne by her to an unnamed lover." The adverbs used by some historians increase one's sense of amazement: she "cheerfully claiming that the Dauphin was a bastard by one of her lovers"; "she said openly, not caring who overheard, that he was a bastard ánd not the rightful heir at all."[54] This scandalous renunciation provided the rationale for the treaty conditions officially making Henry the son of Charles and Isabel and the heir to France. Suddenly it was a wise Dauphin who knew his own father.

That Isabel could make such an assertion and remain queen consort says much about the state of French affairs (in all senses). One thinks by contrast of Henry VIII's treatment of putatively errant spouses a century later. Her action adds another layer of irony to Shakespeare's composition of the lines: "Haply a woman's voice may do some good / When articles too nicely urged be stood on." The "good" no longer sounds like simple peacemaking; indeed, given Isabel's reported desire for vengeance upon her son, it may be a stretch to call her action "good" at all. More generously, one may see Isabel as stalwart on behalf of her daughter's future as the next queen mother — whether she be deemed English, French, or "other."[55] Both objectives invert the gendered hierarchies of the day.

Indeed, Isabel's actions continued to provoke outbursts from French historians centuries later, repeatedly interweaving nationalist and gendered criticisms. Writing in the early twentieth century, Victor Duruy laments (reiterating the "shame" Shakespeare's Bourbon expresses at Agincourt): "On May 21, 1420, the shameful Treaty of Troyes was concluded between Henry V, the Duke of Burgundy, and Queen Isabella of France, by which the last-

54. Pitcher, *Case*, 225; Saccio, *Shakespeare's English Kings*, 87; Seward, *Hundred Years War*, 181; Buchan, *Joan of Arc*, 26.

55. This was also an act of self-preservation for Isabel, who would have no power if her son inherited the throne. Unfortunately for her, less than five years later the premature death of Henry led to the same end, and in 1429 as part of the treaty of Arras, Burgundy retracted his position and recognized Charles VII as rightful heir.

named disinherited her son to crown her daughter. The very summary of the terms may well cause shame to any Frenchman." He avers (rhetoric swelling) that not only hunger and occupation eventually led to the unifying French desire to drive out the English: "the belief grew that the kingdom, betrayed by a woman, the unworthy Queen Isabella of Bavaria, would be delivered by a maid of the people, a virgin. This heroic daughter of the masses, this virgin deliverer, was Joan of Arc." In condemning Isabel, Duruy is not alone in making much of her birth, a reminder that the nonnative queen always remains a suspicious, liminal figure.[56]

The very idea of a betrayed "French nation," more recent historians have observed, is anachronistic; feudal infighting and rebellions made loyalties as personal and fluid in French-speaking territories as they were on the Welsh borders. Yet there was a French crown, and an emergent system of nation-states developed soon after, attaining by Shakespeare's time enough ideological weight for "nation" to become a key word in his play. And the nascent patriotism inspired by Jeanne d'Arc, appearing only eight years after the Treaty of Troyes, required a foreign villain as well as a French heroine (even if the heroine herself arguably came from the Holy Roman Empire, from a border territory outside "la France actuelle"). The figure of the English Duke of Bedford not affording sufficient scope for loathing, who better than a "foreign" female, an Eve to motivate a redeeming Virgin? Aged, bereft of her powerful male allies, and forbidden access to her English grandson Henry VI, Isabel made a promising candidate for mythic transformation. After her death, she became an even more convenient scapegoat. And so in 1982, a French biographer must still begin his more sympathetic account by acknowledging the story so useful to nationalist ideology:

---

56. Victor Duruy, *A Short History of France* (New York, 1917), 1:356, 363. Nor are these nationalist assumptions made only by the French; a nineteenth-century British historian thus describes Troyes: "The unheard-of proceeding by which two foreigners, Philip and the Queen, . . . took upon themselves, for the gratification of their own vindictive passions, to alienate the Crown of France . . . was enough to rouse the most indifferent of French subjects"; *England and France under the House of Lancaster*, 193. Isabel remains a foreigner after spending thirty-five of her fifty years as Queen of France.

Jules Viard summarizes Isabel's later decline as if it were poetic justice for the treaty by which "she surrendered France":

> After her triumphal entry into Paris with [her husband, Henry V, and Katherine], she soon became an object of loathing to the whole French nation. She survived her husband, her son-in-law, and eight out of her twelve children, and she passed the last miserable years of her life in poverty, solitude, and ill health. She died at the end of September 1435 and was interred without funeral honors in the abbey of St. Denis, by the side of her husband.
> (*Encyclopedia Britannica*, 11th ed., s.v. "Isabella, Isabeau, or Elizabeth of Bavaria.")

In fact, Isabel's death was not unattended by peers, although a barge transported her bier to St. Denis so as to avoid hostile Armagnac neighborhoods.

230   Isabeau de Bavière a laissé dans l'Histoire un nom entaché d'ignominie. Pen-
dant des générations, les écoliers ont appris à maudire cette reine de France
qui renia son fils et livra le royaume au roi d'Angleterre. Aucune femme
célèbre de l'Histoire de France n'a été autant haïe, non pas par les contempo-
rains, mais par la postérité. Isabeau, dont le nom même, qui lui a été donné par
les Français, traduit bien une nuance de mépris puisqu'il s'agit d'un sobriquet
désignant en fait *Isabelle* . . . [57]

Having obscured the boundaries of nationhood not only through her German birth but through her alliance with the English, the tainted queen cannot be allowed even the French version of her name intact. Although she
signed "Ysabel," she is known to history—with a "sense of contempt"—as
"Isabeau." The renaming aptly signals the other social boundary she was
perceived to violate, that of conventionally constructed gender: she becomes
the masculine "beau," not the feminine "belle."

The life of "Isabeau de Bavière" thus exemplifies the precariousness of
queenly power, just as the Salic Law institutionalized its paradoxical nature
(necessary to the Crown's reproduction yet not allowed to embody or bestow sovereignty). Her multiple forms of "otherness" were the source of
both her usefulness and her dangerousness within the system of feudal
monarchy.[58] While the structural ambiguity of Isabel's position typifies the
plight of many queens consort, she also brought to the role an exceptional
character.[59] Yet she had never been trained for, or shown any temperamen-
tal interest in, governance. The factional jockeying among the king's male
relatives led to her becoming an active regent in the first place, exercising
authority according to her own predispositions and familial loyalties as well
as those of the (varying) figures who courted her alliance. If Isabeau came
to be seen as a monstrous collaborator, it was the "proper" male aristocracy
that created her.

57. "Isabeau de Bavière left in history a name laden with infamy. For generations, school-
children have learned to curse this queen of France who disowned her son and handed over the
realm to the king of England. No famous woman in the history of France has been so hated, not
only by her contemporaries, but by posterity. The name Isabeau itself, given to her by the
French, imparts a sense of contempt, since it is in fact a nickname for Isabelle"; Markale, *Isabeau,* 7, translation mine with assistance from Gilberte Furstenberg.
58. Aristocratic women played important political roles both because of the vital need to solidify territorial and familial alliances through marriages and because high mortality rates left
them wielding power over duchies and kingdoms; Yolande d'Aragon and Anne de Bretagne are
two fourteenth-century "French" examples.
59. On problems involved in the representations of queens, including finer distinctions between queens consort and queens regnant, see the essays in Louise Fradenburg's volume.

Despite massive changes in political context—from the era of late feudal collapse in which she lived, through the time of emerging nation-states when *Henry V* was penned, into our own day when representational government has made monarchy truly a matter of "ceremony"—one constant adheres in the historical representation of the French Queen: she figures a woman with real, but obscurely legitimated, political power. And in marrying her daughter Catherine to Henry, she created another "French" queen mother whose shadow lurks in English history: the woman who gave birth to Henry VI, but also the widow who married Owain Tudor after Henry's early death. In the end, the French Princess who married "Harry England" herself turned Welsh.[60]

Her mother Isabel's story similarly illustrates the systemic way in which queenship confounded national purity. Looking at the historical record reveals just how much artistic craft and ideological reshaping was required for Shakespeare to make *Henry V* end peacefully. What he leaves out suggests the extent of her threat to his form of gendered resolution, which requires what one might call her "domestication" or "pacification"; at the same time, his decision to include her at all creates a more consistent, less jingoistic play, one attentive throughout to the problematic necessity of claiming through the female and collaborating with the foreign.

Seeking his own peace, Shakespeare omits any reference to "Isabeau's" most unmaternal action at Troyes. Indeed, he omits all the complexities of the Queen's past readily available to him in his chronicle sources.[61] Shakespeare's Isabel may recall the earlier Dauphin's tennis balls jest when she mentions those "fatal balls" that had the power to (as Henry predicted) "mock mothers from their sons" (1.2.287); yet her estrangement and mockery of her own son are removed. As the only mother Shakespeare includes in his play, Isabel in her final speech blessing the marriage acknowledges only the benign role of maternity in perpetuating a royal line.

The chroniclers' Isabeau (as I shall now distinguish the historical figure) more closely resembles those fearsome, wanton women who haunted Shake-

---

60. Hopkins parenthetically notes the connection; "Fluellen's Name," *Shakespeare Studies* 24 (1996): 153.

61. The closest thing to acknowledgment of the hereditary disavowal occurs when the French King temporarily resists "that one article" concerning his naming of Henry as son and heir to France: "*Notre très cher fils Henri, roi d'Angleterre, héritier de France*; and thus in Latin, *Praeclarissimus filius noster Henricus, rex Angliae et haeres Franciae*" (5.2.340, 333–36). But the moment swiftly passes, and even this brief objection remains a concern exclusively between men. Although Latin and French would be the appropriate languages for diplomatic and legal proceedings, the absence of an assertion in English dramatically mutes this transfer of power.

232   speare's imagination in the *Henry VI* plays to which the *Henry V* epilogue returns in sadness. To mention Isabeau's challenge to paternity, however, would rupture the unequal collaboration between English and French, male and female, that Shakespeare's fifth act attempts. After all, as Phyllis Rackin reminds us in a different context,

> The son's name and entitlement and legitimacy all derived from the father, and only the father was included in the historiographic text. But only the mother could guarantee that legitimacy. As bearers of the life that names, titles, and historical records could never fully represent, the women were keepers of the unspoken and unspeakable reality that always threatened to belie the words that pretended to describe it.[62]

Other royal personages in the century before Shakespeare had proclaimed the bastardy of heirs to the throne; Shakespeare himself wrote plays about two such accusers, Richard III and Henry VIII.[63] But here in the time of Henry V, the assertion came not from a rival claimant but from the mother herself, and if granted authority, called into question both her morals and the legitimacy of a slightly older child: the crucial princess Catherine. Most historians dismiss Isabeau's claim about her son's illegitimacy, and given Charles VII's eventual reclamation of that throne it is expedient not only for her honor but for the later Valois dynasty that they do so.[64] But she nevertheless exposed the deep, irremovable contradiction of state reliance on the word and deed of an errant queen—for the English as well as the French. Through the very action by which she became Henry's official mother, Is-

---

62. Rackin, *Stages*, 191.

63. According to Froissart, during deposition proceedings Henry IV imputed that Richard II might have been illegitimate: "'and now the rumour is . . . that you are not the son of the Prince of Wales . . . that when the Prince felt his marriage was a failure . . . she, who had won him in marriage by guile and cunning, was afraid that my uncle the Prince would find some pretext for divorcing her. So she arranged to become pregnant and gave birth to you, . . . whose habits and character are so different from the warlike nature of the Prince, it is said in this country and elsewhere that your father was a clerk or canon. . . . ' King Richard swallowed all these things which the Duke of Lancaster said to him and had nothing to say in reply. He quite saw that neither force nor argument could help him, but only meekness, friendliness and plain dealing"; Froissart, *Chronicles*, 460–61. Even Henry V's lineage was somewhat shady (see Hopkins, "Fluellen's Name," 151).

64. Catherine was a year and a half older than Charles, and both were born at least a decade after the onset of Charles VI's illness. Markale argues that even if Isabeau had an affair with Louis d'Orléans, the most likely candidate, it was not until after Charles's birth. The loose reputation of Louis, "le débauché des années 1390" (Markale, *Isabeau*, 89), and others at court, however, made the accusations plausible in their day (and after). Indeed, the Dauphin Charles himself had nagging doubts about his paternity.

abeau challenged a son's faith in the maternal bond that underwrote English assaults on the Salic Law. Shakespeare artfully finesses the problem of Henry's needing the endorsement of such a woman.[65]

The French Queen carries with her a subtext of fear of the liminal female that extends beyond her own representation; she recalls by name the earlier Queen Isabel (1292–1358) who was the historical source for Henry's French claim.[66] *Her* name is omitted from earlier speeches in the play directly concerning that inheritance, pointedly: Shakespeare's Archbishop of Canterbury—who seems to name everyone he possibly can when recounting the genealogy of the Salic Law itself—does not mention her. Nor does any other character rousing Henry to remember his lineage refer to that crucial French Queen Isabel.[67] This is all the more notable given that Hall's chronicle had the Archbishop assert the connection directly: "Regard well, my sovereign Lord, your just and true title to the realm of France . . . as very heir to Queen Isabel, your great grandmother, daughter to King Philip the Fair and sister and heir to three kings deceasing without issue. This inheritance from the woman is declared to be just by the Mosaical law and used and approved

65. Lisa Hopkins suggests a possible reference to her sexual misconduct, though it is oblique indeed: she posits that the Archbishop's "pointed reference to the 'dishonest manners of . . . life' of German women (1.2.49) may also be recalled by anyone who happens to remember 'Queen Isabel's' nationality"; "Fluellen's Name," 153. Jardine emphasizes the problem of the "mixed nationality" of her daughter Catherine's direct offspring: her Frenchness undermines "the male fiction of the pure and proper blood-line" and "threatens to taint its ethnic purity" (*Reading*, 10). The problem was systemic.

66. The daughter of Philip IV and the sister of the last three Capetian monarchs (all of whom died without a living male heir), she became Edward II's wife and Edward III's mother.

67. Alan Sinfield, *Faultlines: Cultural Materialism and the Politics of Dissident Reading* (Berkeley, 1992), 129ff. Eggert notes: "[Isabella of France's] name appears . . . only as a distant echo in Canterbury's genealogy of the French monarchy, as a different, more distant Isabella, the French 'fair Queen Isabel' from whom 'King Lewis the Tenth' derived his claim to the French throne (1.2.76–82)"; "Nostalgia," 529. In *The Famous Victories*, the Archbishop does refer to "your great grandmother Isabel," though he inaccurately (or wishfully) names her as wife rather than mother to Edward III. The play *Edward III* (which some are now attributing in part to Shakespeare) does mention Isabel in its discussion of the Salic Law.

The Salic Law was revived to justify transferring the crown to Isabella's cousin, Philip VI (the first Valois). Froissart presents this as the reason for subsequent unrest: "The twelve peers and all the barons of France would not give the realm to Isabel the sister, who was Queen of England, because they said and maintained, and still do, that the realm of France is so noble that it ought not to go to a woman, and so consequently neither to Isabel, nor to the King of England, her eldest son. . . . Thus the realm of France went out of the right lineage, as it seemed to many folk, whereby great wars have arisen, and great destructions of people and countries in the realm of France and other places"; F. J. Tickner, ed., *A Shorter Froissart* (London, [n.d.]), 22–23. Markale agrees that the Salic "law" was only a custom, invoked and overlooked strategically: "Le système dans lequel devait évoluer Isabeau de Bavière était ce qu'on pourrait appeler 'phallocratique' . . . l'accent était mis définitivement sur le pouvoir mâle" (*Isabeau*, 18).

234 by the Gallican descent."[68] This inheritance, not simply the hand of Princess Catherine, was always the historical Henry's "capital demand." When the French offered money and the princess, he rejected the offer (as Shakespeare's act 3 Chorus acknowledges, swiftly glossing past why "the offer likes not").[69] Henry instead wanted the princess and the inheritance. But the troubling maternal source for that inheritance is erased from Shakespeare's play, leaving only a (superficially) less daunting namesake.

Regarding the play as "a powerful Elizabethan fantasy simply because nothing is allowed to compete with the authority of the king," Alan Sinfield argues that "dependence upon female influence over inheritance, legitimacy, and the state produces so much anxiety that the English can hardly bring themselves to name it."[70] Knowledge of the changes in representing Isabeau de Bavière reinforces that sense of anxiety within the play (though to call it "Elizabethan" carries obvious ironies). For theatergoers familiar with Marlowe's *Edward II*, a supplementary reason for erasing the "source Isabel" would be clear: to remember Edward's Isabel casts quite a pall over Princess Katherine's impending marriage among the English audience.[71] Nor did one need to look so far back to discover problems in English/French royal marriages. Isabeau's own child and namesake, Catherine's eldest surviving sister, had married the other English king to be deposed and murdered during the fourteenth century. Even after Richard II's death, an ongoing conflict in Anglo-French relations for many years concerned the English failure to return her dower money.[72] Though she was later remarried to Charles, Duc d'Orleans (son of Isabeau's first murdered companion), this young Isabel's

68. Hall, cited in Pitcher, *Case*, 211.

69. If anything, it is implied that the "petty and unprofitable" nature of the dukedoms offered, rather than the French title, was at issue.

70. Sinfield, *Faultlines*, 121.

71. Suffering from Edward's neglect, she became Mortimer's lover and her husband's nemesis. She also became a mythic figure of evil in most English representations. In the eighteenth century, Thomas Gray's Welsh *Bard* apostrophized:

> She-Wolf of France, with unrelenting fangs,
> That tear'st the bowels of thy mangled Mate,
> From thee be born, who o'er thy country hangs
> The scourge of Heav'n.

Henry S. Pancoast, ed., *Standard English Poems* (New York, 1905), 224. The wheel comes full circle: Shakespeare's own slur from *Henry VI, Part 3* returns to haunt an earlier queen than Margaret. Gray's savage representation is starkly rendered late in Derek Jarman's film of Marlowe's *Edward II*. By contrast, Froissart was born in Hainault and aided by its ruling family, who had been the champions of this Isabel; Edward III was to marry Philippa of Hainault. In the early seventeenth century, Elizabeth Cary's *Edward II* also represents the earlier Isabel more sympathetically.

72. E. F. Jacob, *Henry V and the Invasion of France* (London, 1947), 68.

plight provided another unpleasant reminder of a queen consort's uncertain usefulness as a bargaining chip between kingdoms.[73]

One more exceptional but shadowy female informs the appearance of Shakespeare's Isabel; known in England as Joan of Navarre (1370?–1437), she was the other Queen Mother to Henry. Reading the second tetralogy, one would not suspect Henry IV of having a living wife or Hal a stepmother. Yet this was the person Henry V left in power when beginning his French campaign. As act 1 scene 2 makes apparent, the other major concern besides Henry's claim to the French throne is his kingdom's safety from Scottish invasion should he go abroad. It is again the Archbishop who counters such fears:

> Divide your happy England into four,
> Whereof take you one quarter into France
> And you withal shall make all Gallia shake.
> If we with thrice such powers left at home
> Cannot defend our own doors from the dog,
> Let us be worried and our nation lose
> The name of hardiness and policy.
>
> (1.2.215–21)

The name actually lost here is woman—as if England were an all-male nation. The Archbishop's idea of a hardy "we" hardly conjures females among its powerful numbers. The chronicler Hall once more serves as a reminder that historical events transpired differently, and that Shakespeare knew it.[74]

As regent, Henry's stepmother attracted controversy and mistrust—and again the liminal national identification of queens consort played its part.

73. Froissart recounts the girl queen's isolation when Richard was taken, her household being "so broken up that neither man, woman nor child was left to her" (*Chronicles*, 454). She and Catherine remain the only two of Isabel's female children to merit representation on (some) genealogical charts of the French royal family. Princesses enter the historical stage when they succeed as maternal bearers or serve as active consorts, and when alliances fail. Seen thus, the grief born of "nothing" suffered by Shakespeare's version of the young Isabel in *Richard II* emblematizes a childless queen's weighty emptiness—her truly cipherlike status within the "great account" of history (a status *Henry V*'s Chorus transfers to his fellow actors). Howard and Rackin say of her: "the only English queen who appears in the canonical histories [i.e., the second tetralogy] is the wife of Richard II. Nameless, she has very little time on stage and no function in the plot of Richard's fall" (*Engendering*, 24–25). But if we give her back her name and place of birth, this French/English queen, like her mother in *Henry V*, complicates gendered distinction between the tetralogies. Like Margaret of Anjou in the *Henry VI* plays, all these Isabels are liminal figures in international politics, would-be suturers who fail.

74. "When the King had ordered all things for the tuition and safeguard of his realm and people, he, leaving behind him for governor of the realm the Queen, his mother-in-law [*sic*], departed to the town of Southampton"; Hall, f. HV, xi recto, in Pitcher, *Case*, 215.

236 For before Joan of Navarre married Henry IV, she had been Jeanne de Navarre, widow of Jean IV, Duc de Bretagne. Her second son by that marriage even fought with the French at Agincourt and was taken prisoner by the English.[75] Jeanne's situation, guarding England while her stepson fought her son in France, epitomizes the feudal system's awkward use of royal women, creating at least the appearance of split loyalties that could then be held against them. Joan was imprisoned in 1419:

> queene Jone late wife of king Henrie the fourth, and mother in law to this king, was arrested by the duke of Bedford the kings lieutenant in his absence, and by him comitted to safe keeping in the castell of Leeds. . . . About the same time, one frier Randoll of the order of Franciscanes that professed divinitie, and had beene confessor to the same queene, was taken [and slain in a quarrel]. It was reported that he had conspired with the queene by sorcerie and necromancie to destroie the king.[76]

"Witchcraft" had best be confined to the kissing lips of eligible princesses.

Only in an oblique manner does *Henry V* reflect on the historical problems involving royal women with political power: crucial because of their reproductive power and often through their agency as consorts or relatives, yet distrusted, feared, and in the realm of France officially barred from sovereignty. Nevertheless, when the French Queen enters, these issues are granted a shadowy presence. Women often served as regents in a land other than that of their birth. In this instance, a foreign queen mother stands in while the potentially more threatening figure of a corrupted and only adoptively English queen mother is deleted from Shakespeare's story. To have lost both one's parents, in Henry V's case, seems far from an act of carelessness.[77]

Shakespeare's inclusion of a domesticated Isabel suggests a familiar New Historicist antithesis. She can be regarded as an addition who complicates

75. While Brittany was an independent duchy and that son, Arthur de Richemont, was generally a staunch supporter of a unified Anglo-French realm, he was still Henry's enemy on that crucial battlefield.

76. Holinshed, *Chronicles*, 82. E. F. Jacob confirms that Henry was "not exempt from the contemporary fear of necromancy and magic. . . . [H]is own stepmother, Joan of Navarre, was arrested . . . and relegated to seclusion for her suspected share in magical arts against him"; *Henry V*, 44. See also Pitcher, *Case*, 228; Holinshed, *Chronicles*, 1168b, 1198a.

77. Hopkins calls attention to the silence about Henry's mother, Mary Bohun, despite her being the source for his Welshness; after Agincourt, "fittingly enough, it is the fatherless Fluellen who has provided a conduit for this return of the repressed mother"; "Fluellen's Name," 152.

the play's narrative trajectory toward subjugation of the female and France through her political activity and frank commentary, carrying the historical traces of other powerful, even threatening women. Her eventual alliance with Henry dramatizes his acknowledgment of the legal importance of maternity in sovereign claims. Conversely, she can be seen as a carefully tamed version of women's place in history. She testifies to the shaping power of a masculine English presence, and—to the extent we hear a voice onstage that can be called female at all—one that has been thoroughly co-opted by the conqueror to serve the peaceful rather than violent traffic in women.[78] Either way, her presence as a collaborator recalls the labor and struggle involved in history as well as its dramatization, and provides multiple possibilities for modern performance. Remembering these associated princesses as well substantiates the Queen's worries about failed marriages; when she remembers that "ill office or fell jealousy" may "Thrust in between the paction of these kingdoms / To make divorce," a chorus of female voices could join her.

Shakespeare's own monarch, for all her manipulation and savvy in maintaining her status as royal prince rather than married queen, was not exempt from the difficulties of claiming through—or indeed, as—the female. Distancing herself from her slandered mother, Anne Boleyn, could not prevent Elizabeth's enemies from recalling her own official childhood "bastardy." And the Tudors had in the first place made their questionable claim to the English throne through the Beaufort line: indeed, through a female (Margaret Beaufort) descended from a union itself only belatedly legitimized (John of Gaunt and his mistress-made-wife Katherine Swynford). On the paternal side, Henry VII of course derived from that Franco-Welsh alliance of Henry V's widow with Owain Tudor. These ghostly presences from the feudal past continued to shadow Shakespeare's present, the early modern political world to which he overtly refers in *Henry V*.

Soon after the Chorus explicitly invokes "our gracious Empress" (5.0.30) and (in what is famously the only direct reference to contemporary political history in the canon) heralds the return of "the General" "from Ireland coming, / Bringing rebellion broached on his sword" (5.0. 31–32), a fascinating Folio "mistake" creates a connection between Isabel and those events: as she enters, she addresses Henry as "brother Ireland" rather than as "brother

---

78. Because of the substantial literature on cross-dressing, I do not rehearse its implications for Isabel's representation on the early modern stage, although it is worth remembering that Shakespeare's character was always a female impersonation, the representation of gender inherently unstable. But within the conventions of his theater, a character such as Isabel would have been perceived as comparatively female.

238 England" (to which land modern editors universally return him).[79] What these pages have made clear, I hope, is that even in this instance present troubles do not simply replace or erase past anxieties; rather, the disturbing and triumphal elements of historical inheritance create layers of meaning, a palimpsest in which both the kinship and the otherness of the past leave a mark. Simply expunging the "mistake" from memory errs too much on the side (ironically) of antiquarianism, in danger of making the past quaintly nostalgic. But conversely, making Ireland the singular focus of attention skews history too much in the direction of current events alone, overshadowing the gendered collaborator who recalls a historical problem distinct from that of colonization. In more general terms, if scholarship from E. M. W. Tillyard to the archivally based "New Boredom" can sometimes be accused of the former error, much recent New Historicist and "Presentist" work may fall prey to the latter.[80] Better to note, and know, Ireland as an invisible presence hovering alongside Dafydd Gam, unseen and unheard but shadowing the overt assertion of "brother England"—a dark conceit sustaining a hermeneutic circle of interpretation back and forth between times, rather than an allegorical code collapsing back into the false clarity of one discoverable meaning. For considered whole, *Henry V* confounds easy interpretation as mere propaganda or subversion not only because of Shakespeare's remarkable gift for creating ambiguity but also because of his particular willingness to acknowledge and dramatize the collaborative dynamics of the historical process itself. Like both Dafydd and Isabeau transformed into Davy Gam and Isabel, from a position of subordinated power the past collaborates with the present.

Performing History

So what are modern artistic collaborators to do with Davy Gam and the French Queen, or border-crossing Welshmen and Frenchwomen more generally? Like textual variants, historical subtexts cannot easily be performed; when legends fade and back-stories lose their resonance, Shake-shifters try-

---

79. *The Norton Facsimile: The First Folio of Shakespeare*, ed. Charlton Hinman (New York, 1968), Folio 92.

80. The terms New Boredom and Presentism derive from David Kastan (*Shakespeare After Theory*) and Terence Hawkes (*Shakespeare in the Present*), respectively, and have initiated a debate of heuristic usefulness, although the claims of difference between them in critical practice have been exaggerated—and the difference may indeed strike the nonspecialist as far slighter than the rhetorical positions imply. This in itself may signal a reasonable doubled perspective on historiography within the discipline, although saying it that way doesn't sell as many books. The question of what our analyses achieve remains an urgent one for the humanities.

ing to reanimate a four-hundred-year-old play in modern performance venues and new media may understandably object to further complications. They may prefer not to confront any more differences or layers between past and present. Yet there are consequences to late modern collaborations with an early modern Englishman's vision of his country's late medieval past.[81] In some productions, the result is the perpetuation of attitudes that seem at odds with modernity itself, or at least undermine the more equitable, cosmopolitan attitudes that many profess to honor through artistic practice. At a minimum, then, Shake-shifters might seek more awareness of their own place in the performance of history. More ambitiously, they could hope (like Virginia Woolf) to discover new creative possibilities that better capture their beliefs and aspirations (though we have seen the challenges inherent in that process as well). In doing so, the contemporary performers become more nuanced collaborators with Shakespeare, like Shakespeare.

Obviously it helps to have a character from the back-story represented onstage, so let us consider first the more promising figure of the French Queen. Whereas the modern use of actresses in the place of boy actors can aggravate the problems in reproducing *The Taming of the Shrew*, here it is a cause for optimism: "haply a woman's voice may do some good" when placed in dialogue with the masculine military hero, more clearly exposing if not challenging the gendered nationalism that has become the historical correlate to what feudalism was for Shakespeare, our own haunting past-present. In the most recent feature film version, then, we might expect to see her gainfully employed.

But she's not there. Kenneth Branagh's 1989 film, following the precedent of several Royal Shakespeare Company directors, removes the French Queen completely. His screenplay cuts her first substantial speech and gives her final prayer for peace to Henry himself; moreover, it becomes his final triumphant speech of the film, his last words.[82] In the process, Branagh not only reenacts the English conquest but makes it more absolute than did Shakespeare. He also caps his film's systematic presentation of himself as a beneficent, almost disinterested "star of England," asserting his stature as actor/director. Like much scholarship, his film equates *Henry V* with Henry

---

81. On production history, see also Sandra L. Williamson and James E. Person Jr.; Sally Beauman; Brennan; and James N. Loehlin.

82. Branagh makes no comment about this change in his published screenplay. Samuel Crowl, acknowledging a debt to Eggert, notes that Isabel's part is "often cut in production," the last speech "often assigned to the king [of France] as his blessing"; *Shakespeare Observed: Studies in Performance on Stage and Screen* (Athens, OH, 1992), 173, 190. This was true of the RSC's 1975 production directed by Terry Hands and starring Alan Howard. The part was also cut from the 1989 Stratford, Ontario, production. Adrian Noble directed the stage production starring Branagh that helped launch the idea of the film.

240   V, collapsing the play's multiple perspectives into a study of a single psyche. And as in his other conscious choices to reconceive the filmic technique and thematic emphases of his theatrical ancestor Laurence Olivier, Branagh (despite his professed dedication to actorly communalism) outdoes the self-aggrandizing bravado of his forefather.[83] This personal victory comes at a high price, simplifying the play's treatment of gender and removing the figure of the political collaborator.

Given Branagh's stated awareness that *Henry V* is a "depressingly male piece," his "usurpation" of Isabel's final lines might seem a conscious commentary on the play's own pattern of subduing the feminine, were it not for the long performance history of diminution and erasure from which it derives — and the fact that the wooing scene with Katherine is so clearly played as romantic comedy.[84] Furthermore, Branagh's visual choices during Burgundy's speech confirm the scene's focus on Henry's coming of age through his own personal suffering and sacrifice — not through negotiation with nationally challenging "others." While Burgundy speaks of French devastation ("Corrupting in it[s] own fertility," in Shakespeare's suggestive phrasing [5.2.40]), we see only one flashback image of the French dead before moving to multiple images of the friends Henry has had to sacrifice en route, three of whom never even accompanied him to France. Moreover, that single image of the French, grieving over the Constable's corpse after the Agincourt battle, is prefaced by a close-up on the French King (Paul Scofield) and is followed by the corresponding close-up on Branagh prior to the series of English faces: the conventions of flashback thus announce that even now memory is divided by nation, with only the Frenchman recalling his own dead (and at some cost to plausibility, given that king's absence from Agincourt). The sequence thus not only psychologizes Henry's history but makes its primary contents the *English* dead, and — especially by concluding with the face of Falstaff — the private loss within one's self.

Of Branagh's act 5, Samuel Crowl writes: "Henry's French expedition began with the conviction that he inherited his rights there by claiming from the female, and now he completes his multiple mergers by uttering his own dream of union and assimilation; Branagh's Henry and Kate are seen here not only as the makers of manners but as the creators of powerful political

---

83. See Peter S. Donaldson's oedipal comparison of Branagh's film with Olivier's; my reading supplements his sense of Olivier's greater ease in mastering the feminine/woman (less threatening than the agonistic male), whereas Branagh shows more sensitivity for the defeated father. On "actor militancy," see Branagh's *Beginning*, and on the tensions between Branagh's populist impulse and his representational politics in *Hamlet*, see Douglas Lanier's "'Art Thou Base.'"

84. Kenneth Branagh, *Beginning* (London, 1989), 237.

symbols as well."[85] No doubt this aptly captures much of Branagh's project, though it sidesteps even those subordinated gestures at a different French perspective that the film's ending contains: Katherine's anxious looks toward her father and public muteness (Emma Thompson silently looking down, somber and glassy-eyed as in the final pose she becomes a symbol of France); the presence of Michael Maloney's now silenced and impassive Dauphin; and the weary concessions and nearly tragic consciousness of Scofield as the war-haunted, shamed yet dignified French king. Crowl's description also glosses over the play's crucial concern with the difference between "claiming from" the female and removing or usurping power, pushing euphemism to the limits in seeing Henry as one who desires "assimilation" through "mergers." For Branagh's Henry has quite literally "gotten" the girl and taken the woman's part as "his own dream" without giving away a whit of his wit or masculine authority. A collaborating Queen is no longer deemed necessary.

Although I find this self-aggrandizing dimension of his film disappointing, my aim is not to join the pack of Branagh baiters or deny the considerable pleasures of his *Henry V*—to some of which I shall soon return. After all, in muting the potential for gendered criticism within act 5's formal comedy, Branagh is in a sense merely extending a dynamic that has deep roots in modern performance tradition. On the nineteenth-century stage, selective cutting and casting choices unraveled Shakespeare's patterns of gender representation, contributing to the unambiguous celebration of Henry as ideal king. William Charles Macready's promptbook for his Covent Garden production, using Kemble's 1815 edition, crosses out Isabel's three lines most frankly recalling Henry's warfare ("Your eyes which hitherto have borne in them / . . . The fatal balls of murdering basilisks").[86] His was a powerful precedent for others, including Charles Kean. Kean's 1859 production in turn made another influential change that, while motivated by a quite local and pragmatic desire, had gendered as well as nationalistic consequences. Wishing his wife to participate in his final stage production as actor-manager, he transformed the Chorus into Clio, the Muse of History. This alteration gives mythic authority and disinterestedness to Chorus's speeches —which present, as many have noted, a far more exalted and encomiastic view of the English than do the intervening scenes. Additionally, the gender switch diminishes the script's associations of women with an effeminized, conquered France (whereas in the edited text, even Nell Quickly—the only

---

85. Crowl, *Shakespeare Observed*, 173.

86. Kemble's 1806 edition includes the entire first speech but (prefiguring Olivier) cuts her second speech. Information on nineteenth-century productions is drawn from the microfilmed promptbooks at the Folger Library.

242   English female—dies "Of a malady of France" [5.1.83]).[87] The larger associative pattern that Isabel's speech both extends and complicates is thereby
erased, and a benignly motivated act of domestic collaboration between
artists smoothes away the political rough edges.

      Some productions followed Kemble in keeping the basilisk speech but
placing it later, making it substitute for Isabel's second "post-wooing" speech
in the Folio text. Charles Calvert's 1872–75 production split 5.2 into two
parts surrounding the cudgeling of Pistol by Fluellen (5.1 in the Folio); the
Queen's only speech now initiated a scene within the cathedral at which
Katherine and Henry were wed. Her most challenging lines thus occurred
after the treaty negotiations had made the marital solution a fait accompli,
denuding her words of their practical potential to block or resist Henry's
idea of a happy ending. Here again the producer's wife played the Chorus,
this time as a rather lofty version of Rumor (the jester-like tongues of this
figure's *Henry IV, Part 2* costume replaced by a flowing white gown). The
shift from Clio to Rumor does acknowledge the play's ambiguity of perspective regarding the historical truth, although it continues to ignore the symbolic gendering of the two nations. Anthony Brennan observes that in less
stately fashion, "Women continued to play the Chorus in the 1920s and
1930s, Sybil Thorndike strutting about in a brisk performance."[88] All these
production choices muted the text's pattern associating England with victorious masculinity conquering an effeminate and female France.[89] Instead,
the female Chorus combined with a kinder, gentler Isabel makes baldly explicit what remains implicit in the scene of Princess Katherine's wooing:
even voices of potential resistance (because of their gendered or national exclusion) laud Henry's military adventure. Nor does this dynamic fade with
the return to male Choruses. In productions such as Olivier's, Isabel too was
to be enlisted in such celebratory collaboration with the victor.

      Olivier's film at least retains the queen's role, though making her a re-
markably pliant accomplice to Henry. After her matronly recital of the

---

    87. The Folio reads: "my Doll is dead I' th' spital / Of a malady of France," which most edi-
tors attribute to Shakespeare's carelessness (Nell alone appears in *Henry V*, and Doll was at
odds with Pistol in *Henry IV, Part 2*).

    88. Brennan, *Henry V*, xxiii.

    89. By contrast, in some nineteenth-century productions dancing girls in the French camp
extended the association between France and the feminine (and "Gallic looseness of morals,"
wryly notes Brennan, ibid., xxiv). Lewis Waller, W. Bridges-Adams, and Robert Atkins all used
female Choruses in the early twentieth century, though by the 1930s some dressed as men (see
Brennan, xix–xxiv). The 1996 New York Shakespeare Festival production (dir. Douglas
Hughes) distributed the Chorus lines, with some of the richest passages going to female speak-
ers; the need to enrich the roles for actresses (in a play where they speak less than 5 percent of
the lines) often provides incentive.

basilisk speech, Queen Isabel (Janet Burnell) follows the English king's in-
structions as willingly as any actress attending to her director. When he asks
whether she will "go with the princes" to help settle the terms of the peace
treaty, he simultaneously prompts her with a tiny nod of his head; the offered alternative, that she "stay here with us," is accompanied by an equally
understated negative shake which she acknowledges.[90] Thus Olivier creates
a visual joke out of her (i.e., his) decision to contribute "a woman's voice" to
the state negotiations, a joke that confirms his control and domesticates her
political boldness.

Of course, noting the presence or gender of a character is not in itself a
sufficient indicator of the political texture of a production, any more than
"gender" or "nationalism" carries a stable meaning of which performers are
universally cognizant. Specific contexts shape the significance of these
choices, each of which can generate numerous insights and responses. Nevertheless, certain patterns do emerge and create a performance history. The
prominence or absence of Isabel's first speech, for example, correlates with
the comparative emphasis placed upon Henry's opening lines and his general attitude toward the war. This is particularly true of the modern screen
productions: the greater Henry's internal ambivalence or irony, the less
need or opportunity for other characters to confront him. In his opening
scene, Branagh dramatizes Henry's consciousness and concern about the
riskiness of his enterprise by delivering the last clause of "France being
ours, we'll bend it to our awe, / Or break it all to pieces" sotto voce, as if it
were his private reservation. No wonder then that he further deflects attention from Burgundy's speech and entirely erases the figure and basilisk
words of Isabel. What matters in Branagh's film is not so much the material
fate of female France as the cost to the conscience of the king. By contrast,
in the often pedestrian BBC/Time-Life television production, David
Gwillim begins by stating out loud the two seeming alternatives of bending
or breaking France as he addresses an approving court.[91] This interpretation, perhaps more consonant with the play's military tenor, is less overtly
concerned with rendering Henry's actions palatable to a late twentieth-
century audience skeptical about the glories of war.[92] And in line with this,
an elegant but forthright Isabel (Pamela Ruddock) voices her basilisk lines
quite pointedly.

90. *Henry V.* Dir. Laurence Olivier. Two Cities Films Ltd. 1944.
91. *Henry V.* Dir. David Giles. BBC/Time-Life TV. 1979.
92. It also accords better with the historical accounts of Henry's exceptionally brutal actions
during the sieges of Harfleur and Rouen, as on other occasions during his French campaigns
("lenity" was not his hallmark, despite Shakespeare's 3.6.106–12).

244 Olivier's choices hover between. The metatheatricality of his film's opening scene, played as if at the Globe theater in 1600, makes Henry's oratorical flourish overtly performative; the concluding scenes begin to move back from the realism of Agincourt and a meditative Henry to a playful world, muting the seriousness of Isabel's criticism. Prefaced by her jabbing her daft husband to prompt his brief speech and followed by the visual comedy with Henry already mentioned, Isabel's speech includes its harshest lines but is comically framed. Moreover, her second speech is eliminated, the wooing of Katherine being so obviously successful and the ending an unambiguous celebration (with only the epilogue's happier lines to boot).

Despite Olivier's choice to defuse her criticism, film as a medium has great potential to give special pointedness to the visual imagery in Isabel's first speech. Viewed in such a context, the taming of Isabel's potentially disruptive presence in films of *Henry V* becomes all the more intriguing. With close-ups and the ability to cross-cut looks between the French Queen and the English King, one could easily highlight the animosity lurking just beneath the ceremonial surface, or the poignant precariousness of this all too brief peace. Although not connecting this latter dimension with Isabel directly, the end of the BBC's televised *An Age of Kings* episode (1960) artfully suggested how visual juxtapositions can mute the English victory: the camera pans right from the ceremonial conclusion to reveal Chorus standing over the stone tomb marked with Henry V's name.[93] The slab ominously recalls not only the immanent death of the "star of England" but also (like Philip Larkin's poem "Church Monuments") our modern distance from all those who struggled for power so long ago. This jarring shift removes us from the fictional fantasy space in which past and present can seem to merge, leaving the audience to mourn a larger loss than any specific player—the loss of all those who bled and died only to produce a singular abstraction called "England" which would likewise "bleed" (epilogue 6, 12). In this instance, televisual context perhaps afforded the license to end on such a mournful note: because this *Henry V* was presented as part of a larger series dramatizing the entire Shakespearean history cycle, the grim epilogue became a useful transition to the following weeks' episodes.

When it comes to Isabel, however, the existing screen representations are better understood in relation to the classic patterns of Hollywood cinema—notably the paradigm of female representation explored by Laura Mulvey in

93. *An Age of Kings*. Dir. Michael Hayes. BBC television, 1960. Viewed at the British Film Institute Archives.

the mid-1970s. Her theory that the camera encourages spectatorial identification with a male gaze upon woman-as-object has since been strongly modified, by herself and others; but it remains an influential starting point for
gendered analysis of film (and of Shakespeare's histories, via Rackin). Mulvey focuses on how a mysteriously "other" woman typically halts narrative
movement and hence male "success" in two senses of the word. The Isabel of
the playtext, however, complicates that paradigm, in that her words—rather
than her sight or image—carry her disruptive force. Assigning the basilisk
look to Henry, she exposes the location of the actual threat in historical narratives of war: it is not the provocative woman but the man and his men who
destroy the living bodies of the French. Because Isabel's words are resistant
yet elegantly framed, echoing Henry though phrased more critically, she
cannot easily be presented as monstrous or dismissed as irrational. Moreover, because they are spoken by a maternal yet potent female, the words in
Shakespeare's version cannot be defused as sexual invitations or foreplay,
nor do they encourage visual framing of her as an object of desire. Thus both
her words and her position make it difficult to inscribe her as object of the
Hollywood gaze. No doubt this helps explain why she is so thoroughly domesticated by Olivier and erased by Branagh; in both films the fetishized
position of woman-as-image falls to Princess Katherine (quite understandably), and she gets far more attention.

But just as Mulvey's analysis has been challenged as too monolithic, video
productions point toward other screen possibilities for the woman's part yet
to be realized.[94] Paralysis is not the last word, either in the text or in performance. It is nevertheless indicative of recent artistic conventions and conditions that the most innovative representation comes not in an original film or
video production but instead in a recorded stage performance.[95] In the English Shakespeare Company's *Henry V* directed by Michael Bogdanov (1990
video release),[96] Queen Isabel does speak out, challenging Henry's authority and charm. This production also has one actress (June Watson) double

94. See Mary Ann Doane and *Camera Obscura*, vol. 21, for some feminist reconsiderations of
Mulvey's 1975 discussion of the male gaze.

95. For a polemical reading of Branagh's film as an ideological betrayal of Noble's production, see Chris Fitter—who further believes the film's framed rectangle and the modern prosce-
nium stage "invite 'tyranny' of directorial control of meaning"; "A Tale of Two Branaghs: *Henry
V*, Ideology, and the Mekong Agincourt," in *Shakespeare Left and Right*, ed. Ivo Kamps (New
York, 1991), 272. Scholars and practitioners in both media have adequately challenged such
monolithic formal arguments (which would, if true, seem to absolve Branagh of responsibility
over the tyrannizing medium anyway).

96. *King Henry V*. Dir. Michael Bogdanov. English Shakespeare Company. 1990.

246   Mistress Quickly and the French Queen, consequently calling greater attention to Isabel's role in both performance and negotiations.[97] Having altered Shakespeare's text as well as history in order to include the Dauphin in the final scene, Bogdanov makes Isabel's willingness to leave Princess Katherine with Henry—an action that also implies the Dauphin's disinheritance—into a provocation driving the French prince offstage in anger. The Dauphin's displacement reintroduces into Shakespearean performance the historical rupture between Isabeau and her son—though the Dauphin in question was Charles, not (as one must infer here) Louis.

The ESC's choice to keep the earlier Dauphin alive and onstage until this speech reinforces the political significance and humiliation for France that the marriage constitutes and that Isabel's subsequent prayer attempts to transcend; his angry exit prefigures the vexed history to come. Those in the audience familiar with that history will know that the Hundred Years War was eventually won by the very Dauphin whom Isabeau displaced through her alliance with the English monarch. After the wooing scene, when the ESC's Dauphin once again disrupts the marital accord, Isabel repairs the awkwardness by using both speech and physical action to reunite an offended, sulking Henry (Michael Pennington) with the princess. Thus her role becomes all the more important in creating peace between nations, and her gender difference remains functional as part of the production's more critical perspective on Henry.

Branagh likewise extends the earlier Dauphin's life, but quietly; none of the symbolic historical resonance persists here because of the absence of Isabel. Yet while occluding the involvement of gender with nation, Branagh does allow the French contingent some dignity, and consequently the sense of the losing side's suffering does not entirely disappear in his film—nor, more significantly, does the Welsh "subplot" involving Davy Gam and Fluellen at Agincourt. Given his Belfast upbringing and more conventionally realist style of filmmaking, it is not surprising that Branagh's representation of the liminal British characters is less cartoonish than Olivier's. But here, illustratively, a "personal" disposition accords with or indeed reflects a larger cultural change and leads to more fruitful Shake-shifting.

Forty years ago in the film version of Robert Bolt's *A Man for All Seasons*, the actor who would play Branagh's French King made Wales memorable as the punch line of a sardonic jest: upon learning what political office his ac-

---

97. The 1996 New York Shakespeare Festival's production cast Kathleen Chalfont in the double role and similarly had the Dauphin stride off during the final negotiations; perhaps a new twist in performance history is emerging. Nicholas Hytner's 2003 Royal National Theatre production likewise doubled these two women's parts.

cuser's treachery has gained, the doomed Sir Thomas More (Scofield) replies with this chapter's first epigraph. Olivier's film was made at a time when Wales was likewise deemed politically unimportant and drew upon the theatrical tradition of playing "low" characters for easy laughs. As performed by Esmond Knight, Fluellen is a nimbly amusing sprite who forces Pistol to eat his leek and then sashays away. He does hold a dead boy during the battle of Agincourt but is not allowed his lines or access to the King afterward. As a result, his role as remembrancer of Crécy disappears, and with it Henry's triumphant assumption of his Welshness prior to the naming of the English dead. Given the list without prelude, Olivier solemnly surveys it, pausing as if to allow those bereaved by World War II to enter their own loved ones' names among the memorable dead. There is no stylistic connection between his soft-spoken intonation of Davy Gam and the broad antics of his Captain Fluellen, no hint of a repressed history that might connect two of his Welsh-born followers.

Granted, it is more to ask that a modern performance make something of this submerged pattern than of the one involving Isabel. Davy Gam may be named at a climactic moment, after the rising action and violence that have culminated at Agincourt; in a successful production, the audience, like Henry's band of brothers, will listen in hushed awe to the few, the happily few, names of the "English" dead. An actor worth his leading role will make the most of the moment.[98] Nevertheless, Davy remains only a name, not a part—so when several of Branagh's choices, unlike Olivier's, do have the effect of reanimating Gam and the Welsh-French connection, it is all the more serendipitously welcome. As his Henry reads the names, the camera surveys in sequence some of the weary and more familiar surviving members of the army—for once directing attention outward beyond the speaker. Branagh's voiceover warmly embraces the wide syllables of the last remembered name: the familiar "Davy," the simple "Gam," the (relatively) humble "Esquire"— all linger in the memory, more resonant than many French princes.

Just prior, the camera suggests—perhaps unwittingly, but nonetheless effectively—the Franco-Welsh connection. Having just learned from the French Herald Mountjoy that "[t]he day is yours," Branagh stands amazed and exhausted in the foreground with Mountjoy behind, the latter sadly peering at him from the misty battleground in a two-man tableau; the King further asks and learns that the place is called Agincourt (4.7.85). Then as Henry so names the battle and Mountjoy exits from the fixed-angle shot,

---

98. Alan Howard famously made this a moment of near breakdown, as the cost and exhaustion of Henry's massive achievement finally struck home.

Figure 5. The defeated French: Mountjoy (Christopher Ravenscroft) after Agincourt in Kenneth Branagh's *Henry V*

Figure 6. A Welsh correction: Fluellen (Ian Holm) after Agincourt in Kenneth Branagh's *Henry V*

there slowly rises up in his place the figure of Fluellen. He comes forward and replaces the defeated French with the collaborative Welsh, signaling Henry's transition from stalwart fighter to savvy ally (see figures 5 and 6).

Moreover, this is when Fluellen recalls the analogous battle against the French and the Welsh service there; his words serve to link past and present, France and Wales, and also to release the emotions that the King has quietly contained until now. Branagh's Henry bursts out with laughing relief to em-

Figure 7. An international fellowship of death: Mountjoy and Fluellen among the band of brothers

brace his loyal Welshman along with his own Welshness. Overtly depoliticized to allow a slightly patronizing playfulness about ethnic special pleading, the scene aptly translates Shakespeare's mixture of mockery and acknowledgment to a modern medium and context in which identity politics often slide into nostalgic nationalism. Then, recovering his quiet composure (following the interpolation of Pistol's final speech), Henry reads the names of the dead—significantly, with both Mountjoy and Fluellen among those gathered nearest to him (see figure 7). Given the inclusion of Mountjoy and intimacy with Fluellen in this sequence, it becomes less remarkable that Branagh would feel it appropriate for his character to mouth words originally attributed to a French female: he presents this Henry as having grown into international adulthood, though always serving "England."[99]

This pattern in the representation relies upon the sensitive embodiments of Christopher Ravenscroft as Mountjoy and especially Ian Holm as Fluellen, so that even comic exchanges also carry with them a sense of their dignity in difference. While attention certainly remains confined to a gender-specific band of brothers, that band enlarges beyond Pistol's version

99. Branagh's tussle with and tearful embrace of Mountjoy at the battle's end further reinforces the linkage with Fluellen (whom he also embraces in tears). Moreover, it is Mountjoy who protects Henry from attacking French camp followers during the *Non nobis* march. In this regard, the nationalist division of flashback memories between the French and English kings, noted earlier, is a step backward—or another sign of mixed messages.

250   of the nation in order to honor soldiers of other ethnic origins. The importance of Fluellen as more than a secondary comedian, then, comes to the
fore here, even as much of the play's "use" of him is cut: the leek-eating
scene that challenges narrow Englishness is gone, as is Henry's employment
of the Welshman against Williams (also gone in Olivier). The effect, as the
film moves toward resolution, is to make the role of Fluellen more of a piece
in tone and emphasis with the final scenes of French alliance.

I have focused thus far on screen performances because of their medium's
distinctive modernity and also because of the remarkable impact of the two
feature films upon most people's conception of *Henry V* at present. But as
with *The Taming of the Shrew*, film has not yet taken the lead in representing
the political dimensions of state-level collaboration with Shakespeare's histories. In the case of Isabel, this is obviously true, with the ESC video providing one example of a more adventurous modern stage decision. As I have
discussed elsewhere, my interest in this figure was sparked by a far more ex-
perimental stage production by the Company of Women, in which the use of
racial difference and doubling made more evident the French Queen's difficult position.[100] Similarly, in today's Britain, the political ramifications of
making not only Ireland but Wales a joke have become more apparent and
Fluellen is less frequently presented as quaintly foolish. When Tony Blair
ceded the speakership of a newly constituted Welsh assembly to a man he
earlier opposed, the limits of London's ability to control the choices of its
Welsh constituents resurfaced. Rethinking the representation—both political and theatrical—of the "Celtic fringe" is once more a matter of (the) moment, and gives more weight to those choices in representing *Henry V.*

My purpose in analyzing the figure of the political collaborator is not just
to point out two more representatives of "underrepresented" groups (although it does help us move away from exclusive attention to the psyche of
one member of the elite), or to challenge the "great man" view of history (albeit it has certainly informed the modern performance of *Henry V*). What interests me is the way in which the collaborator both blurs the line between
national self and national other, gendered self and gendered other, and reveals the fluidity of categories such as "enemy" and "friend"—both words
reiterated throughout this play. Most crucially, these collaborators reveal
the unequal landscape in which even the "victims" or losers have some space
of agency and responsibility, thus challenging the inevitability of historical
conclusions as well as static thinking about hierarchical oppositions. They

100. This was the Company of Women's 1994 all-female production directed by Maureen
Shea; see my *Shakespeare Bulletin* review and "The Disappearing Queen: Looking for Isabel in
Henry V," in *Shakespeare and His Contemporaries in Performance*, ed. Edward Esche (Aldershot,
UK, 2000), 339–55.

epitomize, in other words, the dynamic temporality and decision making that reshape identities and "nation," and with them art. They are not (as George W. Bush would have it) simply "with" one, or "with" the enemy. Collaborators disturb those who want simple enemies even more than those who want friends—and they force us to think hard.

And thus they are disproportionately troubling if one wants to create a pure hero out of a soldier (or artist). Isabel's may be a small part, but she threatens more than gender roles alone, undoing the symmetry so evident in Branagh's closing scene when "France" and "England" face each other from either end of a long table. Fluellen's recollection of allies whom this very King has recently been fighting troubles the simple contrast between the French and English dead, as does knowledge that one of those latter names is Welsh; Olivier, trying to associate the enemy with Germany (and invisible French collaborators?) does not venture into that murky border territory.[101] Following Shakespeare's own method of simplifying and suppressing the more disturbing dimensions of the historical record, these modern performances collaborate ideologically as well as artistically in the celebration of a British nation-state. Outdoing Shakespeare at his own dangerous game, they translate history into an account primarily of one man's heroic leadership of a coalition of the (mostly) willing, through war.

By looking at two rather than just one collaborative figure, my aim has been to emphasize the inadequacy of single binaries in our critical analyses as well as in historical world affairs, be the chosen terms ones involving gender or nationhood. The Henry plays work to make those terms inseparable, yet seldom is this acknowledged more subtly than by equating Wales and France with femininity in *Henry IV, Part 1* and *Henry V,* respectively. But the military Fluellen and his dead countryman present a challenge to simple equations—and Isabeau's name speaks for itself. As in the artistic play between past and present, these two methods of social categorization are better conceived as continua in dynamic tension over time. Considered thus, Henry's progress is precisely toward recognizing a category neither self nor other: the collaborators, unlike both his brothers and his enemies, turn out to be those who staunch the bleeding.[102]

101. Likewise, Mountjoy gets his mention of the "mercenary blood" drowning the French nobility (4.7.75), but the entire episode involving English treachery for money is cut (Branagh emphasizes the personal betrayal most vigorously). My reference back to those wartime collaborators who gave the word its bad name serves as a reminder that I am not "celebrating" those who collaborate, but instead calling for specific attention to their actions; the larger goal here is to enunciate an alternative model, beyond two-sided conflict as a "solution" to questions of difference.

102. One can make a similar class-based argument regarding the role of Williams, whom Henry does best to see neither as rebel nor as comparable to himself.

252   Shake-shifting, more benignly, likewise creates something neither entirely
of oneself or other, partaking of both past and present and involving multiple layers of representation. What modern artists want to do with this
awareness is of course their own choice, and hence responsibility. But wishing to spur rather than limit creative possibilities, I believe scholars need to
be more active in suggesting routes to help busy practitioners animate history; we could float more ideas, rather than showing up to criticize exclusively after the fact. After all, scholars and teachers too are diachronic collaborators with Shakespeare and have a role to play in conveying whatever
knowledge we value to a wider public. We can document and highlight moments in modern media when the significant complexities of both past and
present are creatively conveyed, such as in Branagh's "Welsh correction."
And we can suggest directions for artists to consider—in their preparations
as well as their final productions.

     In performance, one way to reanimate the historical back-stories is to
present Fluellen's alliance, like the wooing of Katherine, as a dynamic struggle rather than a fait accompli. By simply allowing his character, the third-
largest role within the play, a more substantial proportion of his scenes and
potential seriousness, the thematic import of the Welsh presence emerges,
rather than just its comic side. In conveying the range of tones and issues associated with Fluellen, one also necessarily involves Henry in another more
subtle contest than those on the battlefield; his setting of Fluellen against
Williams suggests more than a little submerged aggression against his potentially challenging followers. Viewed in tandem with the French negotiations to follow, the alliance with Fluellen constitutes another component of
Henry's victory that is less a matter of "God's will" (as he views the miracu-
lously lopsided Agincourt deaths) than a dramatic achievement of human
wills, including but not limited to that of Will Shakespeare.

     My emphasis here would not be on simple revisionism, elevating aspects
of identity now perceived to be undervalued by the playwright. Of course
one can imagine a compensatory rebuttal to English-biased historiography
as well as dramatic tradition if the oddly named Fluellen were transformed
back into the proper Welsh Llywelyn; he might well compete (through association with the last independent Welsh ruler, Llewelyn the Great) with the
play's monarch.[103] If performed in sequence with *Henry IV, Part 1*, the connection would become even clearer—especially if one doubled the role with

---

103. See Hopkins on the absence of a standard Welsh patronymic for "Fluellen"; see also
Hopkins and Hawkes ("Bryn Glas") on the links between his name and that of the last independent Prince of Wales, Llywelyn yr Olaf.

that of Glendower himself. Taken to an extreme, this choice undoes the tensions associated with collaboration as distinct from enmity, and slides back into another reductive version of man-to-man combat. Something akin to this appeared in the Company of Women's treatment of the Frenchwomen other than Isabel. In opposition to the play's performance tradition and formal structure, the "wooing" scene became more rape than romance, as Henry threatened and even assaulted Katherine and Alice. As a result, the Frenchwomen became simple victims of domestic violence and lost their (limited) agency more completely than in conventional productions where heroic Henries seem destined to charm. Although certainly valid as a provocative "female correction," the schematic clarity conspired against split or multiple perceptions, the layering that would seem one of Shakespeare's more useful—indeed, vital—dramatic contributions for our own times.

But even if one finds ways to render the collaborator's challenging status in performance, does it help capture this interplay between past and present? Calling attention to women's roles or the Celtic fringe in performance can become the correlate to those scholarly modes emphasizing only current political categories. Are there other aspects of the text's historicism worth sustaining in performance? To what end does one reproduce such texture in a world where Shakespeare's play now has become part of our own historical inheritance, both disturbing and triumphal?

Recontextualizing Shakespeare's play for the modern stage or screen involves another layer of awareness of time and history: in addition to the historical era represented within the Shakespearean text, and the Elizabethan moment of its composition, one must add (at least) the present moment of performance—as well as, in most cases, some awareness of the theatrical and screen history of productions intervening. For whether we will or no, contemporary performances carry history with them. If they do so unconsciously, they tend to reiterate the "given," leading to clichés and stereotypical representations rather than vital dramatic Shake-shifting. Two stage productions from the later 1990s, directed by Ron Daniels and Richard Olivier, respectively, illustrate the problems that persist even when the past and the present are acknowledged as different and then intermingled. Despite vast contrasts in styles and approach, the two directors still replicated the dominant historically determinist tradition in which *Henry V* is all about men, and in which the French are destined to fail.

At Boston's American Repertory Theater (ART; and later at the RSC), Daniels mounted what in mainstream theater is regarded as a postmodern production: that is, it mixed costumes from historically different periods and alluded to various times and places disjunctively. On occasion, the distinc-

254   tions between two "pasts" became functional. At the same time, the production was quite "modern" in its exposure of Henry's role in war's brutality;
even his own men expressed shock at his ugly threats before Harfleur. Yet
having the English garbed in World War II khakis and using microphones as
they went to fight against medieval French aristocrats exaggerated the distance between the nations, in a way that again ended up reinforcing a sense
of the inevitability—albeit unattractive—of Henry's victory. Chopine-shod
French noblemen riding stylized horses into battle at Agincourt similarly
suggested nostalgic lamentation for the loss of honor and beauty at the
hands of modern technology (even as the production relied on modern theatrical machinery to create such beautiful effects). Using different historical
periods, then, resulted in an even greater sense of fatalism to the English triumph; the effect was antithetical to the politics of disjunctive dramaturgy
advocated by Brecht and other twentieth-century theatrical activists.

The doubled use and critique of modern technologies did create one
haunting gender-related juxtaposition, suggesting the reason for the Frenchwomen's collaboration: after the scene at Harfleur, the set opened back to
reveal Katherine watching Henry's threatening speech broadcast on black-
and-white television within a surreally claustrophobic room; her language
lesson became overtly motivated by fear and pragmatism. Yet the production as a whole maintained stereotypes, without a memorable Isabel and
with Mistress Quickly played (for broad laughs) by a portly man in drag.
Thus the woman's part remained predictably sympathetic and charming
when virtually powerless, and comic or peripheral when publicly assertive.

Whereas Daniels's production broadcast its stylistic (post)modernity, the
production directed by Richard Olivier to inaugurate the Globe Theatre on
London's Southbank advertised its historicity. The very choice of play was
meant to betoken the authentic spirit of the recreated space, as *Henry V* is
purported by some to have been the first Shakespeare play to debut at the
Globe. Uniquely among the four shows produced during this new Globe's
first season, its *Henry V* claimed to replicate Elizabethan costuming and performance practices. All the actors were male. Again, however, many choices
upheld simplified stereotypes of gender and nation, and in a modern rather
than "historical" manner. Mistress Quickly was once more done as drag,
calling attention to the comic potential of cross-dressing in a way reliant
upon contemporary sexual categorization. The French women were not so
represented; here the production helped remind modern audiences that the
early modern convention could allow an actor just as much "transparency"
in representing a woman as when embodying a character of his own sex. Yet
even the emotionally effective doubling of the Boy and Princess Kather-

ine—two vulnerable figures fundamentally affected by yet outside the battle—reinforced the association of the sympathetic woman with political powerlessness.

A small cast reinforced the association between the French and femininity: the act 5 negotiations consisted of a small group of English men confronting the King of France and the three named female characters (Isabel, Katherine, Alice). This might have complicated the representation of power had the director not encouraged melodrama-style mockery of the entire French nobility throughout the four acts prior. Because the silly, effete Dauphin doubled as Isabel (resonating nicely with Isabeau's historical displacement of the Dauphin), those comic overtones persisted even though the Queen was played seriously; national identification took precedence over gender difference. The potential of what is now unconventional casting to emphasize the gendered complexities of the text was overshadowed, if not erased, by a cartoon version of the politics of nationhood—with neither recovering an "historical" closeness to Shakespeare.

Perhaps fears of the European Union lurked behind the comical booing at the French characters. More certainly, the long shadow of Richard Olivier's father, and his film's sanitized version of the English, informed the production: the choice of the younger Olivier to direct the Globe's debut looked back nostalgically not only to the English military triumph of Agincourt but also to a more recent era of artistic and political pride. As such, the jig completing the evening was perhaps the truest manifestation of this performance's rendering of gender and nationhood. With the all-male cast pounding their drums and sticks energetically, the dance seemed less a theatrical recreation than a belated attempt to recover lost potency (with Robert Bly as gender guru and the dead Olivier as departed British spirit). Indeed, the director's program comments confirmed that he hoped to duplicate what he portrayed uncritically as Henry's success: "The story of *Henry V* has remarkable parallels to the reopening of the Globe. One man has a vision of reclaiming something lost; he unites a disparate group of diverse interests into a 'band of brothers' who together cross old boundaries and mortal obstacles in quest of this long lost, fertile territory." What mortal perils faced Olivier's actors remained unspecified, as did the "fertile territory" they sought to conquer. But the imperial project, "an intimation of destiny," remained unchallenged: "With the renaissance of the Globe the second Elizabethan age may yet build upon its predecessor's effort and example." Emptied of political content, history repeats itself as corporate spectacle—the mode in which Olivier has subsequently developed his Shakeshifting career.

256   As in the Daniels production, a local choice at the Globe had the potential
to question the nationalist triumph, but was dwarfed by the performance
context. The choruses were delivered by various characters important to the
act following, and gradually descended the social scale away from the epitome of England: from Henry seeking his "Muse of Fire" to Exeter—and
then Fluellen, Williams, and Pistol. The Epilogue went to Charles of
France, allowing the defeated King (an apt figure for vicarious suffering or
revenge) to speak of blood and suffering to come. Yet the dance gave the
"last word" not to serious questioning but to visceral confirmation: what ultimately mattered in this production was easy theatrical pleasure. Even
when History reared its ugly head and produced an international "real life"
media spectacle involving British nationhood and gender, the play was mar-
keted as a simple comfort: on the day before the funeral of Diana, Princess
of Wales (flown back from France where she, like Henry, died young), the
Globe's artistic director and star, Mark Rylance, announced a schedule
change so that *Henry V* would be performed on the funeral night. As if to
confirm obliviousness to any specific politics or historical distance in Shakespeare's text, he dedicated the show "to Princes and Princesses everywhere."
Whatever this rhetorical flourish meant to convey, it further reduced the
play's concerns with gender and nation to vacuity. Mimicking early modern
stage practices in an utterly changed modern world has little to do with recovering (or revising) the historical thematics of Shakespeare.

If performers and directors choose to bring some consciousness of Welsh
and French history to bear, translating it into their representations of
Fluellen, Isabel, and Henry himself, they may help distinguish their productions—and the attitudes they reproduce and produce—from the English tri-
umphalism of a stage tradition reaching back to the eighteenth century and
on to the new Globe. They may find visual and design cues to signal the in-
terconnection of the Welsh and French material, clarifying the parallelism of
Henry's victories through his mixture of coercion (force) and negotiation. In the
process, they would have to wrestle with the otherness of Shakespeare's
past. Indeed, it is in that very recognition of change over time that the most
effective challenge to all forms of chauvinism (sexist) lies.

Because the historical particulars informing Shakespeare's play are not
commonly remembered, even valiant attempts to incorporate them into performance will sometimes fall flat. Modern audiences may no longer regard
Isabel's entrance and speech as startling; certainly the stories that made the
figure of Isabeau so threatening are no longer common knowledge. John
Pettigrew, in a review of the 1966 Shakespeare Festival production in Stratford, Ontario, not only deemed all referentiality to Anglo/French-Canadian

tensions "irrelevant" but also dismissed a "bad moment": "I'm still wondering . . . why that meaning look between French King and Queen with the
Queen's reference to 'fell jealousy' in her final speech."[104] Scholarship can
recover the genealogy of this figure, but finding contemporary correlatives
to convey the Queen's challenge onstage can be difficult indeed. Similarly,
when leek eating and St. Davy's Day can hardly avoid sounding even
quainter than they would in Elizabethan times, we need to think about contemporary connections in order to convey the more serious topics once suggested by things Welsh.

For of course the terms of internal colonialism have also changed in a
postcolonial era. With unconscious irony, many who live in the territories
associated in Sir Walter Scott's day with "darker" races now vilify those
whom their families' imperial collaborations have displaced or uprooted
around the globe. Across the Atlantic, descendants of those sent off in coffin
boats in the year of the Burnings fight to exclude other refugees in political
and economic distress. With immigration and patriotism again hot-button
political dilemmas, one thinks of other collisions between complacent "na-
tive-born" citizens and new immigrant groups who strive to negotiate between assimilation and their own cultural memories (and to stay alive). It
would be easy to encourage actors to think of current versions of Fluellen-
like behavior: to update the man who quotes his book learning yet taunts
another "newcomer," proudly remembers his ancestry while trying harder
than others to fit in and obey the rules, all the while being both employed
and patronized by the man he most hopes to please, recognized as "a little
out of fashion" yet having "much care and valour" (4.1.84–85). Audiences
need not see all the rehearsal work — any more than they "see" Davy Gam —
for it to have ramifications as part of the larger artistic process. Moreover,
with increasing access to multimedia websites (such as that accompanying
the National Theatre's more topically oriented *Henry V* directed by Nicholas
Hytner and starring Adrian Lester), even this dimension of the collaborative
process is becoming more broadly accessible, arguably now part of the performance "product" itself.[105]

Were more directors, designers, and casts to carry through this kind of
collaborative recontextualization, the analogies between on- and offstage activity encouraged by both historicist and presentist scholars could become
consequential within performance. In short, to remember fifteenth-century

104. John Pettigrew, "Stratford's Festival Theatre: 1966," *Queen's Quarterly* 73, no. 3 (1966):
389.
105. See the weblink at: http://www.stagework.org.uk/webdav/servlet/XRM?Page/

258   Wales, and even the Welsh name of Dafydd ap Llywelyn, alongside Davy Gam, Esquire, may lead us back not solely to the remembrance of things past but also to historically informed analogies within the present, a careful use of history that adds more drama. The comedy will not disappear, but neither will its cost — or the consequentiality of making certain historical figures into putatively timeless "heroes." One comes to see the range of and limits to diachronic collaboration, and how local choices have ramifications reaching beyond a single issue.

As in the case of Branagh's neat Franco-Welsh replacement shot after Agincourt, it may not ultimately matter whether particular artists intend to be truer to history when they make choices that in fact capture the complex interplay of past and present. They may sometimes be unwitting collaborators, reminding us that each rendition encourages interpretive possibilities beyond any single participant's imagination. In this too they may be like Shakespeare himself, picking up pieces of history from chronicle and stage, reshaping them to fit his own dramatic patterns and obsessions, but also revealing more than he might recognize. Here too, there is a role for the scholar as active interpreter. Looking at *Henry V* not only as an early modern artifact but as a collaborative work of diachronic performance moves us beyond that New Historicist chestnut of judging Shakespeare's play as either containment or subversion. Like Brechtian dramaturgy, reading for signs of diachronic collaboration emphasizes history as contingent and multiple rather than inevitable; it allows the opportunity for modern scholars and performers to reconsider the consequences of their own interpretative choices at the present moment — and demands they take some but not all the responsibility for being artistic and political co-workers.

In this artistic process, Shakespeare's playtext itself becomes a kind of Isabeau: available for diverse representations and yet deserving of thoughtful consideration within its own historical contexts. Its modern performance then functions neither as a mere reiteration of a nostalgic past (be it textual, sexist, or national) nor as a narcissistic love affair with a falsely conceived present (allowed absolute originality, individuality, and social equity). Instead performance can negotiate between past and present from its privileged position in that ultimate hierarchy between the living and the dead. For the more we choose to turn a querying rather than a basilisk eye upon the past, and the more we know about that old diachronic collaborator Shakespeare, the more modern and resonant our own collaborations will become.

Bibliography

Abel, Elizabeth. "Narrative Structure(s) and Female Development: The Case of *Mrs. Dalloway*." In Bloom, *Virginia Woolf*, 243–64.

Adelman, Janet. *Suffocating Mothers: Fantasies of Maternal Origins in Shakespeare's Plays, "Hamlet" to "The Tempest."* London: Routledge, 1992.

Aebischer, Pascale, Edward J. Esche, and Nigel Wheale, eds. *Remaking Shakespeare: Performance across Media, Genres, and Cultures.* Houndmills, UK: Palgrave, 2003.

Agnew, Jean-Christophe. *Worlds Apart: The Market and the Theater in Anglo-American Thought, 1550–1750.* Cambridge: Cambridge University Press, 1986.

Alexander, Catherine M. S., and Stanley Wells, eds. *Shakespeare and Race.* Cambridge: Cambridge University Press, 2000.

Alexander, J. H., and David Hewitt, eds. *Scott and His Influence.* Aberdeen: Association for Scottish Literary Studies, 1983.

——, eds. *Scott in Carnival.* Aberdeen: Association for Scottish Studies, 1993.

Allott, Miriam. *The Brontës: The Critical Heritage.* London: Routledge & Kegan Paul, 1974.

Altman, Joel B. "'Vile Participation': The Amplification of Violence in the Theatre of *Henry V.*" *Shakespeare Quarterly* 42, no. 1 (1991): 1–32.

Arata, Stephen. "Scott's Pageants: The Example of *Kenilworth.*" *Studies in Romanticism* 40, no. 1 (2001): 99–107.

Ashmole, Elias. *The Antiquities of Berkshire.* Vol. 1. London: For E. Curll in Fleet Street, 1719.

Baker, David J., and Willy Maley, eds. *British Identities and English Renaissance Literature.* Cambridge: Cambridge University Press, 2002.

Baldo, Jonathan. "Wars of Memory in *Henry V.*" *Shakespeare Quarterly* 47, no. 2 (1996): 132–59.

Ball, Robert Hamilton. *Shakespeare on Silent Film.* New York: Theatre Arts Books. 1968.

Barker, Juliet, "The Haworth Context." In Glen, *Cambridge Companion to the Brontës*, 13–33.

Barnes, Julian. *A History of the World in 10 1/2 Chapters.* New York: Alfred A. Knopf, 1989.

Bartels, Emily. "Making More of the Moor: Aaron, Othello, and Renaissance Refashionings of Race." *Shakespeare Quarterly* 41 (1990): 433–54.

Barthelemy, Anthony. *Black Face, Maligned Race: The Representation of Blacks in English Drama from Shakespeare to Southerne.* Baton Rouge: Louisiana State University Press, 1987.

260   Bate, Jonathan. *The Genius of Shakespeare.* Oxford: Oxford University Press, 1998.

———. *Shakespeare and the English Romantic Imagination.* Oxford: Oxford University Press, 1986.

———. *Shakespearean Constitutions: Politics, Theatre, Criticism, 1730–1830.* Oxford: Clarendon Press, 1989.

———, and Russell Jackson. *Shakespeare: An Illustrated Stage History.* Oxford: Oxford University Press, 1996.

Beauman, Sally, ed. *The Royal Shakespeare Company's Production of "Henry V" for the Centenary Season at the Royal Shakespeare Theatre.* New York: Pergamon Press, 1976.

Beckett, Samuel. *Happy Days.* New York: Grove Press, 1961.

Beer, Gillian. "The Body of the People: *Mrs. Dalloway* and *The Waves.*" In *Virginia Woolf: The Common Ground.* Ann Arbor: University of Michigan Press, 1996. 48–73.

Bendyshe, Thomas, ed. *The Anthropological Treatises of Blumenbach and Hunter.* London, 1817.

Bennett, Susan. *Performing Nostalgia: Shifting Shakespeare and the Contemporary Past.* New York: Routledge, 1996.

Bentley, Gerald Eades. *The Professions of Dramatist and Player in Shakespeare's Time, 1590–1642.* Princeton: Princeton University Press, 1986.

Bergeron, David. *Shakespeare's Romances and the Royal Family.* Lawrence: University Press of Kansas, 1985.

Berry, Edward. "Othello's Alienation." *Studies in English Literature, 1500–1900* (1990): 315–33.

Bleeth, Kenneth, and Julie Rivkin. "'The Imitation David': Plagiarism, Collaboration, and the Making of a Gay Literary Tradition in David Leavitt's 'The Term Paper Artist.'" *PMLA* 116 (2001): 1349–63.

Bloom, Harold. *The Anxiety of Influence.* 2nd ed. New York: Oxford University Press, 1997.

———. *Shakespeare: The Invention of the Human.* New York: Riverhead Books, 1998.

———, ed. *Virginia Woolf.* New York: Chelsea House, 1986.

Bluestone, Max. *From Story to Stage: The Dramatic Adaptation of Prose Fiction in the Period of Shakespeare and His Contemporaries.* The Hague: Mouton, 1974.

Bock, Carol. "'Our plays': The Brontë Juvenilia." In Glen, *Cambridge Companion to the Brontës,* 34–52.

Bolt, Robert. *A Man for All Seasons: A Play in Two Acts.* New York: Random House, 1960.

Bolter, Jay, and Richard Grusin. *Remediation: Understanding New Media.* Cambridge: MIT Press, 1999.

Bolton, H. Philip. *Scott Dramatized.* London: Mansell, 1992.

Bolton, W. F. *Shakespeare's English: Language and the History Plays.* Oxford: Blackwell, 1992.

Boose, Lynda E. "The Father and the Bride in Shakespeare." *PMLA* 97 (1982): 325–47.

———. "Scolding Brides and Bridling Scolds: Taming the Woman's Unruly Member." *Shakespeare Quarterly* 42, no. 2 (1991): 179–213.

———, and Richard Burt, eds. *Shakespeare, The Movie: Popularizing the Plays on Film, TV, and Video.* London: Routledge, 1997.

[Booth, Junius Brutus.] "Mr. Booth's Appeal to the Public." 26 February 1817. Theatre Museum Archive, Covent Garden, London.

Bourdieu, Pierre. *Distinction: A Social Critique of the Judgment of Taste.* Trans. Richard Nice. Cambridge: Harvard University Press, 1984.

———. *The Field of Cultural Production.* Ed. Randall Johnson. New York: Columbia University Press, 1993.

Braddon, Mary Elizabeth. *Aurora Floyd.* Ed. Richard Nemesvari and Lisa Surridge. Peterborough, ON: Broadview Press, 1998.

Bradley, A. G. *Owen Glyndwr and the Last Struggle for Welsh Independence*. New York: Putnam, 1901.

Branagh, Kenneth. *Beginning*. London: Chatto & Windus, 1989.

——. *Henry V by William Shakespeare: A Screen Adaptation*. London: Chatto & Windus, 1989.

Brennan, Anthony. *Henry V*. New York: Twayne, 1992.

Brewer, Wilmon. *Shakespeare's Influence on Sir Walter Scott*. Boston: Cornhill, 1925.

Bristol, Michael. *Big-Time Shakespeare*. London: Routledge, 1996.

——. *Shakespeare's America, America's Shakespeare*. London: Routledge, 1990.

——, Kathleen McLuskie, and Christopher Holmes, eds. *Shakespeare and the Modern Theatre: The Performance of Modernity*. London: Routledge, 2001.

Brontë, Charlotte. *Jane Eyre*. Ed. Beth Newman. Boston: Bedford Books of St. Martin's Press, 1996.

——. *The Letters of Charlotte Brontë*. Vol 1: *1829–1847*. Ed. Margaret Smith. Oxford: Clarendon Press, 1995.

Brower, Reuben. "Something Central Which Permeated: 'Mrs. Dalloway.'" In Bloom, *Virginia Woolf*, 7–18.

Brown, Iain Gordon, ed. *Scott's Interleaved Waverley Novels: An Introduction and Commentary*. Aberdeen: Pergamom/Aberdeen University Press in association with the National Library of Scotland, 1987.

Brown, John Russell. *Shakespeare's Plays in Performance*. Rev. ed. New York: Applause, 1993.

Brown, Pamela Allen. *Better a Shrew Than a Sheep: Women, Drama, and the Culture of Jest in Early Modern England*. Ithaca: Cornell University Press, 2003.

Bruster, Douglas. *Quoting Shakespeare: Form and Culture in Early Modern Drama*. Lincoln: University of Nebraska Press, 2000.

Buchan, Alice. *Joan of Arc and the Recovery of France*. London: Hodder & Stoughton, 1948.

Buhler, Stephen M. *Shakespeare in the Cinema: Ocular Proof*. Albany: State University of New York Press, 2002.

Bulman, J. C., ed. *Shakespeare, Theory, and Performance*. London: Routledge, 1996.

Bulman, J. C., and H. R. Coursen, eds. *Shakespeare on Television*. Hanover, NH: University Press of New England, 1988.

Bunn, Alfred [and Thomas John Dibdin]. *Kenilworth: An Historical Drama, in Two Acts*. London: J. Duncombe, [1832].

Burne, Alfred H. *The Agincourt War*. 1956. Rpt., London: Greenhill Books, 1991.

Burnett, Mark Thornton, and Ramona Wray, eds. *Shakespeare, Film, Fin de Siècle*. Houndmills, UK: Macmillan; New York: St. Martin's Press, 2000.

Burt, Richard. "T(e)en Things I Hate about Girlene Shaksploitation Flicks in the Late 1990s, or, Not So Fast Times at Shakespeare High." In Lehmann and Starks, *Spectacular Shakespeare*, 205–32.

——. *Unspeakable ShaXXXspeares: Queer Theory and American Kiddie Culture*. New York: St. Martin's Press, 1998.

——, ed. *Shakespeare After Mass Media*. Houndmills, UK: Palgrave, 2002.

Burt, Richard, and Lynda E. Boose, eds. *Shakespeare, The Movie, II: Popularizing the Plays of Film, TV, Video, and DVD*. London: Routledge, 2003.

Buzard, James. "Translation and Tourism: Scott's *Waverley* and the Rendering of Culture." *Yale Journal of Criticism* 8, no. 2 (1995): 31–59.

Callaghan, Dympna. "'Othello was a white man': Properties of Race on Shakespeare's Stage." In *Alternative Shakespeares*, vol. 2, ed. Terence Hawkes. London: Routledge, 1996. 192–215.

262   Camden, William. *Britannia*. New York: Johnson Reprint Co., 1971. Facsimile of 1695 ed.

Cameron, Alasdair. "Scottish Drama in the Nineteenth Century." In Gifford, *History of Scottish Literature*, 3, 429–441.

Carlisle, Carol. "Macready's Production of *Cymbeline*." In Foulkes, *Shakespeare and the Victorian Stage*, 138–52.

Cartmell, Deborah. "Franco Zeffirelli and Shakespeare." In Jackson, *Cambridge Companion to Shakespeare on Film*, 212–21.

———. *Interpreting Shakespeare on Screen*. London: Macmillan, 2000.

Cartmell, Deborah, I. Q. Hunter, and Imelda Whelehan, eds. *Retrovisions: Reinventing the Past in Film and Fiction*. London: Pluto, 2001.

Cartwell, Deborah, and Imelda Whelehan, eds. *Adaptations: From Text to Screen, Screen to Text*. London: Routledge, 1999.

Case, Sue Ellen, and Janelle Reinelt. *The Performance of Power: Theatrical Discourse and Politics*. Iowa City: University of Iowa Press, 1991.

Chatterjee, Sudipto, and Jyotsna G. Singh. " Moor or Less? The Surveillance of Othello, Calcutta 1848." In Desmet and Sawyer, *Shakespeare and Appropriation*, 65–82.

Childress, Diana T. "Are Shakespeare's Late Plays Really Romances?" In *Shakespeare's Late Plays: Essays in Honor of Charles Crow*, ed. Richard C. Tobias and Paul G. Zolbrod. Athens: Ohio University Press, 1974. 44–55.

Cochrane, Claire. *Shakespeare and the Birmingham Repertory Theatre, 1913–1929*. London: Society for Theatre Research, 1993.

Coleridge, Samuel Taylor. *Table Talk*. London: George Routledge and Sons, 1884.

Colley, Linda. *Britons: Forging the Nation, 1707–1837*. New Haven: Yale University Press, 1992.

Collick, John. *Shakespeare, Cinema, and Society*. Manchester: Manchester University Press, 1989.

Conquergood, Dwight. "Ethnography, Rhetoric, and Performance." *Quarterly Journal of Speech* 78 (1992): 80–123.

Coursen, Herbert. *Shakespearean Performance as Interpretation*. Wilmington: University of Delaware Press, 1990.

Cowhig, Ruth. "Blacks in English Renaissance Drama and the Role of Shakespeare's *Othello*." In Dabydeen, *Black Presence*, 1–25.

Crawford, Anne. *Letters of the Queens of England, 1100–1547*. Stroud, Gloucestershire, UK: Alan Sutton, 1994.

Creed, G. Letter to the editors, *The Drama; or Theatrical Pocket Magazine*, 1 January 1822, 231.

Critchley, Simon. *On Humour*. New York: Routledge, 2002.

Crowl, Samuel. *Shakespeare Observed: Studies in Performance on Stage and Screen*. Athens: Ohio University Press, 1992.

Cunningham, Michael. *The Hours*. New York: Farrar, Straus, & Giroux, 1998.

Daalder, Joost, ed. *The Changeling*, by Thomas Middleton and William Rowley. New York: Norton, 1990.

Dabydeen, David, ed. *The Black Presence in English Literature*. Manchester: Manchester University Press, 1985.

D'Amico, Jack. *The Moor in English Renaissance Drama*. Tampa: University of South Florida Press, 1991.

Dash, Irene. Review of the BBC *The Taming of the Shrew*. *Shakespeare on Film Newsletter* 5, no. 2 (1981): 7 ff.

Davies, Anthony, and Stanley Wells, eds. *Shakespeare and the Moving Image: The Plays on Film and Television*. Cambridge: Cambridge University Press, 1994.

Davies, J. D. Griffith. *Owen Glyn Dwr*. London: Eric Partridge. 1934.

Davies, R. R. *The Revolt of Owain Glyn Dŵr*. Oxford: Oxford University Press, 1995.

Dawson, Anthony B. "Performance and Participation: Desdemona, Foucault, and the 263
Actor's Body." In Bulman, *Shakespeare, Theory, and Performance*, 29–45.

de Grazia, Margreta. *Shakespeare Verbatim*. Oxford: Clarendon Press, 1990.

de Grazia, Margreta, and Peter Stallybrass. "The Materiality of the Shakespearean Text."
Shakespeare Quarterly 44 (1993): 255–83.

de Lauretis, Teresa. *Technologies of Gender.* Bloomington: Indiana University Press, 1987.

Deleuze, Gilles. *Desert Islands and Other Texts, 1953–1974.* Cambridge: Semiotext(e)/MIT
Press, 2004.

Deleuze, Gilles, and Félix Guattari. *Anti-Oedipus: Capitalism and Schizophrenia.* Minneapolis: University of Minnesota Press, 1983.

de Pisan, Christine. *The Treasure of the City of Ladies.* Trans. and intro. by Sarah Lawson.
London: Penguin, 1985.

De Salvo, Louise. "Shakespeare's 'Other' Sister." In *New Feminist Essays on Virginia Woolf*,
ed. Jane Marcus. Lincoln: University of Nebraska Press, 1981. 61–81.

Desmet, Christy, and Robert Sawyer, eds. *Shakespeare and Appropriation.* New York: Routledge, 1999.

Diamond, Elin, ed. *Performance and Cultural Politics.* London: Routledge, 1996.

DiBattista, Maria. *Virginia Woolf's Major Novels: The Fables of Anon.* New Haven: Yale University Press, 1980.

Doane, Mary Ann. *Femmes Fatales: Feminism, Film Theory and Psychoanalysis.* New York:
Routledge, 1991.

Dobson, Michael. *The Making of the National Poet: Shakespeare, Adaptation, and Authorship,
1660–1769.* Oxford: Clarendon Press, 1992.

Dobson, Michael, and Nicola J. Watson. *England's Elizabeth: An Afterlife in Fame and Fantasy.* Oxford: Oxford University Press, 2003.

Donaldson, Peter S. *Shakespearean Films/Shakespearean Directors.* Boston: Unwin Hyman,
1990.

———. "Taking on Shakespeare: Kenneth Branagh's *Henry V.*" *Shakespeare Quarterly* 42, no.
1 (1991): 60–71.

Dowling, David. *Mrs. Dalloway: Mapping Streams of Consciousness.* Boston: Twayne, 1991.

Drakakis, John, ed. *alternative shakespeares.* New York: Methuen, 1985.

Drury Lane Theatre. Playbills. Spring and fall seasons, 1817. Theatre Museum, Covent
Garden, London.

Duncan, Ian. *Modern Romance and Transformations of the Novel: The Gothic, Scott, Dickens.*
Cambridge: Cambridge University Press, 1992.

Duruy, Victor. *A Short History of France.* Vol. 1. New York: E. P. Dutton, 1917.

Dusinberre, Juliet. *Virginia Woolf's Renaissance: Woman Reader or Common Reader?* London:
Macmillan, 1997.

Eagleton, Terry. *The Ideology of the Aesthetic.* Cambridge, MA: Basil Blackwell, 1990.

Earle, Peter. *Henry V.* London: Weidenfield and Nicolson, 1972.

Eckert, Charles W., ed. *Focus on Shakespearean Films.* Englewood Cliffs, NJ: Prentice-Hall,
1972.

Edwards, Owen Dudley, Gwynfor Evans, Ioan Rhys, and Hugh MacDiarmid. *Celtic Nationalism.* London: Routledge & Kegan Paul, 1968.

Edwards, Philip. *Threshold of a Nation: A Study in English and Irish Drama.* Cambridge:
Cambridge University Press, 1979.

Eggert, Katherine. "Nostalgia and the Not Yet Late Queen: Refusing Female Rule in
Henry V." *ELH* 61, no. 3 (1994): 523–50.

———. *Showing like a Queen: Female Authority and Literary Experiment in Spenser, Shakespeare,
and Milton.* Philadelphia: University of Pennsylvania Press, 2000.

England and France under the House of Lancaster. London: John Murray, Albemarle Street,
1852.

264   *An English Chronicle of the Reigns of Richard II., Henry IV., Henry V., and Henry VI., written before the year 1471.* Ed. John Silvester Davies. London: J. B. Nichols and Sons for the Camden Society, 1856.

Erickson, Peter. *Patriarchal Structures in Shakespeare's Drama.* Berkeley: University of California Press, 1985.

———. *Rewriting Shakespeare, Rewriting Ourselves.* Berkeley: University of California Press, 1991.

Erne, Lukas. *Shakespeare as Literary Dramatist.* Cambridge: Cambridge University Press, 2003.

Erne, Lukas, and M. J. Kidnie, eds. *Textual Performances: The Modern Reproduction of Shakespeare's Drama.* Cambridge: Cambridge University Press, 2004.

Evans, H. T. *Wales and the War of the Roses.* Cambridge University Press, 1915. Rpt. Stroud, Gloucestershire: Alan Sutton, 1995.

Everett, Barbara. *Young Hamlet: Essays on Shakespeare's Tragedies.* Oxford: Clarendon Press, 1989.

Felperin, Howard. *The Uses of the Canon: Elizabethan Literature and Contemporary Theory.* Oxford: Clarendon Press, 1990.

Ferguson, Margaret W. "Juggling the Categories of Race, Class, and Gender: Aphra Behn's *Oroonoko*." In Hendricks and Parker, *Women, "Race," and Writing,* 209–24.

Ferris, Ina. *The Achievement of Literary Authority: Gender, History, and the Waverley Novels.* Ithaca: Cornell University Press, 1991.

Fineman, Joel. *Shakespeare's Perjured Eye: The Invention of Poetic Subjectivity in the Sonnets.* Berkeley: University of California Press, 1986.

———. "The Turning of the Shrew." In *Shakespeare and the Question of Theory,* ed. Patricia Parker and Geoffrey Hartman. New York: Methuen, 1985. 138–59.

Fischlin, Daniel, and Mark Fortier, eds. *Adaptations of Shakespeare: A Critical Anthology of Plays from the Seventeenth Century to the Present.* London: Routledge, 2000.

Fitter, Chris. "A Tale of Two Branaghs: *Henry V*, Ideology, and the Mekong Agincourt." In *Shakespeare Left and Right, ed.* Ivo Kamps. New York: Routledge, 1991. 259–75.

Fleishman, Avrom. *Virginia Woolf: A Critical Reading.* Baltimore: Johns Hopkins University Press, 1975.

Fleming, Juliet. "*The French Garden*: An Introduction to Women's French." *ELH* 56 (1989): 19–51.

Fleney, Ralph, [ed.]. *A Calendar of the Register of the Queen's Majesty's Council in the Dominion and Principality of Wales and the Marches of the Same* [1535] *1569–1591.* Cymmrodorion Record Series no. 8. London, 1916.

Floyd-Wilson, Mary. *English Ethnicity and Race in Early Modern Drama.* Cambridge: Cambridge University Press, 2003.

Folkerth, Wes. *The Sound of Shakespeare.* New York: Routledge, 2002.

Ford, Richard. *Dramatizations of Scott's Novels.* Oxford: Oxford Bibliographical Society, 1979.

Foucault, Michel. "What Is an Author?" In *Textual Strategies: Perspectives in Post-Structuralist Criticism,* ed. Josué V. Harari. Ithaca: Cornell University Press, 1979. 141–60.

Foulkes, Richard, ed. *Shakespeare and the Victorian Stage.* Cambridge: Cambridge University Press, 1986.

Fox, Alice. *Virginia Woolf and the Literature of the English Renaissance.* Oxford: Clarendon Press, 1990.

Fradenberg, Louise, ed. *Women and Sovereignty.* Edinburgh: Edinburgh University Press, 1992.

Freedman, Barbara. *Staging the Gaze: Postmodernism, Psychoanalysis, and Shakespearean Comedy.* Ithaca: Cornell University Press, 1991.

Freud, Sigmund. "'A Child Is Being Beaten': A Contribution to the Study of the Origin of 　**265**
Sexual Perversions (1919)." In *The Standard Edition of the Complete Psychological Works of
Sigmund Freud*, trans. and ed. James Strachey. Vol. 17. London: Hogarth Press, 1955.

Froissart, Jean. *Chronicles*. Ed. Geoffrey Brereton. New York: Penguin, 1979.

Froula, Christine. "Virginia Woolf as Shakespeare's Sister: Chapters in a Woman Writer's
Autobiography." In *Women's Re-Visions of Shakespeare*, ed. Marianne Novy. Urbana: University of Illinois Press, 1990. 123–42.

Frye, Northrop. *Anatomy of Criticism: Four Essays*. Princeton: Princeton University Press, 1957.

Furness, Horace Howard, ed. *The New Variorum Edition of Shakespeare*. Vol. 6: *Othello*.
Philadelphia: J. B. Lippincott, 1886.

Garber, Marjorie, ed. *Media Spectacles*. New York: Routledge, 1993.

——. *Shakespeare After All*. New York: Pantheon Books, 2004.

——. *Symptoms of Culture*. New York: Routledge, 1998.

Garner, Shirley Nelson. "*The Taming of the Shrew*: Inside or Outside the Joke?" In *"Bad"
Shakespeare: Revaluations of the Shakespearean Canon*, ed. Maurice Charney. Rutherford,
NJ: Fairleigh Dickinson Press University Press, 1988: 105–19.

Garrick, David. "Catharine and Petruchio." *The Plays of David Garrick*. Vol. 3. Carbondale:
Southern Illinois University Press, 1981.

Gates, Barbara Timm, ed. *Critical Essays on Charlotte Brontë*. Boston: G. K. Hall, 1990.

Gifford, Douglas, ed. *The History of Scottish Literature*, vol. 3: *Nineteenth Century*. Gen. ed.
Cairns Craig. Aberdeen: Aberdeen University Press, 1988.

——. "Myth, Parody, and Dissociation: Scottish Fiction, 1814–1914." In Gifford, *History
of Scottish Literature*, 3:217–59.

Glen, Heather, ed. *The Cambridge Companion to the Brontës*. Cambridge: Cambridge University Press, 2002.

Goldman, Jane. *The Feminist Aesthetic of Virginia Woolf*. Cambridge: Cambridge University
Press, 1998.

Grady, Hugh. "Disintegration and Its Reverberations." In Marsden, *Appropriation of
Shakespeare*, 111–27.

——. *The Modernist Shakespeare: Critical Texts in a Material World*. Oxford: Clarendon Press,
1991.

——, ed. *Shakespeare and Modernity: Early Modern to Millennium*. London: Routledge,
2000.

Greene, Sally, ed. *Virginia Woolf: Reading the Renaissance*. Columbus: Ohio State University
Press, 1999.

Grierson, Sir Herbert. *Sir Walter Scott, Bart.: A New Life*. London: Constable, 1938.

Griffiths, Ralph A. *Conquerors and Conquered in Medieval Wales*. New York: St. Martin's
Press, 1994.

Guth, Deborah. "'What a Lark! What a Plunge!': Fiction as Self-Evasion in *Mrs. Dalloway*." *Modern Language Review* 84 (1989): 18–25.

Hall, Kim. *Things of Darkness: Economies of Race and Gender in Early Modern England*. Ithaca:
Cornell University Press, 1995.

Halpern, Richard. *Shakespeare among the Moderns*. Ithaca: Cornell University Press, 1997.

Hankey, Julie, ed. *Othello*, by William Shakespeare. *Plays in Performance* series. Bristol:
Bristol Classical Press, 1987.

Hapgood, Robert. "Popularizing Shakespeare: The Artistry of Franco Zeffirelli." In
Boose and Burt, *Shakespeare, The Movie*, 80–94.

Hare, Arnold. "Shakespeare in a Victorian Provincial Stock Company." In Foulkes,
Shakespeare and the Victorian Stage, 258–70.

Haring-Smith, Tori. *From Farce to Metadrama: A Stage History of "The Taming of the Shrew,"
1594–1983*. Westport, CN: Greenwood Press, 1985.

Harries, Frederick J. *Shakespeare and the Welsh*. London: T. Fisher Unwin, 1919.

266 Harries, Martin. *Scare Quotes from Shakespeare: Marx, Keynes, and the Language of Reenchantment.* Stanford: Stanford University Press, 2000.

Hawkes, Terence. "Bryn Glas." In *Post-Colonial Shakespeares*, ed. Ania Loomba and Martin Orkin. London: Routledge, 1998. 117–140.

———. *Shakespeare in the Present.* London: Routledge, 2002.

———. *That Shakespeherian Rag.* London: Methuen, 1986.

Hayden, John O., ed. *Walter Scott: The Critical Heritage.* London: Routledge, 1970.

[Hazlitt, William]. "On Mr. Kean's Iago." *The Examiner*, 24 July 1814. Collected in *Shakespeariana*, vol. 62. Shakespeare Center Library Collection, Stratford-upon-Avon.

Hechter, Michael. *Internal Colonialism: The Celtic Fringe in British National Development, 1536–1966.* Berkeley: University of California Press, 1975.

Hedrick, Donald. "War Is Mud: Branagh's Dirty Henry V and the Types of Political Ambiguity." In Boose and Burt, *Shakespeare, The Movie*, 45–66.

Hedrick, Donald, and Bryan Reynolds, eds. *Shakespeare without Class: Misappropriations of Cultural Capital.* New York: Palgrave, 2000.

Helgerson, Richard. *Forms of Nationhood: The Elizabethan Writing of England.* Chicago: University of Chicago Press, 1992.

Henderson, Diana E. "The Disappearing Queen: Looking for Isabel in *Henry V.*" In *Shakespeare and His Contemporaries in Performance*, ed. Edward Esche, 339–55. Aldershot, UK: Ashgate, 2000.

———. "*Henry V.*" *Shakespeare Bulletin* 12, no. 4 (1994): 24–25.

———. "Learning from Campbell Scott's Hamlet." In Henderson, *Concise Companion*, 77–95.

———. *Passion Made Public: Elizabethan Lyric, Gender, and Performance.* Urbana: University of Illinois Press, 1995.

———. "Performing History: *Henry IV*, Money, and the Fashion of the Times." In *A Companion to Shakespeare and Performance*, ed. Barbara Hodgdon and W. B. Worthen. Oxford: Blackwell, 2005. 376–96.

———. "Rewriting Family Ties: Woolf's Renaissance Romance." In Greene, *Virginia Woolf*, 136–60.

———. "A Shrew for the Times, Revisited." In Burt and Boose, *Shakespeare, The Movie*, II, 120–39.

———, ed. *A Concise Companion to Shakespeare on Screen.* Oxford: Blackwell, 2006.

Henderson, Diana E., and James Siemon. "Reading Vernacular Literature." In *A Companion to Shakespeare*, ed. David Scott Kastan. Oxford: Basil Blackwell, 1998. 206–22.

Henderson Scott, Paul. *Walter Scott and Scotland.* Edinburgh: Saltire Society, 1994.

Hendricks, Margo, and Patricia Parker, eds. *Women, "Race," and Writing in the Early Modern Period.* London: Routledge, 1994.

Henken, Elissa R. *National Redeemer: Owain Glyndwr in Welsh Tradition.* Ithaca: Cornell University Press, 1996.

Hewitt, David. "Walter Scott." In Gifford, *History of Scottish Literature*, 3:65–87.,

———, ed. *Scott on Himself: A Selection of the Autobiographical Writings of Sir Walter Scott.* Edinburgh: Scottish Academic Press, 1981.

Highley, Christopher. *Shakespeare, Spenser, and the Crisis of Ireland.* Cambridge: Cambridge University Press, 1997.

———. "Wales, Ireland, and *1 Henry IV*" in *Renaissance Drama*, n.s., 21 (1990): 91–114.

Hill, Errol. *Shakespeare in Sable: A History of Black Shakespearean Actors.* Amherst: University of Massachusetts Press, 1984.

Hirschhorn, Clive. *Hollywood Musical.* New York: Crown, 1981.

Hodgdon, Barbara. *The End Crowns All: Closure and Contradiction in Shakespeare's History.* Princeton: Princeton University Press, 1991.

———. "Katherina Bound: or, Play(K)ating the Strictures of Everyday Life." *PMLA* 107, no. 3 (1992): 538–53.

——. "Sexual Disguise and the Theatre of Gender." In Leggatt, *Cambridge Companion to* *Shakespearean Comedy*, 179–197.

——. *The Shakespeare Trade: Performances and Appropriations*. Philadelphia: University of Pennsylvania Press, 1998.

Holderness, Graham. *Shakespeare in Performance: The Taming of the Shrew*. Manchester, UK: Manchester University Press, 1989.

——. *Shakespeare Recycled*. New York: Harvester Wheatsheaf, 1992.

——. "What ish my nation?": Shakespeare and National Identities." In *Materialist Shakespeare*, ed. Ivo Kamps, 218–38. London: Verso, 1995.

——, ed. *The Shakespeare Myth*. Manchester: Manchester University Press, 1988.

Holinshed, Raphael. *Holinshed's Chronicles*. Ed. R. S. Wallace and Alma Hansen. Westport, CT: Greenwood Press, 1978. Rpt. of Clarendon Press ed., 1917.

Hopkins, Lisa. "Fluellen's Name." *Shakespeare Studies* 24 (1996): 148–55.

Horkheimer, Max, and Theodor W. Adorno. *The Dialectics of Enlightenment*. Trans. John Cumming. New York: Continuum, 1982.

Howard, Jean E. Introduction to *Cymbeline*. In *Norton Shakespeare*, 2955–64.

——. *The Stage and Social Struggle in Early Modern England*. New York: Routledge, 1994.

Howard, Jean E., and Phyllis Rackin. *Engendering a Nation: A Feminist Account of Shakespeare's English Histories*. New York: Routledge, 1997.

Hughes, Arthur E. *Shakespeare and His Welsh Characters*. Devizes, UK: George Simpson, 1919.

Hussey, Mark. *The Singing of the Real World*. Columbus: Ohio State University Press, 1986.

Ioppolo, Grace. *Revising Shakespeare*. Cambridge: Harvard University Press, 1991.

Jackson, Russell. "Shakespeare's Comedies on Film." In Davies and Wells, *Shakespeare and the Moving Image*, 99–120.

——, ed. *The Cambridge Companion to Shakespeare on Film*. Cambridge: Cambridge University Press, 2000.

Jacob, E. F. *Henry V and the Invasion of France*. London: Hodder & Stoughton, 1947.

Jacobus, Mary. "The Difference of View." In *Reading Woman: Essays in Feminist Criticism*. London: Methuen, 1986.

Jameson, Fredric. *The Political Unconscious: Narrative as a Socially Symbolic Act*. Ithaca: Cornell University Press, 1981.

Jardine, Lisa. *Reading Shakespeare Historically*. London: Routledge, 1996.

Jensen, Emily. "Clarissa Dalloway's Respectable Suicide." In *Virginia Woolf: A Feminist Slant*, ed. Jane Marcus. Lincoln: University of Nebraska Press, 1983. 162–79.

Jones, Edward T. "ACT's *Taming of the Shrew*: A Consciousness-Raising Farce." *Shakespeare on Film Newsletter* 2, no. 1 (1977): 4–5.

Jones, Eldred. *Othello's Countrymen: The African in English Renaissance Drama*. London: Oxford University Press, 1965.

Jones, Gareth, *A New History of Wales: The Gentry and the Elizabethan State*. Swansea: Christopher Davies, 1977.

Jones, J. Gwynfor. *Early Modern Wales, c. 1525–1640*. New York: St. Martin's Press, 1994.

Jorgens, Jack J. *Shakespeare on Film*. Bloomington: Indiana University Press, 1979.

Kahn, Coppélia. "*The Taming of the Shrew*: Shakespeare's Mirror of Marriage." *Modern Language Studies* 5 (1975): 88–102.

Kastan, David Scott. *Shakespeare After Theory*. New York: Routledge, 1999.

Kerr, James. *Fiction against History: Scott as Storyteller*. Cambridge: Cambridge University Press, 1989.

Kliman, Bernice. "Maurice Evans' Shakespeare Productions." In Bulman and Coursen, *Shakespeare on Television*, 91–101.

268   Lamb, Charles. "On the Tragedies of Shakspeare." In *The Portable Charles Lamb*, ed. John Mason Brown. New York: Viking, 1949. 559–82.

Lang, Andrew, ed. *Kenilworth*, by Sir Walter Scott. New York: E. B. Hall, 1893.

Lanier, Douglas. "'Art Thou Base, Common and Popular?' The Cultural Politics of Kenneth Branagh's *Hamlet*." In Lehmann and Starks, *Spectacular Shakespeare*, 149–71.

———. "Encryptions: Reading Milton Reading Jonson Reading Shakespeare." In *Reading and Writing in Shakespeare*, ed. David Bergeron. London: Associated University Presses, 1996. 220–50.

———. *Shakespeare and Modern Popular Culture*. Oxford: Oxford University Press, 2002.

Lascelles, Mary. *The Story-Teller Retrieves the Past*. Oxford: Clarendon Press, 1980.

Laurence, Patricia. *The Reading of Silence: Virginia Woolf in the English Tradition*. Stanford: Stanford University Press, 1991.

Leggatt, Alexander, ed. *The Cambridge Companion to Shakespearean Comedy*. Cambridge: Cambridge University Press, 2002.

Lehmann, Courtney. *Shakespeare Remains*. Ithaca: Cornell University Press, 2002.

Lehmann, Courtney, and Lisa S. Starks, eds. *Spectacular Shakespeare: Critical Theory and Popular Cinema*. Madison, NJ: Fairleigh Dickinson University Press, 2002.

Lethbridge, Charles, ed. *The First English Life of King Henry V*. Oxford: Clarendon Press, 1911.

Levine, Laurence. *Highbrow/Lowbrow: The Emergence of Cultural Hierarchy in America*. Cambridge: Harvard University Press, 1990.

Liddiard, J. S. Anna. *Kenilworth: A Mask*. London: Hibernia-Press Office for Longman, Rees, and Co. [also printed for John Cumming, Dublin], 1815.

Little, Arthur L., Jr. "The Primal Scene of Racism in *Othello*." *Shakespeare Quarterly* 44 (1993): 304–24.

———. *Shakespeare Jungle Fever*. Stanford: Stanford University Press, 2000.

Lloyd, J. E. *Owen Glendower*. Oxford: Clarendon Press, 1931.

Lockhart, J. G. *Life of Sir Walter Scott*. Abridged ed. Edinburgh: Adam and Charles Black, 1853.

Loehlin, James N. *Henry V. Shakespeare in Performance series*. Manchester: Manchester University Press, 1996.

Logan, George M., and Gordon Teskey, eds. *Unfolded Tales: Essays on Renaissance Romance*. Ithaca: Cornell University Press, 1989.

London, Bette. "The Pleasures of Submission: *Jane Eyre* and the Production of the Text." *ELH* 58, no. 1 (1991): 195–213.

Low, Lisa. "'Listen and Save': Woolf's Allusion to *Comus* in Her Revolutionary First Novel, *The Voyage Out*." In Greene, *Virginia Woolf*, 117–135.

MacDonald, Joyce Green. "Acting Black: Othello, Othello Burlesques, and the Performance of Blackness." *Theatre Journal* 46, no. 2 (1994): 231–49.

MacQueen, John. *The Rise of the Historical Novel*. Vol. 2 of *The Enlightenment and Scottish Literature*. Edinburgh: Scottish Academic Press, 1989.

Maguire, Laurie E. "Cultural Control in *The Taming of the Shrew*." *Renaissance Drama* 26 (1995): 83–104.

———. "'Household Kates': Chez Petruchio, Percy, and Plantagenet." In *Gloriana's Face: Women, Public and Private, in the English Renaissance*, ed. S. P. Cerasano and Marion Wynne-Davies. Detroit: Wayne State University Press, 1992. 129–65.

Maley, Willy. *Nation, State, and Empire in English Renaissance Literature: Shakespeare to Milton*. New York: Palgrave Macmillan, 2003.

———. "'This sceptred isle': Shakespeare and the British Problem." In *Shakespeare and National Culture*, ed. John J. Joughin. Manchester: Manchester University Press, 1997. 83–108.

Manvell, Roger. *Shakespeare and the Film*. New York: Praeger, 1971.

Marcus, Jane. *Virginia Woolf: A Feminist Slant*. Lincoln: University of Nebraska Press, 1983.

Marcus, Leah. *Puzzling Shakespeare: Local Reading and Its Discontents*. Berkeley: University of California Press, 1988.

———. "The Shakespearean Editor as Shrew-Tamer." *ELR* 22, no. 2 (1992): 177–200.

———. *Unediting the Renaissance: Shakespeare, Marlowe, Milton*. New York: Routledge, 1996.

Markale, Jean. *Isabeau de Bavière*. Paris: Payot, 1982.

Marsden, Jean I., ed. *The Appropriation of Shakespeare: Post-Renaissance Reconstructions of the Works and the Myth*. London: Harvester Wheatsheaf, 1991.

Marshall, Gail, and Adrian Poole, eds. *Victorian Shakespeare*. 2 vols. Houndmills, UK: Palgrave Macmillan, 2003.

Marshall, Herbert, and Mildred Stock. *Ira Aldridge: The Negro Tragedian*. 1958. Rpt., Carbondale: Southern Illinois University Press, 1968.

Masten, Jeffrey. *Textual Intercourse: Collaboration, Authorship, and Sexualities in Renaissance Drama*. Cambridge: Cambridge University Press, 1997.

McConnell, Frank D. "'Death among the Apple Trees': *The Waves* and the World of Things." In Bloom, *Virginia Woolf*, 53–65.

McEachern, Claire. "*Henry V* and the Paradox of the Body Politic." In *Materialist Shakespeare: A History*, ed. Ivo Kamps. New York: Verso, 1995. 292–319.

McGann, Jerome. *Textual Condition*. Princeton: Princeton University Press, 1991.

McGlinchee, Claire. "Sir Walter Scott: A Man of the Theatre." In Alexander and Hewitt, *Scott and His Influence*, 507–510.

McMillin, Scott. "The Moon in the Morning and the Sun at Night: Perversity and the BBC Shakespeare." In Bulman and Coursen, *Shakespeare on Television*, 76–81.

McMillin, Scott, and Sally-Beth MacLean. *The Queen's Men and Their Plays*. Cambridge University Press, 1998.

Mendelson, Edward. "The Death of Mrs. Dalloway: Two Readings." In *Textual Analysis: Some Readers Reading*, ed. Mary Anne Caws. New York: MLA Publications, 1986. 272–80.

Michie, Elsie. *Outside the Pale: Cultural Exclusion, Gender Difference, and the Victorian Woman Writer*. Ithaca: Cornell University Press, 1993.

Mikalachki, Jodi. "The Masculine Romance of Roman Britain: *Cymbeline* and Early Modern English Nationalism." *Shakespeare Quarterly* 46 (1995): 301–22.

Miller, J. Hillis. "*Mrs. Dalloway*: Repetition as the Raising of the Dead." In Bloom, *Virginia Woolf*, 169–90.

Miller, Jonathan. *Subsequent Performances*. New York: Viking, 1986.

Mitchell, Jerome. "A List of Walter Scott Operas." In Alexander and Hewitt, *Scott and His Influence*: 511.

Moisan, Thomas. "'What's that to you?' or, Facing Facts: Anti-Paternalist Chords and Social Discords in *The Taming of the Shrew*." *Renaissance Drama* 26 (1995): 105–29.

Moon, Michael. *A Small Boy and Others: Imitation and Initiation in American Culture from Henry James to Andy Warhol*. Durham: Duke University Press, 1998.

Morris, Peter. *Shakespeare on Film*. Ottawa: Canadian Film Institute, 1972.

Mowat, Barbara. *The Dramaturgy of Shakespeare's Romances*. Athens: University of Georgia Press, 1976.

Mullaney, Steven. *The Place of the Stage: License, Play, and Power in Renaissance England*. Chicago: University of Chicago Press, 1988.

Mulvey, Laura. "Visual Pleasure and Narrative Cinema." In *Film Theory and Criticism*, ed. Gerald Mast and Marshall Cohen. 3rd ed. New York: Oxford University Press, 1985. 803–816.

Nashe, Thomas. *The Works of Thomas Nashe*. Ed. Ronald B. McKerrow. Oxford: Blackwell, 1958. Rpt., ed. F. P. Wilson.

270   Neely, Carol Thomas. *Broken Nuptials in Shakespeare's Plays*. New Haven: Yale University Press, 1985.

——. "Circumscriptions and Unhousedness: *Othello* in the Borderlands." In *Shakespeare and Gender: A History*, ed. Deborah E. Barker and Ivo Kamps. London: Verso, 1995. 302–15.

Neill, Michael. *Putting History to the Question: Power, Politics, and Society in English Renaissance Drama*. New York: Columbia University Press, 2000.

Nelson, Bonnie. "Much Ado About Something: The Law of Lombardy and the 'Othello Play' Phenomenon." *Studia Neophilologica* 58, no. 1 (1986): 71–83.

Newman, Karen. *Fashioning Femininity and English Renaissance Drama*. Chicago: University of Chicago Press, 1991.

Novy, Marianne. *Engaging with Shakespeare: Responses of George Eliot and Other Women Novelists*. Athens: University of Georgia Press, 1994.

O'Connell, Michael. "The Experiment of Romance." In Leggatt, *Cambridge Companion to Shakespearean Comedy*, 215–29.

Odell, George C. D. *Shakespeare: From Betterton to Irving* Vol. 2. New York: Charles Scribner's Sons, 1920.

Olivier, Laurence. *Confessions of an Actor: An Autobiography*. New York: Simon & Schuster, 1982.

Orgel, Stephen. *The Authentic Shakespeare, and Other Problems of the Early Modern Stage*. New York: Routledge, 2002.

——. *Imagining Shakespeare: A History of Texts and Visions*. Houndmills, UK: Palgrave, 2003.

——"What Is a Text?" *Research Opportunities in Renaissance Drama* 26 (1981): 3–6.

Orkin, Martin. "*Othello* and the 'Plain Face' of Racism." *Shakespeare Quarterly* 38, no. 2 (1987): 166–88.

Oruch, Jack. "Shakespeare for the Millions: Kiss Me, Petruchio." *Shakespeare on Film Newsletter* 11, no. 2 (1987): 7 ff.

Osborne, Laurie. "Romancing the Bard." http://www.colby.edu/personal/l/leosborn/POPSHAK/.

——. *The Trick of Singularity: "Twelfth Night" and the Performance Editions*. Iowa City: University of Iowa Press, 1996.

Oxberry, W[illiam]. "Kenilworth, A Melo-drama." In *The New English Drama, with prefatory remarks, biographical sketches, and notes, critical and exploratory; being the only edition existing which is faithfully marked with the stage business, and stage directions, as performed at the Theatres Royal*. Vol. 19. London: W. Simpkin and R. Marshall, and C. Chapple, 1824.

Pancoast, Henry S., ed. *Standard English Poems*. New York: Henry Holt, 1905.

Parker, Patricia. "Romance and Empire: Anachronistic *Cymbeline*." In Logan and Teskey, *Unfolded Tales*, 189–207.

——. "Uncertain Unions: Welsh Leeks in *Henry V*." In Baker and Maley, *British Identities*, 81–100.

Patterson, Annabel. *Reading Holinshed's Chronicles*. Chicago: University of Chicago Press, 1994.

Pearson, Roberta E., and William Uricchio. "Brushing Up Shakespeare: Relevance and Televisual Form." In Henderson, *Concise Companion*, 197–215.

Pendleton, Thomas A. "Garrick and the Pickford-Fairbanks Shrew." *Shakespeare on Film Newsletter* 12, no. 1 (1987): 11.

Pettet, E. C. *Shakspeare and the Romance Tradition*. London: Staples Press, 1949.

Pettigrew, John. "Stratford's Festival Theatre: 1966." *Queen's Quarterly* 73, no. 3 (1966): 384–97.

Pickford, Mary. *Sunshine and Shadow*. Garden City, NY: Doubleday, 1955.

Pitcher, Seymour M. *The Case for Shakespeare's Authorship of "The Famous Victories," with the complete text of the anonymous play.* New York: State University of New York Press, 1961.

Poole, Adrian. "Northern Hamlet and Southern Othello? Irving, Salvini, and the Whirlwind of Passion." In *Shakespeare and the Mediterranean: The Selected Proceedings of the International Shakespeare Association World Congress, Valencia, 2001.* ed. Tom Clayton, Susan Brock, and Vincente Fores. Newark: University of Delaware Press 2004.

——. *Shakespeare and the Victorians.* London: Arden Shakespeare, 2004.

Potter, Lois. *Othello. Shakespeare in Performance series.* Manchester: Manchester University Press, 2002.

Pratt, Mary Louise. *Imperial Eyes: Travel Writing and Transculturation.* London: Routledge, 1992.

Preston, Mary. "Othello," from *Studies in Shakespeare: A Book of Essays* (1869). In *Women Reading Shakespeare, 1660–1900: An Anthology of Criticism,* ed. Ann Thompson and Sasha Roberts. Manchester: Manchester University Press, 1997. 126–31.

Promptbooks, *Henry V*. Microfilm Collection, Folger Shakespeare Library, Washington, DC.

Punter, David. "'To Cheat the Time, a Powerful Spell': Scott, History, and the Double." In Alexander and Hewitt, *Scott in Carnival*: 1–18.

Pye, Christopher. *The Regal Phantasm: Shakespeare and the Politics of Spectacle.* New York: Routledge, 1990.

Quick, J. R. "The Shattered Moment: Form and Crisis in *Mrs. Dalloway* and *Between the Acts*." *Mosaic 7* (spring 1974): 127–36.

Rabkin, Norman. *Shakespeare and the Problem of Meaning.* Chicago: University of Chicago Press, 1981.

Rackin, Phyllis. *Stages of History: Shakespeare's English Chronicles.* Ithaca: Cornell University Press, 1990.

Raman, Shankar. *Framing "India": The Colonial Imaginary in Early Modern Culture.* Palo Alto: Stanford University Press, 2001.

Raphael, Frederic. "The *Auteurs* behind the *Auteur*." *TLS* 17 January 1997, 4–6.

Reinelt, Janelle G., and Joseph R. Roach, eds. *Critical Theory and Performance.* Ann Arbor: University of Michigan Press, 1992.

Review, unsigned, of *Kenilworth* (stage). *Theatrical Observer,* 26 October 1832.

Review, unsigned, of *Visions of the Bard. Theatrical Observer,* 23 October 1832.

Review, unsigned, of *Visions of the Bard. Theatrical Observer,* 25 October 1832.

Reynolds, Bryan. *Performing Transversally: Reimagining Shakespeare and the Critical Future.* New York: Palgrave Macmillan, 2003.

Roach, Joseph. *Cities of the Dead: Circum-Atlantic Performance.* New York: Columbia University Press, 1996.

Robertson, Fiona. *Legitimate Histories: Scott, Gothic, and the Authorities of Fiction.* Oxford: Clarendon Press, 1994.

Rodenburg, Patsy. *Need for Words: Voice and Text.* London: Methuen, 1993.

Roe, Sue, and Susan Sellers, eds. *The Cambridge Companion to Virginia Woolf.* Cambridge: Cambridge University Press, 2000.

Rosenberg, Beth Carole. *Virginia Woolf and Samuel Johnson: Common Readers.* New York: St. Martin's, 1995.

Rosenberg, Marvin. *The Masks of Othello.* Newark: University of Delaware Press, 1992.

Rothwell, Kenneth, and Annabelle Melzer. *Shakespeare on Screen: An International Filmography and Videography.* New York: Neal-Schuman, 1990.

Rozett, Martha Tuck. *Talking Back to Shakespeare.* Newark: University of Delaware Press, 1994.

Ruotolo, Lucio. "*Mrs. Dalloway*: The Unguarded Moment." In *Virginia Woolf: Revaluation*

272   *and Continuity*, ed. Ralph Freedman. Berkeley: University of California Press, 1980. 141–60.

Rutter, Carol. *Clamorous Voices: Shakespeare's Women Today*. Ed. Faith Evans. New York: Routledge, 1989.

———. "Looking at Shakespeare's Women on Film." In Jackson, *Cambridge Companion to Shakespeare on Film*, 241–60.

Saccio, Peter. *Shakespeare's English Kings: History, Chronicle, and Drama*. New York: Oxford University Press, 1977.

Schlack, Beverly Ann. *Continuing Presences: Virginia Woolf's Use of Literary Allusion*. University Park: Pennsylvania State University Press, 1979.

Schoch, Richard W. *Shakespeare's Victorian Stage: Performing History in the Theatre of Charles Kean*. Cambridge: Cambridge University Press, 1998.

Schwartz, Beth C. "Thinking Back through Our Mothers: Woolf Reads Shakespeare." *ELH* 58, no. 3 (1991): 721–46.

Schwartz, Murray M., and Coppélia Kahn, eds. *Representing Shakespeare: New Psychoanalytic Essays*. Baltimore: Johns Hopkins University Press, 1980.

Scott, Sir Walter. *The Heart of Midlothian*. Ed. Claire Lamont. 1982. Rpt. Oxford: Oxford University Press, 1999.

———. *Kenilworth; A Romance*. Ed. J. H. Alexander. Edinburgh: Edinburgh University Press, 1993.

———. *The Letters of Sir Walter Scott*. Ed. H. J. C. Grierson. London: Constable, 1932–37.

———. "Life of Kemble." In *Critical and Miscellaneous Essays*, vol. 3. Philadelphia: Carey and Hart, 1841.

Seward, Desmond. *The Hundred Years War*. London: Constable, 1978.

Shakespeare, William. *Cymbeline*. Ed. J. M. Nosworthy. 1955. Rpt., London: Routledge, 1996.

———. *Henry V*. Ed. Gary Taylor. Oxford: Clarendon Press, 1982.

———. *King Henry V*. Ed. T. W. Craik. New York: Routledge, 1995.

———. *The Norton Facsimile: The First Folio of Shakespeare*. Ed. Charlton Hinman. New York: Norton, 1968.

———. *The Norton Shakespeare*. Ed. Stephen Greenblatt, general editor, and Walter Cohen, Jean E. Howard, Katharine Eisaman Maus. New York: W. W. Norton, 1997.

———. *Othello*. Ed. E. Honigmann. Arden 3. Walton-on-Thames: Thomas Nelson, 1997.

———. *Othello*. Ed. M. R. Ridley. Arden 2. London: Methuen, 1958.

———. *The Taming of the Shrew*. Ed. Ann Thompson. Cambridge: Cambridge University Press, 1979.

———. *The Taming of the Shrew: Texts and Contexts*. Ed. Frances E. Dolan. Boston: Bedford/St. Martin's, 1996.

Shakespeare and the Stage. Series 1: Prompt Books from the Folger Shakespeare Library, Washington, DC. Harvester Microform, 1985.

Shakespeare's Globe Theatre, London. Playbill for *Henry V*, directed by Richard Olivier. September 1997.

Shaughnessy, Robert, ed. *Shakespeare on Film. New Casebooks Series*. New York: St. Martin's Press, 1998.

Shershow, Scott Cutler. "New Life: Cultural Studies and the Problem of the 'Popular.'" *Textual Practice* 12, no. 1 (1998): 23–47.

Sidney, Philip. *Who Killed Amy Robsart? Being Some Account of the Life and Death, with remarks on Sir Walter Scott's "Kenilworth."* London: Elliot Stock, 1901.

Siemon, James. "'Nay, that's not next': *Othello*, V.ii in Performance, 1760–1900." *Shakespeare Quarterly*, 37, no. 1 (1986): 38–51.

Silver, Brenda. *Virginia Woolf Icon*. Chicago: University of Chicago Press, 1999.

Sinfield, Alan. *Faultlines: Cultural Materialism and the Politics of Dissident Reading.* Berkeley: University of California Press, 1992.

Slights, Camille Wells. "Slaves and Subjects in *Othello.*" *Shakespeare Quarterly* 48 (1997): 377–90.

Smallwood, Robert. "Directors' Shakespeare." In Bate and Jackson, *Shakespeare,* 176–96.

Smith, Hallett. *Shakespeare's Romances.* San Marino, CA: Huntington Library, 1972.

Spivak, Gayatri Chakravorty. "Three Women's Texts and a Critique of Imperialism." *Critical Inquiry* 12 (autumn 1985): 243–61.

Stanton, Kay. "Nell Quickly, Doll Tearsheet, and the Sexual Politics of the Henriad's Subplot." *Proceedings of the Third Annual California State University Shakespeare Symposium,* ed. Edward L. Rocklin and Joseph H. Stodder. Pomona: California State University Press, 1993.

Stepan, Nancy. *The Idea of Race in Science: Great Britain, 1800–1960.* Hamden, CN: Archon, 1982.

Stocking, George W., Jr. *Victorian Anthropology.* New York: Free Press, 1987.

Stott, William, with Jane Stott. *On Broadway.* Austin: University of Texas Press, 1978.

Studlar, Gaylyn. "Barrymore, the Body, and Bliss: Issues of Male Representation and Female Spectatorship in the 1920s." In *Fields of Vision: Essays in Film Studies, Visual Anthropology, and Photography,* ed. Leslie Devereaux and Roger Hillman. Berkeley: University of California Press, 1995. 160–80.

Surrey Theatre, London. Playbill for *Kenilworth,* directed by Thomas Dibdin. 5 and 6 March 1821. Folger Shakespeare Library, Washington, DC.

Sutherland, John. *The Life of Walter Scott: A Critical Biography.* Oxford: Blackwell, 1995.

Sypher, Wylie, ed. *Comedy.* Garden City, NY: Doubleday, 1956.

Taylor, Gary. *Reinventing Shakespeare.* New York: Oxford University Press, 1989.

Taylor, Gary, and Michael Warren, eds. *The Division of the Kingdoms: Shakespeare's Two Versions of "King Lear."* Oxford: Clarendon Press, 1986.

Tennenhouse, Leonard. *Power on Display: The Politics of Shakespeare's Genres.* New York: Methuen, 1986.

Theatre Royal, Covent Garden. Playbill for *Visions of the Bard,* directed by Sheridan Knowles. Inserted between 24–25 October 1932, *Theatrical Observer.* Folger Shakespeare Library, Washington, DC.

Thomson, Peter. "What Scots Say." *Times Literary Supplement* 13 December 1996, 20.

Tickner, F. J., ed. *A Shorter Froissart.* London: Thomas Nelson, [n.d.].

Tronch-Pérez, Jésus. *A Synoptic "Hamlet."* Valencia, Spain: Sederi/Universistat de Valéncia, 2002.

Trumpener, Katie. *Bardic Nationalism: The Romantic Novel and the British Empire.* Princeton: Princeton University Press, 1987.

Urkowitz, Steve. *Shakespeare's Revision of "King Lear."* Princeton: Princeton University Press, 1980.

Van Watson, William. "Shakespeare, Zeffirelli, and the Homosexual Gaze." *Literature/Film Quarterly* 20, no. 4 (1992): 308–25.

Vaughan, Virginia Mason. *Othello: A Contextual History.* Cambridge: Cambridge University Press, 1994.

Vitkus, Daniel J. "Turning Turk in *Othello*: The Conversion and Damnation of the Moor." *Shakespeare Quarterly* 48 (1997): 145–76.

Walker, Marshall. *Scottish Literature since 1707.* London: Longman, 1996.

Wang, Ban. "'I' on the Run: Crisis of Identity in *Mrs. Dalloway.*" *Modern Fiction Studies* 38, no. 1 (1992): 177–91.

Warner, Marina. *Joan of Arc.* Harmondsworth: Penguin, 1983.

Warren, Roger. *Staging Shakespeare's Late Plays.* Oxford: Clarendon Press, 1990.

274   Waswo, Richard. "Scott and the Really Great Tradition." In Alexander and Hewitt, *Scott and His Influence*, 1–12.

Watson, Nicola J. "Kemble, Scott, and the Mantle of the Bard." In Marsden, *Appropriation of Shakespeare*, 73–92.

Watt, Ian. *The Rise of the Novel: Studies in Defoe, Richardson and Fielding.* London: Chatto & Windus, 1957.

Wayne, Valerie. "The Woman's Parts in *Cymbeline*." In *Staged Properties in Early Modern Drama*, ed. Jonathan Gil Harris and Natasha Korda. Cambridge: Cambridge University Press, 2002. 288–315.

Wells, Stanley. "Television Shakespeare." *Shakespeare Quarterly* 33 (1982): 261–77.

———, ed. *Shakespeare in the Theatre: An Anthology of Criticism.* Oxford: Oxford University Press, 2000.

White, Henry Adelbert. *Sir Walter Scott's Novels on the Stage.* New Haven: Yale University Press, 1927.

Wikander, Matthew. *The Play of Truth and State.* Baltimore: Johns Hopkins University Press, 1986.

Wilcox, Lance. "Katherine of France as Victim and Bride." *Shakespeare Studies* 17 (1985): 61–76.

Williams, Glanmor. *Renewal and Reformation Wales, c. 1415–1642.* Oxford: Oxford University Press, 1993.

Williamson, Sandra L., and James E. Person Jr. *Shakespearean Criticism: Excerpts from the Criticism of William Shakespeare's Plays and Poetry, from the First Published Appraisals to Current Evaluations.* Vol. 14. London: Gale Research, 1991.

Willis, Susan. *The BBC Shakespeare Plays: Making the Televised Canon.* Chapel Hill: University of North Carolina Press, 1991.

Wise, Thomas James, ed. *The Brontës: Their Lives, Friendships, and Correspondence.* London: Porcupine Press, 1980. Originally published in the Shakespeare Head Brontë, ed. Wise and J. A. Symington. Oxford: Blackwell, 1933.

Woolf, Virginia. *The Diary of Virginia Woolf.* Ed. Anne Olivier Bell and Andrew McNeillie. 5 vols. New York: Harcourt Brace Jovanovich, 1977–84.

———. *Essays.* Ed. Andrew McNeillie. New York: Harcourt Brace Jovanovich, 1987.

———. Introduction. *Mrs. Dalloway.* New York: Modern Library, 1928.

———. *The Letters of Virginia Woolf.* Ed. Nigel Nicolson and Joanne Trautmann. New York: Harcourt Brace Jovanovich, 1977.

———. "The Leaning Tower." In *The Moment and Other Essays*, 128–54. New York: Harcourt Brace, 1948.

———. *Mrs. Dalloway.* New York: Harcourt, Brace, and World, 1953. Rpt. of 1925 U.S. ed.

———. *Mrs. Dalloway.* London: Vintage, 1992.

———. *Orlando.* 1928. Rpt., New York: Harcourt, Brace, 1973.

———. *A Room of One's Own.* New York: Harcourt Brace Harvest, 1989.

———. *To the Lighthouse.* New York: Harcourt Brace Jovanovich, 1955.

———. *Women and Writing.* Ed. Michèle Barrett. New York: Harcourt, 1979.

———. *A Writer's Diary.* Ed. Leonard Woolf. New York: Harcourt Brace Jovanovich, 1954.

Worth, Christopher. "'A Very Nice Theatre at Edinburgh': Sir Walter Scott and Control of the Theatre Royal." *Theatre Research International* 12, no. 2 (1992): 86–95.

Worthen, W. B. *Shakespeare and the Authority of Performance.* Cambridge: Cambridge University Press, 1997.

———. *Shakespeare and the Force of Modern Performance.* Cambridge: Cambridge University Press, 2003.

———. "Shakespeare and Performance Studies; or, What Is Performance (Criticism) Performance (Criticism) of?" Paper circulated to the "Writing About Performance" Seminar, Shakespeare Association of America meeting, 1997.

Wyatt, Jean M. *"Mrs. Dalloway*: Literary Allusion as Structural Metaphor." *PMLA* 88   275
   (1973): 440–51.
Zeffirelli, Franco. *Zeffirelli*. New York: Weidenfield and Nicolson, 1986.
Zwerdling, Alex. *Virginia Woolf and the Real World*. Berkeley: University of California
   Press, 1986.

Films and Videos

An Age of Kings. Dir. Michael Hayes. BBC television. British Film Institute Archives.
   1960.
All About Eve. Dir. Joseph L. Mankiewicz. 20th Century Fox. 1950.
Henry V. Dir. Laurence Olivier. Two Cities Films Ltd. 1944.
———. Dir. David Giles. BBC/Time-Life TV. 1979.
———. Dir. Kenneth Branagh. BBC/Renaissance Films. 1989.
The Hours. Dir. Stephen Daldry. Paramount/Miramax. 2002.
King Henry V. Dir. Michael Bogdanov. English Shakespeare Company. 1990.
Kiss Me, Petruchio. Dir. Christopher Dixon. PBS/New York Shakespeare Festival. Aired 7
   January 1981. Films Incorporated Video 1982. Stage production, dir. Wilford Leach,
   1978.
"Atomic Shakespeare." *Moonlighting*. Dir. Will McKenzie. 1986.
Mr. I. Magination: The Taming of the Shrew. CBS. Museum of Film and Television Archives.
   Original air date 2 July 1950.
Mrs. Dalloway. Dir. Marleen Gorris. First Look/Bergen/Newmarket/BBC films. 1997.
The Philadelphia Story. Dir. George Cukor. Metro-Goldwyn-Mayer. 1940.
The Taming of the Shrew. Dir. D. W. Griffith. Biograph. 1908.
———. Dir. Sam Taylor. United Artists. 1929.
———. Dir. Paul Nickell. Westinghouse Studio One Theater. 1950.
———. Dir. George Schaefer. NBC Hallmark Hall of Fame. 1956.
———. Dir. Franco Zeffirelli. FAI/Royal Films/Columbia Pictures. 1967.
———. Dir. Kirk Browning. PBS Great Performances/ACT. Original air date 10 Novem-
   ber 1976. Stage production, dir. William Ball.
———. Dir. Jonathan Miller. BBC/Time-Life TV. 1980.
———. Dir. Peter Dews. CBC. 1986. Stage production, Shakespeare Festival at Stratford,
   Ontario,1981.
10 Things I Hate About You. Dir. Gil Junger. Jaret/Mad Chance/Touchstone Pictures. 1999.

Index

About the Author

Diana E. Henderson is a member of the Literature Faculty at MIT and also teaches in the Women's Studies and Comparative Media Studies Programs. She is the author of *Passion Made Public: Elizabethan Lyric, Gender, and Performance* (University of Illinois Press, 1995) and the editor of *A Concise Companion to Shakespeare on Screen* (Blackwell, 2006). She has published numerous articles on early modern poetry, drama, and culture and is currently editing *Alternative Shakespeares: 3* for Routledge.